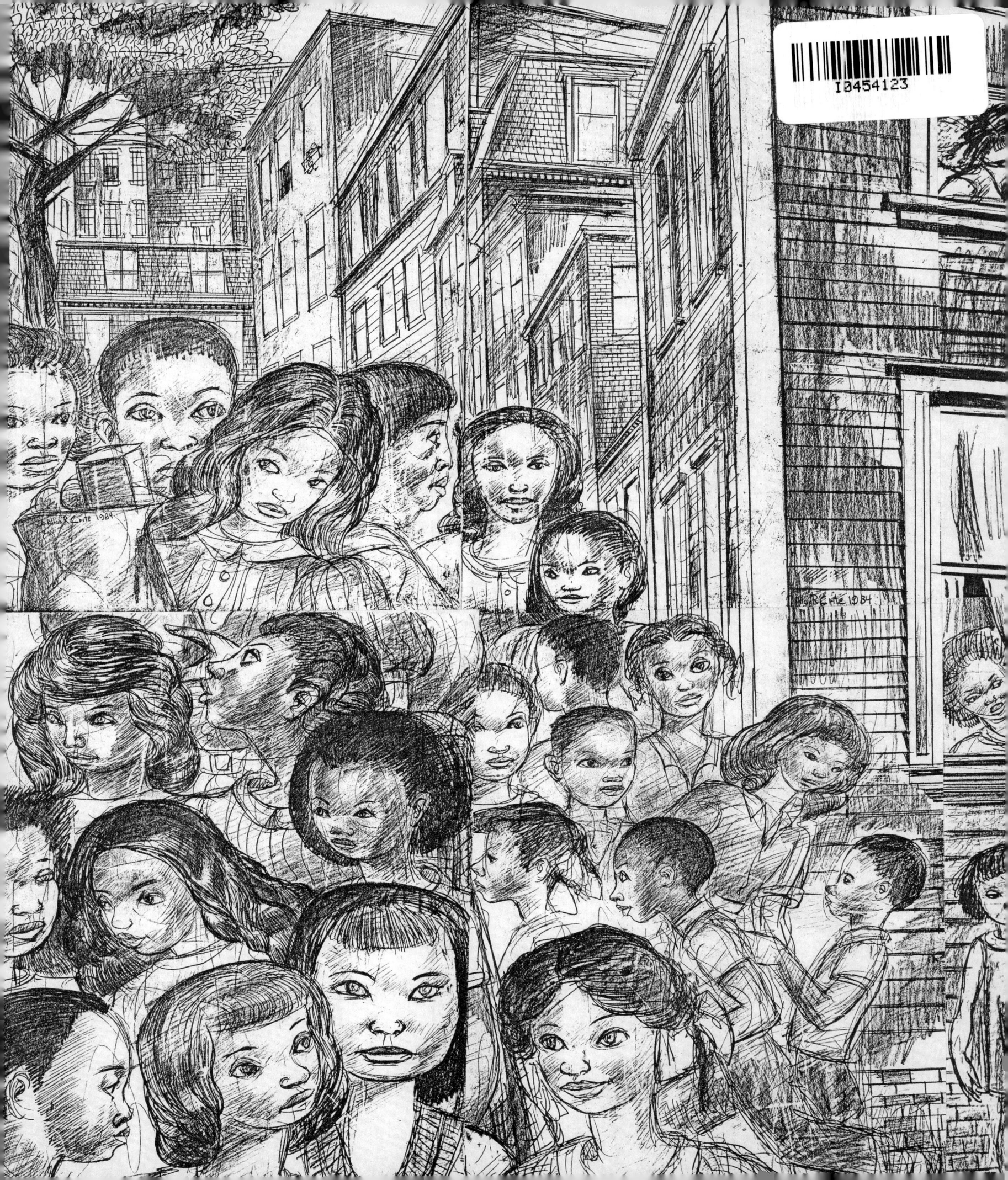

ALLAN ROHAN CRITE

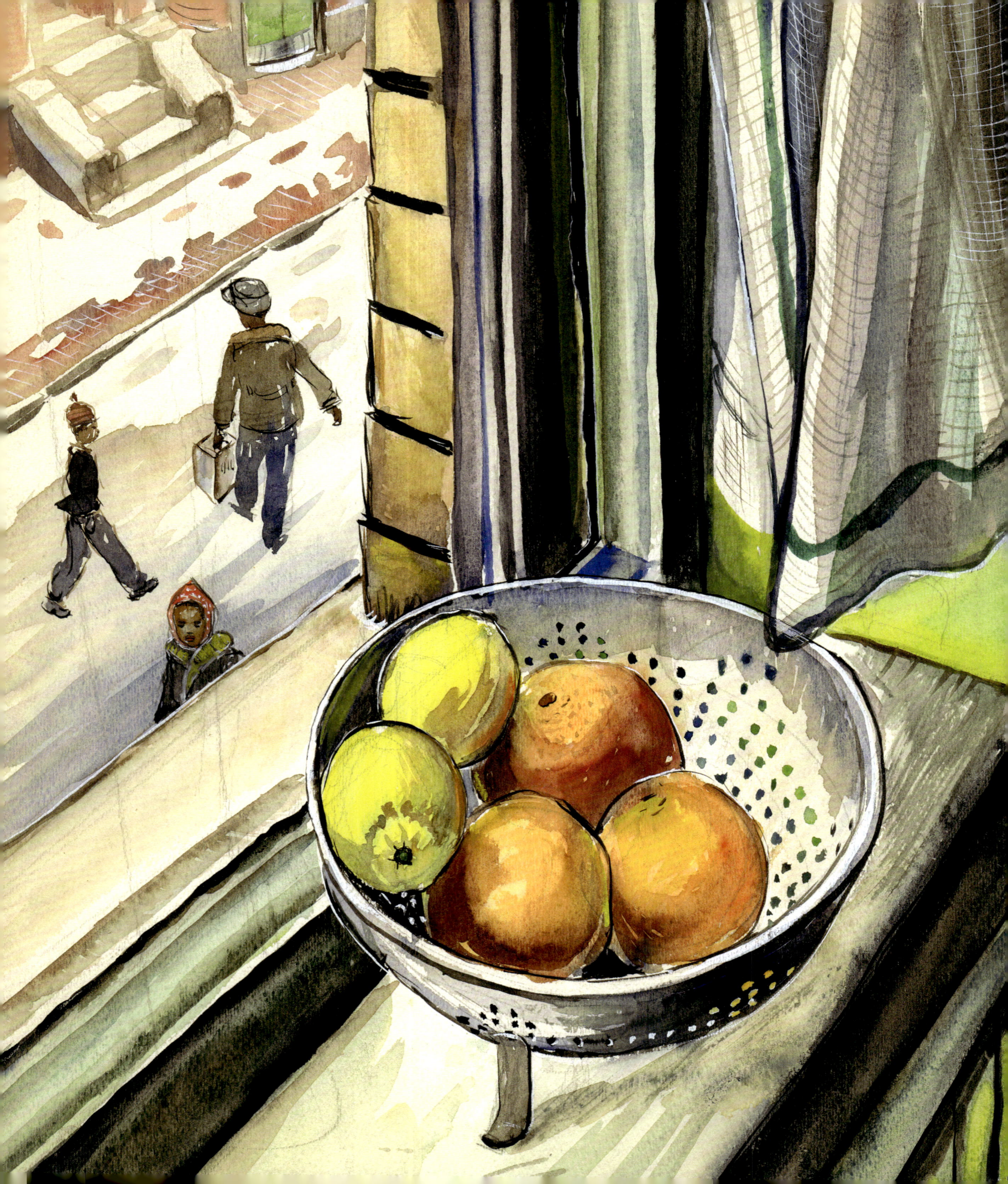

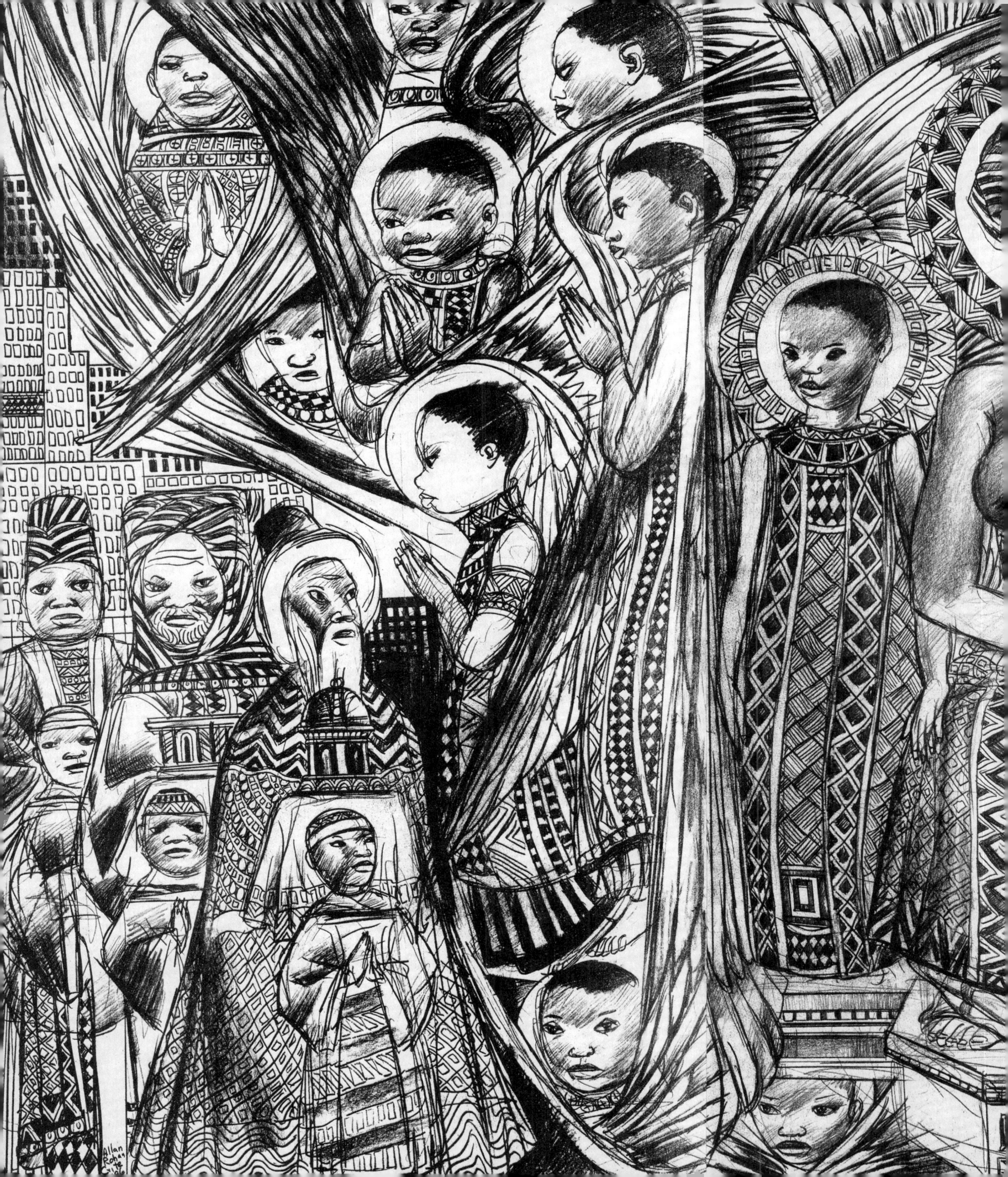

First published to accompany the exhibitions

Allan Rohan Crite: Griot of Boston
Curated by Christina Michelon
Boston Athenaeum, 15 October 2025–24 January 2026

Allan Rohan Crite: Urban Glory
Curated by Theodore C. Landsmark, Distinguished Professor, Northeastern University
and Diana Seave Greenwald, William and Lia Poorvu Curator of the Collection
Isabella Stewart Gardner Museum, Boston, 23 October 2025–11 January 2026

Allan Rohan Crite: Neighborhood
Zimmerli Art Museum, Rutgers, The State University of New Jersey
4 February–31 July 2026

Allan Rohan Crite: Griot of Boston is supported in part by the Terra Foundation for American Art,
the Henry Luce Foundation, The 'Quin Impact Fund, and The Gladys Krieble Delmas Foundation.

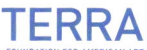 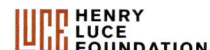 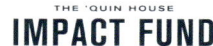 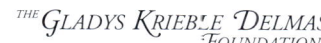

Allan Rohan Crite: Urban Glory is supported in part by Barbara and Amos Hostetter, the Barr Foundation,
the Henry Luce Foundation, the Ford Foundation, the Wyeth Foundation for American Art, The Tom and
Katherine Stemberg Fund for Exhibitions and Programs, Fredericka and Howard Stevenson, and by
an endowment grant from the Mellon Foundation and the National Endowment for the Humanities.

The Museum receives operating support from the Massachusetts Cultural Council, which is
supported by the state of Massachusetts and the National Endowment for the Arts.

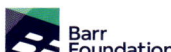 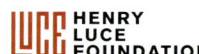 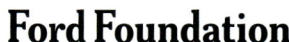

 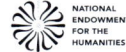 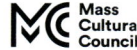 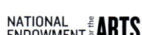

ISBN 978-0-691-97394-4

Library of Congress Control Number 2025936365
British Library Cataloging-in-Publication Data
is available.

Published by the Isabella Stewart Gardner
Museum, 25 Evans Way, Boston MA 02115 and
the Boston Athenaeum, 10 1/2 Beacon Street,
Boston MA 02108

Distributed by Princeton University Press
41 William Street, Princeton, NJ 08540-5237
99 Banbuy Road, Oxford OX2 6JX
press.princeton.edu

GPSR Authorized Representative: Easy Access
System Europe Mustamäe tee 50, 10621 Tallinn,
Estonia, gpsr.requests@easproject.com

Isabella Stewart Gardner Museum Publications
Elizabeth Reluga

Miko McGinty Inc.
Produced by Miko McGinty
Designed by Rita Jules
Typeset by Tina Henderson

Production management by Matthew Harvey
Color correction by Thomas Bollier
Printing by Conti Tipocolor, Florence, Italy

Cover: *Streetcar Madonna*, 1948 (detail of fig. 90).
Back cover: *Columbus Avenue*, 1937 (detail of
plate 9). Page 2: *Fruit and Snow: From My Window
at 2 Dilworth St.*, January 1940 (detail of plate 17).
Page 6: *Groton Street, South End, Boston*, 1946
(detail of plate 24). Page 8: Allan Rohan Crite on
Columbus Avenue, 18 April 1981 (fig. 92). Pages
12–13: *Settling the World's Problems*, 1933 (detail
of plate 3)

10 9 8 7 6 5 4 3 2 1

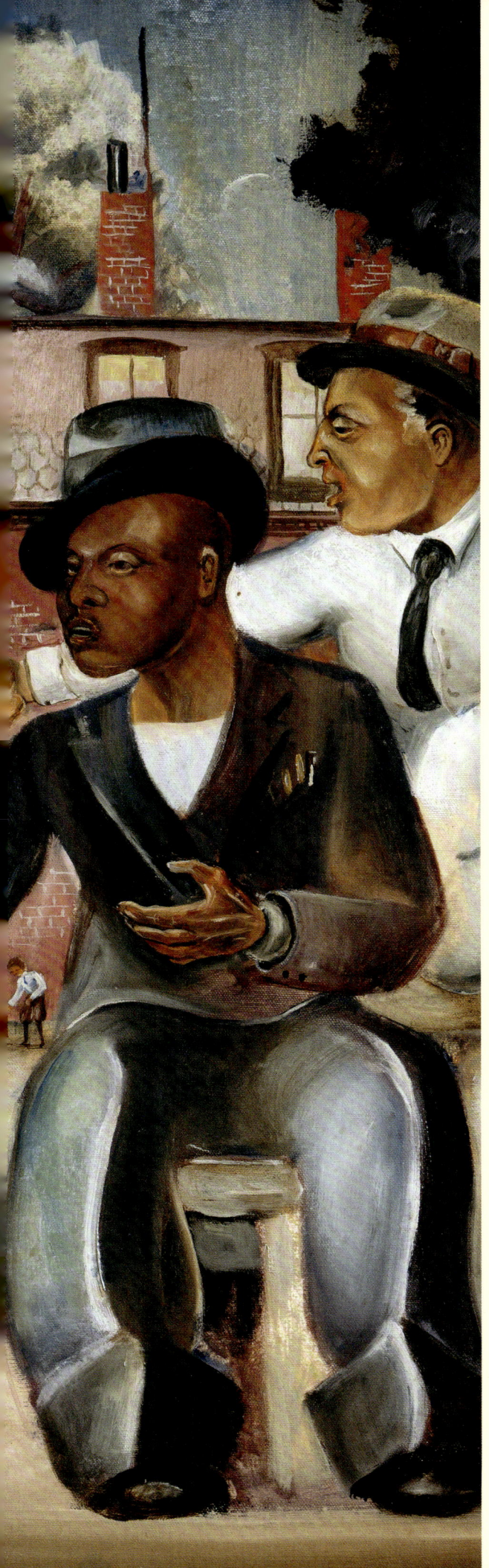

RECOLLECTIONS OF ALLAN ROHAN CRITE

SELECTIONS FROM INTERVIEWS CONDUCTED BY ARIELLE GRAY

As part of a collaboration with WBUR, Boston's NPR station, Arielle Gray interviewed many of Crite's friends and colleagues throughout 2024. These recollections are excerpts of hours of audio that she expertly recorded.

Fig. 10. Allan Rohan Crite, *Mary,*
from the personal sketchbook of
Allan Rohan Crite, 1932. Pencil on
paper, 12.5 × 19.4 cm. Boston
Athenaeum

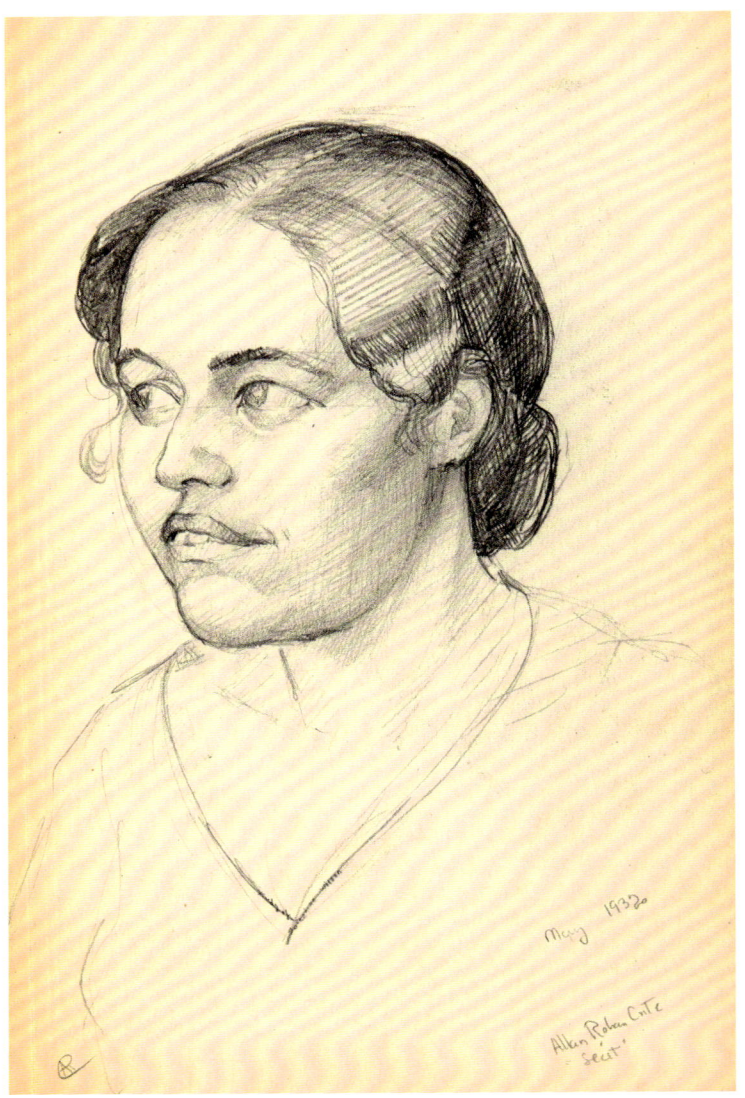

In her essay in this volume, Julie Levin Caro describes how the paintings Crite created
between approximately 1934 and 1945 engage with and enact the particular social values
of Boston's Black community between the wars. They reflect an attachment to certain
middle-class values and a reaction against what Crite viewed as the self-exoticizing
impulses of some fellow Black artists of the period. However, this opposition between
the academically trained Crite, who was dedicated to naturalism, and the painters of the
Harlem Renaissance, who were dedicated to a more abstract aesthetic inspired by African
art and Black folk art, is complex. Digging further into Crite's early-career *Neighborhood
Series,* we find engagement with many threads of the Black arts world and witness his
stylistic evolution. Caro describes some of these works, but there are many poignant
examples to choose from. Two examples in particular stand out in this period: first, the
juxtaposition of a work called *Ice* (May 1939) with one of Crite's best-known canvases,
Harriet and Leon (1941) (see fig. 56); and second, Crite's liturgical work from the late
1930s to the early '40s, in which he depicted holy figures with black skin.

Since the artist donated it in 1971, *Harriet and Leon* has long held pride of place
at the Boston Athenaeum, one of Crite's favorite institutions in Boston (fig. 11). The street
scene focuses on a couple striding through the snow-covered South End, recognizable
with its bow-fronted brick row houses. They are well dressed, and Crite relishes the
details of their clothing: the elaborate plaid of Harriet's green coat and the contoured felt

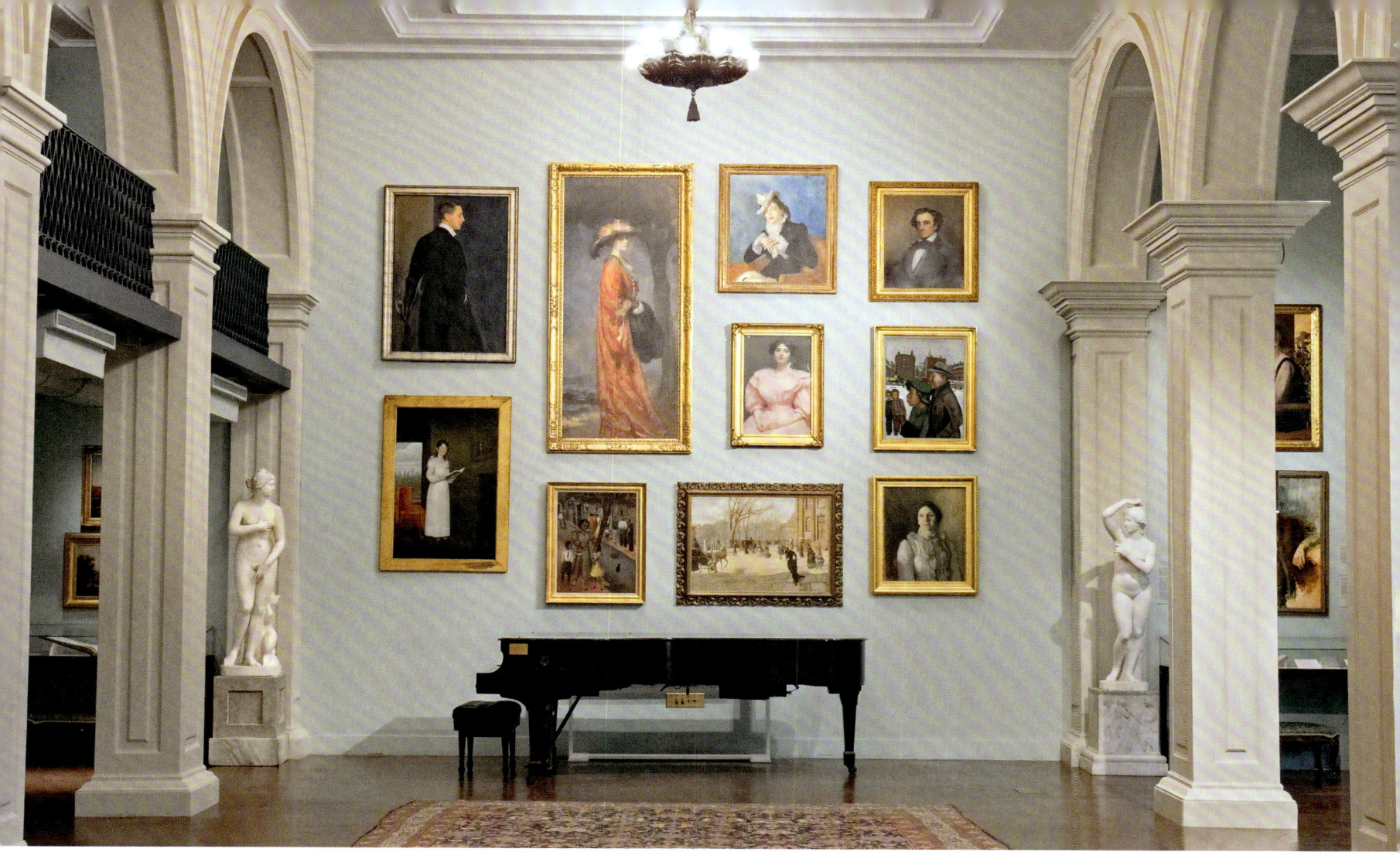

Fig. 11. Salon Wall in the Long Room, Boston Athenaeum, showing *Harriet and Leon,* 2024

of Leon's hat. Many of Crite's neighborhood scenes feel like genre painting—inspired by life, but not featuring specifically identified sitters among the crowd. In this way, they echo the work of one of his favorite artists: Pieter Bruegel the Elder, a connection that Efe Igor Coleman discusses in this volume.[15] This painting, by contrast, is clearly a double portrait. The sitters were two of the artist's friends—the architect Leon Bailey and soprano Harriet Jackson—and not actually a couple. In contrast to the children looking on, who resemble the typical neighborhood kids Crite often included in his paintings, the adults are distinctive: their profiles, her hairstyle, and his glasses are naturalistic and unique. This painting, completed toward the end of Crite's *Neighborhood Series,* shows the artist embracing realism and actively resisting what he considered a self-exoticizing impulse in other Black artists' works.[16] Yet *Harriet and Leon* tells only half the artistic story.

Ice, completed before *Harriet and Leon,* has been in the collection of Boston's Museum of African American History since the 1980s, donated by a couple who purchased a lot of Crite's works from a local dealer (fig. 12).[17] However, it has been barely studied compared to *Harriet and Leon,* to which it is clearly related. In *Ice,* Crite deploys many of the same elements: the same snowy street in the South End and the same yellow ice-delivery truck—although its direction is reversed. The gawking kids are gone, as are most of the playful figures in the background. The biggest changes, however, are in Harriet and Leon, who are not recognizably Harriet Jackson and Leon Bailey. It is unclear whether Jackson and Bailey even posed for this work; instead, another man and woman occupy their position. The figures are abstracted, with large eyes and sculpted features reminiscent of the Yoruba art Crite had sketched in the 1930s (see plate 2).[18] *Ice* looks like a version

Opposite: Fig. 12. Allan Rohan Crite, *Ice,* May 1939. Oil on canvas board, 76.2 × 50.5 cm. Courtesy of Museum of African American History Boston | Nantucket

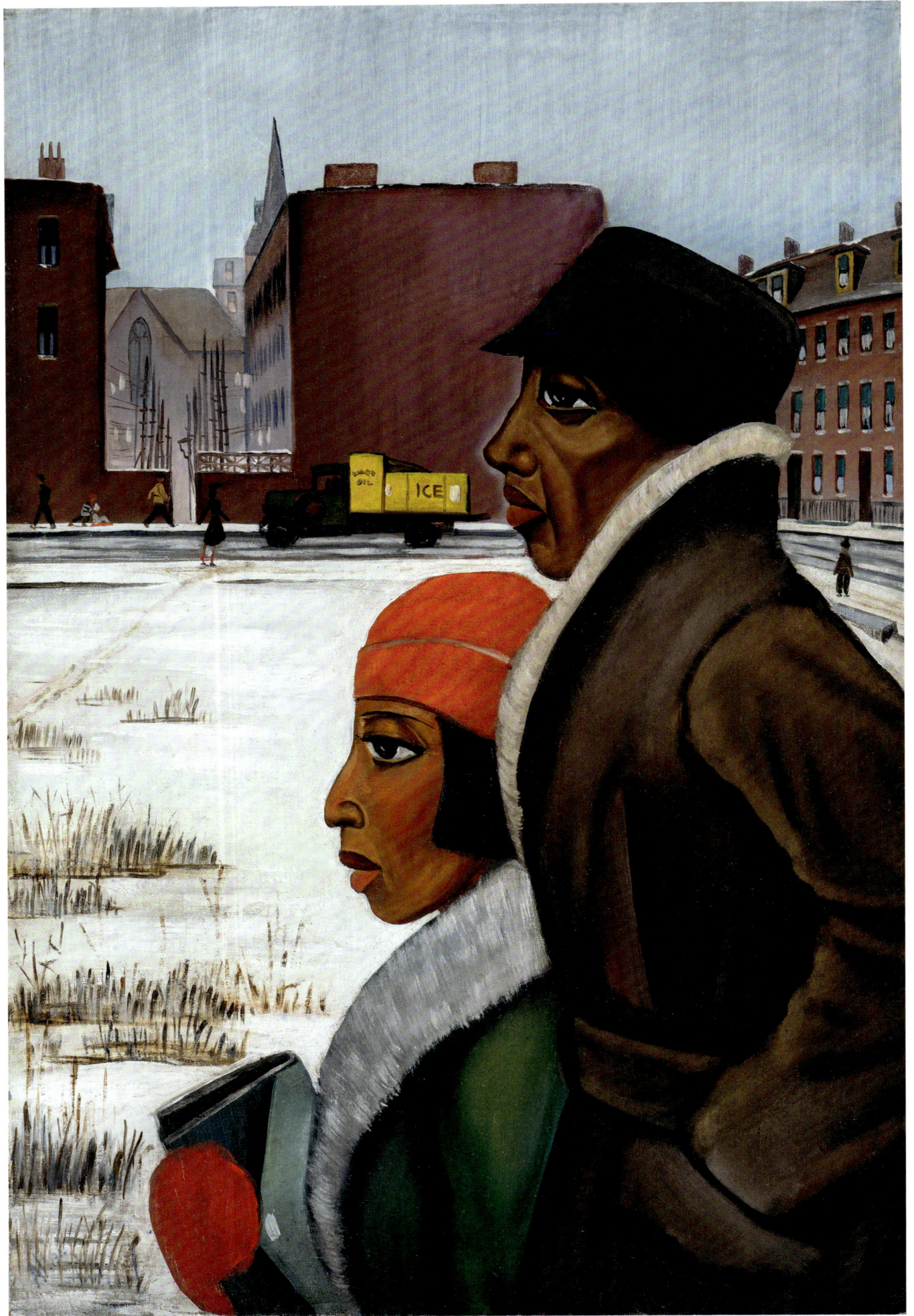

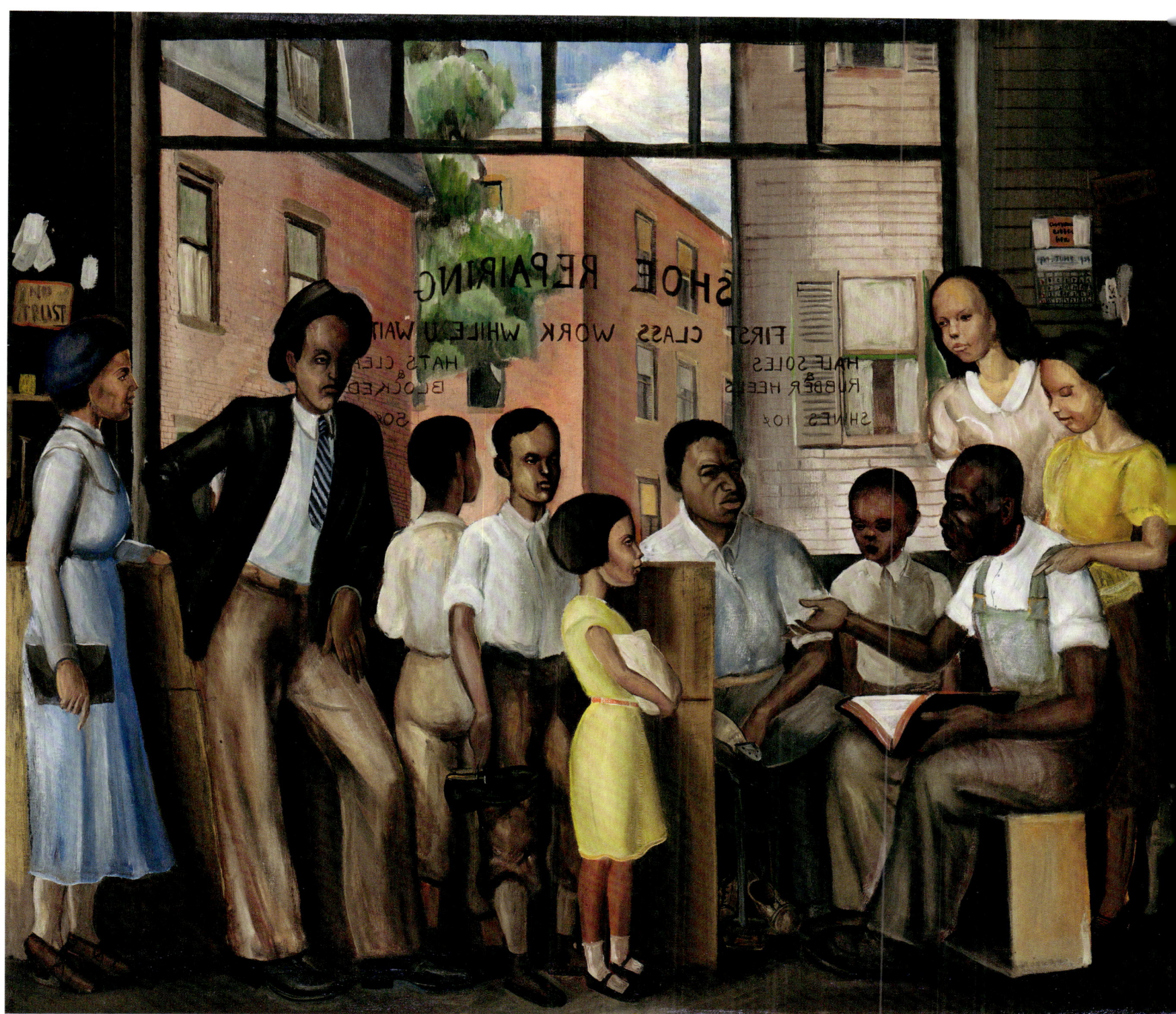

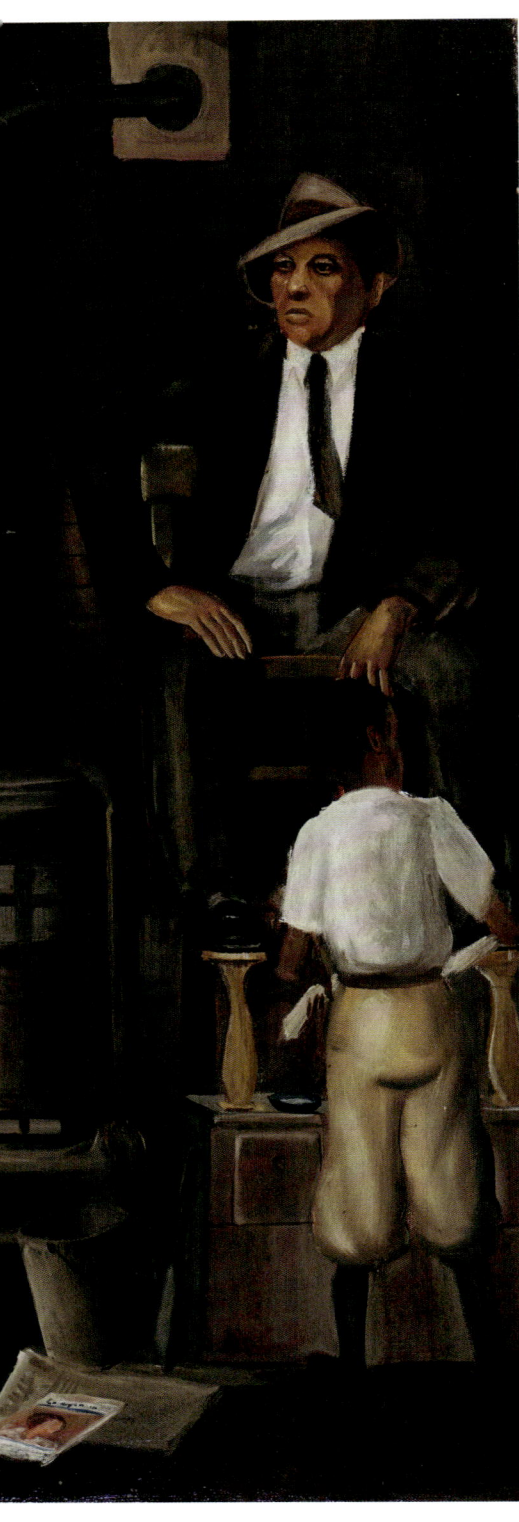

of *Harriet and Leon* deeply influenced by the charge of the Harlem Renaissance to look for inspiration in African artifacts—the faces of the couple are almost masklike. Crite did not in fact fully eschew the stylistic approach most associated with the "jazz person up in Harlem,"[19] which he described retrospectively in the 1970s. In his "Note on African Art" in *The New Negro: An Interpretation* (1925), scholar and critic Alain Locke wrote: "The African art object . . . has now become the corner-stone of a new and more universal aesthetic that has all but revolutionized the theory of art and considerably modified its practice."[20] He continued, "Since African art has had such a vitalizing influence in modern European painting, sculpture, poetry and music, it becomes finally a natural and important question as to what artistic and cultural effect it can or will have upon the life of the American Negro. . . . In the struggle for a racial idiom of expression, there would come to some creative minds among us, from a closer knowledge of it, hints of a new technique . . . incentives toward fresher and bolder forms of artistic expression."[21]

Crite experimented with Locke's exhortation to follow this aesthetic, though in the 1940s he seems to have decided to resist it: he did not give *Ice* to an elite Boston institution—ensuring its future survival and its centrality to his legacy—instead, he lost track of it for decades. In this period, Crite chose a naturalism closer to his academic training, one that he felt was truer to the depiction of his community. This would not, however, always be the case. *Ice* was actually a harbinger of stylistic approaches to which he would later turn that were more self-consciously modern and more clearly indebted to African art. Another foreshadowing of his interest in this aesthetic—and in a range of Locke's exhortations—came from perhaps unexpected quarters: liturgical art specifically designed to be used for worship in the Episcopal Church.

As Annamae Palmer Crite noted, one of her two loves was the Episcopal Church. Her son inherited this love. Crite began creating religious works in childhood and kept making them for the rest of his life. As a young artist, his engagement with religious life was related to genre paintings showing a range of different kinds of worship: from store front bible study (fig. 13), to parades of people headed to church on Sunday (fig. 14), to interiors of Catholic and Episcopal churches. Most paintings prominently feature a neighborhood church or focus on community gatherings before or after worship, as if the neighborhood were an extension of the bonds formed among congregants. In this way, these works are intertwined with the *Neighborhood Series*.

In the religious work from this period, Crite began to show some perhaps unexpected radicalism—a radicalism that did not follow the lead of the Harlem Renaissance but took its tenor from Crite's response to his environment. In *The Children's Mass* (1936), the congregants and young altar boys are all Black, but the priest and nun are white (fig. 15). While this religious genre painting depicts a hierarchical reality that Crite witnessed in which priests were white and worshippers Black, in liturgical works designed to be used for worship, the artist flipped this hierarchy on its head. In *The Stations of the Cross* and other religious works from the 1930s and '40s, the holy figures are Black. The radical nature of this innovation was not lost on the interviewer who took Crite's oral history for the Archives of American Art. The exchange is revelatory:

Allan Rohan Crite: The liturgical drawings—those of the Mass, the story of the Way of the Cross, and so forth—I was telling the story of man through a Black figure. In that area, you might say, the Black people went beyond racial parochialism. Now, there's a literal aspect of the liturgical drawings—why I used a sort of Catholic medium—was that I went through a sort of personal "Oxford revival" [the nineteenth-century movement that reasserted the Catholic heritage of Anglicanism]. . . . So, I found that the Catholic expression—Christianity as a viable medium through which to depict spirituals, etc.—that was my background. People were speaking about "Black is beautiful" in the 1960s as a sort of spark,

Fig. 13. Allan Rohan Crite, *And the Lord Said,* 1934. Oil on canvas, 76.2 × 114.9 cm. Courtesy of Museum of African American History Boston | Nantucket

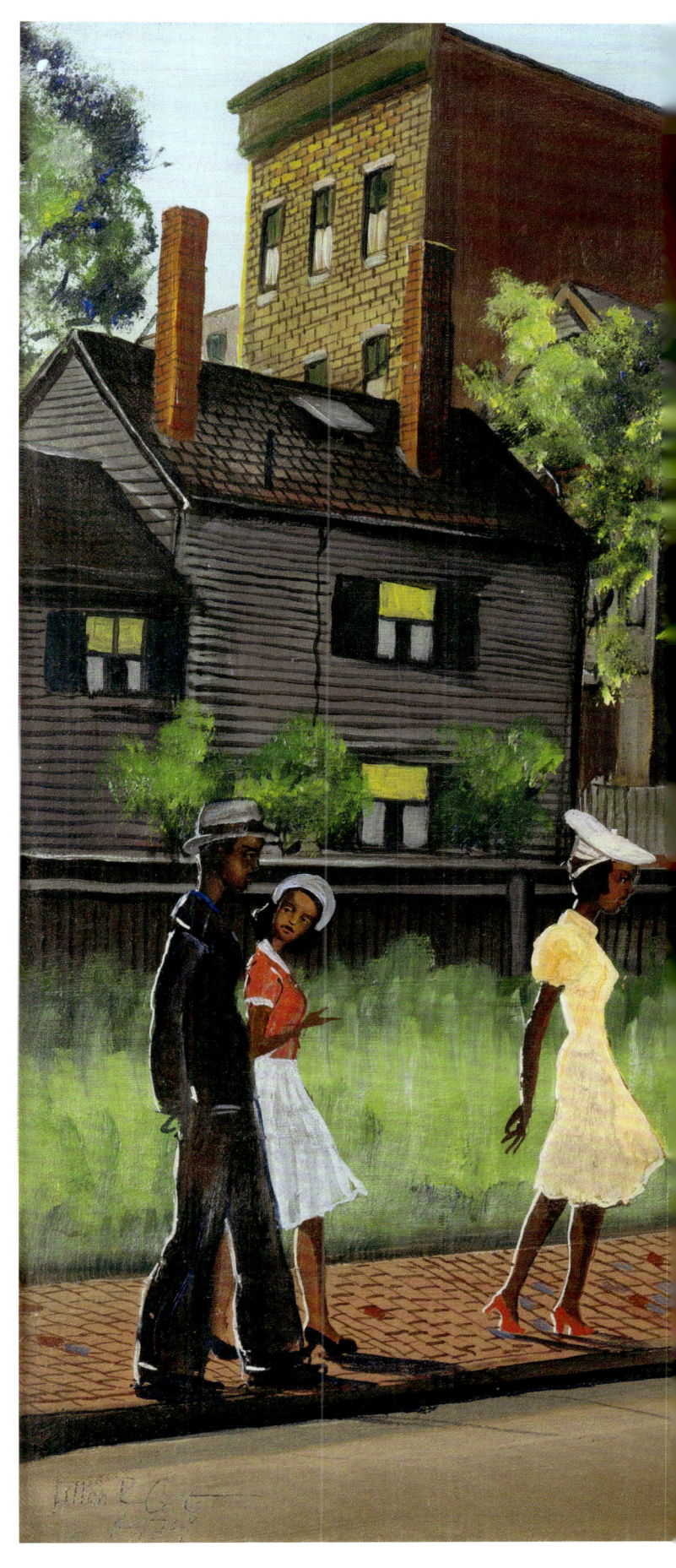

Fig. 14. Allan Rohan Crite, *Cambridge, Sunday Morning,* 1939. Oil on board, 57.5 × 67.5 cm. Boston Athenaeum

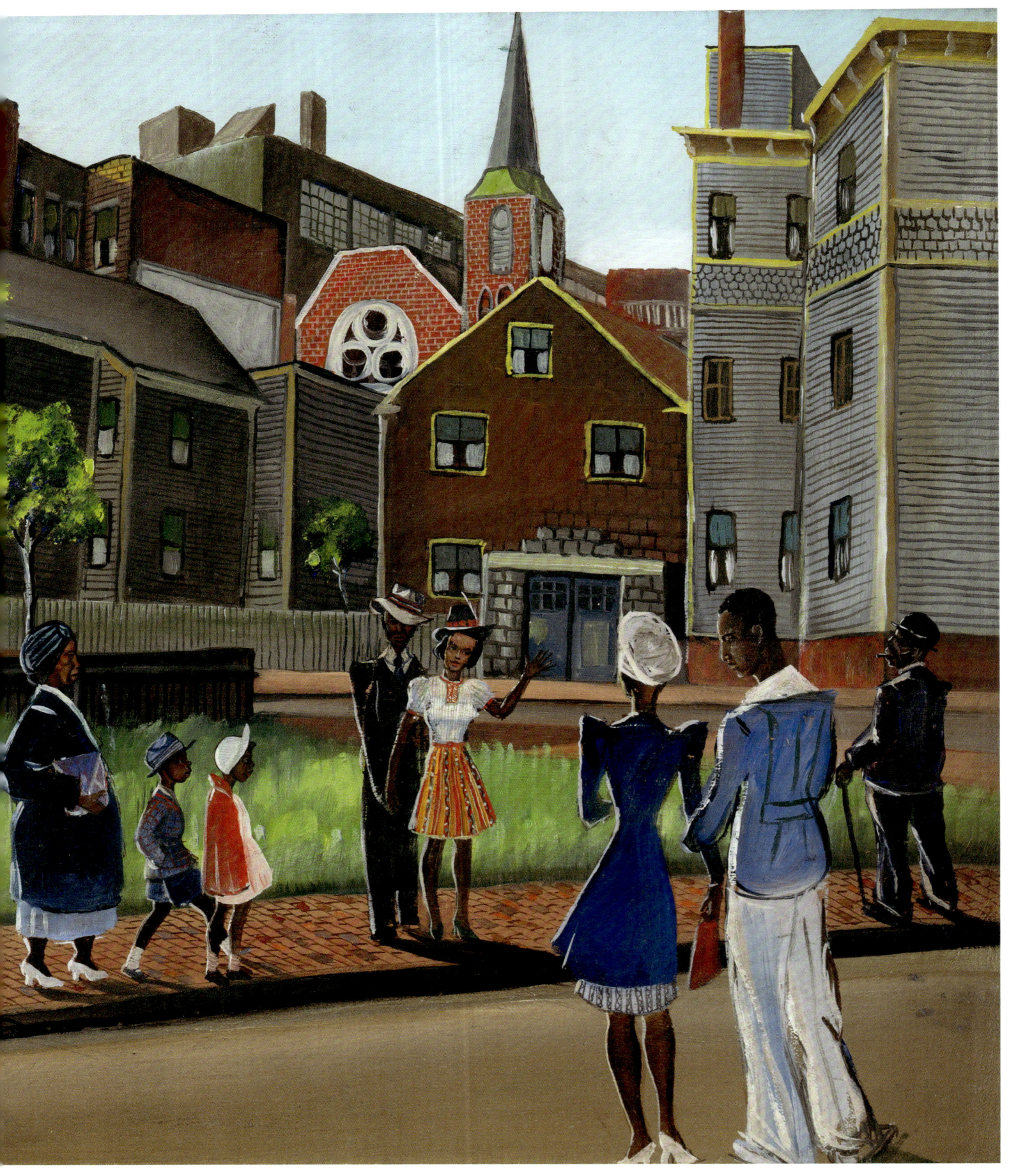

and I'd been saying that since the 1930s. At the time when I made the drawings, there were areas of controversy. People asked me, "Why do you make them Black?" "Well, it makes a good composition," and let it go at that. [Laughs]

Interviewer: You felt that Black people were part of humanity and you might as well use them as any other to illustrate, say, the Mass.

Crite: Oh yes.

Interviewer: To white people particularly, you had to say, simply, "Well, for compositional reasons."

Crite: [Laughing again] I say that partly to be facetious, partly being sardonic, and partly getting the message across.[22]

The works from this era include the elaborate *Stations of the Cross I–XIV* (plate 25), in which the holy figures' race is ambiguous, paper altarpiece-like compositions (plate 26), and the illustrations for Crite's book *All Glory: Brush Drawing Meditations on the Prayer of Consecration,* featuring drawings from the 1930s but published in 1947 by the Anglican

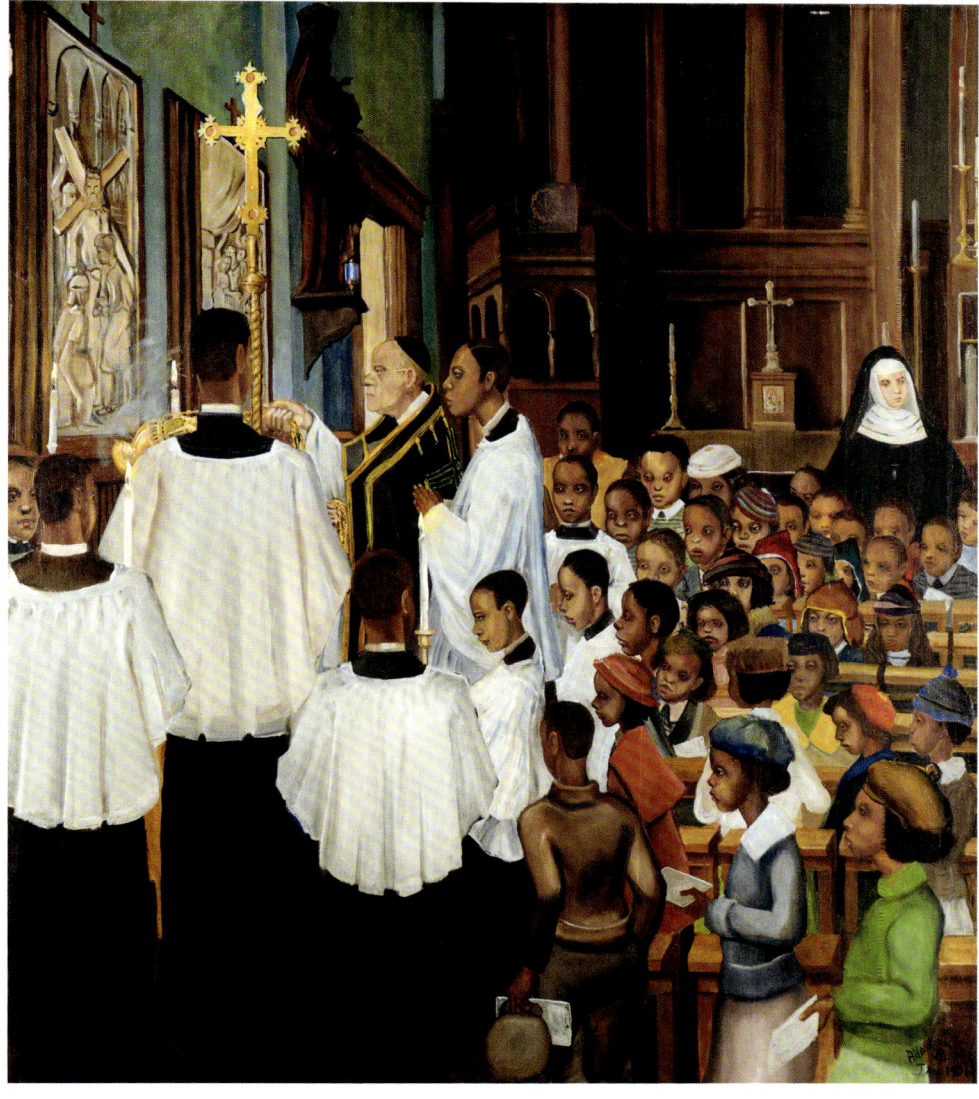

Fig. 15. Allan Rohan Crite, *The Children's Mass,* 1936. Oil on canvas, 110.8 × 88.6 cm. Church of St. Augustine and St. Martin, Boston

Fig. 16. Allan Rohan Crite, *Everybody's talking about heaven,* illustration for *Three Spirituals from Earth to Heaven* (Cambridge, MA, 1948), 1937. Ink on paper, 51 × 38 cm. Houghton Library, Harvard University

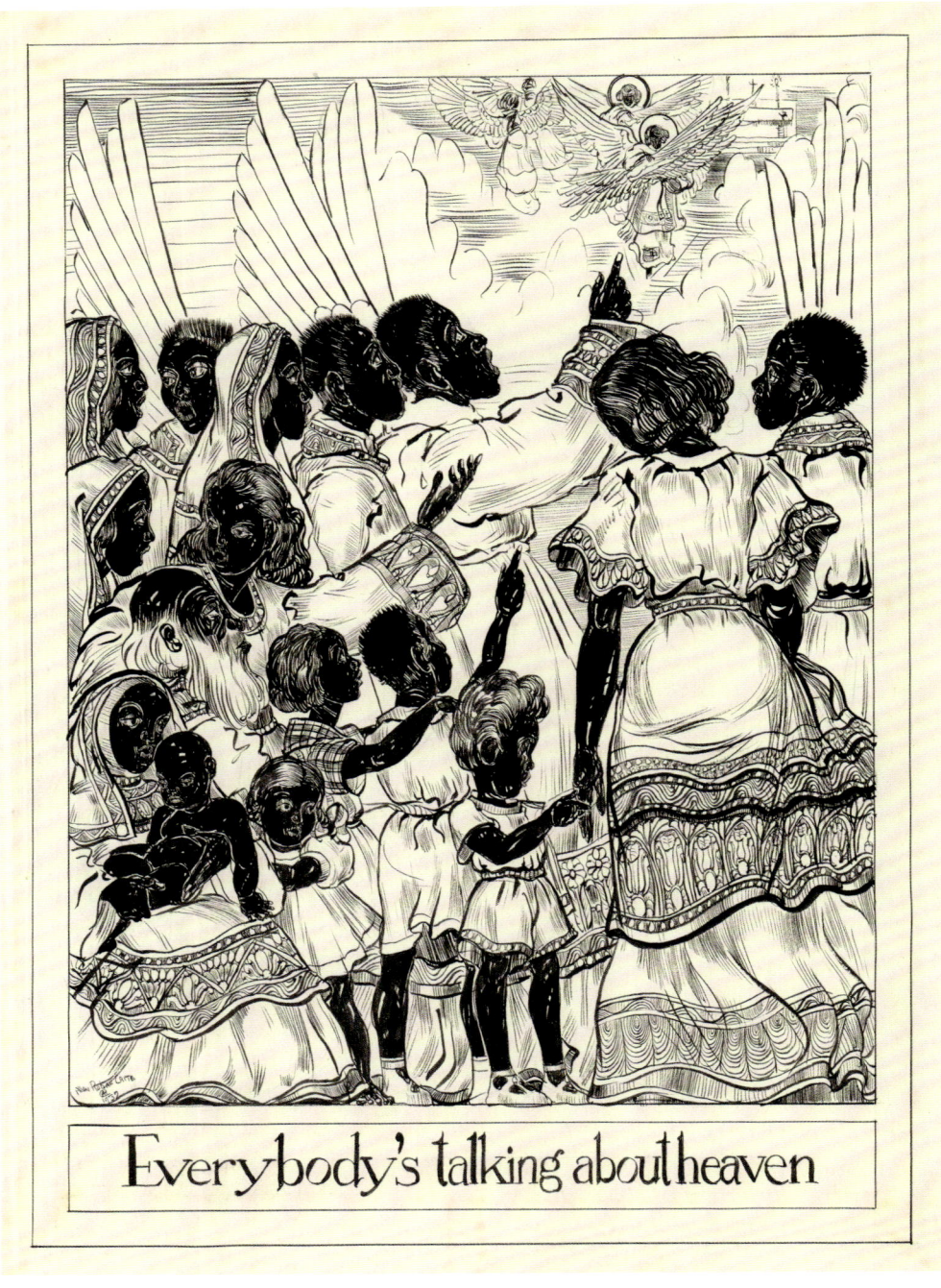

Everybody's talking about heaven

order the Society of St. John the Evangelist. In these pieces, Crite inserts Black figures into traditional church settings.

Perhaps most radically, he published a book that not only featured dark-skinned holy figures but also glorified Black religious song and culture. *Three Spirituals from Earth to Heaven* (1948) (figs. 16, 87, and plate 12), published by Harvard University Press with a foreword by the renowned opera singer Roland Hayes, features drawings from 1937. Crite described this book as an effort to clarify the importance of Black spirituals:

> The other thing was the illustrating of the spirituals. There of course I was deal-
> ing with the hymns of Black people but presenting them as being part of the
> world-wide religious musical literature. I did that because I felt that certain
> aspects, the message of the spirituals, were being lost; because when you

get spirituals mixed up with such things as "folksongs" like "Ole Black Joe," presented as a spiritual by one of the well-meaning in the 1920s and '30s, you have a problem.[23]

Not only did he seek to insert Black people into religious worship, but he showed the ways in which they had made important contributions to "world-wide religious musical literature." In his quiet, intellectual way, Crite was making a radical point that foreshadowed the Civil Rights and Black Power movements of the second half of the twentieth century. These were just two of the many social movements he would later engage with, not as a young artist but as an elder statesman and mentor, as Paula Austin discusses in this volume. But before that moment arrived, Crite accomplished, witnessed, and responded artistically to many more things.

THE CHARLESTOWN NAVY YARD AND THE COMMITMENT
TO WORKS ON PAPER: 1940–1969

In addition to his work as a scholar and artist, Crite had a day job. He began working at the Charlestown Navy Yard as an engineering draughtsman and technical illustrator in 1940 (see plate 36). Immersed in the war effort, Crite was tasked with making highly technical renderings of battleship parts, such as propellers and steam turbines, and creating what were essentially portraits of naval vessels.[24] Years later, Crite recalled, "I looked upon my work in the Navy Department as a means towards an end of promoting myself as an artist. It gave me a more secure financial basis, in a way. It really helped me a great deal."[25] Alongside his oil paintings of the late 1930s and early 1940s, Crite produced a prolific number of watercolors, a practice he continued during his early years at the Navy Yard. In *Consultation in the Drafting Room,* we see a dense composition of men and women employed by the Navy Yard, the man at center scrutinizing a blueprint and sitting opposite a likely Crite self-portrait (fig. 17). As in most of Crite's watercolors, the brushwork is loose and gestural, in marked contrast to the tight angularity often present in his oil paintings. In his ink drawing of the destroyer USS *Mitscher,* the more linear sections of Crite's black-and-white composition, such as the sky and ship itself, incorporate techniques used for much of his liturgical illustration, while the fluid brushstrokes used to articulate the churning sea evoke his work in watercolor (fig. 18).

Newly versed in a job for the federal government that engaged with cutting-edge transportation technology, Crite began to reference some sort of transport in much of his work, from the manual (carts and bicycles) to the mechanized (boats, planes, trolleys, and cars). As his career progressed, he often achieved this by including an airplane in the sky—even rendering an airplane from his vantage point inside one in the 1940s, relatively early in the history of civilian commercial aviation (fig. 19).[26] Some of these forms of transportation were therefore familiar, while others were novel. In Boston, a trolley system that had been active since the late 1800s was rapidly supplemented with new subway trains and tunnels, buses, and elevated railways during the first four decades of the twentieth century—by the 1950s, the system covered more than one hundred square miles throughout the Boston area.[27] This growing transport system suffused Crite's work. From early oil paintings such as *The Carstop* (about 1940) (fig. 20) and watercolors of bus travel, to portfolios of lithographed prints made later in life, mundane modes of travel appear repeatedly in Crite's work. In the self-published portfolio *Recollections of My Childhood* (1978), various forms of transportation feature in almost every composition, often accompanied by musings on Crite's experience as a traveler. He even integrated transportation into his church murals, such as the one at Grace Church on the island of Martha's Vineyard, a longtime vacation community for Black Americans. This latter work—beyond the immediate vicinity of Boston but within Massachusetts—focuses on both the religious and secular comings and goings at Vineyard Haven Harbor (fig. 21).

Opposite: Fig. 17. Allan Rohan Crite, *Consultation in the Drafting Room,* 1943. Watercolor with black ink and white highlights over graphite on paper, 36.5 × 28.6 cm. Boston Athenaeum

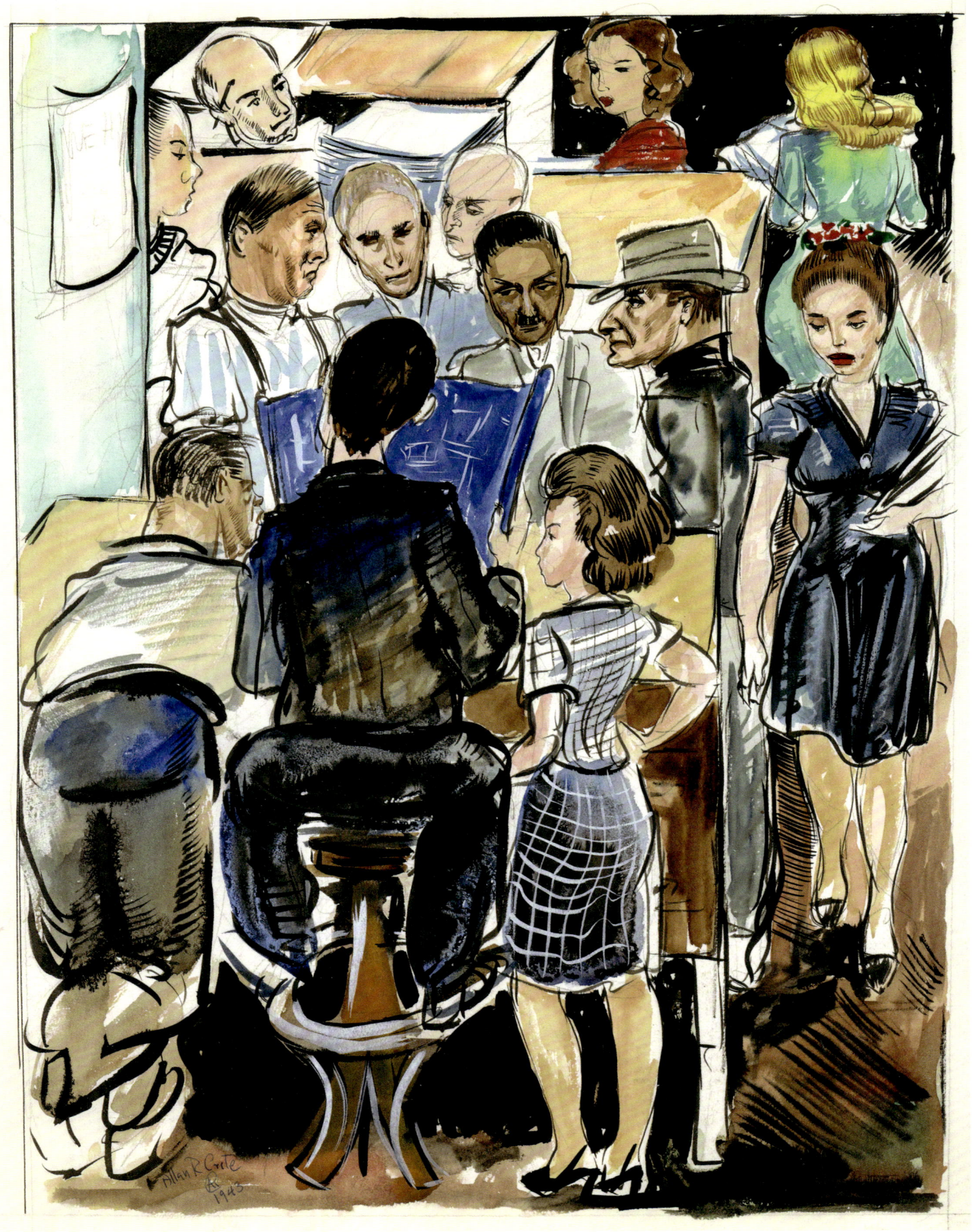

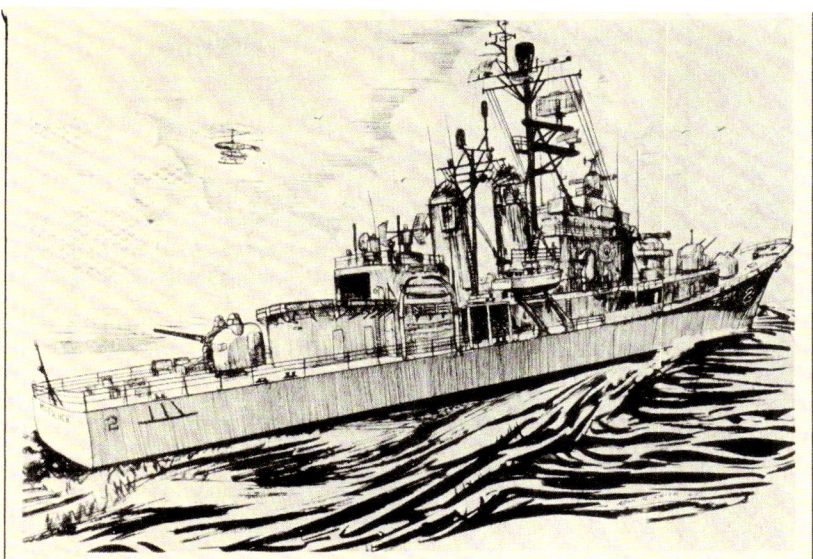

ARTIST'S CONCEPTION of USS Mitscher (DL-2) as she will look when shipyard craftsmen have completed her overhaul shows the new helicopter landing platform on the stern from which drone helicopters will take off. These helicopters are a part of the Navy's DASH (Drone Anti-Submarine Helicopter) weapons delivery system. The helicopter hangar doors will work much like garage overhead doors — they will lift and slide up into the overhead.

Fig. 18. Allan Rohan Crite, *USS Mitscher*, from the *Boston Naval Shipyard News*, 6 May 1960 4. National Park Service, National Parks of Boston, Charlestown Navy Yard

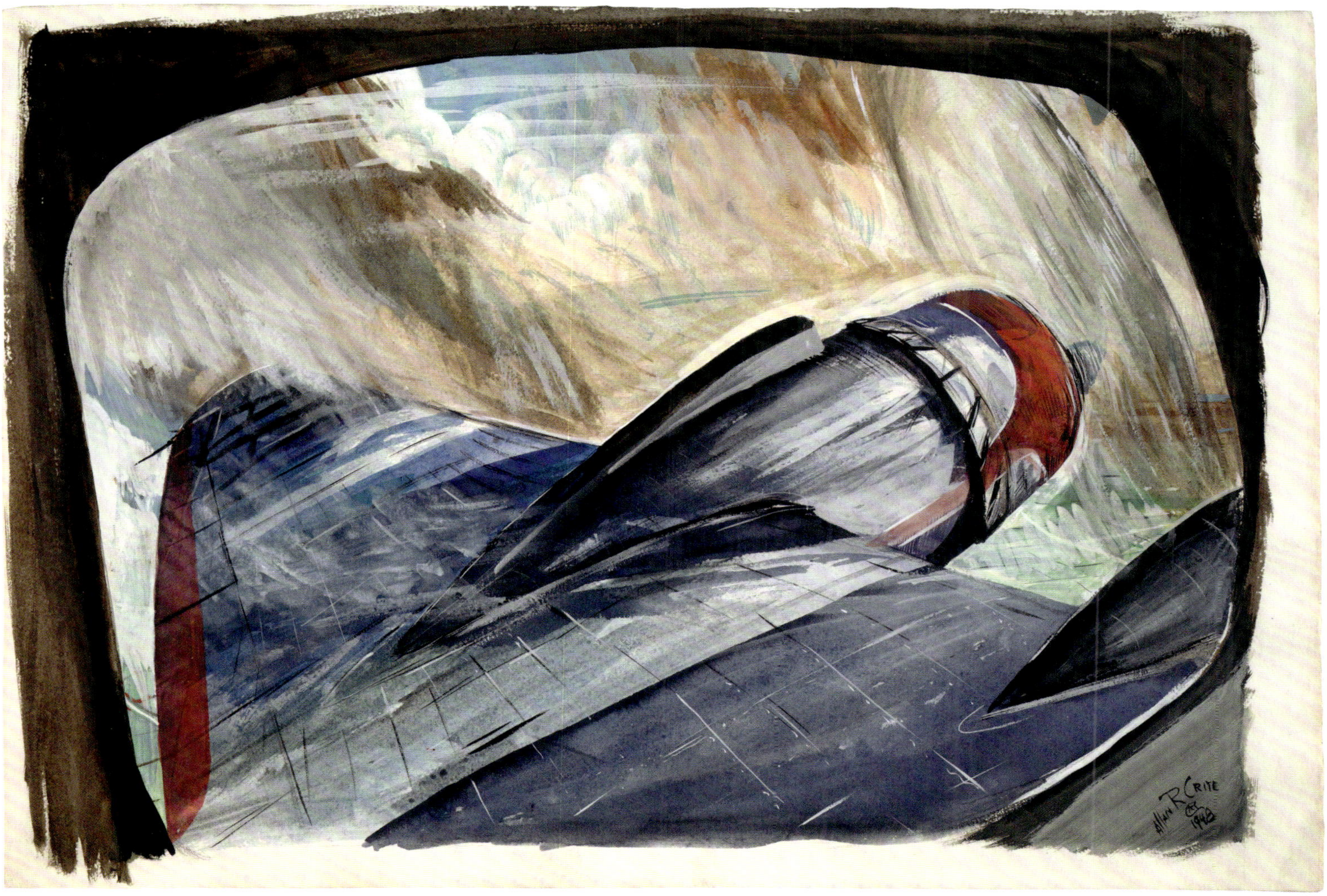

Fig. 19. Allan Rohan Crite, *View from an Airplane Window*, 1948. Watercolor with black ink and gouache over graphite on paper, 37.8 × 54 cm. Boston Athenaeum

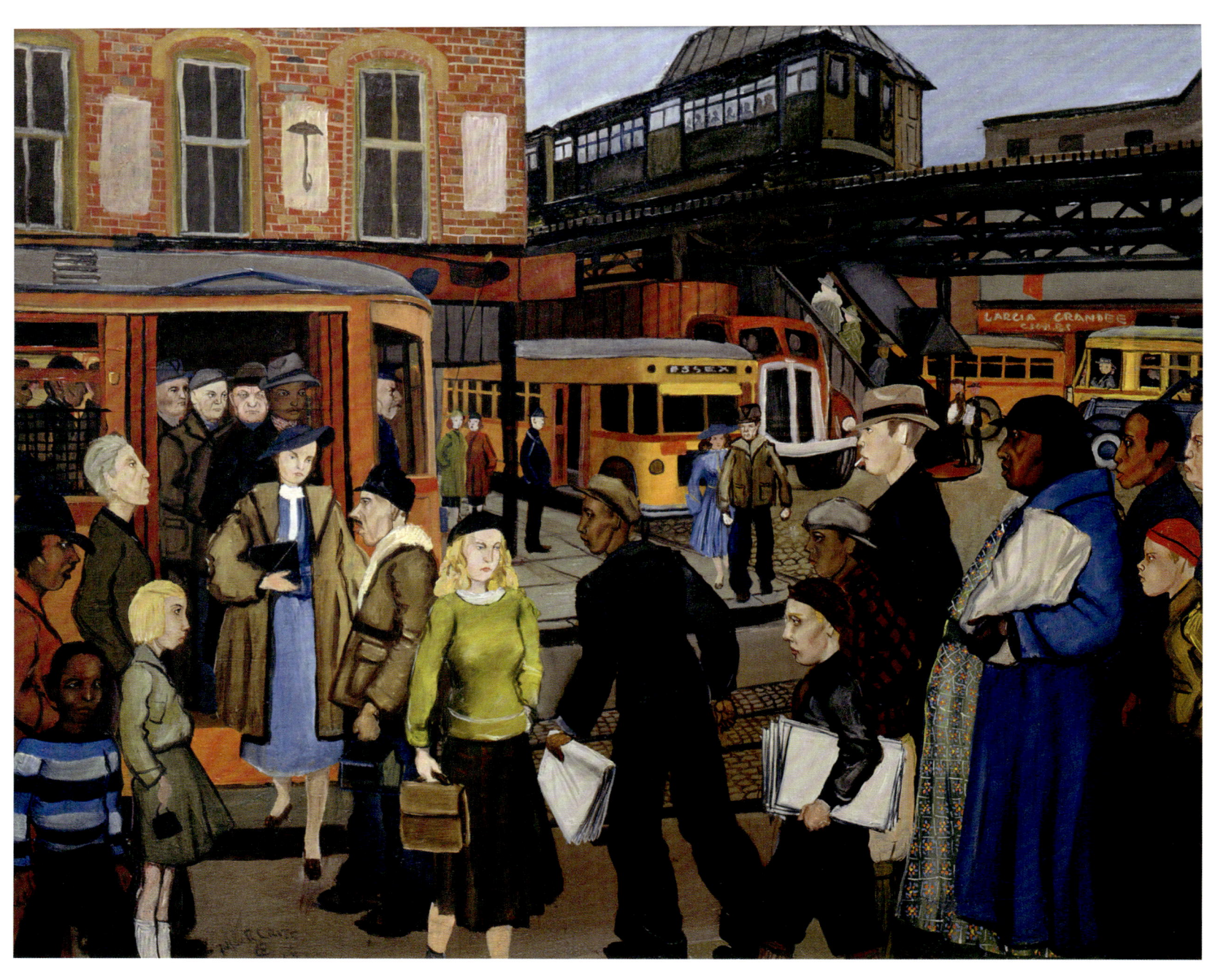

Fig. 20. Allan Rohan Crite, *The Carstop,* about 1940. Oil on canvas, 63.5 × 78.4 cm. Boston Athenaeum

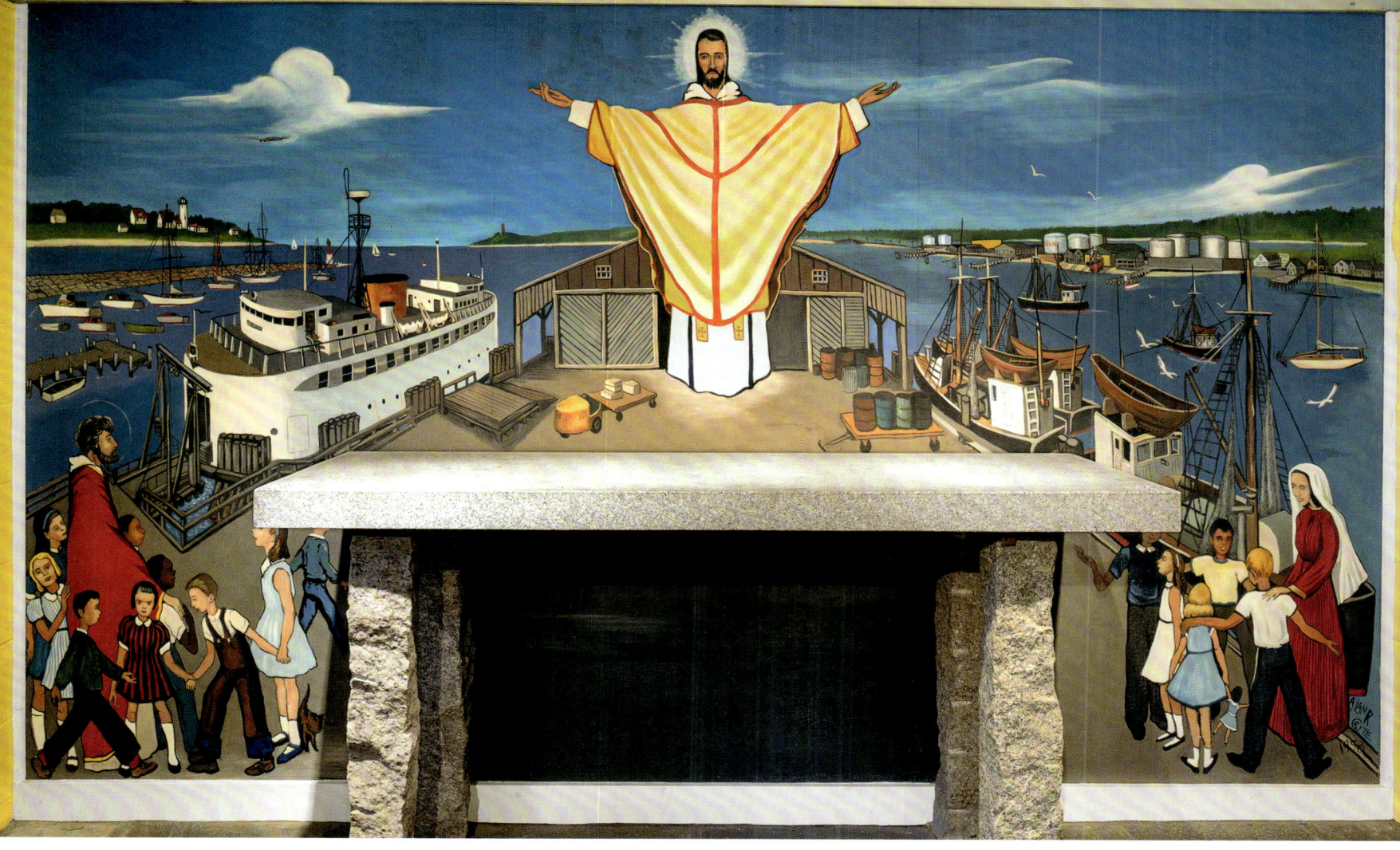

ND ALL THAT MOVE IN THE WATERS, BLESS YE THE LORD

Fig. 21. Allan Rohan Crite, *Untitled (Vineyard Haven Mural),* 1958. Grace Episcopal Church, Vineyard Haven, Massachusetts

Crite's oeuvre embraces not just movement but migration. At the same time that the transportation system in Boston was expanding, the city's Black population was growing rapidly. Boston was a less common destination than New York, Detroit, or Chicago for the first wave of the Great Migration of Black Americans from the South to the North during World War I. But it was an important destination for migrating Black Americans during and in the wake of World War II. Employers like the Charlestown Navy Yard, Crite's own workplace, and the Gillette Safety Razor Company provided well-paying secure industrial jobs during the war. This boon to what had been a largely stagnant economy for three decades continued after the war, as Boston established itself as a hub for high-tech manufacturing. From 1940 to 1950, Boston's Black population doubled—this growth was largely driven by Black residents who had been born in the South.[28]

The News (1945), the last known oil painting of Crite's *Neighborhood Series,* subtly engages with these themes (fig. 22). On the corner of Columbus Avenue and Northampton Street in Boston's Roxbury neighborhood, four men read the news of President Franklin Delano Roosevelt's death. Roosevelt died on 12 April 1945, three months into his fourth term and during the final months of World War II. Crite reproduced the front pages of Boston newspapers, including actual headlines from the *Boston Post* and others, complete with miniature portraits of the late leader. Three of the four men, one of whom appears to be a Black soldier on leave—many Black soldiers were posted to Fort Devens outside Boston—cluster together to read the news, while another man reads independently

Opposite: Fig. 22. Allan Rohan Crite, *The News,* 1945. Oil on canvas, 83 × 72 cm. Boston Athenaeum

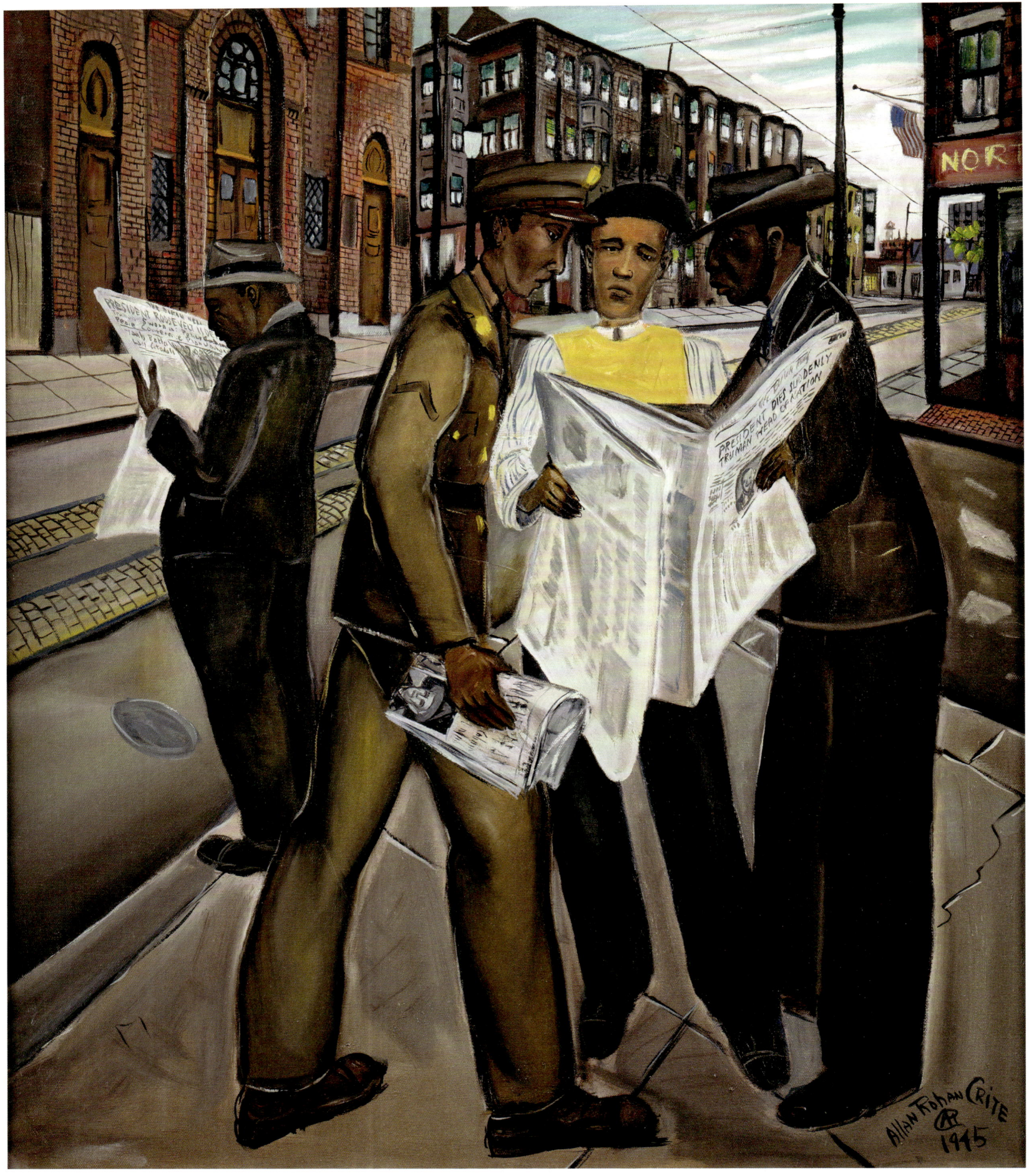

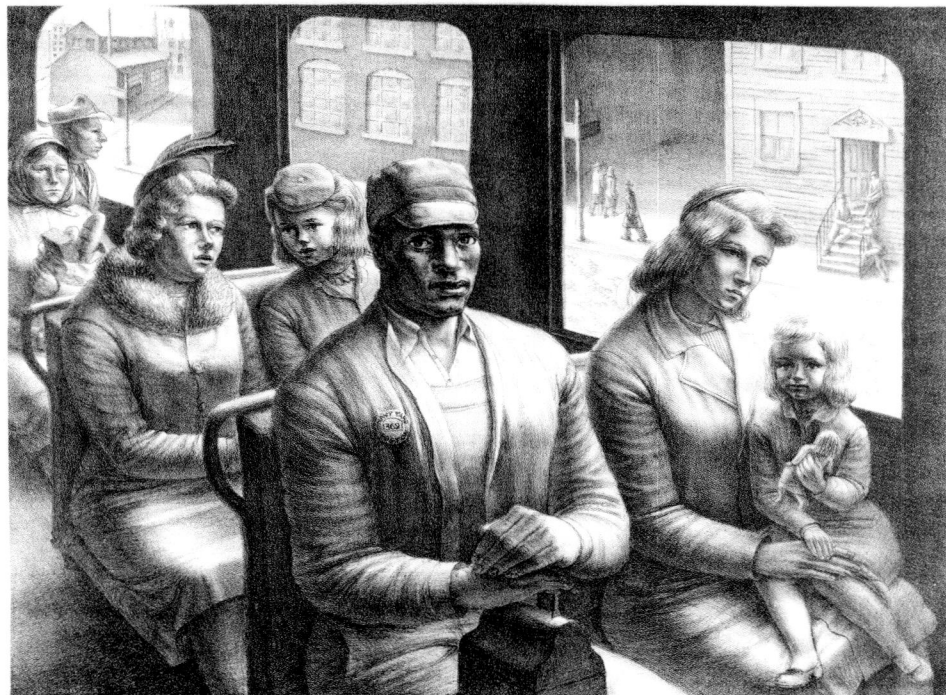

Fig. 23. John Wilson, *The Passing Scene (Streetcar Scene)*, 1945. Lithograph, 36 × 46 cm. Boston Athenaeum

beside them and an American flag waves at half-mast nearby.[29] Crite often included highly specific details in his paintings from the 1930s and early 1940s, such as accurately rendered buildings, signs, and other spatial markers, but this painting's direct connection to a major world event makes it an outlier, even as Crite offers a local viewpoint on an international news story. The fact that the men are reading emphasizes their literacy—a point of tension surrounding the arrival of new Black residents in Boston, many of whom were from the South and were less educated than Boston's existing Black population.[30] While it is impossible to distinguish these men as new arrivals or longtime Bostonians, the man in uniform hints at one of the drivers of the change in Black demographics: migration fueled by federal government policies during and after World War II. Jobs like Crite's at the Navy Yard made Boston desirable in a way that it had not been during earlier waves of migration from the South to the North. Finally, the focus on Roosevelt's death may be a nod to the president's particularly important role in the Black community. Under his leadership, African American voters realigned their primary allegiance from the Republican Party—the party of Abraham Lincoln—to the Democratic Party and New Deal liberalism. The election of 1936 in particular was a watershed moment.[31] This one painting subtly and elegantly engages with many political and social issues affecting Boston's Black community.

Other Black artists in Crite's orbit also chose to address racial dynamics in Boston during this moment of change in the 1940s. Two important works from this period speak to the city's social climate and the centrality of the streetcar to it. John Wilson, who graduated from Crite's alma mater, the School of the Museum of Fine Arts, in 1945, considered the elder artist an important mentor.[32] Wilson's powerful lithograph *The Passing Scene (Streetcar Scene)* (1945) centers on a young Black man on his way to work at the Navy Yard, as evidenced by the badge pinned to his jacket (fig. 23). The man is surrounded by other passengers—mostly white women, one of whom may be a recent European immigrant—but is the only one to look directly at the viewer. Just one year later, Crite united his interest in transportation and devotional imagery in the striking watercolor

Fig. 24. Allan Rohan Crite, *Our Lady of Marblehead,* 1948. Offset lithograph with white gouache, 36.6 × 28.4 cm. Boston Athenaeum

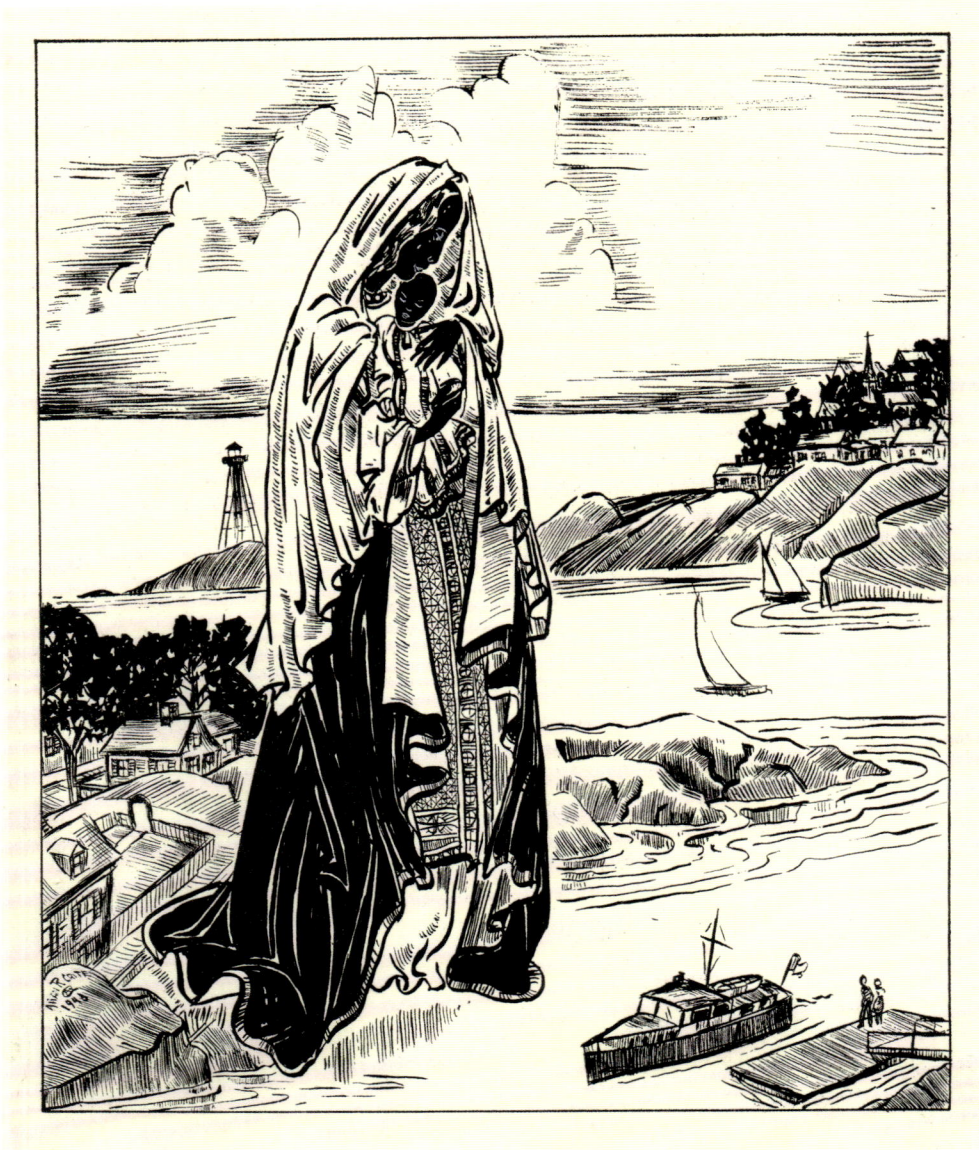

Streetcar Madonna (1946) (see fig. 90). Part of a series that depicts Madonnas in mundane urban settings (see plate 24), *Streetcar Madonna* pictures a Black Madonna and Child seated on a streetcar, the other riders apparently oblivious to the divinity in their midst. As Efeoghene Igor Coleman writes in this volume, *Streetcar Madonna* can be read not only as an elevation of Black motherhood but as trenchant social commentary on racial violence. This holds true also for John Wilson, whose graphic work was more immediately political. These two pictures, striking in their similar compositions and themes, were created at a time when racial tensions were especially high at the Navy Yard, following the unwarranted beating of twenty-five-year-old driller Isaac Cummings by white security guards.[33] Racial tension in Boston was roiling—and would continue to seethe as the demographics and economy of the city shifted after the war and FDR's death, the event that Crite documents in *The News.*

    It was another urban Madonna, however, that marked a significant shift in the artist's practice: *Our Lady of Marblehead* (1948). Here, Crite renders the sky in much the same way that he did in *USS Mitscher,* but instead of a singular drawing in pen and ink, this work is a lithograph (fig. 24). This print shows Crite at the beginning of his embrace of lithography as the primary medium for his work. Crite had made woodcuts and other

relief prints in the past, noting in an oral history that the graphic contrast of those media seemed especially apt for his liturgical work, whereas lithography allowed both ease of image making and substantially higher print runs.[34] Though Crite still occasionally painted (notably in gouache during the 1950s) (see plate 27), he had turned almost exclusively to printmaking with an offset lithography press by midcentury. The process of drawing for a printing plate afforded him the same gestural freedom that ink and watercolor did, but he traded the singularity of these media for the multiples offered by offset lithography.

Crite began collaborating with printers at local Episcopalian churches to produce brilliantly illustrated bulletins. As he explained in a letter to Reverend Tom Lehman of Grace Church in Vineyard Haven, however, he soon acquired his own press and began to do his own printing:

> Since I have seen you, I have acquired a Multilith press 1250 class and am now printing up my church bulletins. . . . It is quite an experience to learn the operation of this foolish machine, but it does eliminate the somewhat frustrating experience which I have had at times in the past waiting for my printer friend to find the time in his overworked schedule to print the bulletins for me. He had reached a stage in his work [in the] latter part of 1960 wherein he simply couldn't handle it and so with his guidance I was able to secure a Multilith at a very reasonable cost and with his instructions learned the beginnings of how to operate it. I will be able to proceed I hope with greater confidence with the supporting knowledge that I will be able to produce the various devotional material for the Church.[35]

Crite used a "paper master" as the printing plate for his offset lithography press. Multilith masters looked like regular sheets of paper but came prepared with a special coating that facilitated image duplication through the press. The sheets also had a row of holes along the edge so that the plate could be hooked onto the press for printing. By using paper masters, Crite was able to sketch directly on the plate with immediacy, as he did in more traditional sketchbooks, but now with the capability of being able to reproduce the image immediately. According to friends, Crite would often make a number of sketches on the masters at a dinner party and the next day share printed portraits of the attendees as a thank-you.[36]

During the 1950s and 1960s, Crite not only balanced his day job at the Navy Yard with his work for the Episcopal Church; he also took classes at Harvard University's Extension School. After fourteen years of study, he graduated with his degree in 1968. Soon thereafter, Crite began a series of exhibitions, publications, and lectures that sought to reintroduce the general public to the interconnectedness and shared cultural foundations of humanity. In a letter to then Boston Athenaeum director Walter Muir Whitehill, Crite explained:

> It has been my opinion that for the most part our sense of the history of the United States is Anglo-Saxon oriented almost to the exclusion of the other major cultural factors such as Indian, Spanish and African elements which are also a part of the principal cultural foundations of the nation. The migrations of the nineteenth century from Europe and the importation of Chinese and Japanese from the orient came on to an "ongoing situation." Hence therefore the stressing of cultural foundations![37]

In focusing again on migration and obscured histories, Crite illustrated the complicated, centuries-long movement of peoples across North America. His views on this subject fueled two related publications in 1968: Crite's self-published *Towards a Rediscovery*

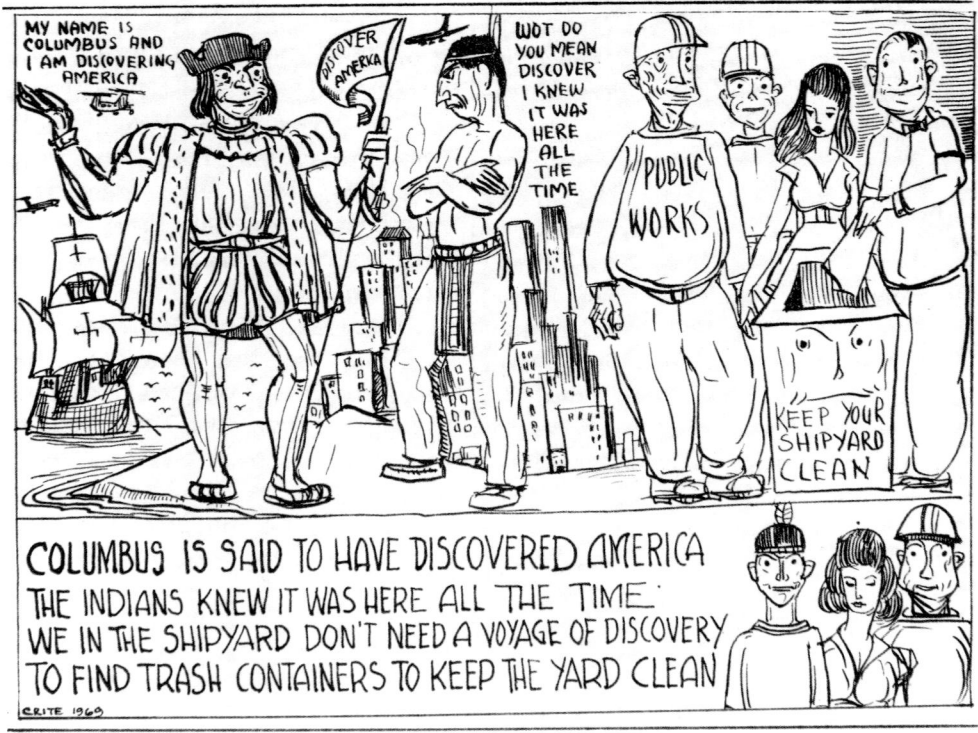

of the Cultural Heritage of the United States and *The Cultural Foundations of America,* a series of pamphlets published by the Boston Athenaeum in conjunction with a series of exhibitions (see plates 32–35). As Paula Austin writes in her essay in this volume, the turbulent social climate of the late 1960s in Boston and beyond was undoubtedly on Crite's mind as he pursued these projects.

By the late 1960s, Crite was also contributing illustrations to the Navy Yard's staff bulletin, the *Boston Naval Shipyard News.* Commissioned by the Navy Yard, these illustrations took the form of comics and urged employees to keep the yard clean. His contributions are often immediately obvious, as he borrowed motifs from his church bulletins and his projects exploring the history of human civilization and migration. In his Columbus Day comic, Crite countered the common discovery narrative, while loosely connecting it to the usual message of cleaning the shipyard. In the comic, a foppish European man says, "My name is Columbus and I am discovering America," to which an Indigenous man replies, "Wut do you mean discover I knew it was here all the time [*sic*]" (fig. 25). This kind of revisionist approach to inherited historical narratives was a crucial part of Crite's cultural heritage projects in the late 1960s.

Following his studies at Harvard's Extension School, Crite returned to campus frequently, both as a librarian for the Grossman Library and as an artist-in-residence at the Semitic Museum, now the Harvard Museum of the Ancient Near East. There, Crite's penchant for close object study and his interest in the history of civilization and migration were nourished. Indeed, these institutions, along with the Boston Athenaeum, would provide an intellectual home to Crite during the 1970s, an era of immense change in the artist's life.

DEAN OF BOSTON'S AFRICAN AMERICAN ARTS COMMUNITY: 1970S–1990S

In the span of one decade starting in 1970, Crite lost his mother, produced some of his most radical work, and ensured a lasting legacy by gifting art to local institutions and helping establish a group of young local artists of color called the Boston Collective. One of the biggest changes occurred in 1971, when mother and son were forced to move from their home of forty-six years, 2 Dilworth Street in Lower Roxbury, owing to urban

redevelopment—or "urban removal," as Crite called it.[38] This moment would remain a touchpoint in Crite's work for years to come, and it fomented a shift in the way Crite thought about his life, art, and legacy. Some clues about this shift appear in a poignant self-portrait set in front of his old street corner, which he included in his *Autobiographical Sketch* (1977) (see fig. 75). He wrote in the caption:

> Such big chunks of this city have become a memory so big chunks of my life is memory. Forgotten in this fast receding past, such is this street . . . forty-six years of my life here has vanished in the dust of bulldozers and hungry cranes as I join the other millions of redevelopment refugees. But now an empty lot full of weeds and forgetfulness is here, and few careless empty beer cans. Buildings, homes have to make way for trash flowering lots until some faceless somebody decides decrees to fill in the lots, which then sprout new buildings for other people who know nothing of those before whose lives and stories are sepulchered beneath, covered over with ever deepening layers of forgetfulness into a fossilization of geologic time.[39]

It was painfully ironic that Crite had become one of the "millions of redevelopment refugees." Urban redevelopment, residential displacement, and the destruction of old houses was not a new theme for Crite. In a series of watercolors from January 1940, he documented destruction in the South End. *Wrecking Old Houses; The Last of Dillon Street; Burning and Digging: South End Housing Project* (fig. 26), and others picture heavy machinery demolishing buildings. Crite's frenetic brushwork contrasts with a vibrant palette that almost aestheticizes the destruction.

There had been efforts dating to the Progressive Era to "improve" the lives and living conditions of urban dwellers—often recent immigrants and people of color— in addition to clearing paths in the early twentieth century for public transit systems to connect Boston to its growing (mostly white) suburbs. Crite's watercolors probably depict some of these early moments, but the full force of the government turned to questions of "urban renewal" after World War II. With federal legislation like the Housing Act of 1949 and the Housing Act of 1954, Boston and other cities were encouraged and provided with funding to demolish "slums" in their city centers. This was done with little respect for the communities there or their displacement, and these projects often replaced historic buildings with modernist ones.[40] The first major project was the 1954–57 demolition of the northeastern section of the South End for industrial redevel-opment. This area was called the "New York Streets" because the roads were named after towns in the state of New York; it ultimately became home to parts of the Mass Pike and Route I-93.[41] Boston's West End—one of the city's most vibrant multicultural neigh-borhoods—was systematically demolished in the late 1950s and early 1960s to make way for new development, including the brand-new City Hall.[42]

Roxbury and other parts of the South End were targeted for redevelopment after the West End, but the communities and their leaders—like activist Mel King and the Emergency Tenants Council—fought back.[43] Crite's distress at the changes wrought on the neighborhood is apparent in a 1961 letter to Athenaeum director Walter Muir Whitehill, in which Crite expressed concern about an abandoned historic house in Roxbury and included sketches of the building.[44] In this way, he shared the concerns of historic preservation in cities advocated by activists like Jane Jacobs.[45] His opposition to urban redevelopment and displacement was further galvanized after he was forced to move, possibly to make way for the construction of Boston's Southwest Expressway and the proposed Inner Belt, a project that Massachusetts governor Francis W. Sargent ultimately halted thanks to fierce community resistance.[46] Unfortunately, it was too late for the Crites to save their home at 2 Dilworth Street.

Opposite: Fig. 26. Allan Rohan Crite, *Burning and Digging: South End Housing Project,* January 1940. Watercolor with ink and white highlights, 38 × 28 cm. Boston Athenaeum

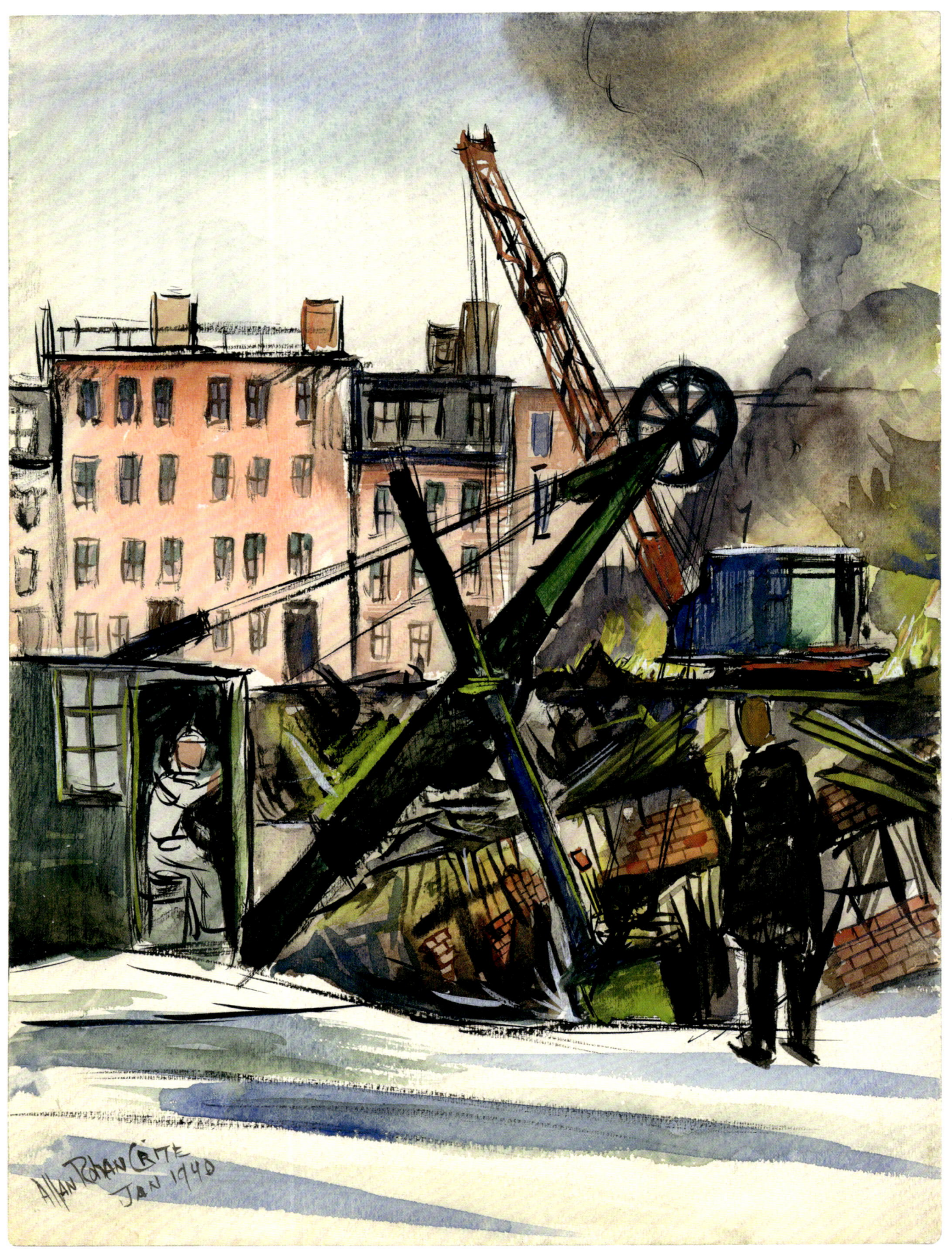

Allan Rohan Crite
Jan 1940

Crite and his mother moved in December 1971 to their new home, just a stone's throw from those of community activists like King and Crite's good friend Byron Rushing. In February of the following year, Crite sent Walter Muir Whitehill and others an illustrated New Year's card, designed and printed by the artist. It noted the change of address and featured small renderings of each of his homes, past and present (fig. 27). In a personal note to Whitehill, Crite wrote of 410 Columbus Avenue, "The house has presented interesting possibilities." This would certainly ring true when Crite situated his printing press in the home rather than keeping it at a local church, as he had before. With the purchase of his brownstone at 410 Columbus Avenue in 1971, Crite's commitment to community preservation seems to have ramped up considerably. He would henceforth dedicate himself to creating new spaces for gathering and establishing new communities of artists in his orbit. The space became a hub for artistic and civic learning.[47]

Crite's life continued to shift as he retired from the Charlestown Navy Yard in 1974 and was able to dedicate more time to making his own art. His mother, Annamae, died in 1977—another major change for the artist, who had always lived with her. Even in old age, she remained a force in his life. Art historian Edmund Barry Gaither recalled in an interview for this volume:

> I visited his home on Columbus Avenue quite a number of times, and my first visits there were before the death of his mother, who was a very large figure in his life. Visiting in the time of his mother had a protocol. You came in, his mother . . . was bedridden, and she would be in place in her receiving room and bedroom on the second floor. So the first thing you did was to go up to the second floor and present yourself essentially at the foot of her bed with greetings, and she sort of stamped your approval and then you got to see everything else.[48]

After his mother's passing, Crite cultivated community in the role of elder and mentor in the Boston arts community, assuming a paternal mantle after his own parent had died.

In particular, he focused on participating in a resilient and dynamic Black artistic community that would explicitly *not* "know nothing of those before whose lives and

Fig. 27. Allan Rohan Crite, New Year's card to Walter Muir Whitehill, 1972. Offset color lithograph with ballpoint additions, 13.5 × 21.5 cm. Walter Muir Whitehill Papers, Collection of the Massachusetts Historical Society

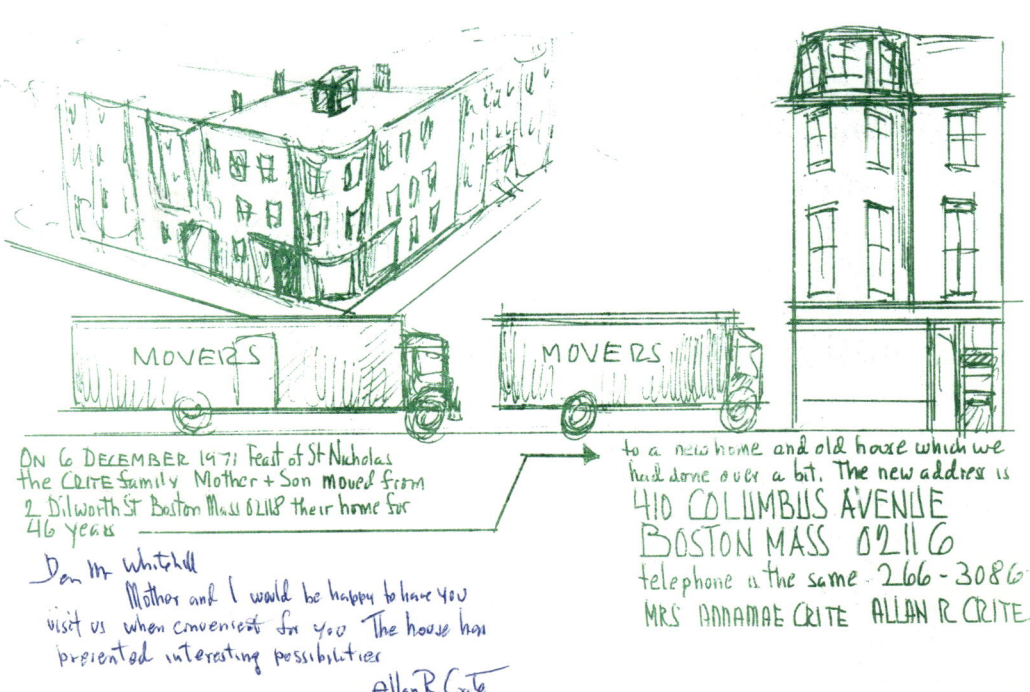

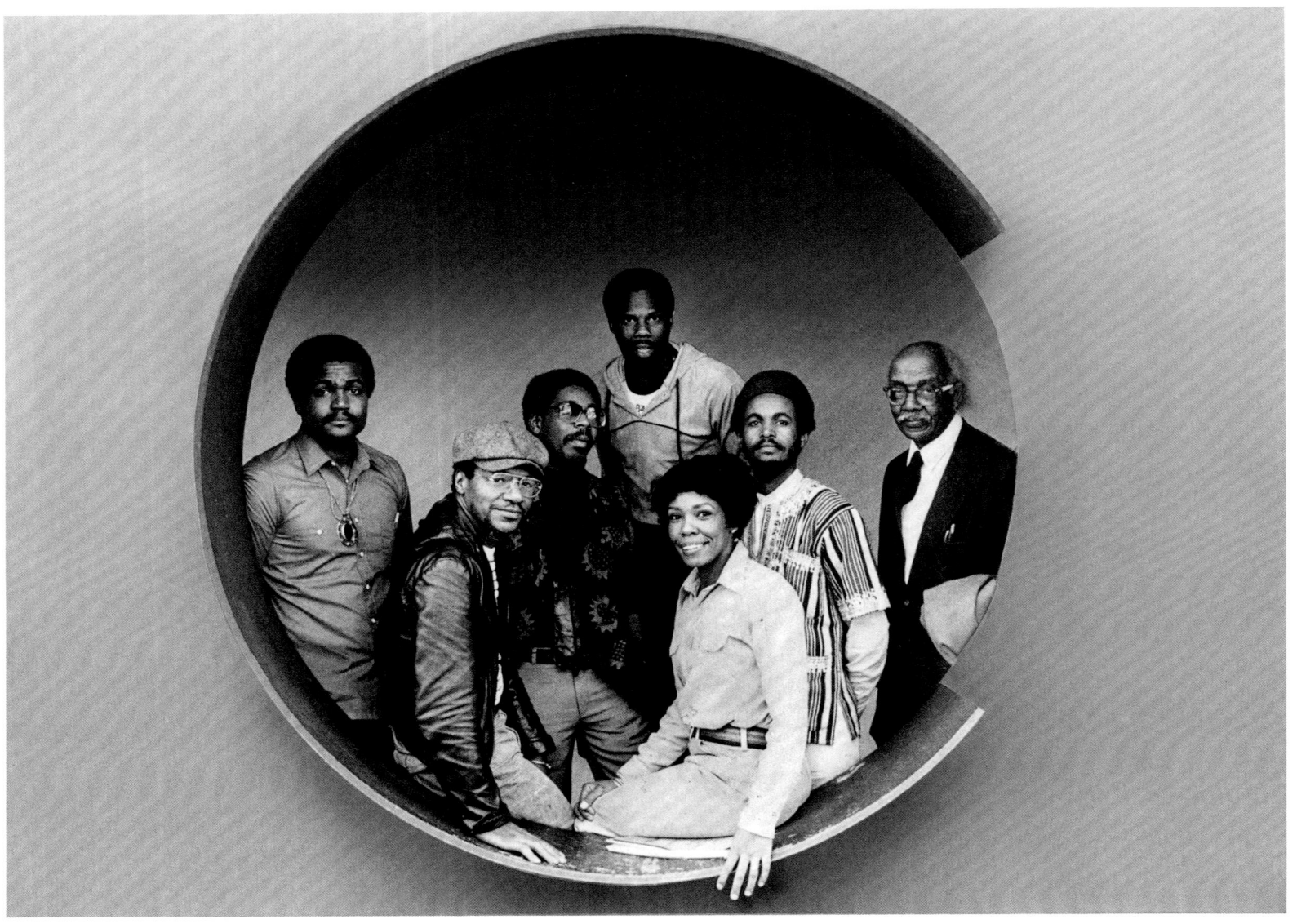

Fig. 28. The Boston Collective, May 1980. *left to right:* Aukram Burton, Vusumuzi Maduna, Reginald Jackson, Paul Goodnight, Susan Thompson, Napoleon Jones-Henderson, and Allan Rohan Crite. Photograph by Aukram Burton

stories are sepulchered beneath." In fact, it would engage with, glorify, and preserve those stories. As Martina Tanga has written, the 1970s saw the creation of a number of institutions that provided support to the Black arts scene in Boston, including the African American Master Artists-in-Residence Program, the Harriet Tubman House Art Gallery at the United South End Settlements, and community organizer Mel King's Community Fellows Program at MIT.[49] In this flourishing ecosystem, Crite helped to organize the Boston Collective around 1979 (fig. 28). This group of artists, all younger than Crite, included Aukram Burton, Vusumuzi Maduna, Paul Goodnight, Reginald Jackson, Napoleon Jones-Henderson, and Susan Thompson; soon, a parallel group called What in the World formed; it included Thompson, Lotus Do, Weeta Lopes, and Johnetta Tinker. Several of these artists have provided recollections for this catalogue about working with Crite and his impact on their lives and artistic practice. Their words are reproduced and resonate throughout this volume, both a touching tribute and a wealth of primary source material. What emerges from these recollections is something core to Crite's practice in these years: a generosity that helped fuel a group of young artists for decades.

Nestled in and to some extent presiding over this ecosystem, Crite was notably prolific from the late 1970s through the 1980s. In this period, he produced a number of printed portfolios, ranging from depictions of the "Combat Zone" (see fig. 80), the adult entertainment district in downtown Boston that was home to strip clubs and pornography shops, to a series titled *Madonnas of Transportation* (1987) (fig. 29). The images

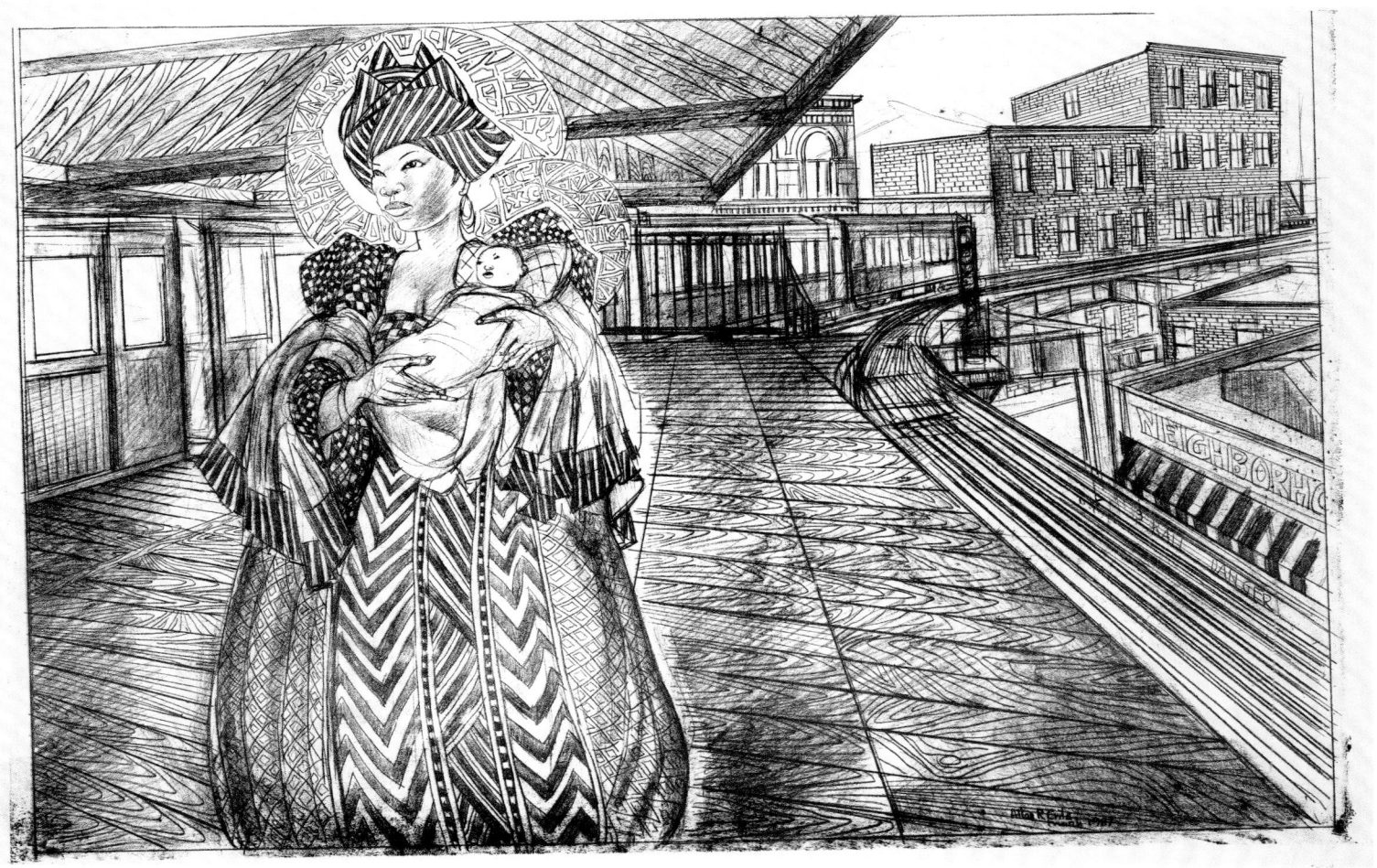

Fig. 29. Allan Rohan Crite, *Madonna of Dudley Station (Curve in the Tracks), No. 4*, from the series *Madonnas of Transportation*, March 1987. Offset lithograph, 27.9 × 43.2 cm. Museum of Fine Arts, Boston

of the Combat Zone specifically portrayed sex workers—evidence of the growing presence of sexuality in Crite's work after his mother's death. Always attentive to the female form in his earlier work, in later life he created elaborate, explicitly erotic works and cautioned friends not to be ashamed of depicting nudity and sexuality (fig. 30). As his mentee Johnetta Tinker recalled, "He always said the human body is our body. Why are we ashamed of the human body? There's something wrong with the human mind if you think there's something wrong with the human body."[50]

In these years Crite developed a new visual language that was self-consciously graphic, almost like graphic novels or zines. Meticulous line drawings show his ability as a draughtsman. The seriality of the work and the frequent inclusion of detailed captions are related to his skill as a prolific writer. Finally, his engagement with the younger generation and his awareness of broader trends in the Black art world are clear in his increasing inclusion of the signifiers of Black power, such as African art and dress.[51] The women in the *Madonnas of Transportation* series are clad in traditional West African garb, like head ties and dashikis. Crite's references to African art and the language of Black power are even more explicit in a series of drawings and prints that juxtapose Black residents of the South End and totemic African art (see plate 37), like *Ancestor Figure, Bambara, Mali, Wood* (1974) (fig. 31).

Two works from this period in Crite's life are particularly illustrative, one for the insight into his artistic process and one for evidence of his doubling down on the importance of neighborhood and neighborhood institutions. Though it is the later of the two, it is interesting to start with a work from the 1980s that provides unique insight into Crite's "artist-reporter" identity. In 1982, Crite was invited to participate in Mel King's

Opposite: Fig. 30. Allan Rohan Crite, *Untitled (Embracing Couple)*, 1977. Colored Multilith print, 35.6 × 21.6 cm. Courtesy of the private collection of Johnetta Tinker

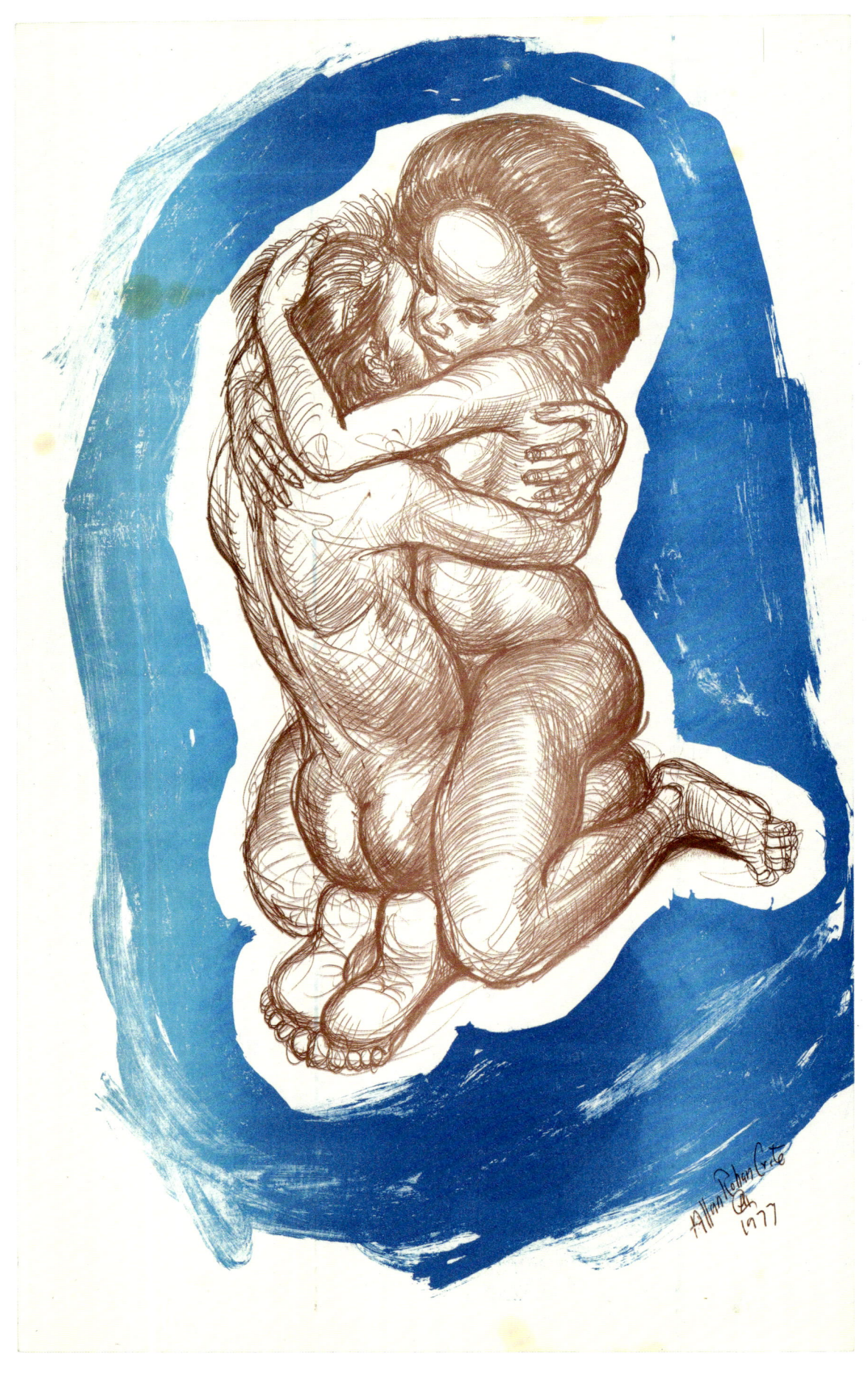

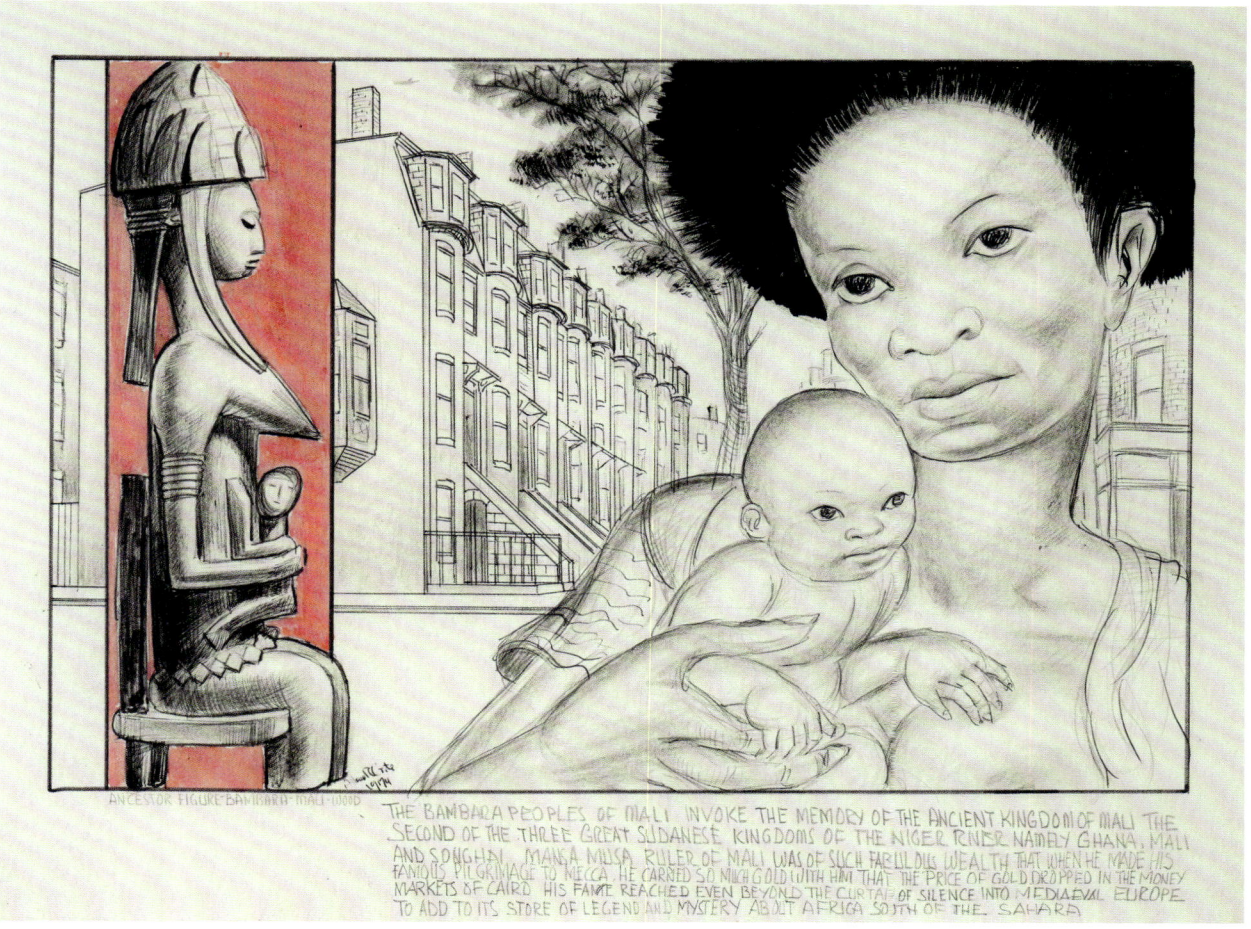

ANCESTOR FIGURE BAMBARA MALI WOOD

THE BAMBARA PEOPLES OF MALI INVOKE THE MEMORY OF THE ANCIENT KINGDOM OF MALI THE SECOND OF THE THREE GREAT SUDANESE KINGDOMS OF THE NIGER RIVER NAMELY GHANA, MALI AND SONGHAI, MANSA MUSA, RULER OF MALI WAS OF SUCH FABULOUS WEALTH THAT WHEN HE MADE HIS FAMOUS PILGRIMAGE TO MECCA, HE CARRIED SO MUCH GOLD WITH HIM THAT THE PRICE OF GOLD DROPPED IN THE MONEY MARKETS OF CAIRO. HIS FAME REACHED EVEN BEYOND THE CURTAIN OF SILENCE INTO MEDIAEVAL EUROPE TO ADD TO ITS STORE OF LEGEND AND MYSTERY ABOUT AFRICA SOUTH OF THE SAHARA.

Community Fellows Program at MIT, which provided residencies for recognized community leaders. During his participation in that program, Crite became interested in how the Chinese Communist Party engaged with the many officially recognized ethnic and linguistic minorities in China. With the help of other Collective members—notably Aukram Burton and Susan Thompson—the group was able to organize a trip to China in 1983 to study this topic.[52] Crite assiduously recorded everything he saw on this trip, creating a comprehensive record that resembles a graphic novel, a form that was just coming to prominence at the time (fig. 32).[53]

Crite would soon return to China, this time as part of an effort by the Commonwealth of Massachusetts to establish a "sister state" relationship with Guangdong Province in the country's southeast. The Boston Collective, with the help of Aukram Burton in particular, proposed an artistic exchange that involved a weeks-long trip to China and included the exhibition of the Collective's work at the Guangzhou Academy of Fine Arts. On this trip, one of Crite's mentees, the artist and educator Johnetta Tinker, observed the artist at work and saw how he created a comprehensive record of what he saw. In recording her recollections for this volume, Tinker said:

> When we went to China together, I saw him look at something 'cause we were on the bus and he would see something, he had his own shorthand. So he always would do a sketch or something [that] looked like scribble to me and then we would get back to the hotel.... The young ones, we went out to party and he would stay back and draw.... When we got back, it looked exactly like what he saw. I was so amazed ... it [was] like his memory.... He called [his

Fig. 31. Allan Rohan Crite, *Ancestor Figure, Bambara, Mali, Wood*, 1974. Black pen and ink, brush-applied red ink, and graphite with porous-tipped black pen on paper, 26 × 35.6 cm. Museum of Fine Arts, Boston

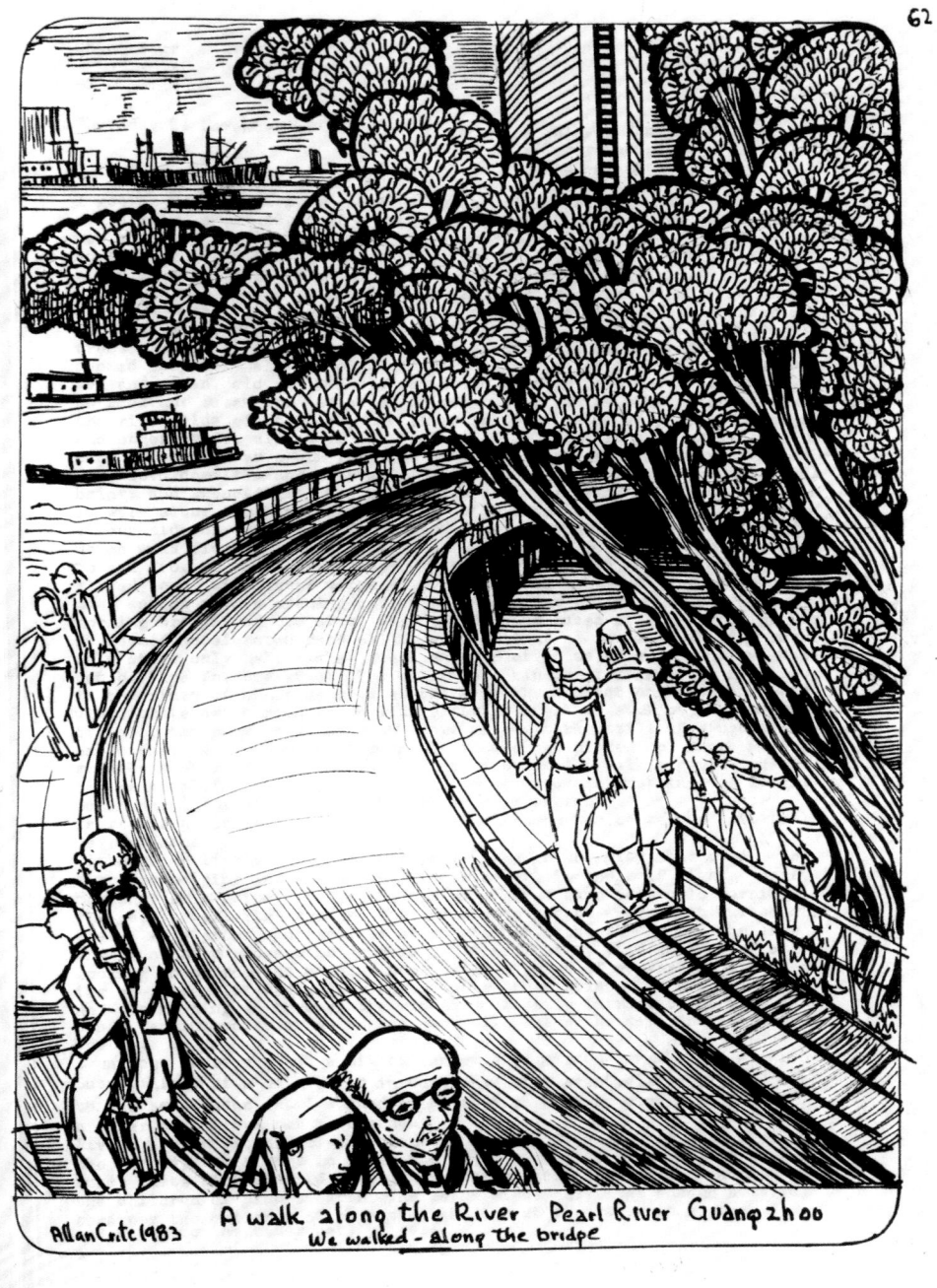

sketchbook] his brains. . . . And he would put it down, then he was, like, "Where are my brains? Where are my brains?" "Your brains are over there, Mr. Crite." So he called it his brains, and he always had a sketchbook with him.[54]

While a sketchbook and drawings from Crite's early life survive, there are comparatively few original drawings and sketchbooks from his later career—printed versions of portfolios proliferate, but the original sketches are lost to time or, in the case of his Multilith press, were drawn directly onto a paper plate and worn down through the printing process. Tinker's recollection provides insight into Crite's process that is not in the visual record, at least not in terms of the works that we know of currently.

Created in the years before the China trip, another of Crite's late-career projects is the most powerful evidence of how he came to focus on the importance of his neigh-

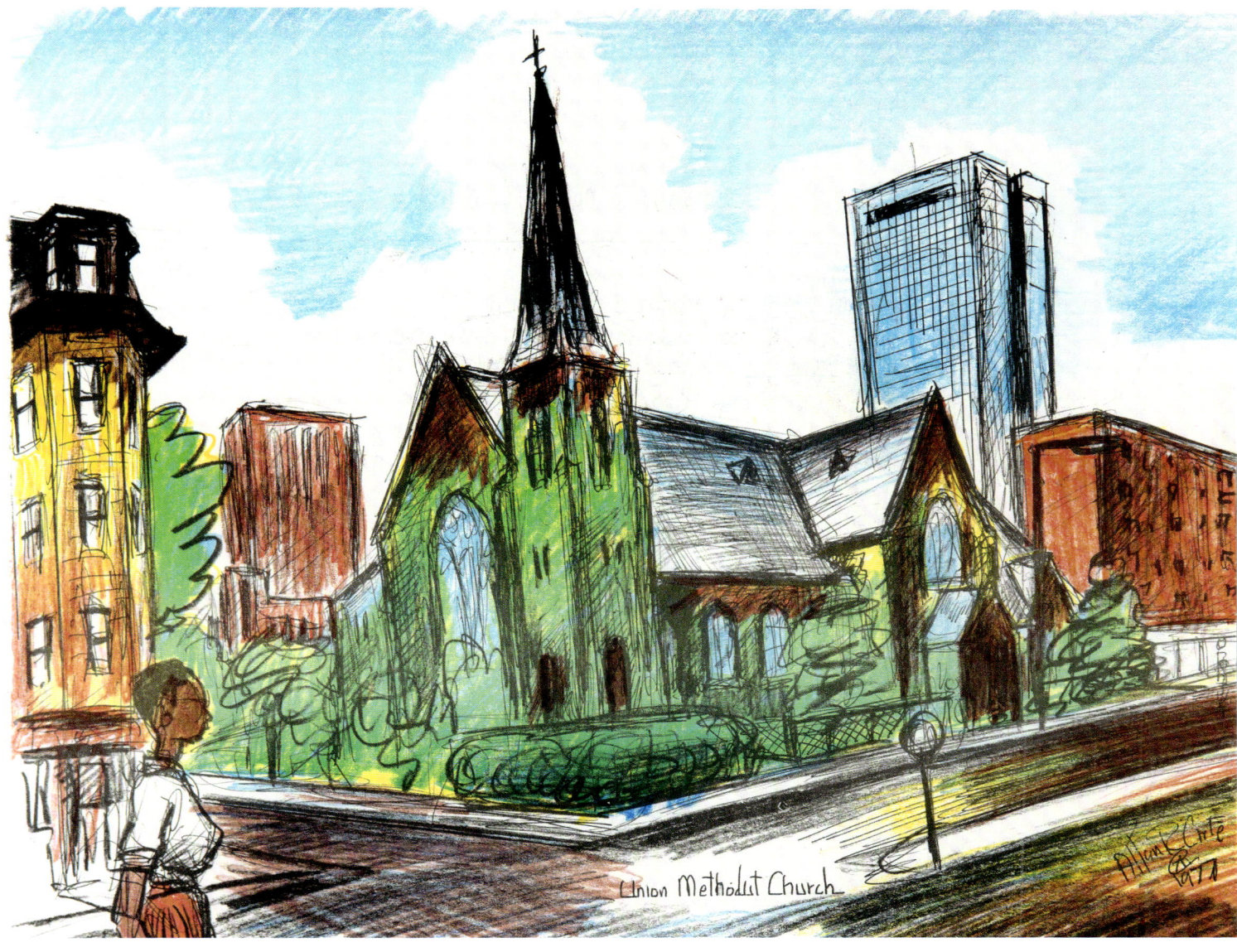

Fig. 33. Allan Rohan Crite, *Union United Methodist Church,* from *An Artist's Sketchbook of the South End: A Walking Tour about Black People,* 1977. Offset color lithograph, 21.7 × 27.9 cm. Boston Athenaeum

borhood and its institutions: *An Artist's Sketchbook of the South End: A Walking Tour about Black People* (1977) (plate 38). The project was the result of an invitation from Byron Rushing, then director of the Museum of African American History on Boston's Beacon Hill, to complete an artist's residency at the institution.[55] The group of maps, captions, and thirteen offset color lithographs—many of which Crite chose to present in a limited run of hand-bound books—represents a tour of sites that were important for the broader Black community in the South End and Lower Roxbury, as well as sites specifically significant to Crite.

The project blended both past and present, nostalgia and reportage. For example, the John Hancock Tower, completed in 1976, looms in the skyline over Crite's plate dedicated to the Union United Methodist Church, home to one of Boston's oldest Black congregations (fig. 33).[56] This clearly dates the image to the moment in which Crite was making it, but other elements of the series seem more ambiguous in their setting in time. The book starts with Crite's childhood home at 2 Dilworth Street. After a description of the home, the view it provided of planes flying in and out of Boston's Logan Airport, and some of his own biography, Crite writes, "Today in 1977 the street no longer exists. It is all a vacant lot. The street is a memory along with all of the other vanished streets of the city."[57] Crite's walking tour is, in part, a walk through a mix of the Black present and a

melancholy Black history of the South End, one in which community, landmarks, and elements of the neighborhood had disappeared. This artistic engagement with the physical institutions of Black Boston may have inspired a project that would dominate Crite's final years: the establishment of the Allan Rohan Crite House Museum. In the walking tour, Crite says of his house simply, "410 Columbus Avenue is my present studio-home, an old bow-front house of the early 1870s."[58] Within a few years, he would be referring to the home as a museum (see figs. 102 and 103).

CONCLUSION: CRITE HOUSE MUSEUM AND FINAL YEARS

As Crite entered his ninth and tenth decades of life, he remained active. He illustrated *The Revelation of Saint John the Divine* (1995) with the specialty publisher the Limited Editions Club and mounted a range of exhibitions at institutions both around Boston—including UMass Boston and the Boston Athenaeum—and nationally. He was the subject of a solo show at the Frye Art Museum in Seattle in 2001. He also got married for the first time, to Jackie Cox, whom he had met when she was working for the National Center of Afro-American Artists. They wed in 1993, and of their first meeting she said, "He was charming, and he was very, very bright, and never would I have dreamt that an eighty-four-year-old had so much life and vitality."[59] In the years before and after his marriage, one project became his primary preoccupation: the establishment of his home as a museum.

During his time as a Community Fellow at MIT, Crite decided that he wanted to make his studio-home—which he had long opened to friends, neighbors, artists, and children—officially into a museum. A newsletter produced by the Community Fellows Program, which lists Crite as a fellow in 1982–83, quotes the artist describing his fellowship project: "Hundreds of people have toured my house and viewed the art and history displayed there. . . . I would love to establish my home [as] a house museum (see fig. 105) to permanently exhibit the artistic history of people of color in New England."[60] He turned to his friend, the lawyer, activist, and higher education leader Ted Landsmark, to help him incorporate and establish the museum. Landsmark recalled:

> The Crite House Museum was a very interesting challenge because at that point in time there really weren't any other living artists in Boston who were interested in opening their homes and studios on a full-time basis to young and emerging artists in the community. And Allan was really in the leadership of a group of artists who were beginning to think about how their work could be transmitted to the community and to other emerging artists by creating house museums and galleries. . . . Entering the house gave one a sense that he was incredibly prolific. . . . He collected the work of other artists in the Greater Boston area, but his own work filled the house. Every drawer, every wall, every crevice, had some drawing or book that he had produced. And so walking into the house was like walking into a culture that he had created . . . his vision of what Boston was (see fig. 104).[61]

Crite's home was, in essence, a natural culmination of his decades of earlier work, which had documented, glorified, and reimagined his neighborhood. As Landsmark astutely recognized, the house itself was like a work of art, a *Gesamtkunstwerk*—a total work of art—designed to become an institution in a community that Crite had long envisioned. In some ways—in its density, its domestic feel—it echoed the Gardner Museum, which he had loved since childhood. Recollections of the house gathered in this volume recall its role as a hub for Crite's printing and how he provided studio space for young artists (notably Susan Thompson) (see fig. 102). Mostly, people recall that it was transporting. Professor Denise Patmon, who was one of Crite's close friends, said, "You just go into a different orbit in his house."[62]

There were, however, many bureaucratic hurdles to making the home into a museum. As Landsmark recalled:

> It was very difficult to turn a studio space into a living museum of the work of a living artist. The tax code, the city's building codes, and regulations that existed that limited the way you could work. . . . In fact, when you look around the city, you find that there are relatively few house museums that are dedicated to the work of a single artist. Turning a personal home into a museum, particularly when that home is not designed for large crowds . . . structure, access, and financial management [are] . . . a real challenge.[63]

As Crite aged, the challenges of running the house museum mounted—even with the dedicated help of his wife, Jackie, who was committed to supporting his vision. As Landsmark said, establishing an institution "takes a huge amount of work, tremendous staff time, and capital to continue to function." Ultimately, several years after Crite's death in 2007 at age ninety-seven, the home was sold and converted into three condo units.[64]

That Crite's house museum fell victim to increasing property values in the rapidly gentrifying South End and the bureaucratic hurdles associated with creating a public institution is a true loss for the cultural landscape of Boston. Never again will a child have the experience of stepping into Crite's home to be transported "into a different orbit." There is no one central place, as Crite envisioned, "to permanently exhibit the artistic history of people of color in New England," or, as Landsmark put it, to present the artist's unique and utopian "vision of what Boston was." Yet, Crite, his art, and his legacy live on in myriad ways.

Research for this catalogue has revealed that Crite's work is truly *everywhere.* As the exhibition checklist in this volume shows, it is in a wide range of institutions around the country, it is all over Boston, it is in churches, and it is in the homes of private individuals who love and care for it. This omnipresence was accelerated by Crite's embrace of the multiple—the lithograph, photocopy, and other printed media. His work is in and of the communities of which he was a part. Beyond the reach of his art, there is the impressive reach of his memory and legacy—the impact he had during his life and the ways in which he continues to inspire people today, almost two decades after his death. The recollections within this catalogue by those who knew him attest poignantly to that impact. Yet his art, his commitment to his community, and his optimism about the beauty of ordinary life continue to resonate with new generations. Crite's ability to inspire is his greatest contribution, one that we are only just beginning to understand and celebrate properly.

Notes

1   See Boone 2008; Caro 2008; Caro 2017, 101–13; Murrell 2024, 30, 75.
2   Crite 1979–80, 29.
3   Abdul-Fattah 2020.
4   Clark 1979, 70.
5   The Children's Art Centre was founded by a curator at the MFA. A history of the program is available at https://uses.library .northeastern.edu/history/. In Crite's recounting in the Archives of American Art oral history interview (Crite 1979–80), he credited Woodbury and Perkins with founding the Art Centre. This seems not to be the case, but Woodbury and Perkins certainly were art instructors for children and seem to have taught groups there, and Crite could have accompanied them on field trips to the Gardner. See Woodbury and Perkins 1925, which includes some of Crite's drawings. There are surviving letters from Woodbury and Perkins to Isabella Stewart Gardner at, e.g., https://www .gardnermuseum.org/experience /collection/31857 and https://www .gardnermuseum.org/experience /collection/30502.
6   Crite 1979–80, 4.
7   Quoted in Caro 2008, 62n47. The quotation is cited as appearing in Culver 1998, no page number given.
8   The Addison Gallery of American Art at Andover has extensive holdings of childhood drawings by Crite showing both fantastical and biblical scenes. These were all given by Elizabeth Ward Perkins. See https:// addison.andover.edu/search-the -collection/.

9   Woodbury and Perkins 1925, frontispiece, 41, 219. Decades later, Crite would self-publish his own drawing manual.

10 See Caro's essay in this volume, 79.

11 Caro 2008, 66.

12 Clark 1979, 70.

13 See Caro's essay in this volume, 81–2.

14 This painting is now in the Smithsonian American Art Museum but was transferred from the General Services Administration. This means that it was completed for the government while Crite was part of the Federal Art Project. See the provenance for the painting at https://americanart.si.edu/artwork/schools-out-5965.

15 See Coleman's essay in this volume, 161–2.

16 See Caro's essay in this volume, 89–96.

17 It was donated by William and Ellen Greenbaum as a group of several canvases acquired from a Boston art dealer.

18 A watercolor sketch titled *Study of African Image, Goddess of Thunder "Shango"* (1933) is in the collection of the Museum of the National Center of Afro-American Artists (plate 2). The authors are grateful to Barry Gaither for showing us this work on 10 April 2024.

19 Crite 1979–80, 29.

20 Alain Locke, "A Note on African Art," in Locke 2012, 99.

21 Ibid., 103–4.

22 Crite 1979–80, 66. Definition of the Oxford Movement from https://www.episcopalchurch.org/glossary/oxford-movement-the/.

23 Crite 1979–80, 66.

24 Original drawings and designs from his work at the Navy Yard are extremely hard to come by for a number of reasons. In some cases, they were destroyed for reasons of national security, while at other times they were simply discarded or given away to co-workers. Our thanks to Jared Chamberlin and his colleagues at the National Archives for aiding our search.

25 Crite 1979–80, 10.

26 For a general overview of the period, see Smith 1942.

27 MBTA 1981, 2–4.

28 Gumprecht 2023, 13–15.

29 Ibid., 15.

30 Ibid., 10–11.

31 Schickler 2016.

32 John Wilson, notes for a talk on Allan Rohan Crite, n.d., John Wilson Archive, Brookline, MA.

33 "Brutal Beating Stuns Navy Yard Workers," *Boston Chronicle,* 27 January 1945. Our thanks to Sarah Woods of the National Parks of Boston for this source.

34 Crite 1979–80, 13–14.

35 Allan Rohan Crite to Reverend Tom Lehman, Grace Church, Vineyard Haven, MA, 26 March [Palm Sunday] 1961, Allan Rohan Crite Papers, Boston Athenaeum, folder 1, MS L757. Crite reportedly convinced St. John's Episcopal Church in Roxbury Crossing to allow him to store the press there, until the building was sold in 1967 owing to a planned highway expansion. In 1971, Crite's home at 2 Dilworth Street was demolished, forcing Crite and his mother to move. He relocated the press to his new home at 410 Columbus Avenue. We are grateful to Byron Rushing for this information.

36 Conversation between Christina Michelon and Reginald Jackson, 27 June 2024.

37 Allan Rohan Crite to Walter Muir Whitehill, 23 May 1968, Walter Muir Whitehill Papers, Collection of the Massachusetts Historical Society.

38 See Johnetta Tinker's recollection in this volume, 122.

39 In August 2021, this caption was transcribed from the original drawing for this image when the work was on long-term loan at the MFA Boston. See authors' reference photographs and image at https://www.groganco.com/auction-lot/allan-rohan-crite-american-1910-2007-set-of_F03A90A123.

40 Levine 2021, 37.

41 Ibid., 38; West End Museum 2017.

42 O'Connor 1993, 113–209.

43 Levine 2021, 38.

44 Allan Rohan Crite to Walter Muir Whitehill, 2 December 1961, Allan Rohan Crite Papers, Boston Athenaeum, MS L664.10.

45 For an overview of this history, see Meeks and Murphy 2016, 25–42.

46 Nally 2022.

47 Perhaps as part of his preparation for the move to Columbus Avenue, Crite made a momentous gift of his art to the Boston Athenaeum. Primarily representing his *Neighborhood Series,* Crite presented sixteen oil paintings, thirty-nine watercolors, and fifteen ink drawings to the institution in February 1971. A letter from Whitehill to Crite dated 19 January 1971, with recommendations for studio space/apartments, suggested that Crite contact Boston artist Ives Gammell and mentioned that Donald Kelley was asking around too. The letter ended with the statement "I am delighted to think that your south end things will eventually be coming to us," a clear reference to the forthcoming gift the following month.

48 See Barry Gaither's recollection in this volume, 154.

49 Tanga 2024a, 26; MIT Colab 2022.

50 See Tinker's recollection in this volume, 121.

51 For a recent comprehensive overview of artists' engagements with the Black Power movement, see Godfrey and Whitley 2017.

52 Tanga 2024b.

53 Baetens et al. 2018, 1–18.

54 See Johnetta Tinker's recollection in this volume, 70.

55 The museum was then called the Museum of Afro-American History; we are grateful to Byron Rushing for this recollection. The frontispiece of the *Sketchbook* also notes its creation for the museum.

56 See O'Connor 2023.

57 Crite 1977b, 1.

58 Ibid., 2.

59 See Caro in this volume, 186. Jackie Cox-Crite described their first meeting in an online event called "Jackie Cox-Crite and Cristela Guerra, 'In the Neighborhood: A Celebration of Allan Rohan Crite,'" hosted by the Boston Athenaeum and held on Zoom on 25 March 2021. See https://vimeo.com/543597745, quotation from time stamp 22:41–22:57.

60 Duran 1983.

61 See Ted Landsmark's recollection in this volume, 179.

62 See Denise Patmon's recollection in this volume, 178.

63 See Ted Landsmark's recollection in this volume, 179.

64 According to Boston property records, the home stopped being assessed as a single-family home in 2011, and the individual condo units began to pay property taxes in 2012. City of Boston, Assessment Records for Parcel 0400422000. https://www.cityofboston.gov/assessing/search/?pid=0400422000.

PLATES 1930–1935

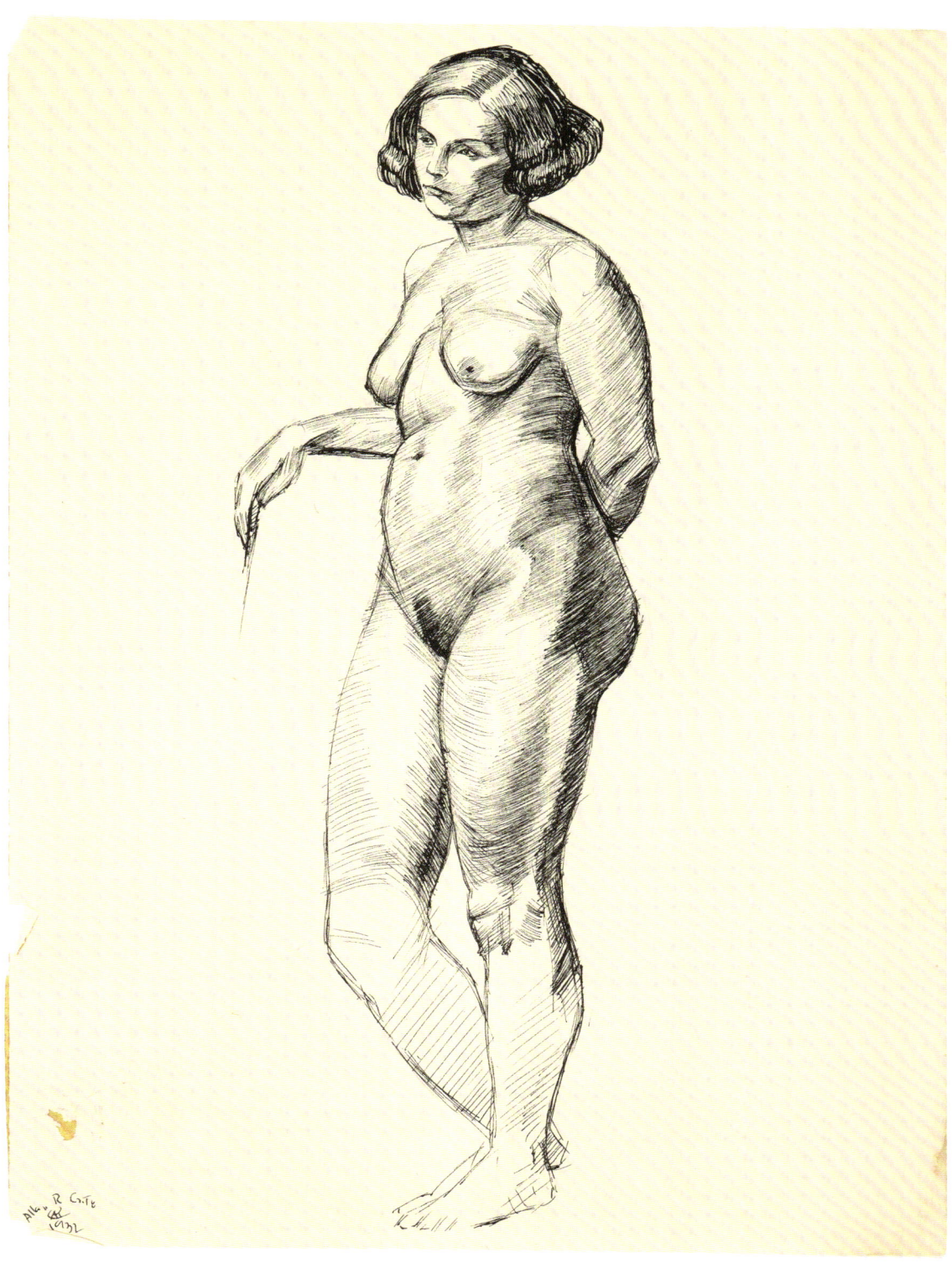

Plate 1. Allan Rohan Crite, *Nude Female Figure,* 1932. Ink on paper, 30.5 × 22.9 cm.
National Center of Afro-American Artists (NCAAA), Roxbury

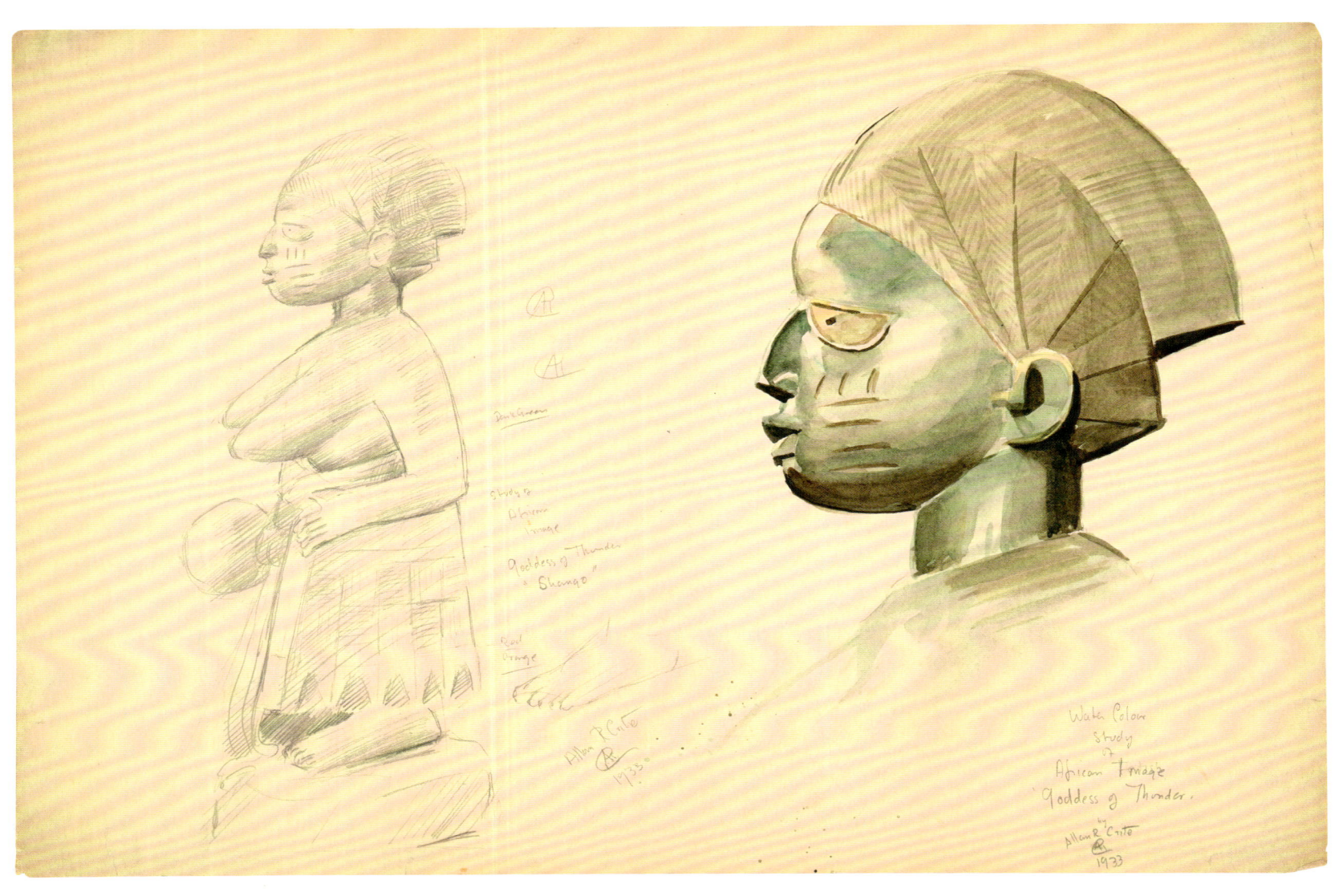

Plate 2. Allan Rohan Crite, *Study of African Image, Goddess of Thunder "Shango,"* 1933.
Watercolor and pencil on paper, 30.5 × 45.7 cm. National Center of Afro-American Artists
(NCAAA), Roxbury

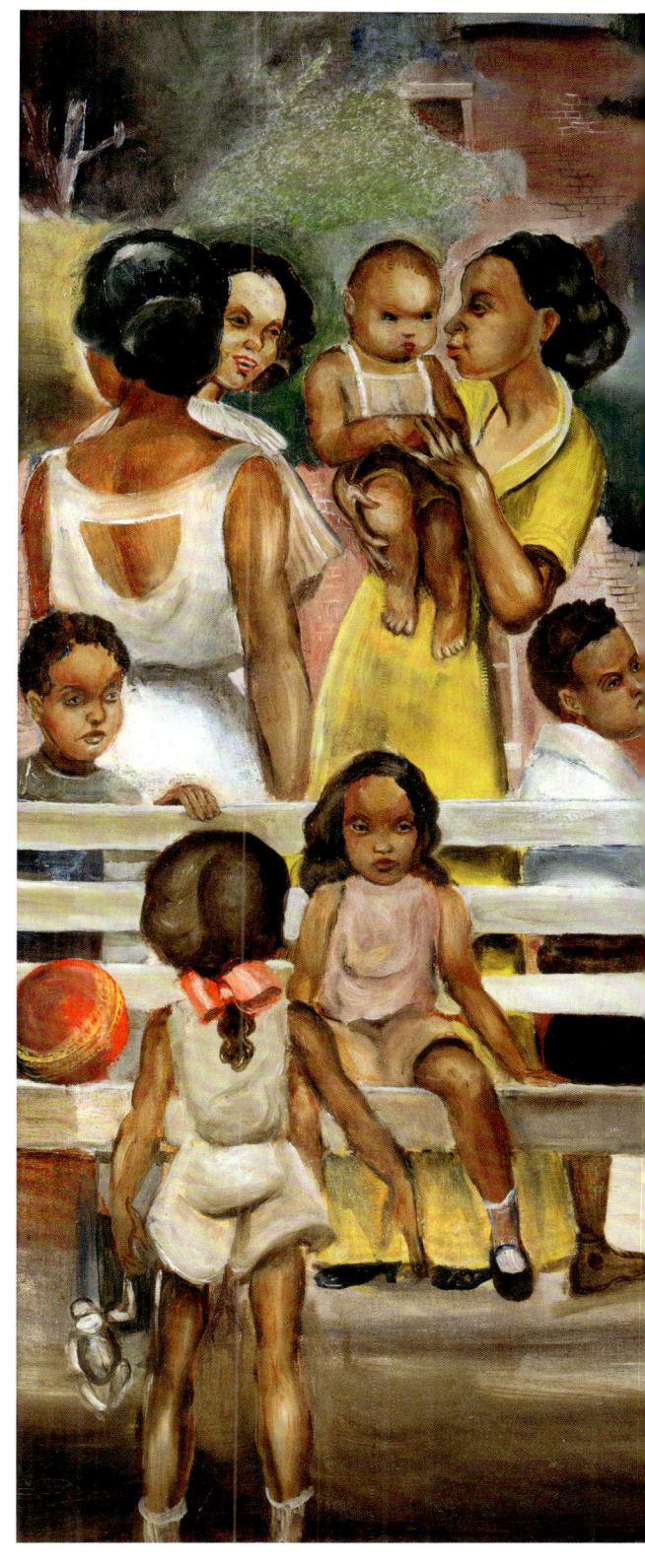

Plate 3. Allan Rohan Crite, *Settling the World's Problems,* 1933. Oil on canvas, 75.9 × 113.7 cm. Courtesy of Museum of African American History Boston | Nantucket

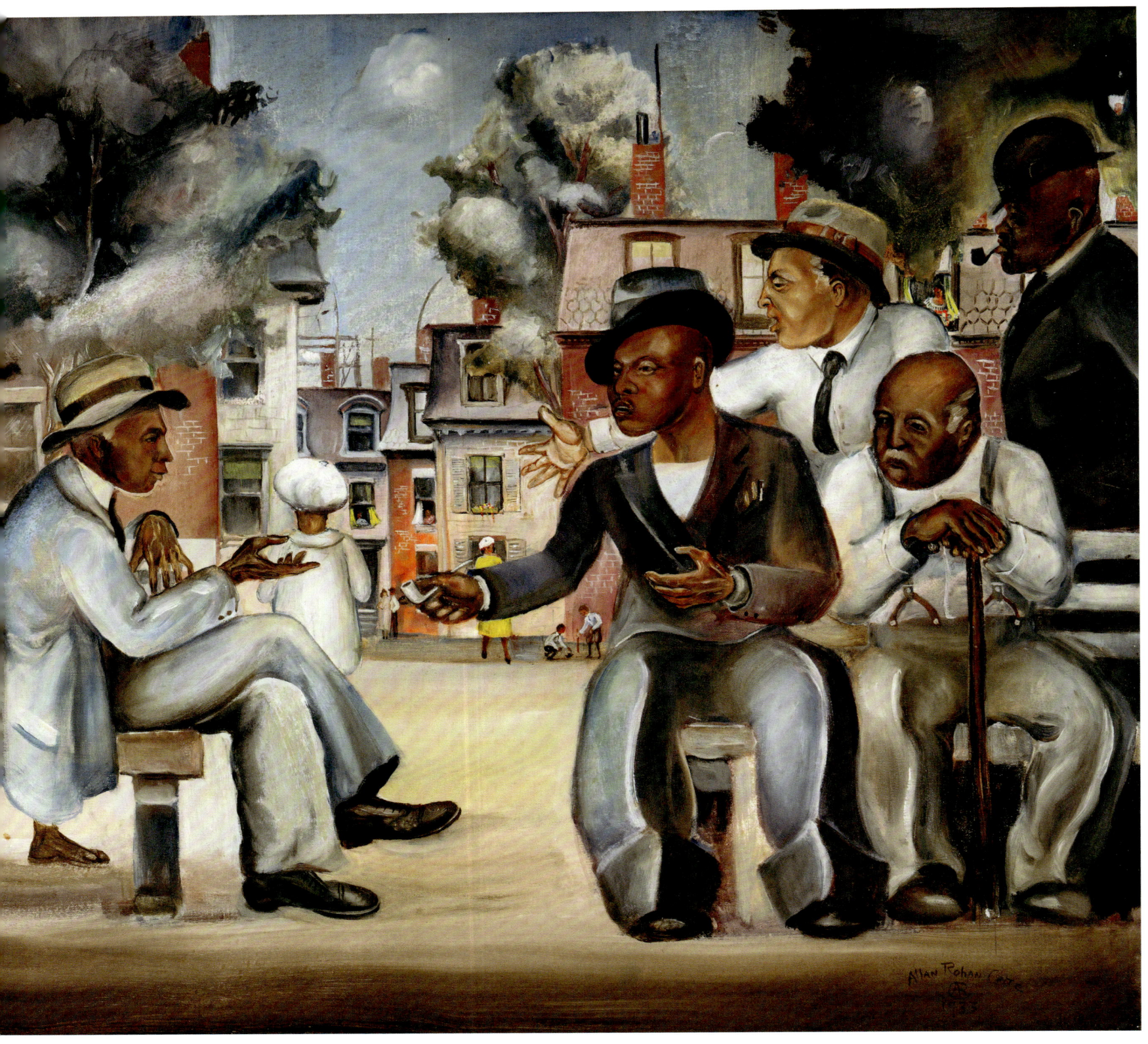

Plate 4. Allan Rohan Crite, *Late Afternoon,* 1934. Oil on canvas, 82 × 61.5 cm.
Boston Athenaeum

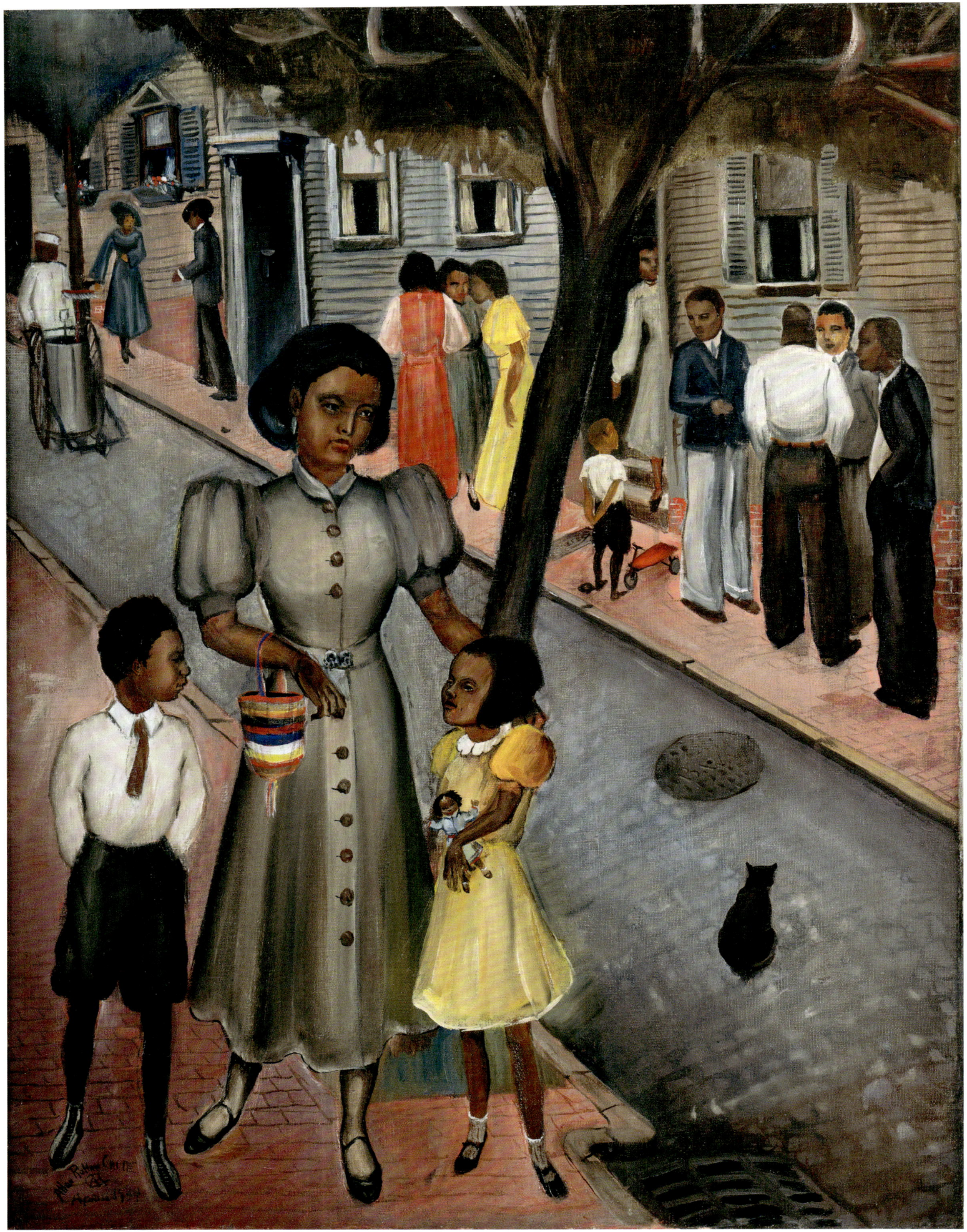

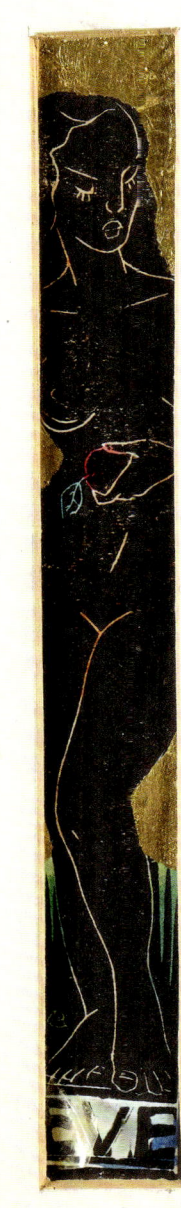
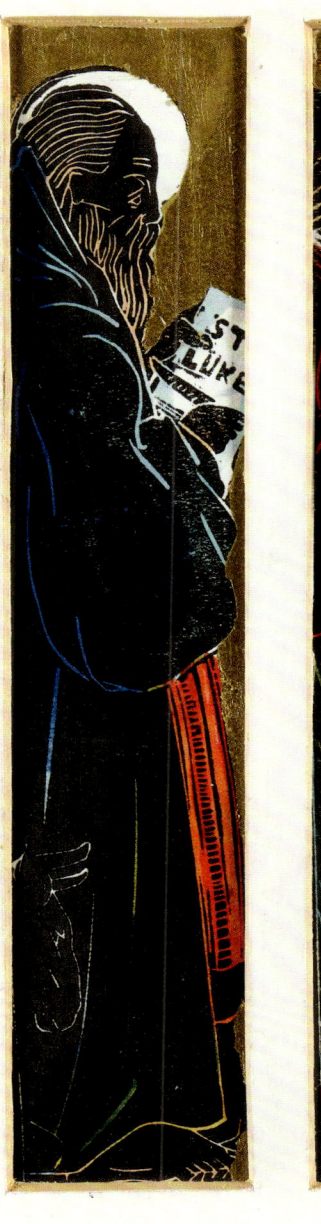
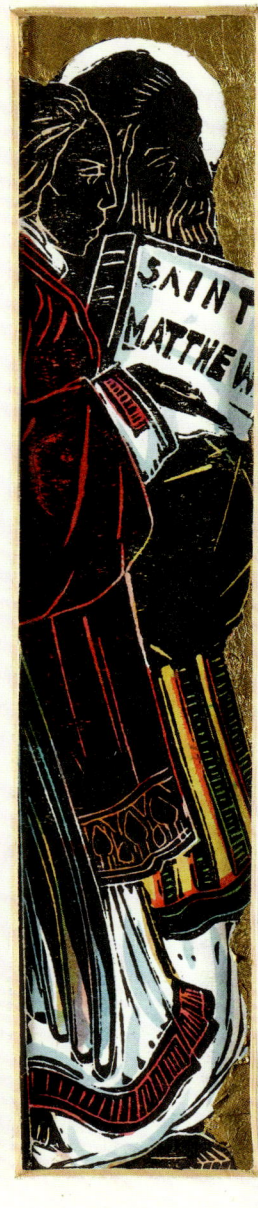

Plate 5. Allan Rohan Crite, *Madonna and Child; 4 Evangelists Saints Luke, Matthew, Mark, and John; Adam and Eve,* about 1934. Linoleum block print hand-colored with marker and gold leaf, 37.5 × 51.1 cm matted. Arts Department, Special Collections, Boston Public Library

Madonna and Child; 4 E

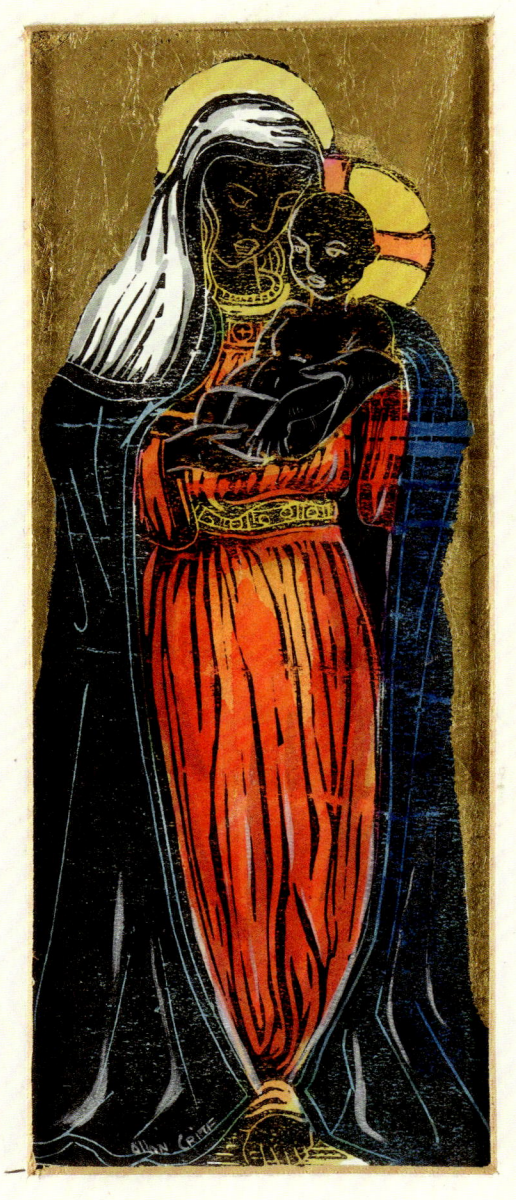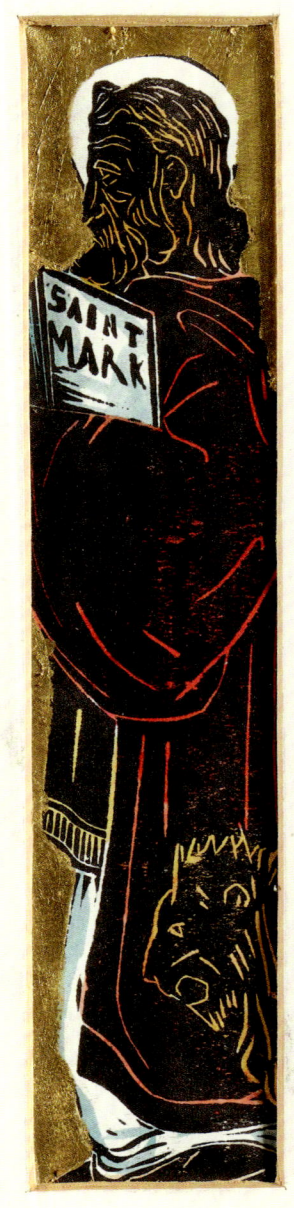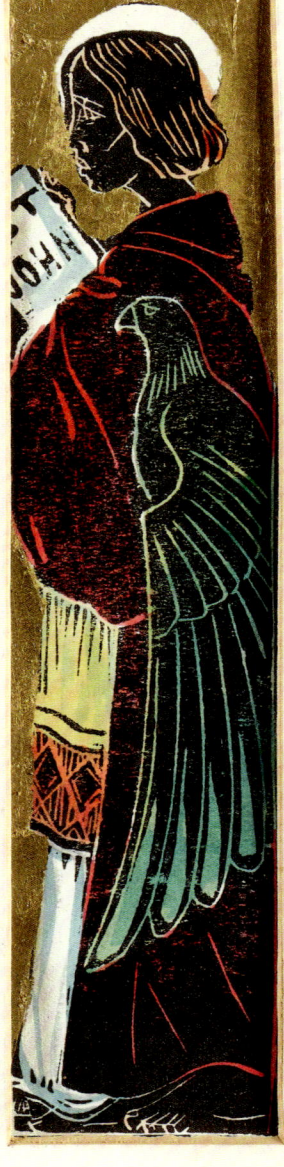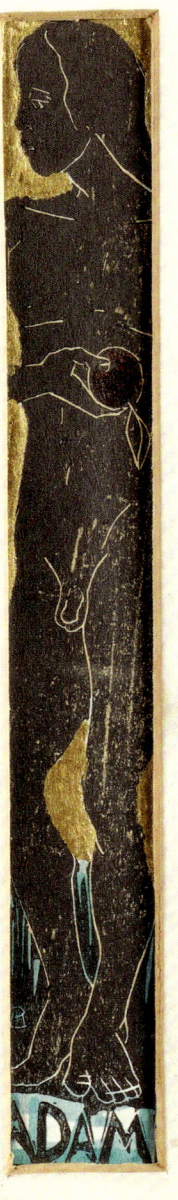

ngelists Saints Luke, Matthew, Mark and John; Adam and Eve

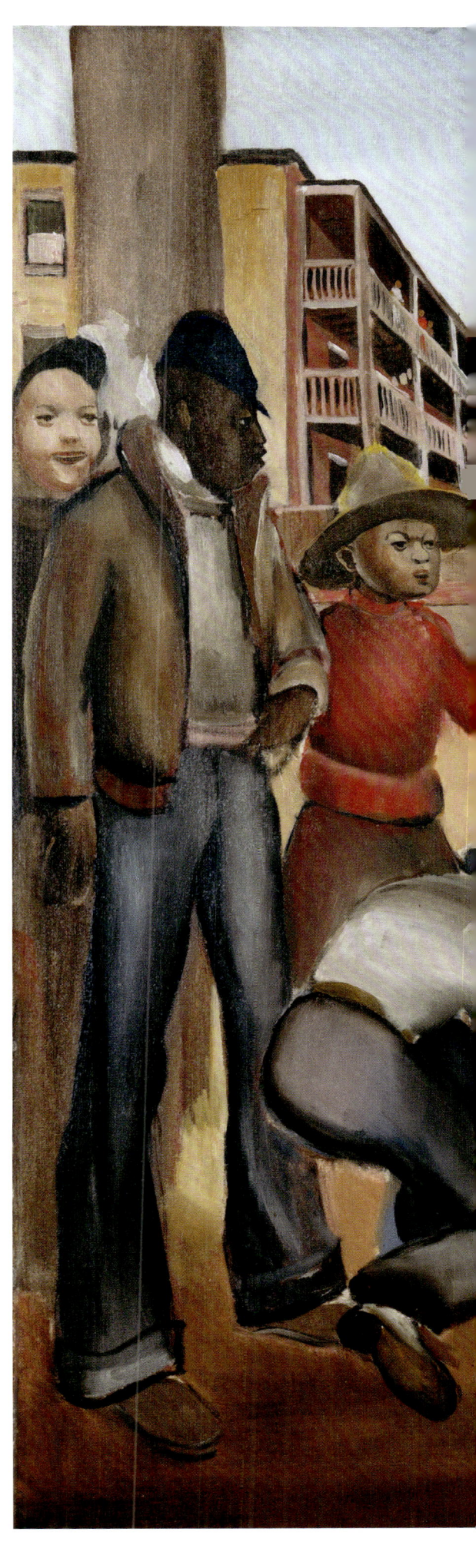

Plate 6. Allan Rohan Crite, *Marble Players,* 1934. Oil on canvas, 76 × 89 cm.
Boston Athenaeum

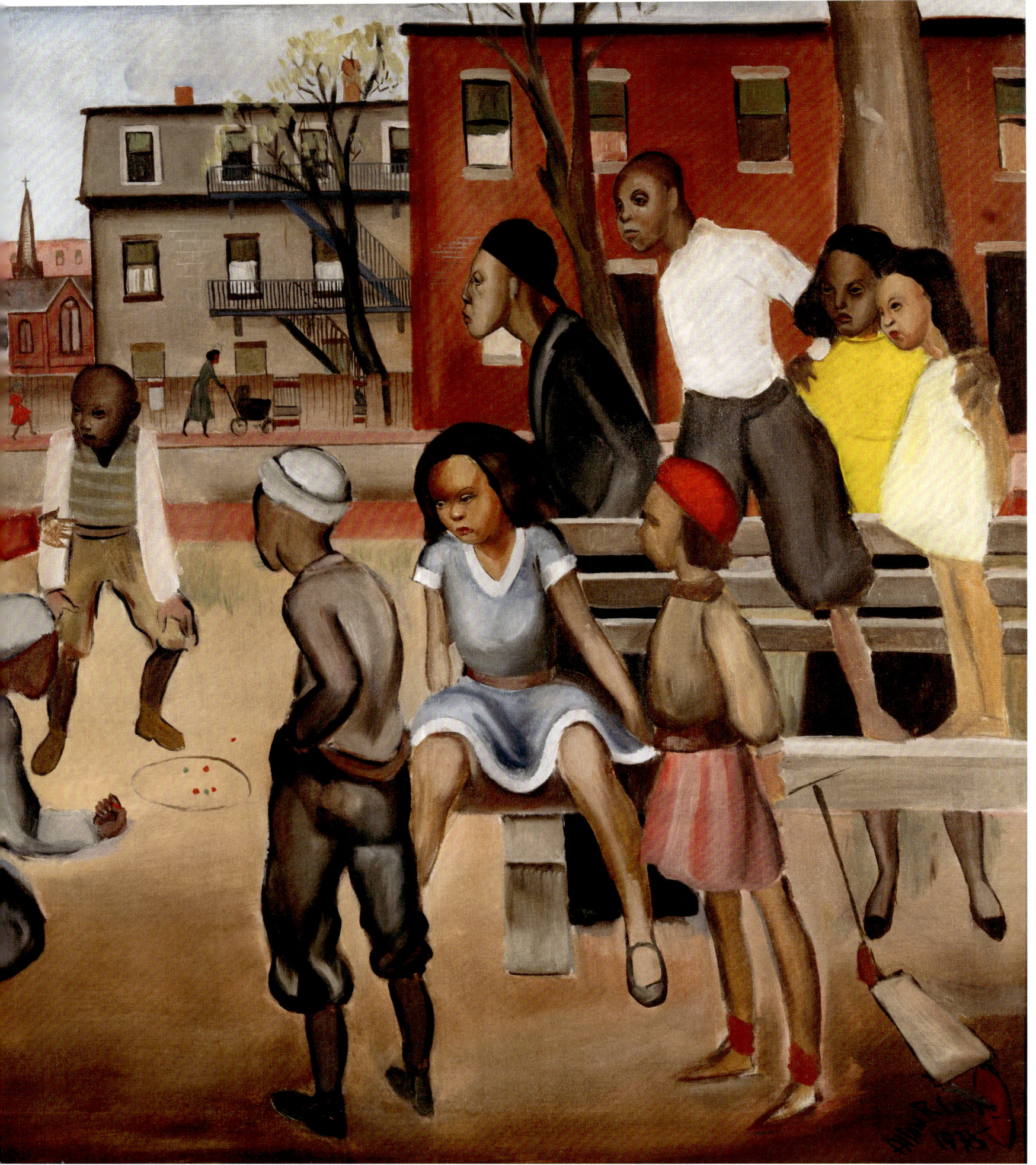

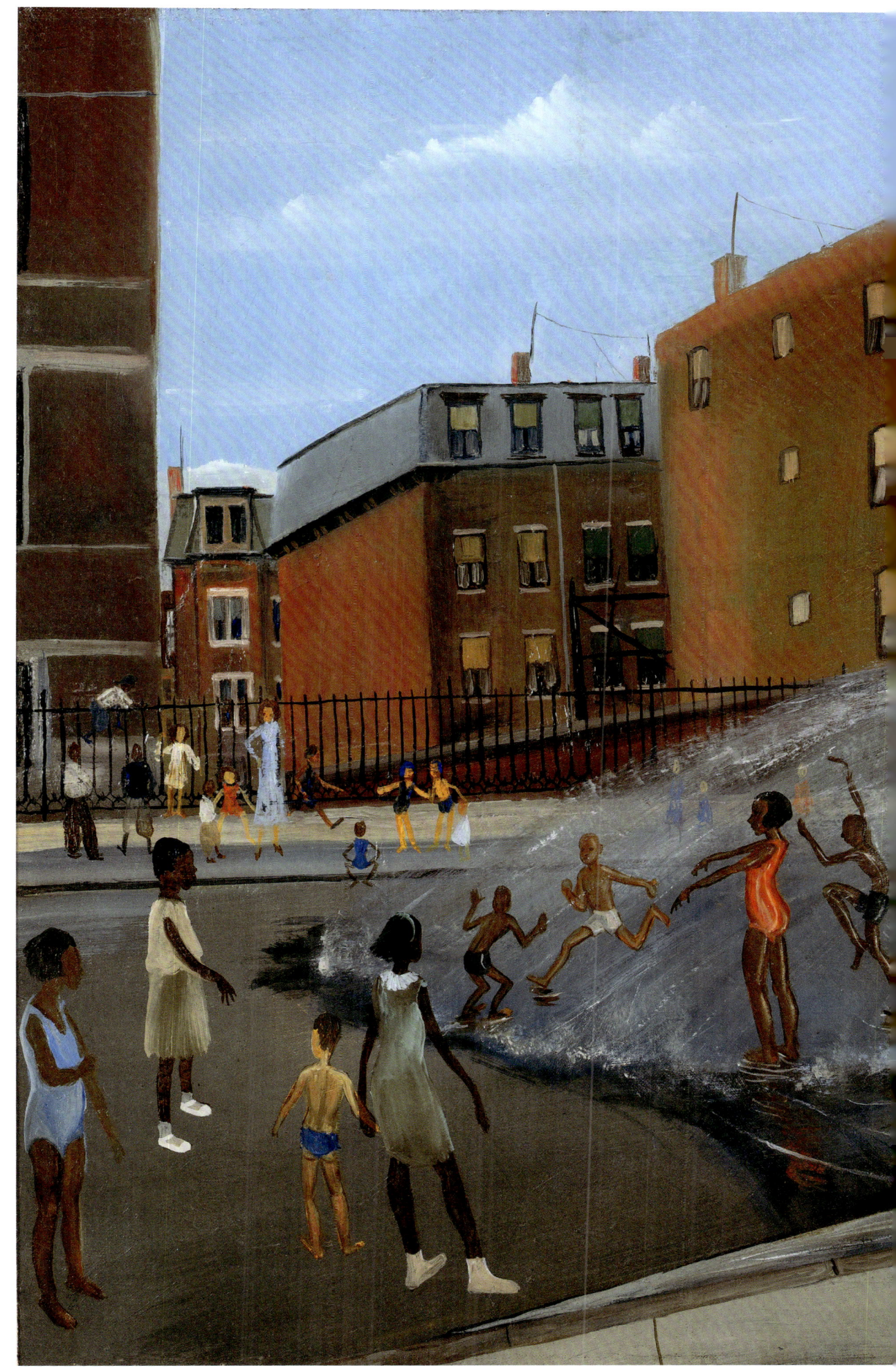

Plate 7. Allan Rohan Crite,
The Shower, Ruggles St., 1935.
Oil on canvas, 61 × 92 cm.
Boston Athenaeum

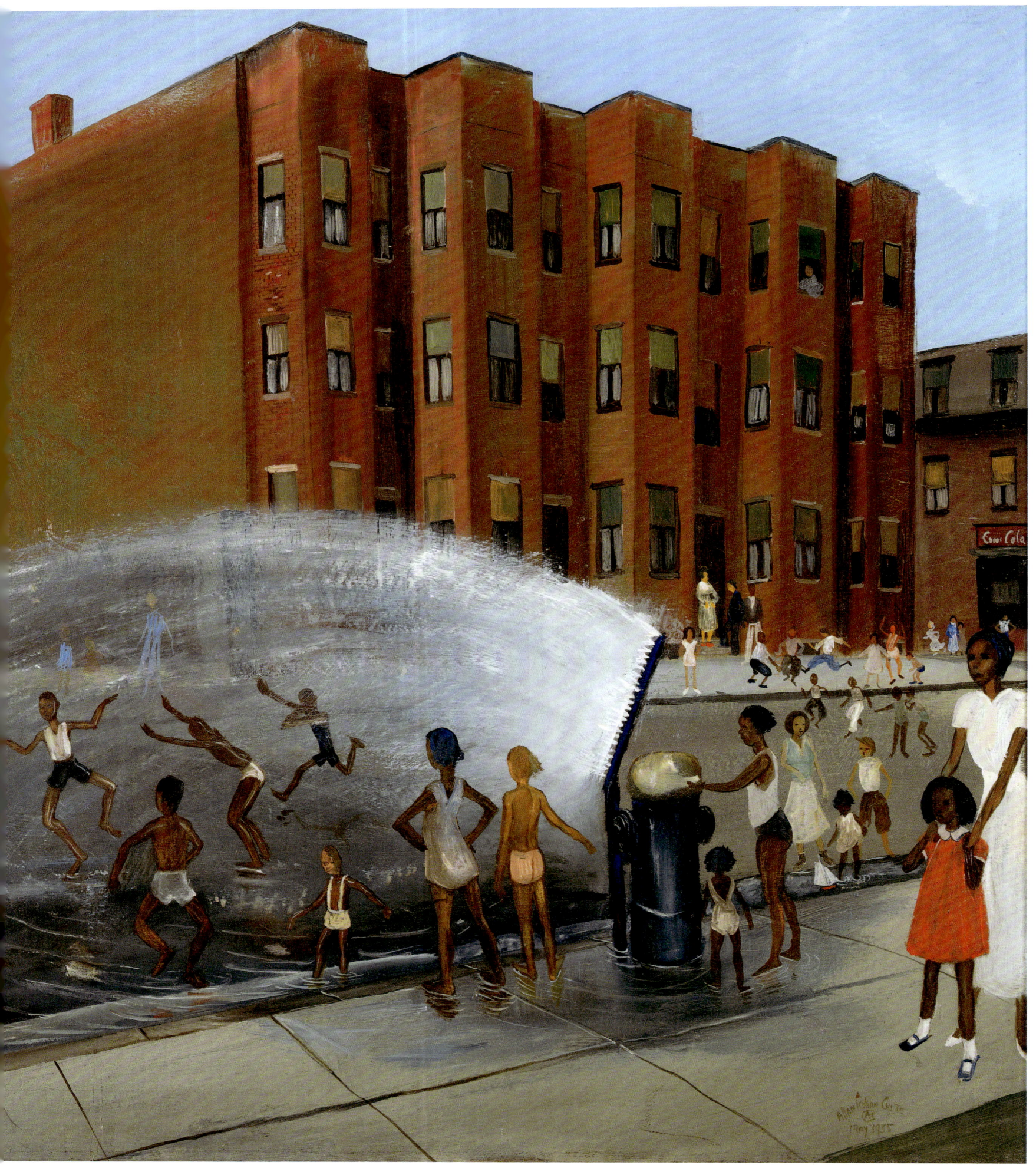

CRITE'S WORKING METHOD

"From the beginning, the very beginning, he was interested in making his art available to ordinary people. He was not interested in making it precious and difficult to access. So he made work on his own machine that he controlled and where he could produce work much more cheaply than if he were tied to a regular professional art press. I remember sort of chiding him a time or two that I thought he should really only be working with better materials and [in a] real studio environment. But he was really more interested that people had the work in hand and that they saw themselves in the work." (Fig. 34)

Barry Gaither

"There was a sense of independence that he had . . . having his own printing press. So he would not need to go out and seek the services of others. . . . He loved depending upon himself."

Denise Patmon

"After the [School of the Museum of Fine Arts], he knew how to produce ecclesiastical work using gold foil and gold paints, and how to take something that was precious in its smaller expression and re-create it on a grand scale where needed." (Fig. 35)

Barry Gaither

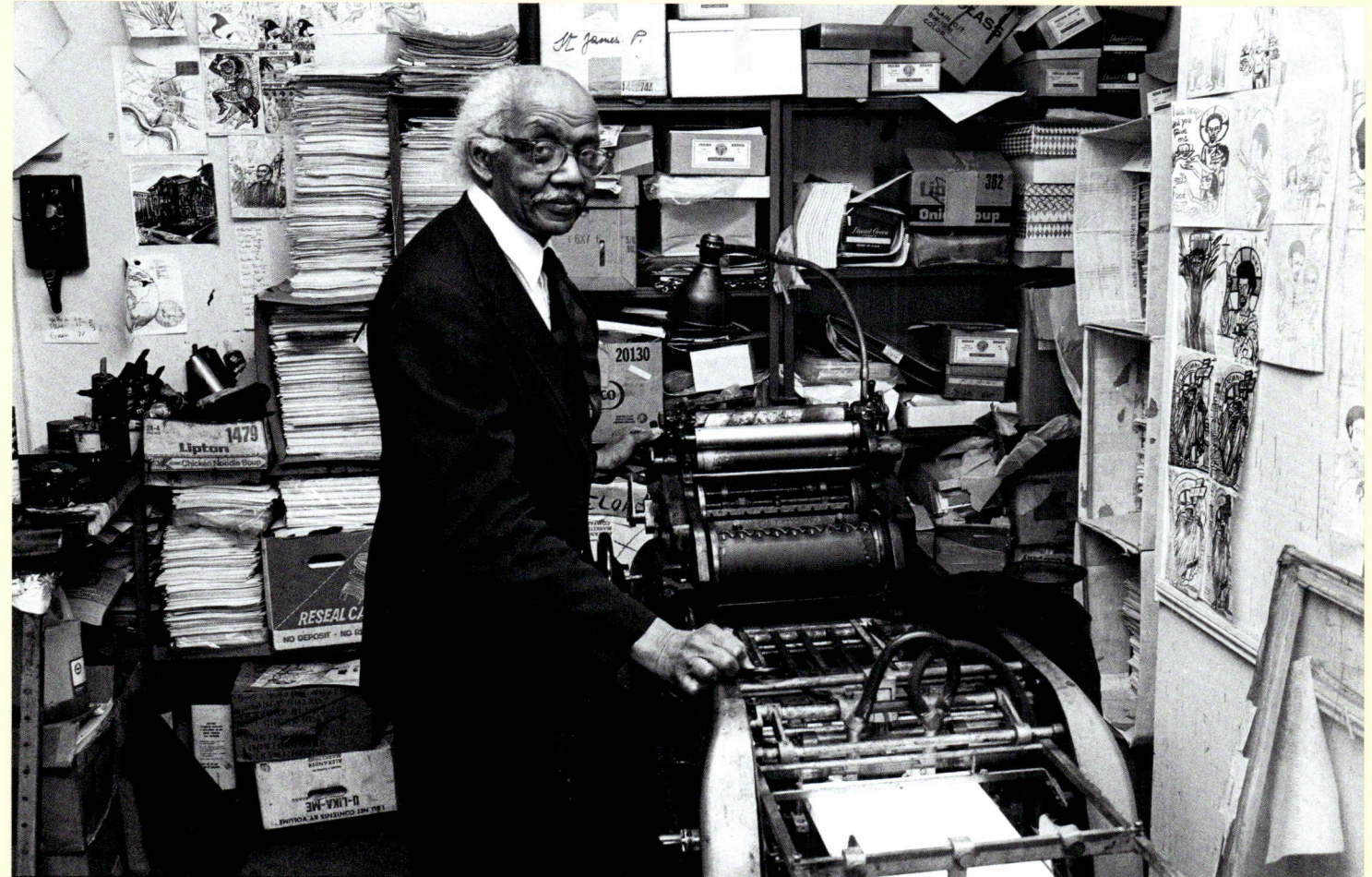

Fig. 34. Allan Crite standing in front of his Multilith 1250 offset printer, which he purchased in 1955 to print weekly church bulletins, May 1985. Photograph by Aukram Burton

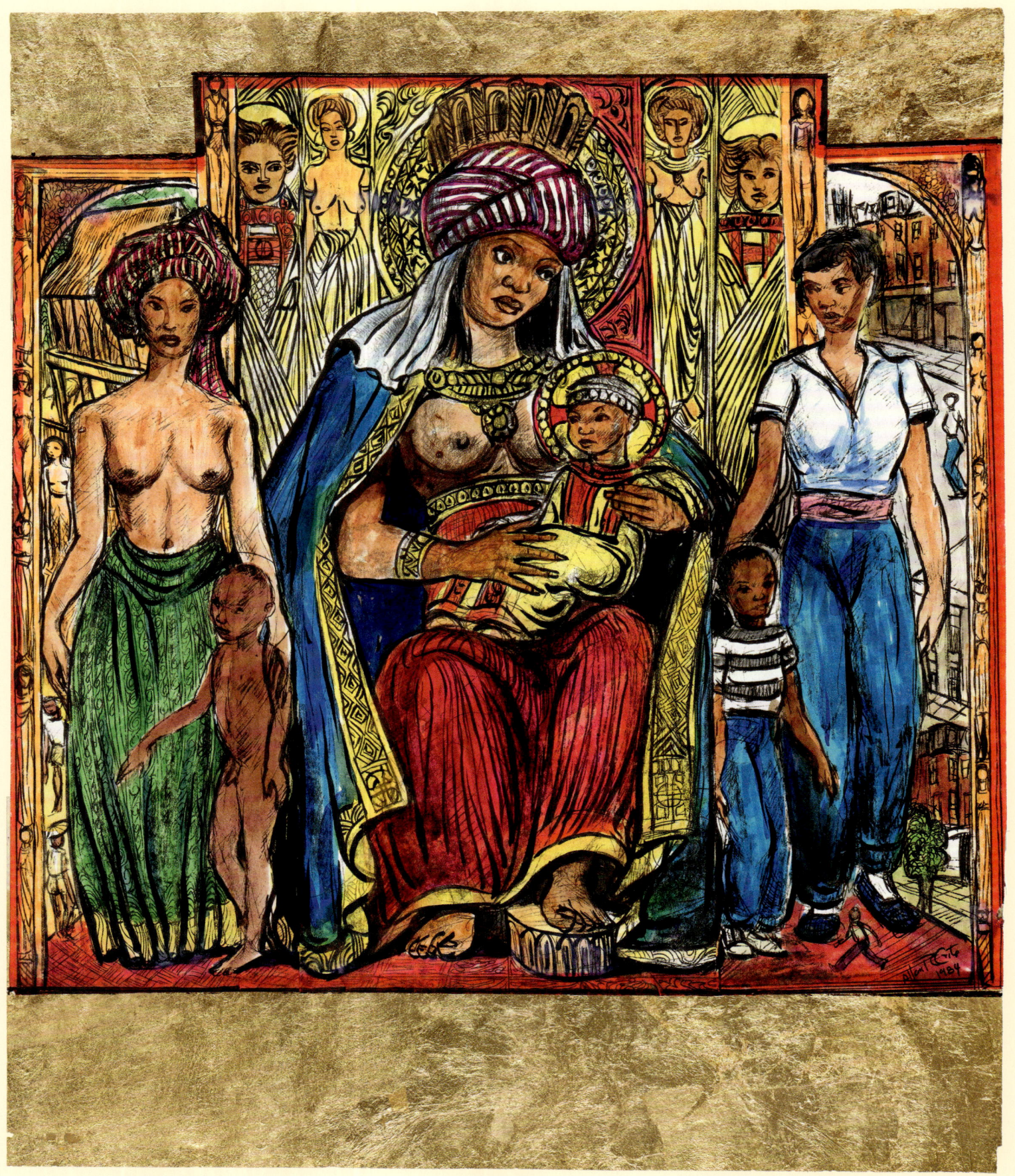

Fig. 35. Allan Rohan Crite, *Untitled (Madonna and Child)*, 1984. Hand-colored and gilded Multilith print, 41.3 × 34.9 cm. Collection of Susan Thompson

"He and I would sit in our regular spot [in a local tea room] and just talk. Just talk about . . . how things were going in college and what I was doing and that kind of thing. But the sketchbook was always there. And, you know, he might think something or see something and draw a little something. And then come back to the conversation. Those were really important early learnings for me about the importance of recording what you're seeing, what you're living, what you're feeling, because you want to pass on those stories. So he was a formidable character in my life."

Denise Patmon

"When we were in China, while we were all out hanging out and, you know, having fun, Allan would be in his room. And I said, 'You okay, Mr. Crite?' He says, 'I got to catch up on my notes and everything.' Because he's thinking he's going to come back and do a book, which he did, you know." (Fig. 36)

Aukram Burton

"He was dedicated to his craft. He was exemplary. . . . If you look at my pictures, we're in the southern part of the Yunnan Province, which is [near] Burma and Vietnam. So we're, like, right there around the equator. It's hot. And Allan, he's there [in his] trench coat with all of these folks around him, sketching, you know, in a trench coat. So yeah, he was dedicated." (Fig. 37)

Aukram Burton

"When we went to China together, I saw him look at something 'cause we were on the bus and he would see something, he had his own shorthand. So he always would do a sketch or something [that] looked like scribble to me and then we would get back to the hotel. . . . The young ones, we went out to party and he would stay back and draw. . . . When we got back, it looked exactly like what he saw. I was so amazed . . . it [was] like his memory. . . . He called [his sketchbook] his brains. . . . And he would put it down, then he was, like, 'Where are my brains? Where are my brains?' 'Your brains are over there, Mr. Crite.' So he called it his brains, and he always had a sketchbook with him."

Johnetta Tinker

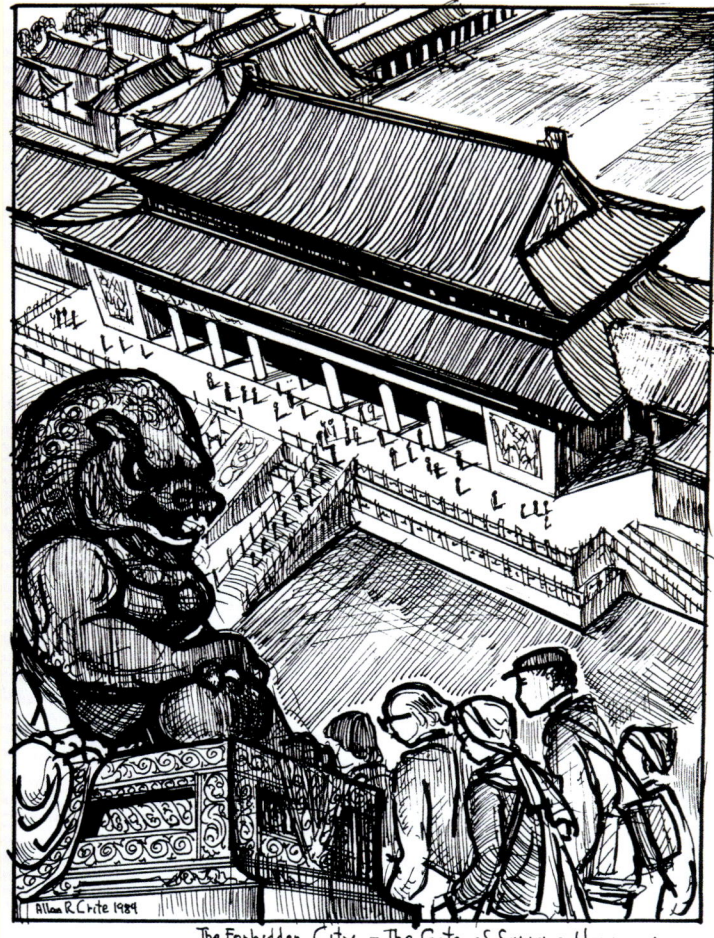

Fig. 36. Allan Rohan Crite, *The Forbidden City—The Gate of Supreme Harmony,* from *A Journal of Community Leaders' Tour to China,* 1983. Photocopy, 28 × 21.3 cm. Boston Athenaeum

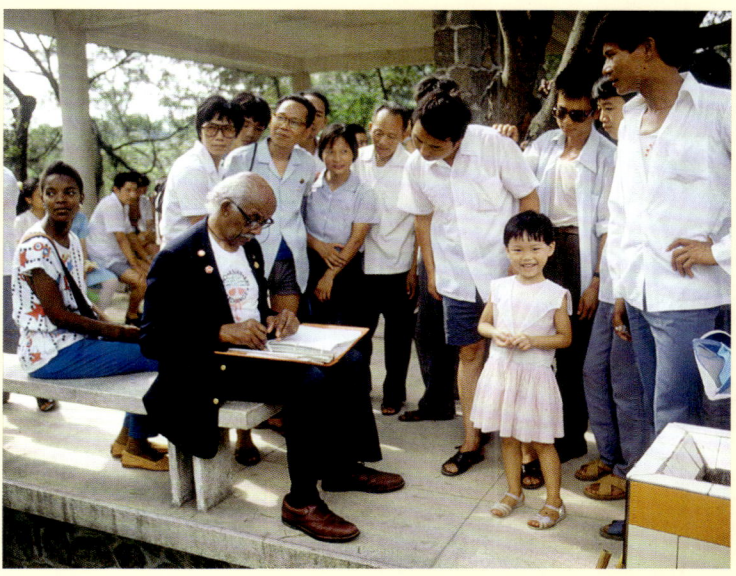

Fig. 37. Allan Rohan Crite sketching in Yuexiu Park, where the legendary Five Goats Statue is situated, during his second visit to Guangzhou, China as part of the Massachusetts-Guangdong Art Exchange Exhibition at the Guangzhou Academy, Academy of Fine Arts, July 1986. Photograph by Aukram Burton

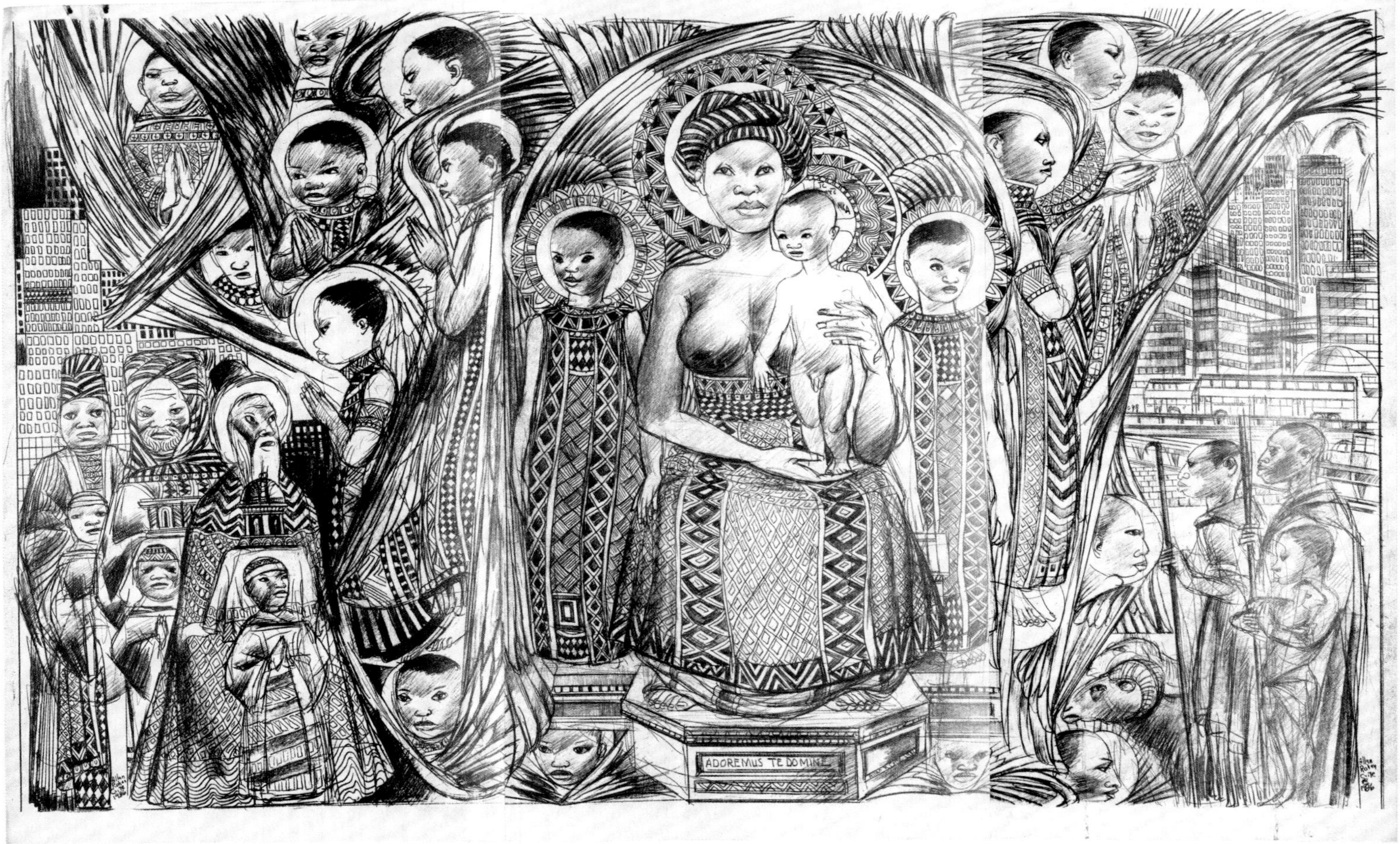

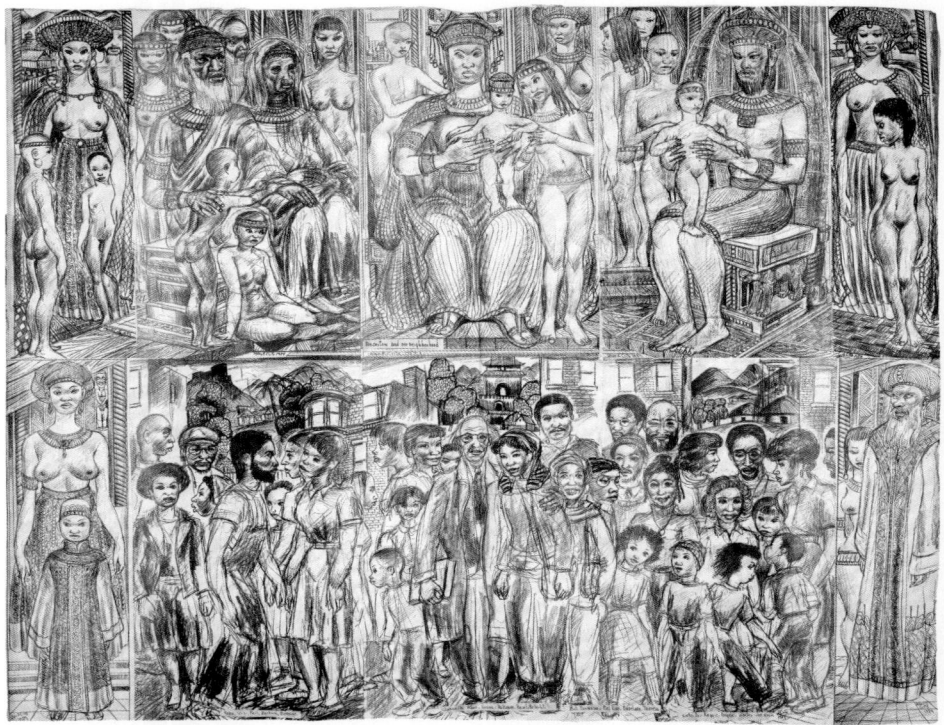

Fig. 38. Allan Rohan Crite, *Untitled (Madonna and Child with Wings),* 1986. Multilith print collage printed on paper from unused church bulletins, 35.6 × 56.5 cm. Collection of Susan Thompson

Fig. 39. Allan Rohan Crite, *Ancestors and Our Neighborhood,* 1984. Multilith print collage, 64.1 × 81.6 cm. Collection of Susan Thompson

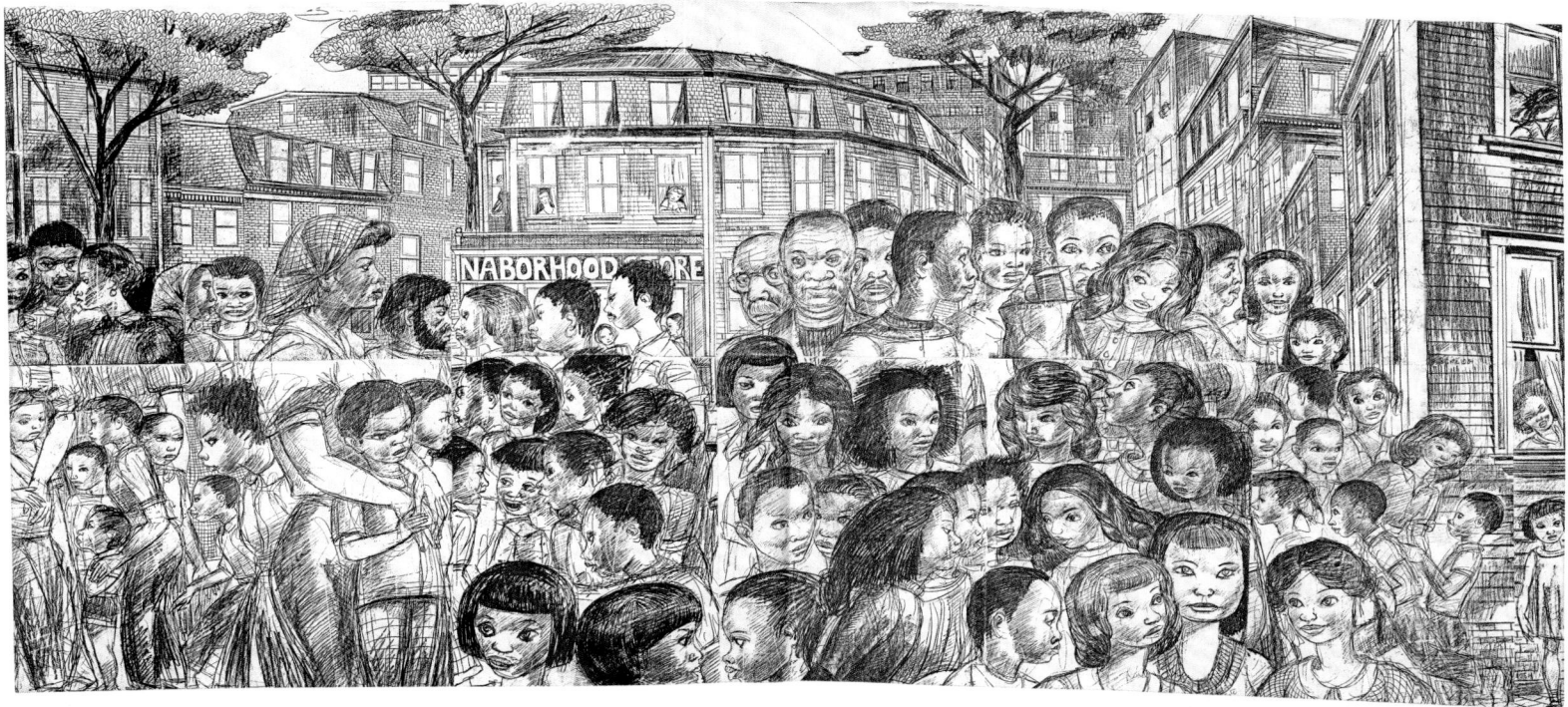

Fig. 40. Allan Rohan Crite, *Portrait of a City*, pp. 7–8, 1986. Multilith print collage in a hand-bound book, 36.2 × 85.1 cm. Collection of Susan Thompson

"To me, his work in brush and ink, just in terms of painterly accomplishment, is the pinnacle of his work. I've never seen anyone be able to do what he did . . . it's so crisp and complex and beautiful, you won't believe he did it with a brush and black ink." (plate 12)

Arthur Dion

"One day [his wife, Jackie] brought him [to my house] and we had dinner. And then I said, 'Allan, would you like to draw on the computer?' And he said, 'I'll draw. Yeah, I want to draw on the computer.' I had a tablet so he could draw on the tablet and see it on the screen. So he did a couple of quick pencil—well, digital—sketches and I printed it out for him and gave him copies of the sketches."

Susan Thompson

"He did not believe in wasting paper or anything. So you print on both sides." (Fig. 38)

Johnetta Tinker

"He was less interested in making a lot of money from his art than in seeing to it that the community got to share in both the production and the distribution of those documents that really showed what the community was like." (Fig. 39)

Ted Landsmark

"The background was just as important as the foreground, all the detail and a lot of the lines and the brushstrokes and everything . . . it's just so much fine work, the quality of it was so superb and it always made me feel like, okay, you got to do more." (Fig. 40)

Johnetta Tinker

"He thought that the Xerox machine was the invention of the world. He would Xerox everything. I'm like, 'Mr. Crite, this is not like museum quality.' But he just felt like [it was great] to be able to reproduce things so quickly." (Fig. 41)

Johnetta Tinker

"Allan had a good nine generations. Nine decades of working, and just thinking about that, Allan did more work in a week than most artists do in a year."

Napoleon Jones-Henderson

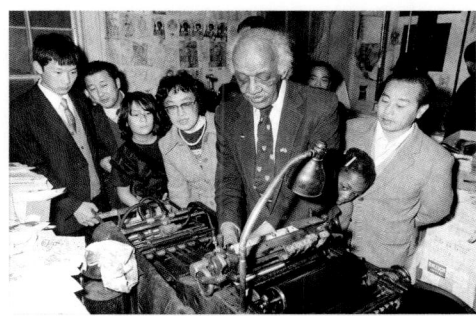

Fig. 41. Allan Crite demonstrates to Chinese artists how he uses a Multilith 1250 offset printer to produce his artwork during their visit to the Crite House Studio. The Chinese artists were in Boston as part of the *China: 7,000 Years of Discovery* exhibition at the Boston Museum of Science, May 1985. Photograph by Aukram Burton

CRITE AND BOSTON'S MUSEUMS

"At the Boston Athenaeum, I went to the Boston Festival Orchestra, one of their performances, and to sit there and to see an oil painting of his in the great room made my heart flutter, because I know how much that institution meant to him."

Denise Patmon

"Allan was very generous with his time and very willing to open his home to meetings of artists so that they could talk about the Boston art scene and about the challenges that Black artists in particular were having [getting] their work exhibited and recognized by the major arts institutions within the city."

Ted Landsmark

"[Crite] always told us that we needed to support our local [institutions], like the African American Museum and the National Center of Afro-American Artists. . . . He said, 'Always support your neighborhood museums, they're the ones . . . that are going to give you the exhibitions. These big museums like the Museum of Fine Arts and all that, it's going to be much harder for you to get exhibitions in there.'" (Fig. 42)

Johnetta Tinker

"We used to play a game no matter what museum we were in. I remember we were in DC at a museum. And he would go and sit down and I'd walk around. [I would ask,] 'Who did this painting?' 'That's a Monet.' 'Who did that sculpture? 'That's a Remington.' He was right all the time. . . . He knew all the artists. . . . He just knew museums. He knew the Gardner in and out. He knew the MFA in and out. He must have gone to every room throughout his lifetime. And what he told me you should do, he said, 'Don't try to see the whole museum in one day.'"

Johnetta Tinker

"He always said that people don't always go into museums. And when they do, it's on free days, and they don't have a lot of time to spend, because museums are expensive. How can families get a chance to go into museums if they don't have the funds? . . . He felt as though murals [and] public art were very important because it brought [in] people that normally would not go into museums. They would have an interaction with art. So he was always, you know, encouraging murals and things like that. He felt as though people will say, 'I can't afford your art. I want it, but I can't afford it.' So he made sure that people had a chance to have a piece of his artwork, even if it was a Xerox copy."

Johnetta Tinker

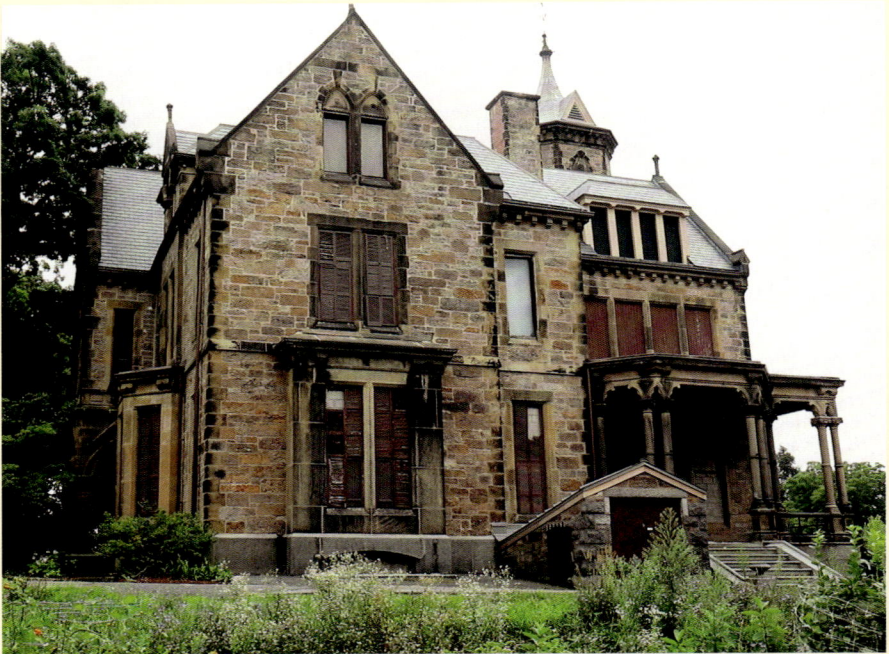

Fig. 42. The National Center of Afro-American Artists (NCAAA), July 2024. Housed since 1980 in the historic Abbotsford Estate in Boston's Roxbury neighborhood, the NCAAA has provided a continual platform for established, new, and underrepresented artists of the African diaspora, harnessing the power of art to bring people together, catalyzing movements, and addressing issues of social justice, race, and power. Photograph by Aukram Burton

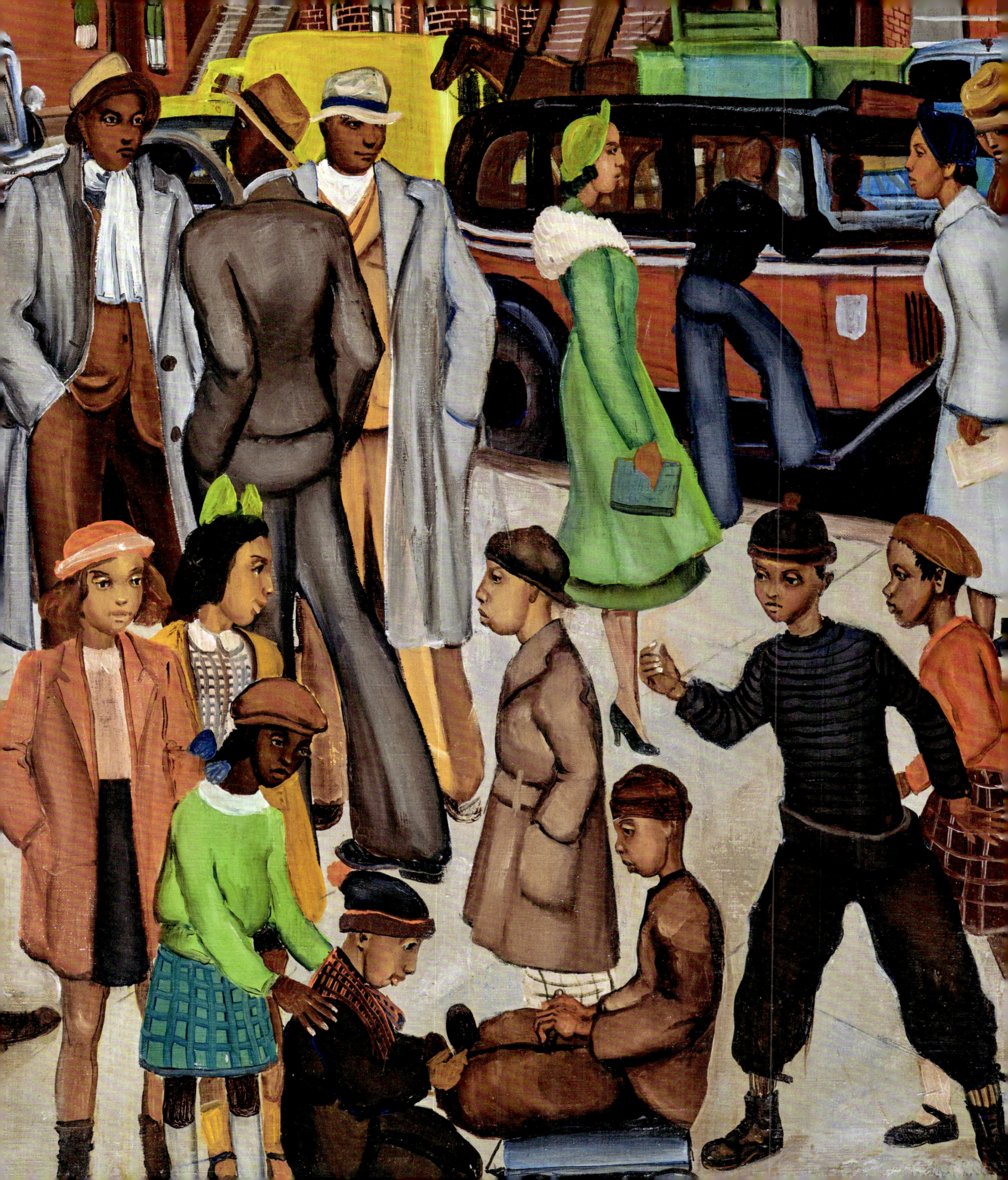

RE-PRESENTING THE BLACK URBAN SCENE

ALLAN ROHAN CRITE'S
NEIGHBORHOOD SERIES IN BOSTON

Julie Levin Caro

> I was making studies of Black people just as ordinary human beings, because the usual picture that one had—at least that's my impression—was that the artist was strongly influenced by, you might say, the jazz person up in Harlem, or of the sharecropper in the deep South. There was nothing in between—of just the ordinary middle-class person who goes to church, does the work, etc. What I decided to do back in those days—and as a matter of fact I'm still doing it—was just simply to record the life of Black people as I saw them in the city where I lived, which happened to be Boston.
>
> —Allan Rohan Crite

Allan Rohan Crite (1910–2007) made this statement in the late 1970s as he reflected on his goals as an artist working forty years earlier.[1] Discussing his well-known *Neighborhood Series* of paintings, drawings, and prints from the mid-1930s to the 1940s, his insistence that he depicted Black people as "ordinary human beings" as opposed to as "the jazz person" or "the sharecropper" can be read in multiple ways. It may be an indictment of the exoticization of Black people as artistic subject matter—by both white and African American artists who were Crite's contemporaries. It can be read as a perspective deeply grounded in the values of Boston's small early twentieth-century Black community, which, as we will see, was committed to striving for racial and socioeconomic integration. Finally, the emphasis on the "middle-class person who goes to church, does the work, etc." might be read as an implicit critique of people who do not do those things. However, to see Crite as someone dedicated to hidebound conservative social values would be a mistake. Instead, through a close look at several of Crite's *Neighborhood Series* canvases, one can track his shifting outlook on Black life, an outlook deeply grounded in and dedicated to Boston. One can also track how this outlook and Crite's artistic presentation of his community changed during this extremely productive decade in his career.

    Crite's depictions of the Black experience, and his comments about those depictions, have not always fit easily into existing histories of African American art. Much of the scholarship on African American artists over the past fifty years has been concerned with expanding the canon and documenting Black artists' contributions to the Harlem

Opposite: Detail of *Columbus Avenue*, plate 9

Renaissance and other contemporaneous art movements, like the American Scene and Regionalism.[2] One foundational strategy for enlarging the art historical canon was to expand the terms in which African American artists and their works are judged by introducing critical theory based on an independent Black aesthetic.[3] This strategy goes back to the 1920s. In his 1925 essay "The Legacy of the Ancestral Arts," African American cultural critic and Harlem Renaissance leader Alain Locke urged Black artists to take pride in their cultural heritage by drawing inspiration from the technical principles and themes of African art as well as from African American folk music and other vernacular cultural forms.[4] Inherent in Locke's call for a "racially expressive art" and for the establishment of a "racial school of art" was a critique of Black middle-class standards of art and excellence, which he believed were too tied to the mainstream to produce an original art.

Using Locke's criteria, Crite's contribution to American art is both present in and absent from the literature on African American art. In the earliest histories written by Locke (*Negro Art: Past and Present,* 1936) and by James Porter, artist, art historian, and Howard University professor (*Modern Negro Art,* 1943), Crite is present as an example of a group of academically trained Black artists who achieved professional recognition.[5] At the same time, Crite's relationship to the history of art is absent in these texts because neither Locke nor Porter analyzed his artistic choices or compared his artworks to those of his contemporaries. More recent survey texts by Sharon F. Patton (*African-American Art,* 1998), Richard J. Powell (*Black Art: A Cultural History,* 1999), and Lisa Farrington (*African-American Art: A Visual and Cultural History,* 2016) ignore the artist's work altogether. While Crite has received some attention in exhibition catalogues focused on the history of early twentieth-century American art movements and the history of art in Boston, these texts also distort the artist's place within that history. On the one hand, studies that focus on the Harlem Renaissance consistently characterize Crite's work as driven by an interest in documenting the Black experience in his Boston community.[6] In this context, Crite's work is understood as idiosyncratic rather than as expressive of a more commonly experienced Black identity based on an interest in connecting with African and Black folk roots.[7] On the other hand, when broad studies of American Regionalism, Social Realism, and New Deal–era art include Crite, the authors focus exclusively on Crite's images of the Black urban scene and describe his work as representative of a singular African American experience.[8] Likewise, studies of the early twentieth-century art scene in Boston characterize the artist as a spokesperson for the city's Black community and situate him and his art outside the local, predominantly white artistic and cultural establishment and stylistic traditions.[9] More recently, scholars have come to focus on understanding the artistic production of Black Americans in the context of global African diasporas—diasporas often created through the forced movement of enslaved and colonized peoples.[10] With this global turn, Crite's often local focus has further marginalized him in the art historical literature.[11]

This essay makes an argument for Crite's importance in the history of African American art and complicates his depiction of Black middle-class life. It begins with an introduction to Crite's biography, artistic training, and career through the 1940s (fig. 43), and introduces some of the tenets of what Crite's understanding of "just the ordinary middle-class person" would have been, as informed by both broader historical research and his individual family experience, particularly the influence of his mother. The core of the essay traces Crite's engagements with his understanding of the Black middle-class Bostonian across three canvases: *Parade on Hammond Street* (1935), *The Handy Street Bridge* (1939), and *Harriet and Leon* (1941).

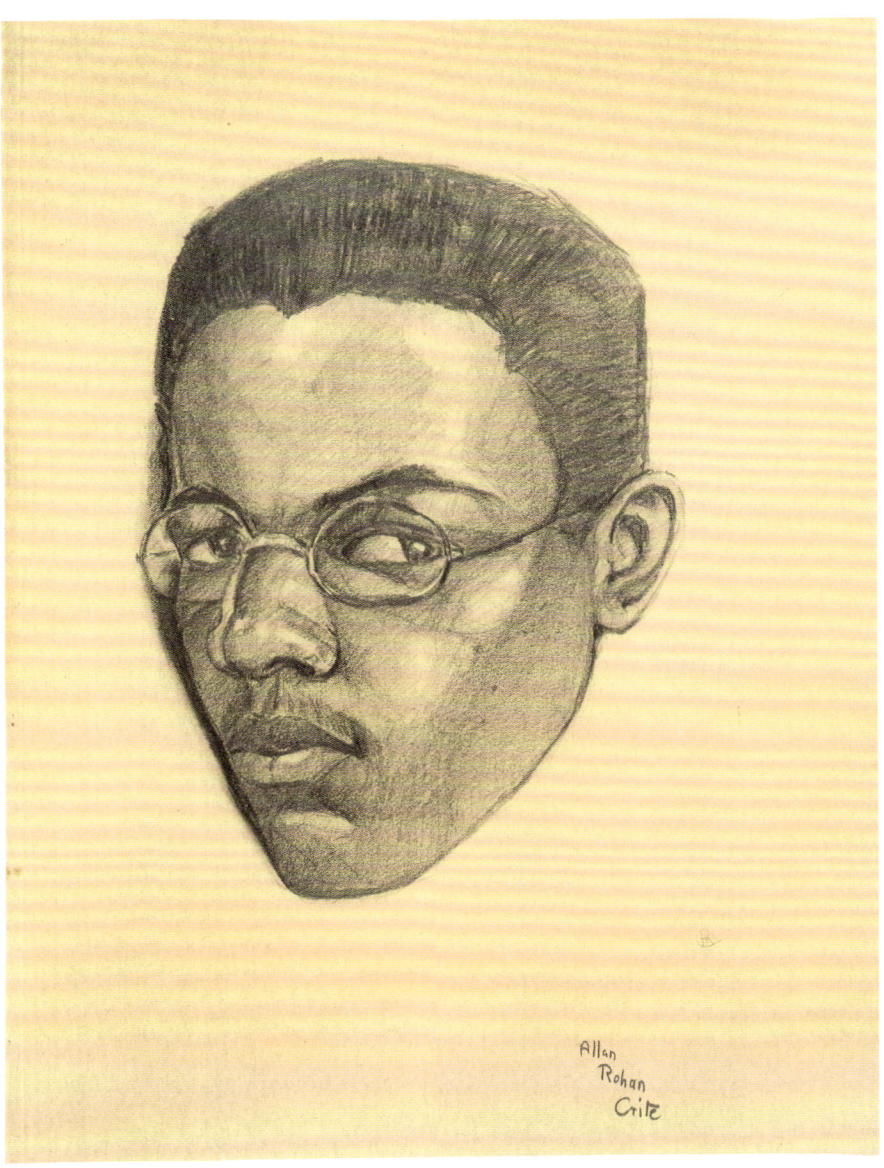

Fig. 43. Allan Rohan Crite, *Self-Portrait,* about 1932. Charcoal and pencil on paper, 46.4 × 34.3 cm. National Center of Afro-American Artists (NCAAA), Roxbury

A BOSTON UPBRINGING

Although Crite was born in North Plainfield, New Jersey, he and his parents, Oscar and Annamae Crite, relocated to Boston before his first birthday. This New England city, specifically the African American neighborhoods of Lower Roxbury and the South End, remained home to the artist for his entire life. Like many African Americans living around the turn of the twentieth century, Crite's parents had middle-class aspirations. The desire for upward mobility not only prompted African Americans to migrate from the rural South to the urban North but also inspired northern Blacks to seek opportunities in new cities. The Crites were probably attracted to Boston for its reputation as a place of unprecedented educational and cultural opportunities for African Americans.[12] At the time, the city was known nationally for its well-established community of free Blacks, which dated back to the seventeenth century, its history as the birthplace of abolitionism, and its superior public education system, the first in the nation to be integrated.[13] Yet the positive assessment of Boston's Black community that informed the Crites' point of view was based largely on its nineteenth-century reputation. Up until World War I, Boston's African American community was one of the most highly regarded in the nation, and the city was understood as a progressive center of Black politics, culture, and educa-

tion. However, during the Great Migration of African Americans from the rural South to the urban North between 1915 and 1945, Black migrants avoided Boston because of its lack of industrial jobs. As a result, Boston's African American population remained small during the period between the world wars, while the Black communities in cities like New York and Chicago became large and diverse centers of politics, literature, art, and music.

Crite's parents came from different social and geographic backgrounds—Annamae Palmer Crite (1891–1977) was from a working-class Methodist family in Philadelphia, while Oscar William Crite (1875–1937) was raised in a rural county in North Carolina by parents who were former slaves—but both came to Boston with the expectation of raising their status to middle class. However, while Mr. Crite sought economic advantages unavailable to him in the South, Mrs. Crite understood the New England city's social milieu in relation to the Black society she knew from her childhood and adolescence in another northern city. She regarded Boston as a place where she could further her class standing through education and membership in the Episcopal Church. Crite's early family life typified a Bostonian Black middle-class upbringing. Crite's father worked as a stationary engineer, and he owned his home, a small brownstone in the center of Boston's Black neighborhood of Lower Roxbury.[14] Crite's mother was a housewife and was actively engaged with local charities and the Episcopal Church. She was a central influence on the artist's life, particularly his understanding of Bostonian attitudes of respectability.

Crite's mother was also particularly enamored of Boston's association with the nation's oldest and most prestigious institution of higher learning, Harvard University. According to Mrs. Crite:

> When I arrived [in Boston], of course, I went directly to Harvard. . . . Harvard University and the Episcopal Church have been my two loves. I went to church, that was on a Sunday, and the next day went to Harvard. I visited the museums . . . and [studied] in the evening Extension [School]. . . . I love Harvard. . . . My son has inherited the same affection for Harvard.[15]

Several of the country's most influential Black leaders had graduated from Harvard, including W. E. B. Du Bois, Alain Locke, and local newspaper publisher and activist William Monroe Trotter. For Mrs. Crite, Harvard symbolized the cultured Bostonian lifestyle she desired for herself and her son. Crite and his mother maintained a lifelong affiliation with Harvard University through its Extension School, where Mrs. Crite took classes from 1910 until the 1950s. A devoted member of her parish of St. Bartholomew's Episcopal Church in Cambridge, one of the area's oldest Black Episcopal congregations, composed largely of middle- and upper-class Black families, Mrs. Crite taught Sunday school, where she took charge of educating the children about history and culture through outings around Boston. Allan also belonged to St. Bartholomew's.

Like many middle-class African Americans, Mrs. Crite disliked jazz music and what she perceived as its attendant culture of vice. She preferred classical music and the fine arts and instilled an appreciation of these cultural expressions in her son. Crite's mother exposed him from an early age to all the cultural attractions of Boston. They were frequent visitors to the Museum of Fine Arts, the Isabella Stewart Gardner Museum (fig. 44) and Harvard University's art and science museums. Crite and his mother walked in the gardens of the Boston Common and toured the State House. They attended concerts of the Boston Symphony Orchestra and private performances at the home of the renowned African American tenor Roland Hayes. Mrs. Crite also viewed her son's interest in the performing arts as an appropriate pursuit. As a teenager, Crite joined a local Black theater group, the Allied Arts Players, and sang concert versions of the spirituals with a local choir. Mrs. Crite instilled her middle-class orientation in her son by encouraging him to

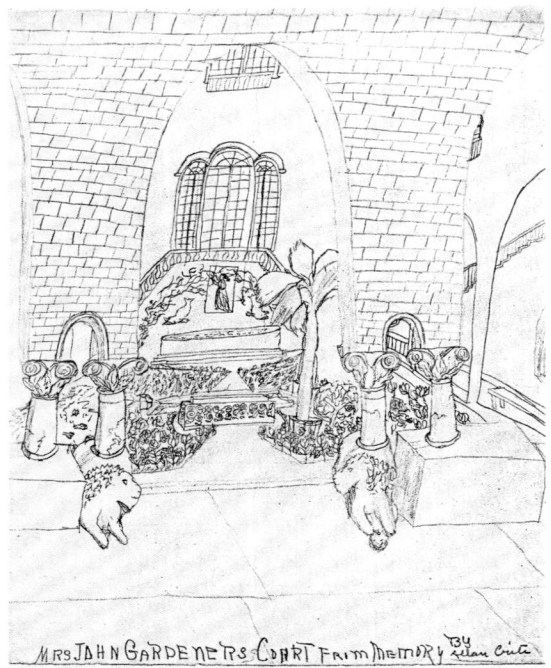

Fig. 44. Allan Rohan Crite, *Mrs. John Gardner's Court from Memory,* 1921. Photocopy, 26.5 × 20 cm. Arts Department, Special Collections, Boston Public Library

engage in these cultural and leisure activities as aspects of a Bostonian way of life. Crite's parents placed a high value on education, and they sent their son to two of the city's most prestigious public schools, the Boston Latin School and English High School, where he graduated in 1929. From childhood, Crite was an avid library patron. His mother especially encouraged him to pursue a career as a professional artist, for she saw this as a suitable cultural endeavor.[16]

In 1929, just after Crite began his studies at the School of the Museum of Fine Arts, known as the Museum School, his father suffered a severe stroke from a work-related accident. The incident left Crite Sr. paralyzed and bedridden for the next seven and a half years, until his death in 1937. The impact of Crite Sr.'s infirmity was devastating to his young wife and son, who immediately saw their family roles change to those of caregivers and their economic circumstances worsen. With Mr. Crite no longer able to provide for the family, they lost ownership of their brownstone and were left in the more precarious position of leasing their house. Against the judgment of her husband and friends, Mrs. Crite decided to step out of her comfortable middle-class lifestyle as a housewife and went to work as a domestic to support her son's art education.[17]

WHAT DID THE BLACK MIDDLE CLASS MEAN TO CRITE?

Crite's understanding of his racial, class, and regional identity as a Black middle-class Bostonian drew from two related concepts prevalent during his formative years in the 1910s and 1920s, the "talented tenth" and the "race" man or woman. First defined in 1903 by W. E. B. Du Bois, the "talented tenth" was an educated professional class of elite Blacks in the top 10 percent of Black society, who bore the responsibility of racial leadership.[18] Similarly, the "race" man and woman felt a strong sense of responsibility, to themselves, their families, and their communities, to be a model of excellence, both personally and professionally, in order to demonstrate the potential of "the race" to both African Americans and whites.[19] Underlying the concepts of the "talented tenth" and the "race" man is the notion of racial uplift, the obligation felt by the Black middle and upper classes to elevate the Black lower class by providing it with a model of achievement and respectable behavior, while at the same time demonstrating to whites the potential of all African Americans to merit the full rights of citizenship.

Crite's artistic project reflects the outlook of the "talented tenth" and the "race" man in the way that it reveals the dual allegiance felt by the Black middle class to uphold white standards of respectability while also affirming a sense of pride in African American identity. The value that Crite's family and community placed on maintaining, displaying, and encouraging a respectable appearance and code of behavior underlies the goals that Crite set for his life and work. As the artist wrote in his diary in 1936:

> There must be a school of thought and a school of Negro artists with a conviction similar to my own to depict and preach the doctrine of the "real" Negro . . . . For as long as the incomplete and picturesque ghost of the "Exotic Negro" is held up to our white friends, all efforts towards understanding between the white and Negro races will fail.[20]

As we will see, in his *Neighborhood Series,* Crite used a set of visual conventions, including a realist style and the representation of qualities of formality, reserve, and gentility, to define the members of his community in terms of a Black middle-class sensibility.

However, two descriptions of the Black middle class, written immediately before and after the period of Crite's early career in the 1930s and 1940s, strongly influenced the perception that the Black middle class was an inauthentic source for Black subject matter or a Black aesthetic. In his essay "The Negro Artist and the Racial Mountain" (1926), the African American writer Langston Hughes argued that the middle-class artist

adopts the sensibilities of white mainstream culture and is therefore incapable of experiencing or representing a genuine Black culture. In contrast, Hughes positions the lower or folk class of African Americans as a source of Black artistic expression:

> Then there are the low down folks, the so-called common element. . . . [They] are not too important to themselves or to the community, or too well fed, or too learned to watch the lazy world go round. . . . They furnish a wealth of colorful, distinctive material for any artist because they still hold their individuality in the face of American standardizations.[21]

While Hughes's desire to elevate Black folk subject matter is an attempt to release it from demeaning stereotypes, his argument simultaneously negates Black middle-class experience as a legitimate basis for an original art. African American sociologist E. Franklin Frazier's *Black Bourgeoisie* (1957) proved to be even more damaging to the reputation of the Black middle class. Long considered to be the definitive study of this social group, its comprehensive scope enabled its biased and negative assertions to go unchallenged for decades. According to Frazier, by acquiring a measure of economic status, middle-class African Americans forgot their true second-class position in American society, as well as their sense of responsibility to provide leadership to the Black masses.

Crite's expression of Black middle-class identity contradicts the assertions of Hughes and Frazier in two important ways. First, the precarious economic situation in which Crite and his community found themselves in the 1930s distinguishes his experience from Hughes's and Frazier's characterization of the Black middle class as a group that had lost contact with the Black masses owing to their relative comfort and advancement. As we will see, an important motivation for Crite's artworks was his class anxiety, which resulted in a desire to fix in place an idealized vision of Boston's Black middle class created from his memory of an earlier, more stable time in his community, along with his creative invention.

Second, Hughes's and Frazier's assertions that the Black middle class, in its desire to reject a Black racial identity, mimicked white social mores and aesthetic values does not account for the strong element of racial pride that many sociologists, writing in the early twentieth century, described as hallmarks of Black middle-class identity. The "middle-class" identity that best applies to Crite's neighborhood paintings fuses these elements of respectability and racial pride. And it is this type of Black middle-class identity that should inform our analysis of Crite's neighborhood paintings.

In this context, the impact of Crite's conservative art training on his stylistic development and artistic goals cannot be overestimated. After completing the Boston MFA's high school vocational arts program, Crite won one of two scholarships awarded each year to attend the MFA's prestigious art academy, known as the Museum School. He continued to receive tuition scholarships throughout his seven-year tenure at the Museum School between 1929 and 1936.[22] Founded in 1877, the Museum School featured a curriculum based on traditional academic principles and with a strong emphasis on drawing skills, and Crite's coursework included classes in cast and life drawing, perspective, design and color theory, anatomy (plate 1), figure and still-life painting, mural decoration, and the history of Western art.[23]

One of Crite's graphite figure drawings from his student years, *Emma Nixon* (1933) (fig. 45), demonstrates how Crite used his grounding in academic principles and an understanding of the human form to convey a sense of the dignity of his subject. In particular, the artist pays careful attention to the distinctive aspects of the young woman's African American physiognomy and hair. Throughout his career, Crite's emphasis on the physical beauty and refinement of his subjects reflects an approach taken by the Boston School of Painters, which emphasized the upper-class status of sitters with aestheticized depictions

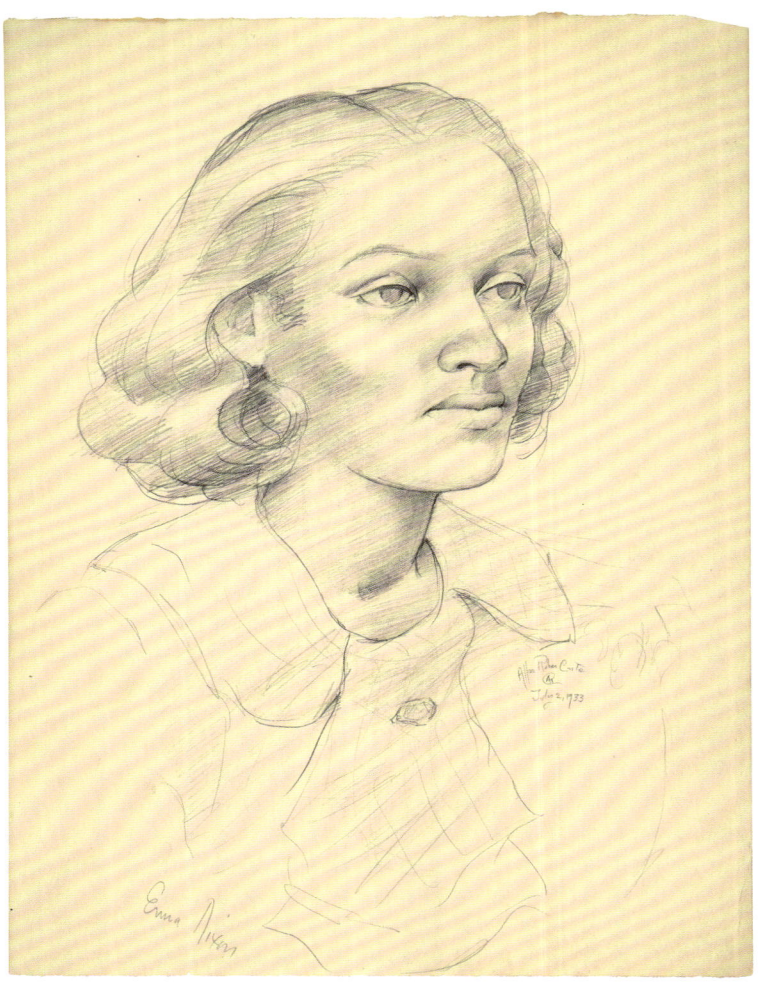

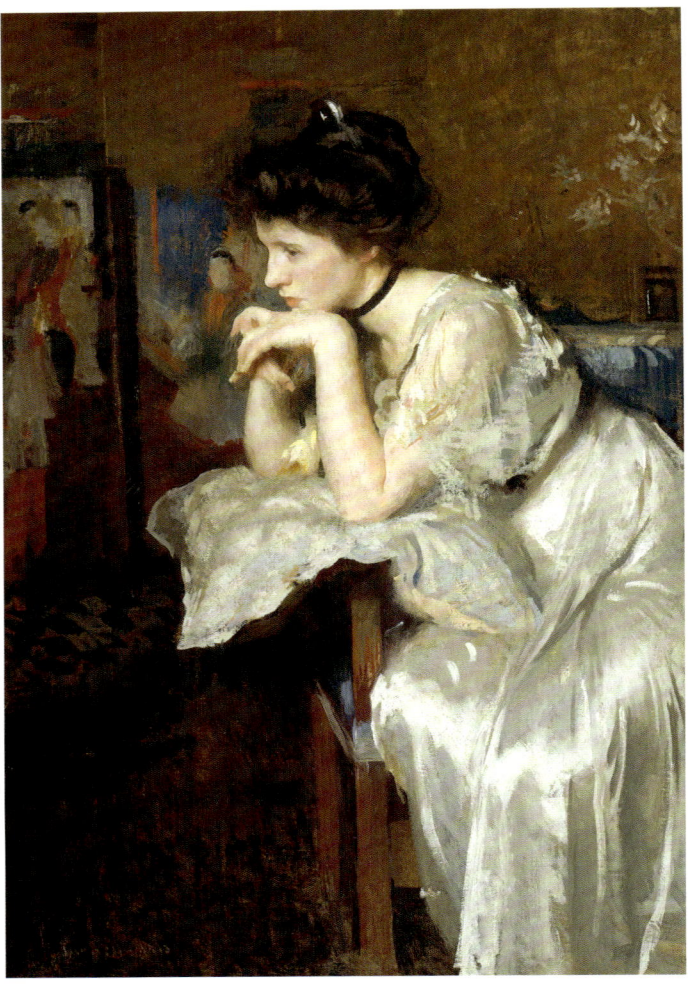

Fig. 45. Allan Rohan Crite, *Emma Nixon,* 1933. Graphite pencil on paper, 40.6 × 30.5 cm. National Center of Afro-American Artists (NCAAA), Roxbury

Fig. 46. Edmund C. Tarbell, *Reverie (Katharine Finn),* 1913. Oil on canvas, 127.3 × 86.7 cm. Museum of Fine Arts, Boston

of visage, dress, and surroundings.[24] Crite learned the Boston School approach directly from its members, many of whom had been instructors at the Museum School since the 1890s. A typical example includes Edmund C. Tarbell's *Reverie (Katharine Finn)* of 1913 (fig. 46). Bathed in diffused light, dressed in the latest fashion, and surrounded by beautiful objects, the female subjects that Tarbell and his fellow painters routinely depicted showed them engaged in leisure activities—daydreaming, sewing, drinking tea, reading—that situated them in the domestic sphere and solidified their status as ladies of fine taste and wealth.

In Crite's final year at the Museum School, he won the coveted Boit Prize for Painting, a confirmation of his high level of achievement in the context of the institution's academic teachings. From this initial grounding in a traditional art approach, Crite maintained a preference for using a realist style throughout his career. Furthermore, his affiliation with the Museum of Fine Arts and its prestigious school was an important professional asset to the young artist. It helped launch his early career, even in the midst of the Depression.

A PERFORMATIVE RATHER THAN DOCUMENTARY APPROACH

In the mid-1930s, Crite, just finishing at the Museum School, produced a number of neighborhood paintings under the patronage of the Public Works of Art Project (PWAP) and the Federal Art Project (FAP), two government-funded programs that supported visual artists as part of President Franklin Delano Roosevelt's New Deal.[25] Although Crite participated in the FAP for a little less than a year, from February to December 1936, he

used this opportunity, along with his brief tenure on the PWAP (February to May 1934), to create ten oil paintings, two watercolors, four drawings, and one linocut print, a substantial portion of his total output of neighborhood street scenes.

Crite exemplified the type of artist that FAP director Holger Cahill wished to support. Formally trained at one of the country's leading art schools, Crite had already exhibited professionally with the Boston Society of Independent Artists and the Harmon Foundation's traveling exhibitions of African American art.[26] By the time Crite began his tenure with the FAP, he had established the essential content and style of the neighborhood paintings. Crite's approach to depicting Black urban life in his street scenes reflected many of the democratic ideals that Cahill wanted FAP artists to promote to the American public. Some of Crite's FAP paintings, such as *Corner of Washington & Northampton Sts.* (1935–1943), emphasize the theme of racial integration and shared Americanness by including scenes of Black and white Bostonians interacting equally in public spaces (fig. 47).

Crite's FAP painting *School's Out* (1936) illustrates the way in which his street scenes enact a Bostonian version of a middle-class outlook through his depiction of Black Bostonians enjoying the full rights and privileges of American citizenship (fig. 48). In this scene, students emerge from a small, one-story redbrick building, an all-girls annex to the Bancroft Elementary School. Some walk hand in hand in lines, while others bound down the street or stop in the alley for a game of jump rope. A few of the girls are met by their mothers, shapely and fashionable women who walk purposefully ahead or stand chatting with one another. The women seem detached from the laughter and activity around them. Their facial expressions and turned backs suggest the separate mental spaces of adults and children. *School's Out* fulfilled the goals of the government-sponsored art projects as well as the prevailing American Scene and Regionalism art movements in using art to envision a pluralist American society in which racial and ethnic participation is the shared goal. As depictions of specific Boston locales that also portray widely shared American experiences, Crite's neighborhood paintings express cultural nationalism by emphasizing his rootedness in his Black middle-class community and his sense of place in his New England city and region.[27]

Central to the success of both American Scene and Regionalist imagery was the collective experience of the Depression. During the 1930s, many artists and writers turned to depictions of everyday life to demonstrate the capacity of ordinary Americans to persevere through difficult times. In *School's Out,* Crite focused on the ritual aspects of daily life that seemed to transcend the social and economic uncertainties of the period. Crite's neighborhood paintings reassured viewers that despite the economic and social hardships of the Depression, the fabric of community life and its American values of education, hard work, and leisure remained intact.

We find additional proof of Crite's dedication to his middle-class values in a decision he made to voluntarily end his employment with the Federal Art Project. This important form of patronage gave the artist a degree of prestige and confidence similar to his affiliation with the Museum School. Moreover, the PWAP and FAP provided him with his first national art exposure by including his work in exhibitions at Washington, DC's Corcoran Gallery and the Museum of Modern Art in New York.[28] Despite the importance that his monthly salary of $94 must have had for his family's strained financial circumstances in the mid-1930s, Crite voluntarily chose to leave the FAP after only eleven months, when cutbacks in the nonrelief-worker category funding would have required that he register for relief assistance to continue his participation. According to the artist, the designation "relief worker" was synonymous with "being on the dole" and, he explained, "My mother and I, we didn't quite like that connotation. So we took the painful decision to not continue."[29]

The painting *Parade on Hammond Street,* completed a year before *School's Out,* in June 1935—during the period between his participation in the PWAP and his involvement

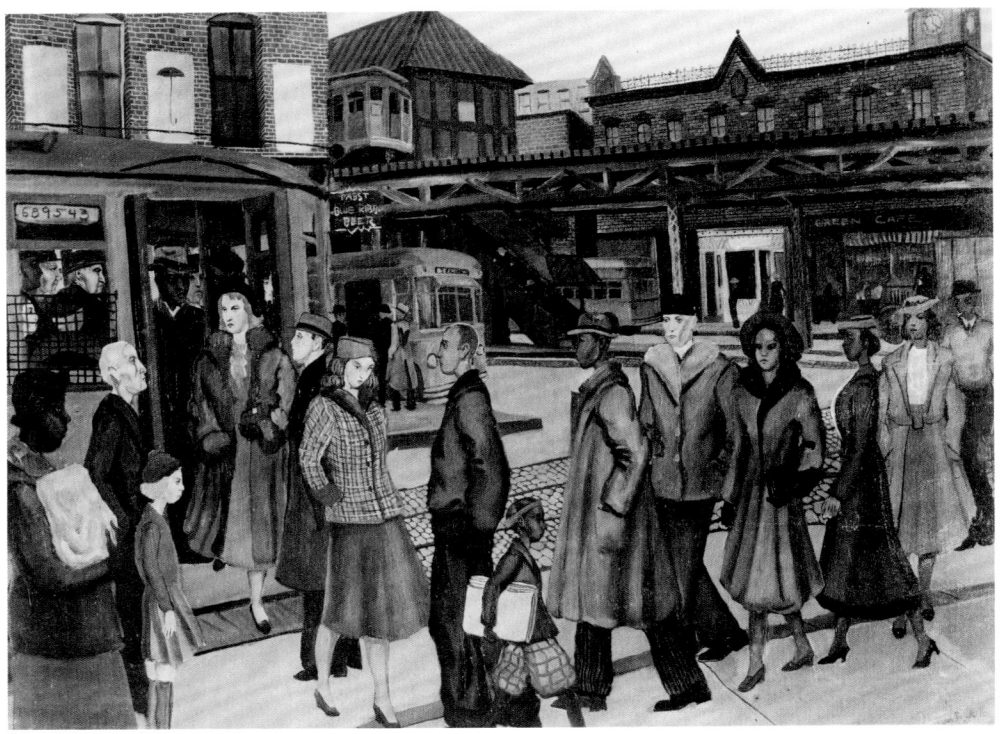

Fig. 47. Allan Rohan Crite, *Corner of Washington & Northampton Sts.,* 1935–43. Gelatin silver print of an oil painting, 21 × 26 cm. Arts Department, Special Collections, Boston Public Library

in the FAP—best demonstrates Crite's interest in presenting Boston's middle-class Black community, even when he was not working in the context of the federal government's aesthetic agenda (fig. 49). In this painting, Crite constructs a scene of leisure and civic pride that identifies Black Bostonians with the values and ideals of an American way of life. With its upbeat mood and use of detailed naturalism, *Parade on Hammond Street* is typical of the *Neighborhood Series* as a whole. As the artist explained, the painting records his memory of a parade in the heart of Boston's African American community in Lower Roxbury: "The parade was one of those district conventions of the Elks, a fraternal order, and the parade was a feature of the festivities. They would be at times on a Sunday preceding a service at one of the churches. It was a festive affair and everyone [was] in the Sunday best of attire."[30] On the right side of the composition, the tall Black man leading the parade captures our attention with his perfect posture, blue and white baton, and striking yellow plumed hat. The open foreground space on either side of the bandleader allows us to view more of the crowd and the physical space of neighborhood, which are as important to Crite's enactment of Black middle-class life as the parade itself.

Parade on Hammond Street is notable for the various performative levels of its visual imagery. The parade participants perform music for the crowd, and they also perform their identity as members of a local chapter of the Elks Lodge, a national fraternal organization associated with white middle-class Americans. The audience members also act out their individual identities as well-dressed professionals, housewives, and citizens. The neighborhood itself, with its immaculate sidewalks and streets and pristine building façades, also plays a role by reflecting the decorous nature of the people who reside there.

Crite's meticulous reconstruction of the setting in *Parade on Hammond Street* helps to ground its narrative in reality and make his imagery accessible to a wide audience. But it is important to remember that *Parade on Hammond Street* and Crite's other neighborhood paintings are not documentaries, for the artist's use of a direct descriptive approach was limited to the planning stages of his compositions. Crite's research process involved taking daily walks through his neighborhood and recording details of the architecture and topography in a sketchpad. In fact, Crite's sketchbooks from this period have very

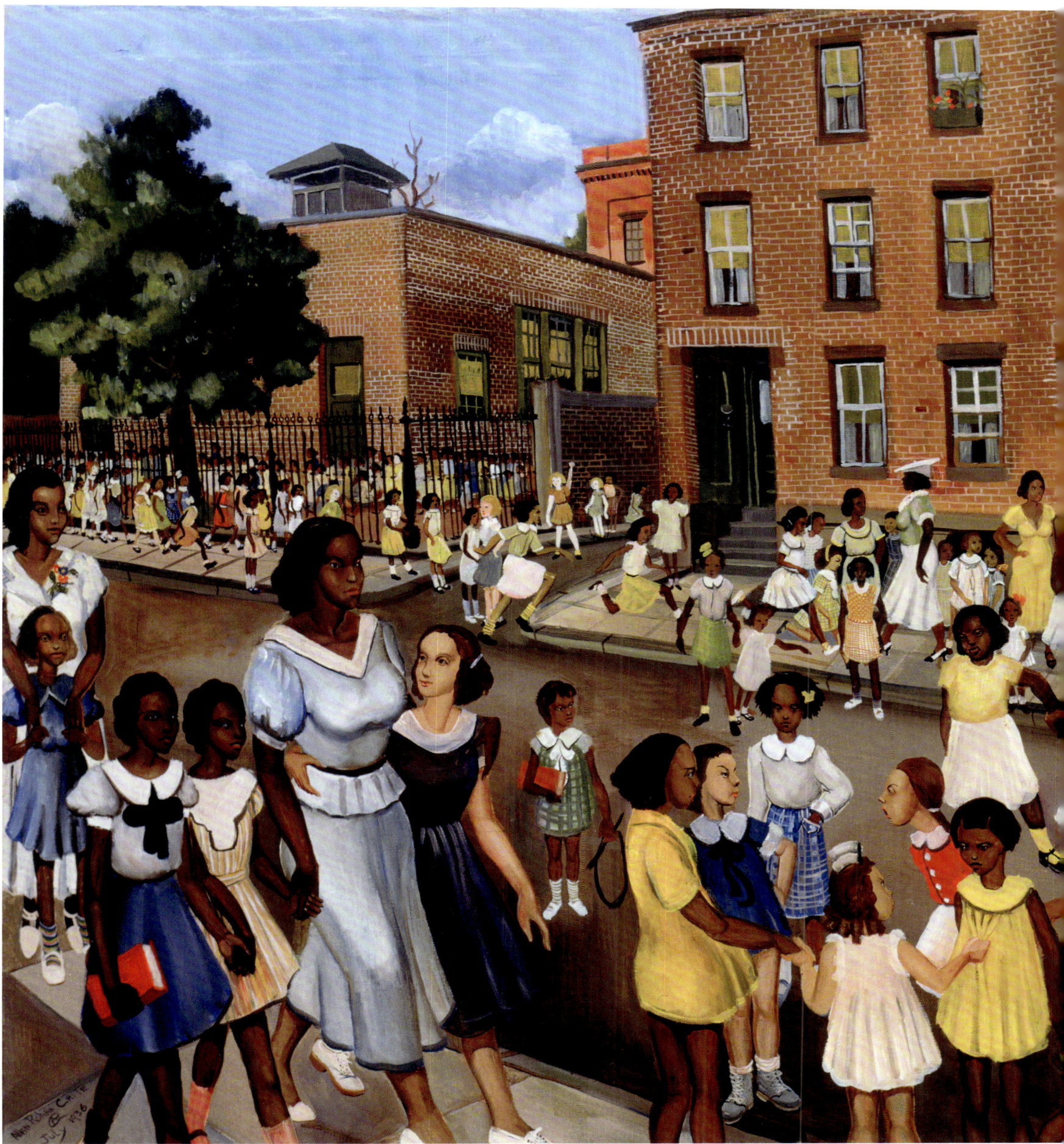

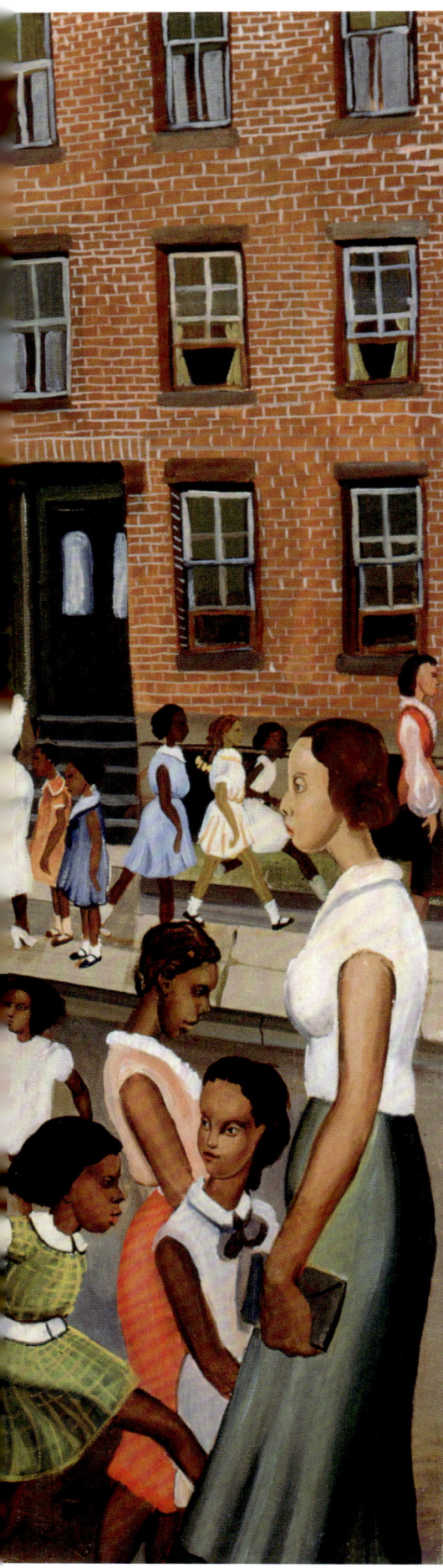

few portrait drawings of people, and the artist has said that when creating individual figures for the final paintings, he referred to a mental file of faces that interested him.[31] The final paintings, then, are carefully constructed compositions executed entirely in the artist's studio from a combination of his on-site drawings, memories, and imagination.

Given their reportorial style, much of the existing scholarship on Crite's neighborhood paintings ascribes a documentary quality to their meaning. In reading Crite's street scenes as visual documentaries, art historians have relied almost exclusively upon Crite's comments about this body of work post-1970, after several decades of city-sponsored urban renewal projects that removed or dramatically altered many sections of Crite's neighborhood, including his home of nearly fifty years at 2 Dilworth Street in Roxbury. In retrospect, the artist reevaluated the meaning of his neighborhood paintings and emphasized their preservationist value as documents of a lost era in the city's history.

It is true that in many cases the neighborhood paintings are some of the only remaining visual records of the buildings, alleyways, and parks that once defined Crite's community. But the revisionist account that Crite gave of his neighborhood paintings has influenced the historiography of his early career. In using Crite's post-urban-renewal description of himself as an "artist-reporter," and in focusing on the descriptive qualities of his street scenes, scholars have assumed that these paintings are unmediated documents of Black urban experience.[32] Rereading the paintings as demonstrations of Crite's pride in his middle-class community, by contrast, gives the artist a greater amount of agency as the inventor of his imagery and allows for a broader interpretation of his style and iconography.

Crite's use of a realistic documentary style in his neighborhood paintings was the result of his application of the skills he learned from his academic art training at the Museum School. In such works as *Parade on Hammond Street,* he began by applying a graphite sketch to the surface of a primed canvas.[33] He then added a thin layer of pink, over which he applied a rich oil medium using varied brushstrokes. Typically, Crite built up his image from back to front in the traditional manner, completing the buildings first and then the figures. Crite's approach relied on his understanding of figure modeling, perspective, and naturalistic color and lighting. In *Parade on Hammond Street* and other neighborhood paintings, the artist often used a limited palette of primary and secondary colors arranged in a balanced manner throughout the composition. He further activated his compositions by repeating forms and figures across the surface of the picture plane and by contrasting the bright colors of the figures' clothing with the bleached-out reds of brick façades and the sober tans and grays of sidewalks and streets. Crite's decision to portray an Elks parade resonates with viewers then and now, as parades were (and are) a familiar American public activity undertaken both for leisure and to demonstrate civic pride. Dating back to the beginning of the country's history as an independent republic, parades were part of a distinctive brand of American democracy.[34]

Parades and marches also have a long and significant history within the African American community as public statements of equal rights and expressions of racial pride, as in the late nineteenth-century parades celebrating Emancipation and the early twentieth-century parades of uniformed members of Marcus Garvey's separatist organization, the Universal Negro Improvement Association (fig. 50).[35] Crite's Elks parade, by

Fig. 48. Allan Rohan Crite, *School's Out,* 1936. Oil on canvas, 76.9 × 91.8 cm. Smithsonian American Art Museum

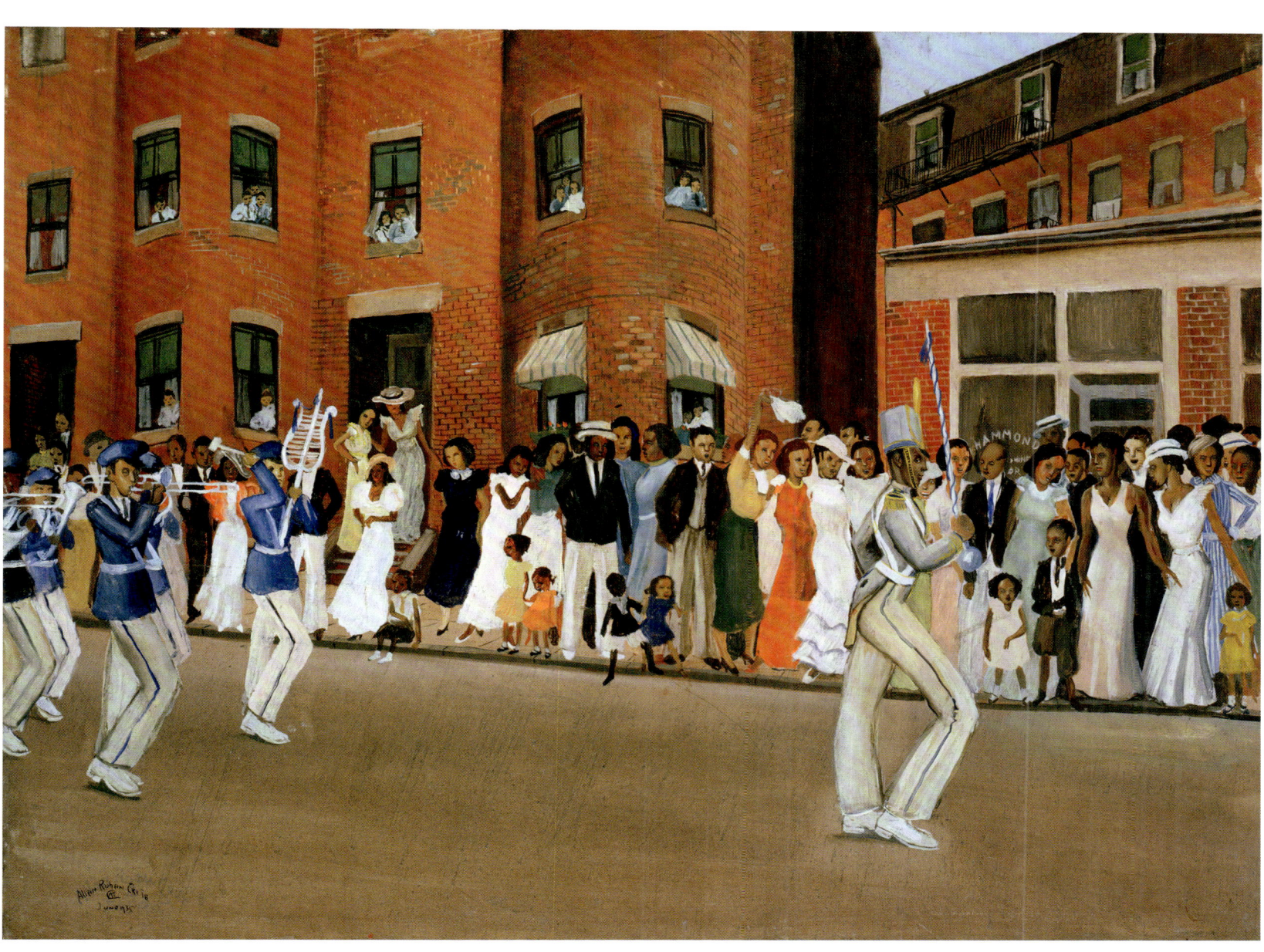

Opposite: Fig. 49. Allan Rohan Crite, *Parade on Hammond Street,* June 1935. Oil on canvas board, 45.7 × 61 cm. The Phillips Collection, Washington, DC, Acquired 1942

contrast, demonstrates his community's involvement in the pursuit of leisure, a hallmark of upper-class status and, in the 1930s especially, Americanness.[36]

Fashion was a signifier of class status in the midcentury Black community. In *Parade on Hammond Street* and countless other neighborhood paintings, Crite identifies the figures as Black middle-class Bostonians through the depiction of various types of clothing. It's Sunday afternoon just after church, and Crite shows figures at the parade as they see themselves, rather than as how they might have been seen by the white world during the workweek. The men appear in dark jackets and ties with white shirts and light-colored pants. The girls are dressed smartly in sailor dresses with white bobby socks, the boys in jackets, ties, and knickers. The women, however, depart from the traditional Bostonian convention of wearing sensible dresses with subdued colors and simple styling.[37] While some of the women's solid or pinstripe dresses with high or lace collars do exemplify this standard, many of the dresses pictured are long, sleeveless, tightly fitted gowns in white or bright colors. Although all the women in *Parade* behave with a degree of decorum and refinement, the women in gowns seem alluring, even sexy, and their appearance complicates the notion of middle-class respectability that forms the ideological basis of Crite's neighborhood paintings. Given the artist's own middle-class Bostonian sensibilities and his strong desire to identify his community with these values, it might seem curious that he would include portrayals of female sexuality in *Parade on Hammond Street* and a number of other neighborhood paintings, such as *School's Out* and *Sunlight and Shadow* (1941) (fig. 51). In these representations, Crite expresses his own subjectivity as a young single male who appreciates the women of his neighborhood; their youth and beauty are important aspects of his community's vibrancy. These sensual women may represent Crite's sublimated desire to be romantically attached. By the mid-1930s, when *Parade* was completed, Crite's family had been living in financially straitened circumstances for six years, since his father's accident at work and subsequent stroke in 1929. The artist had abandoned his long-standing desire to marry his childhood sweetheart, Lois Porter Clue, because he felt he could not financially support the lifestyle she enjoyed as a member of a leading Black family in Roxbury.[38] Deciding instead to devote himself to caring for his parents, his religious studies, and his art, Crite's neighborhood paintings, with their disproportionate number of images of women and children,

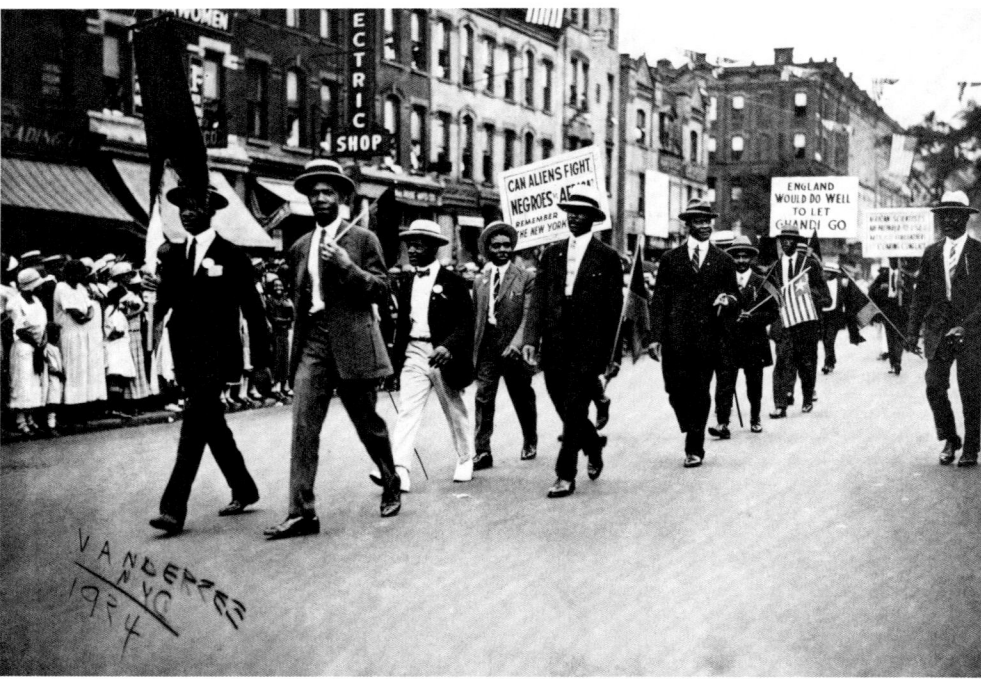

Fig. 50. James Van Der Zee, *UNIA Convention Parade,* 1924. Gelatin silver print, 17.2 × 24.2 cm. James Van Der Zee Archive, The Metropolitan Museum of Art; Gift of Donna Van Der Zee, 2021 (TR.101.165–.556.2021)

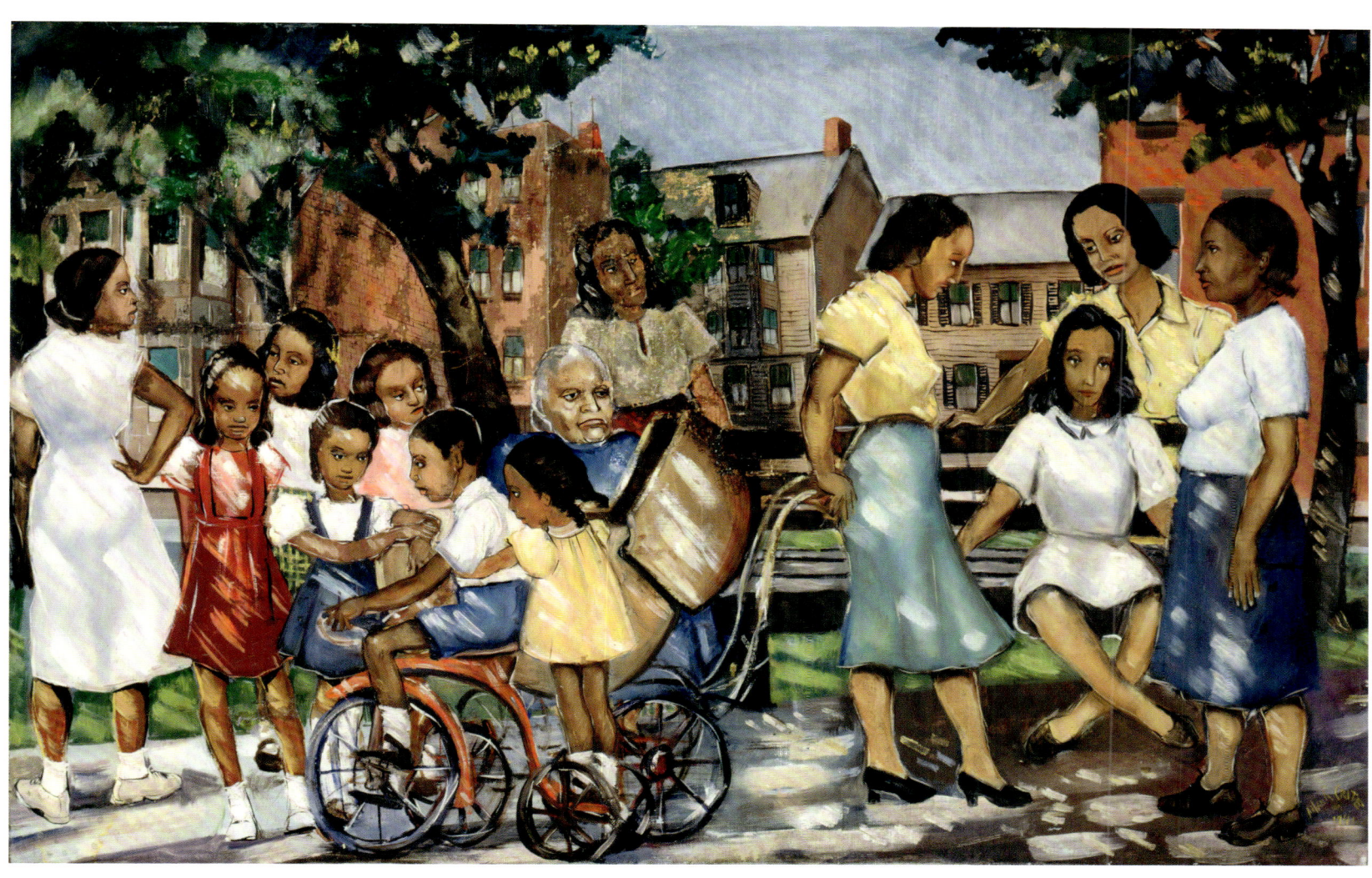

may have enacted his desire to have a family of his own and to achieve the middle-class norm of being a husband and father.

Crite's representation of Black Bostonian street life contrasts with the approach of many of his African American contemporaries, who created images that celebrated the urban folk masses and their participation in the culture of jazz. Archibald John Motley Jr.'s *Untitled (Street Scene, Chicago)* of 1936 (fig. 52), a work from his *Bronzeville Series* of paintings depicting Black life in Chicago, is characteristic of the type of imagery Crite sought to refute with his paintings. In contrast to Crite's preference for creating daytime scenes illuminated by natural light and color, most of Motley's Bronzeville paintings take place after dark, allowing the artist to explore the formal qualities of the artificial light of streetlamps and neon signs and to highlight some of the grittier aspects of urban life.[39] Much of the imagery in *Street Scene, Chicago* depicts the exoticizing stereotypes of African Americans that Crite's paintings consciously avoided. Motley's canvas portrays people performing, listening, and dancing to jazz music, often while smoking or engaging in other vices. Moreover, many of Motley's compositions appear as if they were painted at some physical distance from the action, enhancing the feeling that the figures depicted are on display. By contrast, Crite's use of naturalistic color, modeled figures, and perspective allows viewers to identify the figures as real people and to easily imagine entering the space. Further, the vantage point the artist establishes is that of a witness but also a participant in the daily life of a community. The resulting intimacy and directness of Crite's representations remain unique among the work of his fellow artists.

That *Parade on Hammond Street* successfully communicated these ideals is supported by the work's provenance. First shown in the 1930s at Boston's Grace Horne Gallery, which represented Crite at the time, it was later included in the historic exhibition *American Negro Art,* organized in 1941 in New York by Edith Halpert and Harlem Renaissance leader Alain Locke. Shown alongside some of the major African American artists of the day, *Parade* was purchased by Washington, DC collector Duncan Phillips for his growing collection of contemporary American painting.[40]

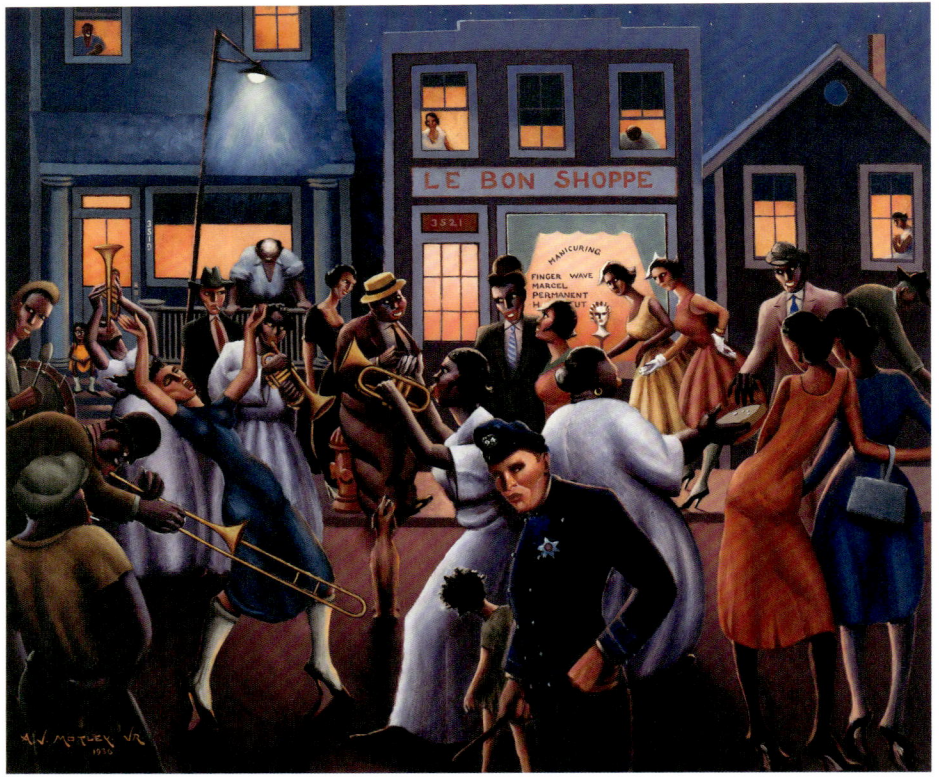

Fig. 52. Archibald John Motley Jr., *Untitled (Street Scene, Chicago),* 1936. Oil on canvas, 91.4 × 106.7 cm. Courtesy of Michael Rosenfeld Gallery LLC, New York, NY

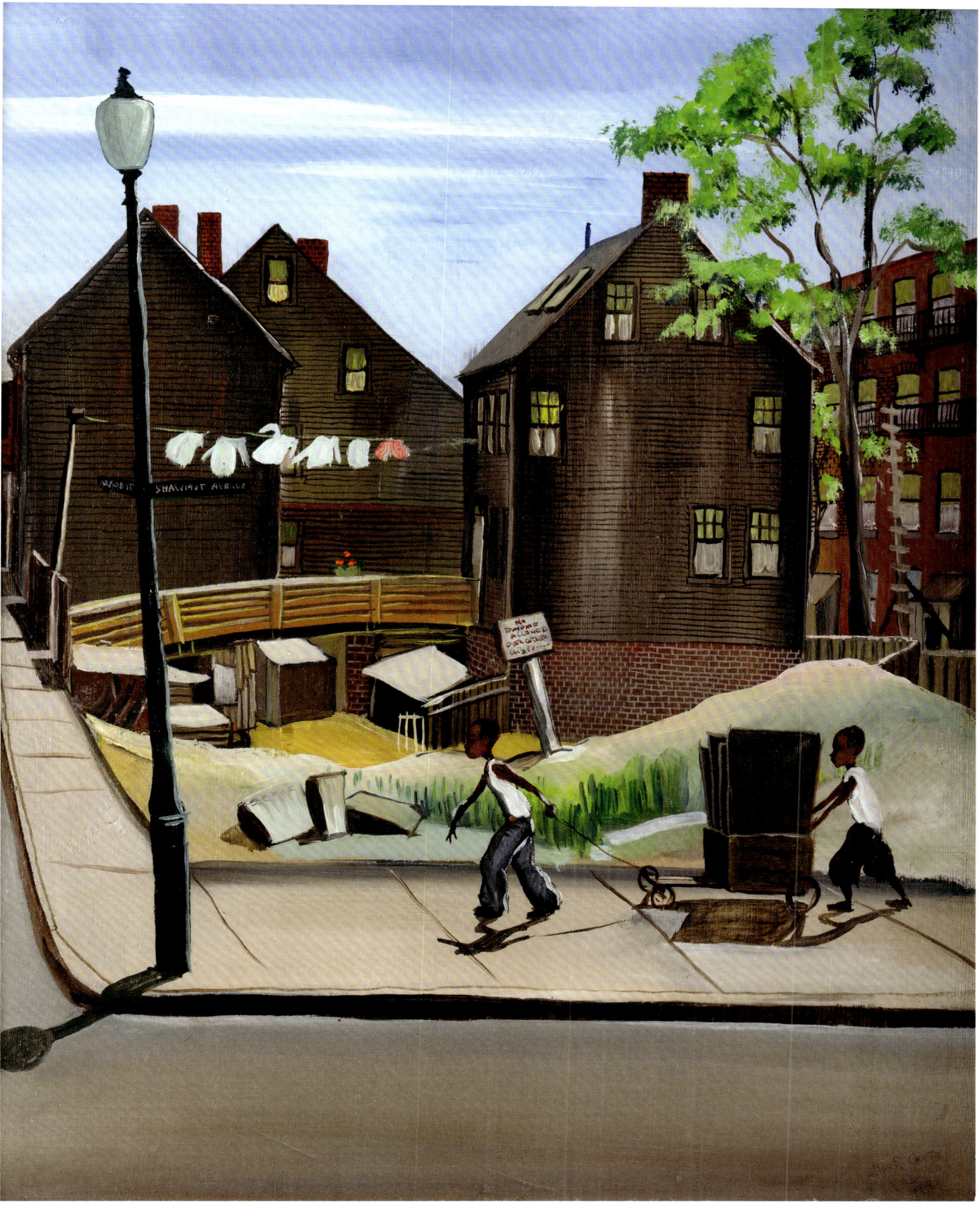

AN EVOLVING PICTORIAL STYLE, AN EVOLVING COMMUNITY

Much of the existing Crite scholarship fails to acknowledge the artist's stylistic development within the more than fifty neighborhood oils and watercolors he created between 1933 and 1945. Art historians tend to refer to the upbeat mood of paintings from the early to mid-1930s to describe the entire series. However, when we compare the mid-1930s compositions to those created between 1939 and 1945, several distinct transitions in the artist's style become evident. Many of the shifts in his personal style parallel the general stylistic tendencies among FAP, American Scene, and Regionalist painters of the period as well as locally among Boston artists.

While neighborhood paintings such as *Parade on Hammond Street* (1935) and *School's Out* (1936) display dense compositions, solidly painted forms, and an abundance of visual detail, later works, like *The Handy Street Bridge* (1939), reflect an interest in flattened surfaces, silhouetted forms, and simplified composition (fig. 53). During this period, American painters Charles Sheeler, Yasuo Kuniyoshi, Charles Demuth, and Jacob Lawrence, along with many sculptors, were inspired by the geometric forms and bold designs of American folk art and by the flat, pared-down style of fifteenth-century Dutch and Flemish Masters and fourteenth-century Italian Primitives—the latter a particular strength of the Isabella Stewart Gardner Museum, which Crite visited often (fig. 54). For his part, Crite said he was drawn to the scenes of daily life by Dutch artists Pieter Bruegel the Elder and Rogier van der Weyden, which contemporary critics noted.

Crite's artist contemporary in Boston Yvonne Twining Humber explained the appeal that early European art had for American artists working in the 1930s and 1940s. "The Italian primitives took me away from the influence of Impressionism," she said. "I wanted to consciously paint forms rather than impressions of forms so I began hardening up the lines."[41] Humber's *Suburban Street* of 1940 (fig. 55), like Crite's *Handy Street Bridge,* displays an interest in creating a streamlined effect through the use of a simplified composition and the repetition of flattened forms that emphasize the two-dimensionality of the canvas surface.

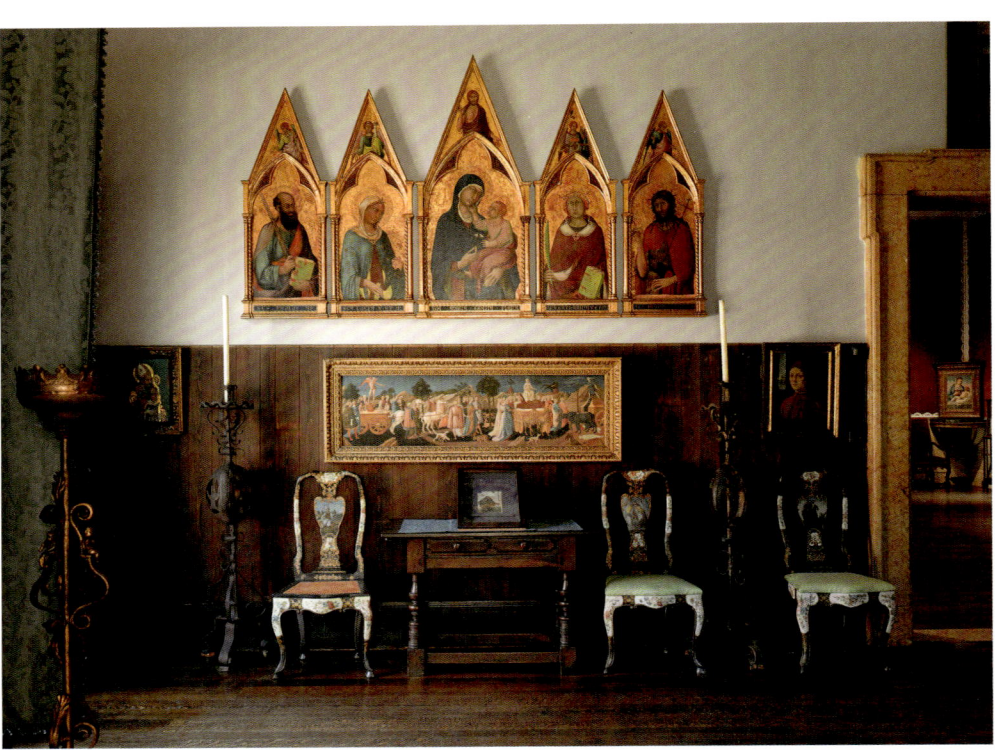

Fig. 54. Early Italian Room, Isabella Stewart Gardner Museum, Boston

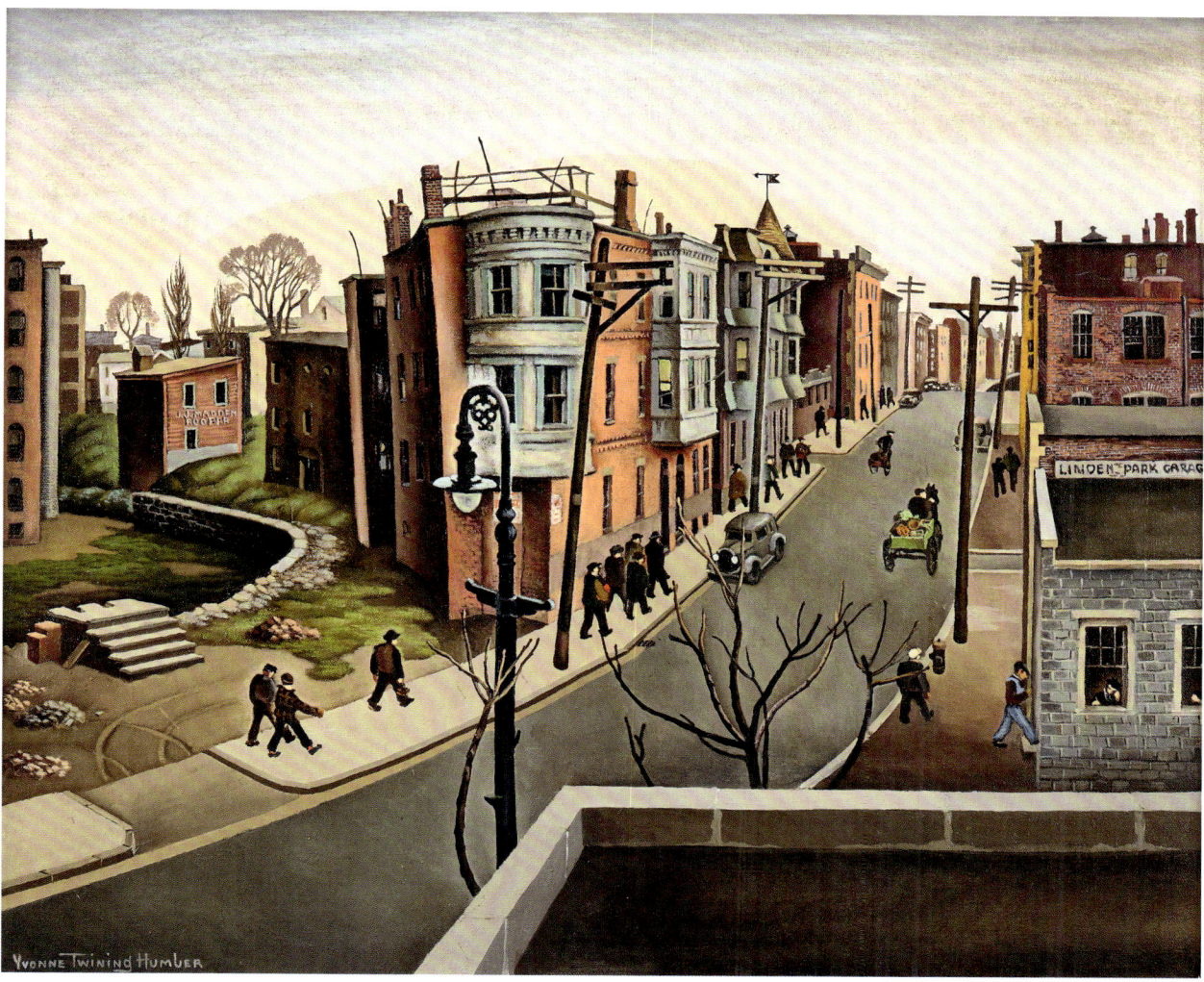

Fig. 55. Yvonne Twining Humber, *Suburban Street,* 1940. Oil on canvas, 50.8 × 73.7 cm. Seattle Art Museum. Margaret E. Fuller Purchase Prize, 31st Annual Exhibition of Northwest Artists (45.84)

The figures in Crite's paintings from the late 1930s, like *Handy Street Bridge,* are more animated than those in his earlier compositions because they are constructed with fewer details and with the use of visible brushstrokes that appear to have been applied quickly. The later *Neighborhood Series* works also feature pronounced and elongated shadows that highlight the two-dimensionality of the canvas. Crite's growing ability to suggest forms and figures without relying on detailed physical description bespeak an increased confidence, which allowed him to depart from his previous pictorial formulas and drew praise from local art critics. In her review of Crite's one-man show at the Grace Horne Gallery, Dorothy Adlow described *The Handy Street Bridge* as a breakthrough in his imagination and artistry:

> The painter has relaxed in his literalness, given more prominence to one detail at the expense of another, stressed major factors of design, arranged hues in harmonic tonalities. He is no longer the faithful journalistic recorder of the South End; he is an artist taking familiar material [and] rearranging it so that it will relate with greater effectiveness his distinctive response to it. . . . The departure is a most significant one and marks a new phase of his career, which puts him into the artistic society of artists like John Sloan and George Grosz.[42]

Although *Handy Street Bridge* depicts children, a major theme of the *Neighborhood Series,* the painting bears witness to the artist's growing sense of unease about his community's future. Unlike Crite's earlier depictions of the main thoroughfares in Boston's

African American community, which brim with life, this scene takes place in a small alley that appears empty and lonely. Two boys pull a makeshift cart filled with wooden boards along a street that a sign identifies as Shawmut Avenue. The dark palette and swept surfaces obscure the sense of depth that contributed to the inviting atmosphere of the earlier street scenes. The elongated shadows, buildings, and streetlamp make the boys appear small in comparison to the background, and as a result they are overwhelmed by the neighborhood structure rather than integrated into it. The streets and sidewalks are still characteristically immaculate, but the dark brown wooden apartment houses in the background do not seem as stable or affluent as the tall brick houses featured in *Parade on Hammond Street* or *School's Out*. The boys are not dressed in the same class-conscious, up-to-date fashions pictured in the earlier canvases. There is a sense of ambivalence in this scene that differs from the carefree mood of Crite's previous neighborhood works. Although the title refers to a wooden bridge visible in the background, it is unclear what the boys are doing. Are they engaged in innocent childhood play, or are they gathering wood for more practical purposes related to the hardships of the period?

BLACK BOSTON: A CONTESTED REALITY

Crite's new approach to representing his neighborhood in works like *The Handy Street Bridge* reflects not just stylistic evolution but also changes to his environment. In the 1930s and into the 1940s, Black Boston experienced increased uncertainty caused by the Depression, the approaching world war, the early stages of government-sponsored urban renewal projects, and a sharp rise in the number of working- and lower-class southern migrants arriving in the city.[43] These changes, particularly the drastic increase in the size and social makeup of Boston's African American community, challenged Crite's perception of his neighborhood as a monolithic, close-knit society of middle-class people. Crite observed in his autobiography:

> During the 1930s, there was in the Boston community of Blacks, a Black society, that is a group of those in the professions, educated and . . . elite. There were the coming out parties for debutantes and there was an attitude towards those with no "social standing" of a sense of difference, and the difference was real and not imagined. . . . After World War number one . . . the elements of change in the Black community started, namely at first a slow migration from the south. This accelerated considerably during World War number two, so that the close-knit, small Black community . . . [and] the influence of a social class of an earlier period diminished and finally vanished.[44]

While *Handy Street Bridge* may allude to these changes, one of Crite's last neighborhood paintings—and his most famous—seems determined to highlight the artist's concept of a Bostonian middle-class way of being even in the face of its being "diminished."

Harriet and Leon (1941) is set on the streets of Boston's Black neighborhood in the South End (fig. 56). The artist posed two of his friends, architect Leon Bailey and soprano Harriet Jackson, as a couple who walk purposefully down Columbus Avenue. As they stride toward the left of the frame, all the other elements in the composition—the man delivering ice, the boy pulling a sled, the bodies of the two curious children, and the receding angles of the buildings and the street between them—track in the direction of their movement. Crite's commitment to conveying details, including the portrait faces of Harriet, Leon, and the children, their clothing, and the neighborhood itself, creates a believable space that the viewer can imagine inhabiting. The wide street is lined with the South End's characteristic brick apartment houses and a church façade and steeple. Crite's inclusion of a church reflects his goal of emphasizing the moral values of his community. Moreover, as in nearly a third of his neighborhood paintings, the presence

Fig. 56. Allan Rohan Crite, *Harriet and Leon,* 1941. Oil on canvas, 91.4 × 66 cm. Boston Athenaeum

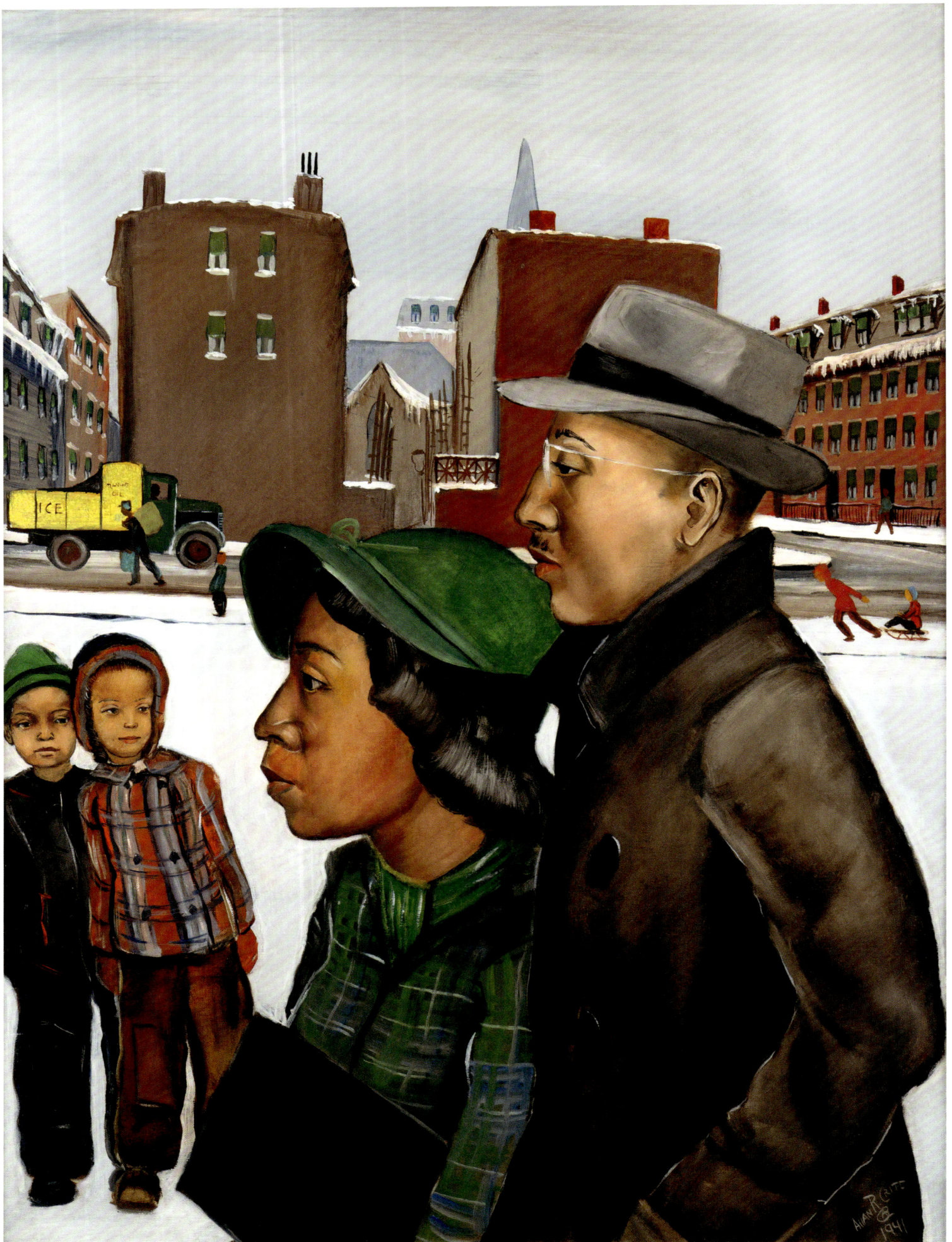

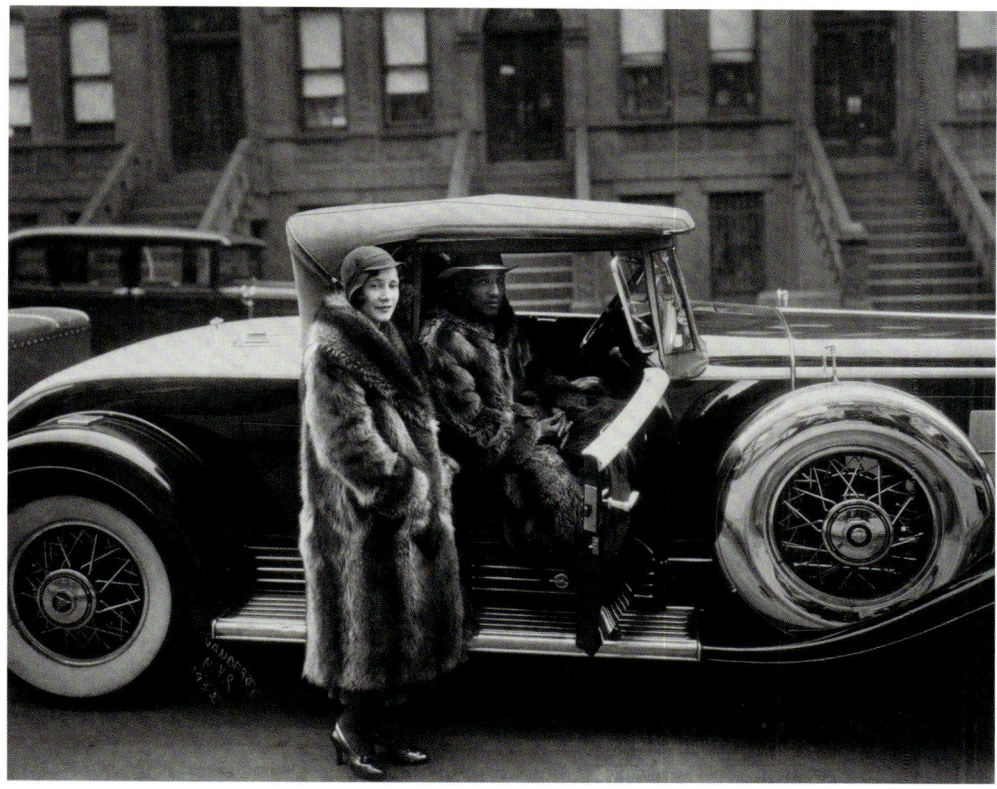

Fig. 57. James Van Der Zee, *Couple, Harlem,* 1932, printed later. Gelatin silver print, 20.3 × 25.2 cm. James Van Der Zee Archive, The Metropolitan Museum of Art; Gift of Donna Van Der Zee, 2021 (2021.446.1.2)

of a large, freestanding church building made of brick or stone masonry suggests that Boston's Black Christian community is large, successful, and, most important, established—in contrast to the characteristic storefront churches of large numbers of migrants who arrived in Boston during the 1940s.[45]

Crite's Bostonian couple is different from the many images of Harlem couples, including James Van Der Zee's iconic 1932 photograph of the stylish modern couple in *Couple, Harlem* (fig. 57) and William H. Johnson's folk and collage Cubist-inspired canvas *Street Musicians* (fig. 58) and other works. Crite's images of Black Bostonians also depart from typical presentations of Black life in the South, such as Harlem Renaissance painter Malvin Gray Johnson's *Brothers* (fig. 59) and Regionalist painter Thomas Hart Benton's *Romance* (fig. 60), which feature figures who are typically barefoot, clad in overalls, and situated outdoors, on farms or in fields. As Crite himself noted in the opening epigraph of this essay, none of these depictions of African Americans resonated with his experience or outlook on his own community in Boston. However, his own view of his community remained selective.

That Crite's outlook was unusual even for Boston is evidenced by the contrasting views of his artist contemporary John Wilson (1922–2015). Like Crite, Wilson grew up in Lower Roxbury and attended the Museum School, but the younger artist had an entirely different impression of life in Boston's Black community, which he pointedly referred to in interviews as the "ghetto."[46] Wilson stated that his own early portraits include a visual language that strives to translate the painter's feelings of disconnection from and disillusionment with white American society as expressed in the contemporary Social Realist writings of Black author Richard Wright.

Characteristic of Wilson's particular approach to representing Black Bostonian identity is *My Brother* of 1942 (fig. 61). In this image, the artist utilizes a realist style to portray the visage of a young man staring at the viewer with an expression of anger and hopelessness. In the background, an impressionistic image of a tenement building reflects the social realities of Boston that may contribute to the young man's despair.

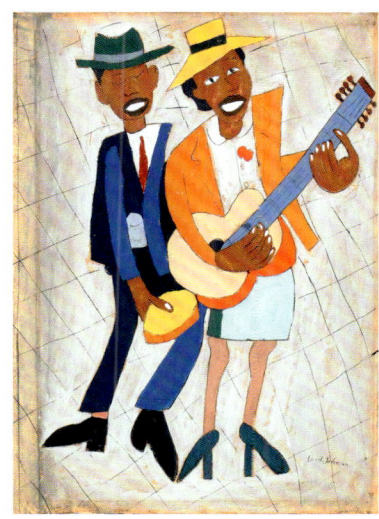

Fig. 58. William H. Johnson, *Street Musicians,* about 1939–40. Gouache and pen and ink on paper, 45.9 × 33.3 cm. Smithsonian American Art Museum

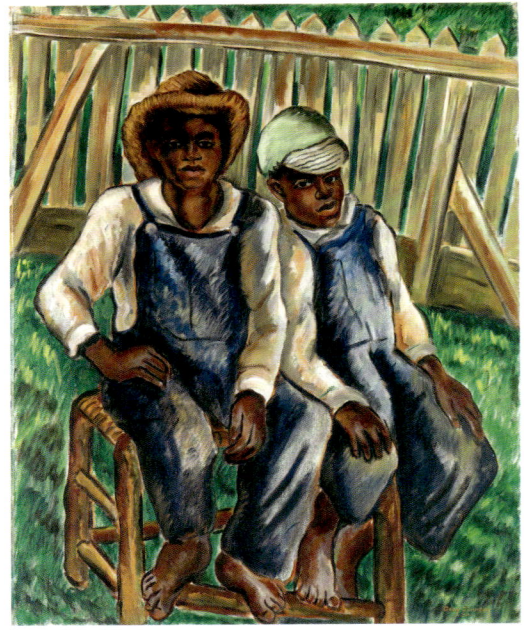
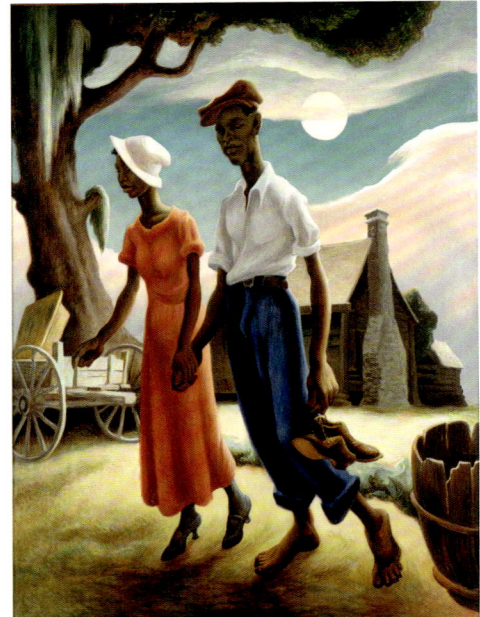
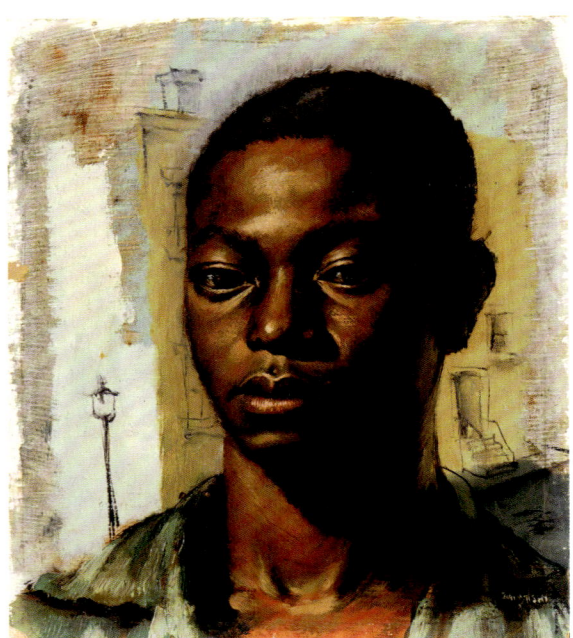

Fig. 59. Malvin Gray Johnson, *Brothers,* 1934. Oil on canvas, 96.5 × 76.3 cm. Smithsonian American Art Museum

Fig. 60. Thomas Hart Benton, *Romance,* 1931–32. Egg tempera, gesso, and oil varnish glazes on board, 115 × 84.5 cm. Blanton Museum of Art, The University of Texas at Austin, Gift of Mari and James A. Michener (1991.187)

Fig. 61. John Wilson, *My Brother,* 1942. Oil on panel, 30.5 × 27 cm. Smith College Museum of Art, Northampton, Massachusetts (SC 1943.4.1)

Crite and Wilson, two Black artists from the same neighborhood who studied at the same art school and painted their community at the same moment, present radically different images. Reflecting on both his own work and Crite's, Wilson stated:

> There was [a] sense of the impossibility for a Black male to get a job and live a kind of, well, you didn't even use the word "middle class." I mean, if you were Black, you just didn't make enough money. So there was this sense of being part of this left-out community. That was my reality, which made it impossible for me to ignore, and for whatever reason Allan's background was such that his mother, especially, gave him this ability to ignore [the poverty of the Black neighborhood].[47]

Wilson's comment points to the continued influence of Crite's mother. She encouraged her son, upon his completion of art school, to study at the Harvard University Extension School for his bachelor's degree, which he received in 1968. After Crite retired in 1974 from a thirty-year career as a draughtsman at the Charlestown Navy Yard, he went back to Harvard, working as a part-time librarian in the Extension School's Grossman Library. Perhaps most important, by encouraging his early and frequent interactions with elite, mostly white institutions, Annamae ensured that Crite had a keen ability to move within the city's elite educational and cultural circles. Early on, he established relationships with the Boston Athenaeum, the Boston Public Library, and the Episcopal Divinity School in Cambridge. He maintained these associations throughout his career and showed a willingness to cross racial and class lines to maintain them.

While Wilson credits Crite's outlook and behavior as rooted in his ability to "ignore" poverty and ghettoization, Crite framed things differently in the same oral history that provides the epigraph that begins this essay. That history was recorded in 1979–80, at a time when his Boston neighborhood was, if anything, suffering even more from crime and poverty than it had in the 1930s and '40s. In response to a question about his interest in Black pride and its relationship to a pluralistic, integrated society, Crite responded:

> You know, we use the term "melting pot," which is untrue. A melting pot assumes that everybody is sort of made alike. . . . It would be better if you looked at the

thing as like a salad. . . . There's a certain individuality in each element . . . yet the salad as a whole represents a unit. . . . That's the real tragedy of segregation— that we cut ourselves off from each other, and cut ourselves off from the gifts that each of us has. . . . In other words, for example, I probably have a dim view of the people in [predominantly white] South Boston. But the trouble is that if they're cut, I bleed. If I'm bruised, they're hurt. . . . We are part of each other. . . . We're thinking we're doing to somebody else, but it's happening to us. That, in my opinion, is the real tragedy. [We are not] enjoying each other, all the gifts that we have for each other, to make the whole thing a much richer experience.[48]

What emerges from this statement is a fundamental optimism in Crite's view of an integrated society in which people from all walks of life can cohere and interact with one another. He was not naïve or ignorant of issues—consider his comment about South Boston in the wake of that neighborhood's virulent opposition to school integration. He was optimistic, and this view not only shaped how he moved through Boston's society and art institutions; it also informed his performative depictions of middle-class Black life in the city. It is perhaps this optimism about an integrated society, coupled with Crite's insistence on portraying his own rootedness in Boston's Black social and artistic community, that has, until now, relegated him to the margins of the history of Black art.

Notes

1 Crite 1979–80, 6–7.

2 See Pinder 1999; Francis 2003, 4–5; Smalls 1994.

3 See Wardlaw 1989 for recent scholarship that addresses this past strategy.

4 See Locke 1925.

5 See Locke 2020; Porter 1992.

6 See Murrell 2024; Haygood et al. 2018, 156–57.

7 See Perry 1992.

8 See Hills 1983; Truettner and Stein 1999.

9 See Tonelli 1990. One important exception is Edmund Barry Gaither's scholarship over the past thirty years, including essays and exhibitions about Crite. See, e.g., Caro et al. 2001; and the exhibition *Allan Rohan Crite: A Retrospective, 1924–1989* (1990) at the National Center of Afro-American Artists in Boston.

10 See Murrell 2024; Nelson and Copeland 2023; Powell 1999.

11 For an exception, see Murell 2024, which includes brief mention of Crite (30, 75).

12 The major studies on the social history of Boston's African American population in the early twentieth century are Daniels 1914; Cromwell 1994.

13 For more on the early history of African Americans in Boston, see Horton and Horton 1979; Hayden 1991.

14 For more history of African American life in Crite's neighborhood, see Bailey et al. 1993; MAAH and NCAAA 1974.

15 Clark 1979, 70.

16 Crite said that his father was less enthusiastic about his career choice, questioning its practicality. The artist's decision to take business courses at night at Tufts University and to complete the Museum School's program in industrial arts alongside his fine arts courses may have reflected his father's influence. Allan Rohan Crite, interview by author, 16 October 2001, Boston, MA.

17 Caro 2008, 66.

18 Du Bois 1969.

19 For a description of the term "race man" as part of Black middle-class psychology, see Drake and Cayton 1962, 394–95.

20 Diary entry, 22 February 1936, in Crite 1977b, "Appendix I: The Works Progress Administration," 1.

21 Hughes 1926.

22 Crite recalled that he was one of the only African American students at the Museum School. However, when he enrolled in 1929, Crite certainly would have been aware of its recent Black alumna Lois Mailou Jones (1905–1998), who attended the Museum School from 1923 to 1927. See Crite 1979–80, 78; Benjamin 1994.

23 Although Crite's school records have been lost, one can surmise the scope of his coursework from the curriculum descriptions printed in the Museum School's bulletins between 1929 and 1936.

24 See Fairbrother 1986.

25 Crite was one of a small group of Black artists on the roster of roughly 3,700 artists supported by the PWAP. An experimental art program, the PWAP was short lived and ended in May 1934 owing to limited funding. In 1935, the government established the FAP, a larger program that operated in all the states and supported artists until 1943. For more on the New Deal art programs, see Park and Markowitz 1977; for more on Black participation in the government-supported art programs of the 1930s, see Fraden 1987.

26 Crite had joined the Boston Society of Independent Artists in 1929 and exhibited neighborhood oil paintings in nearly every annual exhibition between 1934 and 1948. He also showed watercolors and pencil drawings in the Harmon Foundation's annual exhibitions in 1930, 1931, and 1933. See Reynolds and Wright 1989, 166–71.

27 Harris 1995, 49–53.

28 Through the PWAP, Crite participated in exhibitions of government-supported art at the Grace Horne Gallery in Boston and the Corcoran Gallery of Art in Washington, DC, and Crite's FAP painting *School's Out* was included in the exhibition *New Horizons in American Art,* held in 1936 at MoMA.

29 Crite, 1979-80, 31.

30 Crite to Janice Miller, 10 December 981, quoted in Rubenfeld 1999, 496.

31 Crite 1979–80, 47.

32 Crite's retrospective statements about these works originate in his papers and self-published autobiography from the 1970s, and he repeated them to me in the 1990s. As art historian Jacqueline Francis points out, "Too often, imagery by African-American artists is regarded as being transparent. The work is, in effect, framed as a direct translation of cultural experience or an unmediated documentary of it." Francis 2000, 152.

33 My analysis of Crite's artistic style in *Parade on Hammond Street* is based upon the findings of a 1998 X-ray study of the work by Phillips Collection conservator Elizabeth Steele, whose findings are summarized in the endnotes of the catalogue entry for the painting in Passantino and Scott 1999, 784. My firsthand study of *Parade* and a number of contemporaneous neighborhood paintings confirms that Crite routinely used this painting process throughout his early career.

34 As Alexis de Tocqueville wrote in his two-volume study *Democracy in America* (1835–40), a defining feature of American social and political life was the inclination of ordinary Americans to express their individual and communal identities by organizing civic groups and public parades.

35 Oral histories and interviews of Black Bostonians describe the regular occurrence in Roxbury of Black marches for equal rights and UNIA parades. See Carden 1989.

36 As Stephen L. Recken points out, in addition to promoting happiness through a sense of belonging, mass media images and popular psychology advice columns and books of the 1930s encouraged Americans to enjoy life and engage in leisure activities. Recken 1993.

37 Fashion in Boston's Black community in the 1930s is described in Cromwell 1994, 167–68; West 1982.

38 Crite n.d. [after 1970], "Non-Western Art," 2.

39 Bronzeville, also known as the Black Belt, was a colloquial name for Chicago's African American neighborhood. Motley's *Bronzeville Series,* which comprises approximately twenty paintings created between 1929 and 1943, provides an interesting parallel to Crite's neighborhood paintings. For more on this body of work, see Wolfskill 2017.

40 A letter from Phillips to Halpert dated 23 February 1942 describes the sale of *Parade* along with several other important works of African American art, including half of the forty panels of Jacob Lawrence's *Migration Series* (1940–41); see the Allan Rohan Crite curatorial file at the Phillips Collection. Also see Passantino and Scott 1999, 496.

41 Yvonne Twining Humber, interview by author, 9 March 2001, Seattle, WA.

42 See Adlow 1939.

43 Between 1940 and 1960, Boston's Black population increased from 23,000 to 63,000, which is striking when compared to the marginal growth between 1900 and 1940 (11,591 to 23,679). Thernstrom 1973, 179.

44 Crite n.d. [after 1970], 17.

45 The notion of being "established," an "old settler," was a key marker of upper-class status in Boston and other northern cities, such as Chicago. Cromwell 1994, 85–86.

46 John Wilson, interview by author, 17 October 2001, Brookline, MA.

47 Ibid. In this interview, Wilson also explained to me that Crite was an important role model of a professional Black artist and that Crite introduced him to the existence of a larger community of Black artists by lending him a copy of Alain Locke's anthology *The New Negro.*

48 See Crite 1979–80, 59.

PLATES 1936–1945

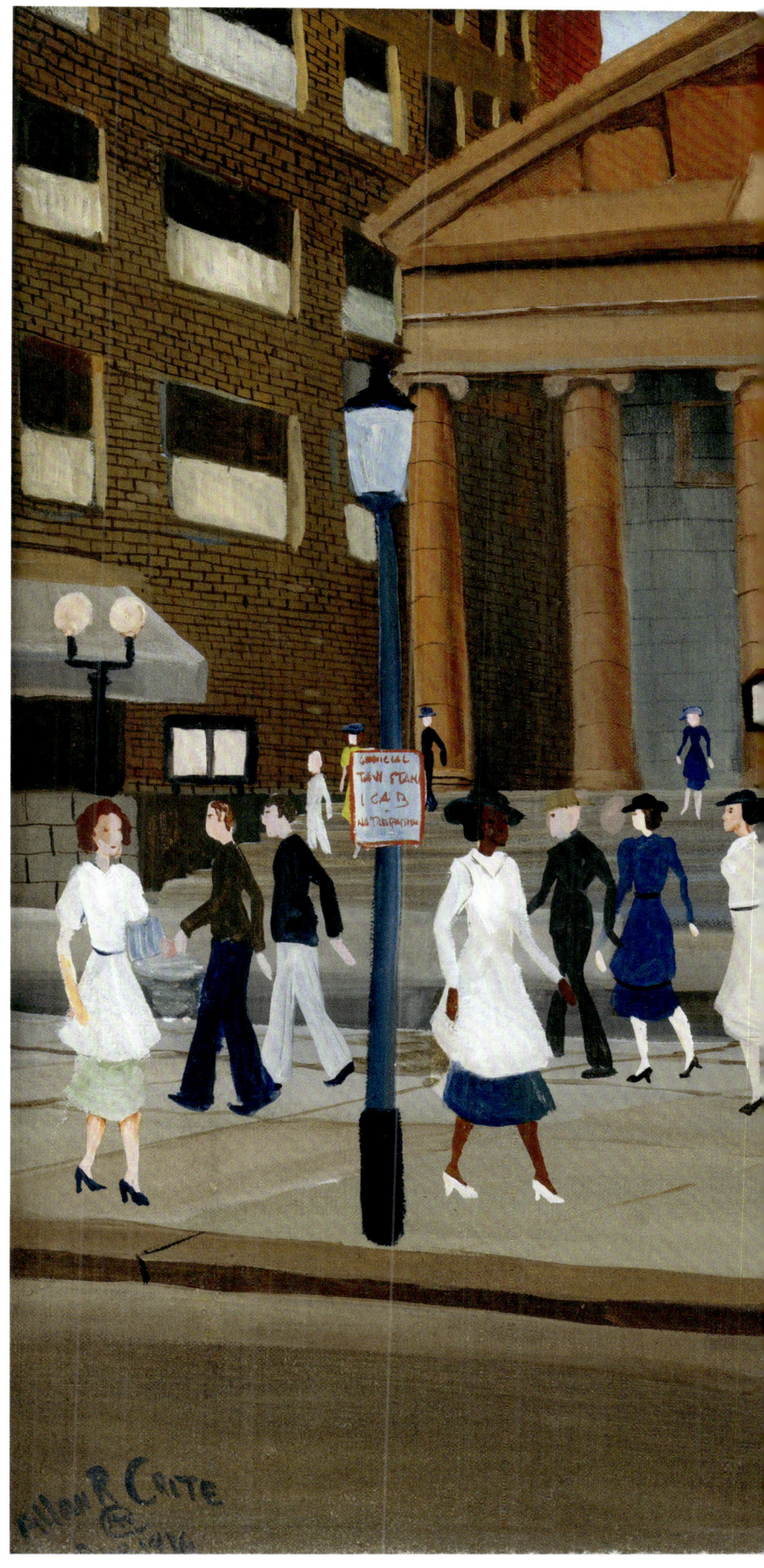

Plate 8. Allan Rohan Crite, *Front of Saint Paul's Cathedral, Tremont Street,* 1936. Oil on board, 46 × 61 cm. Boston Athenaeum

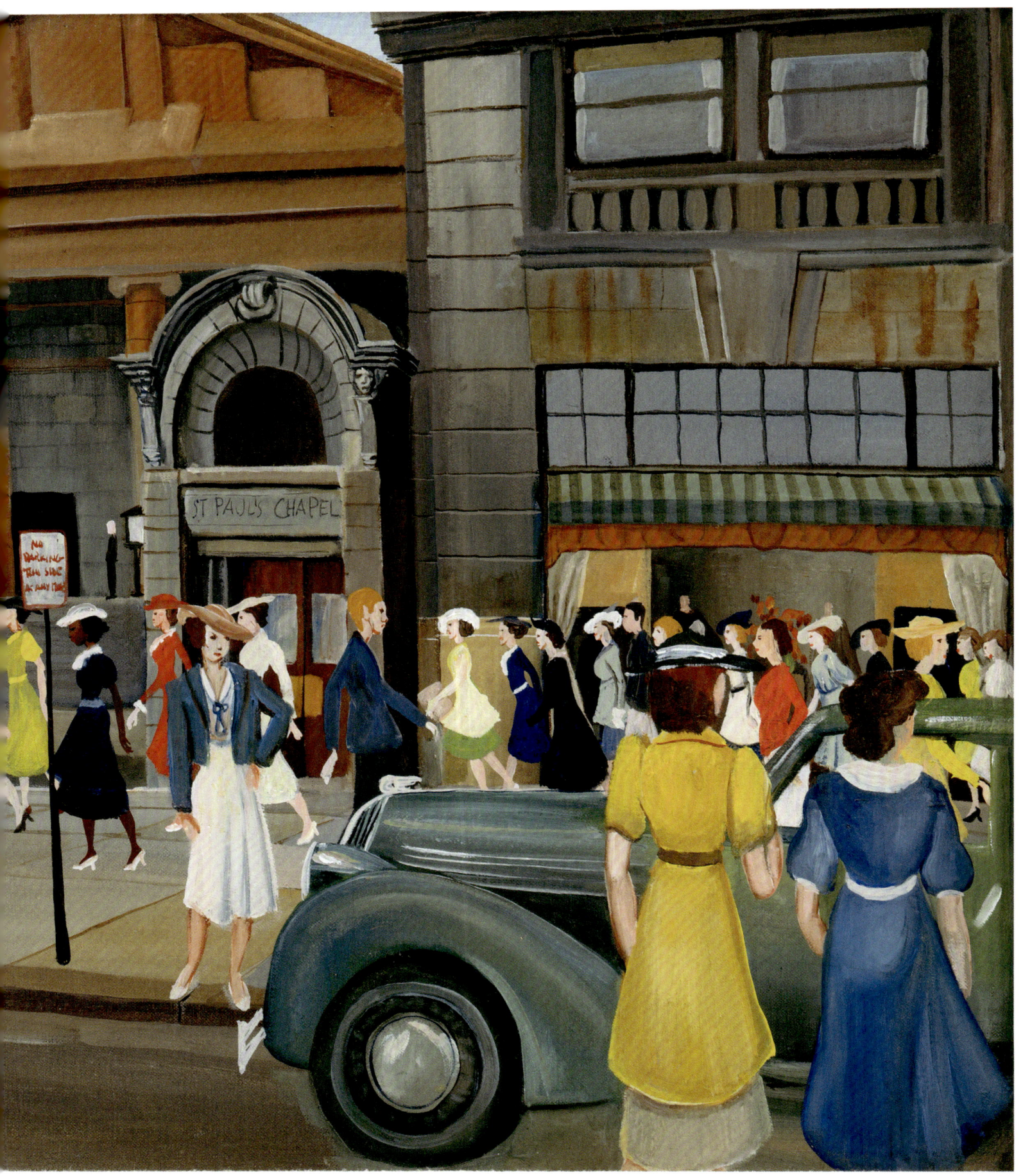

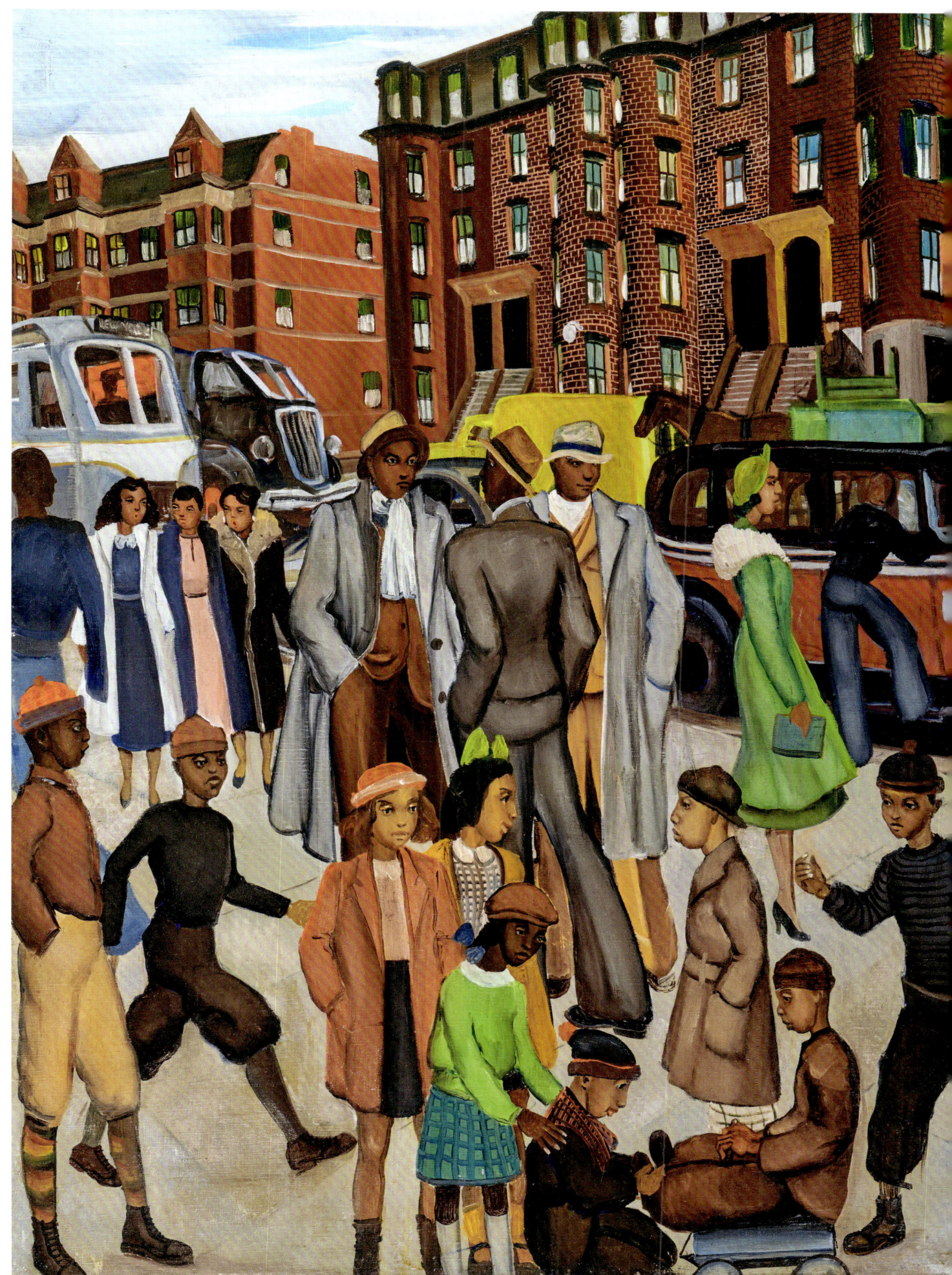

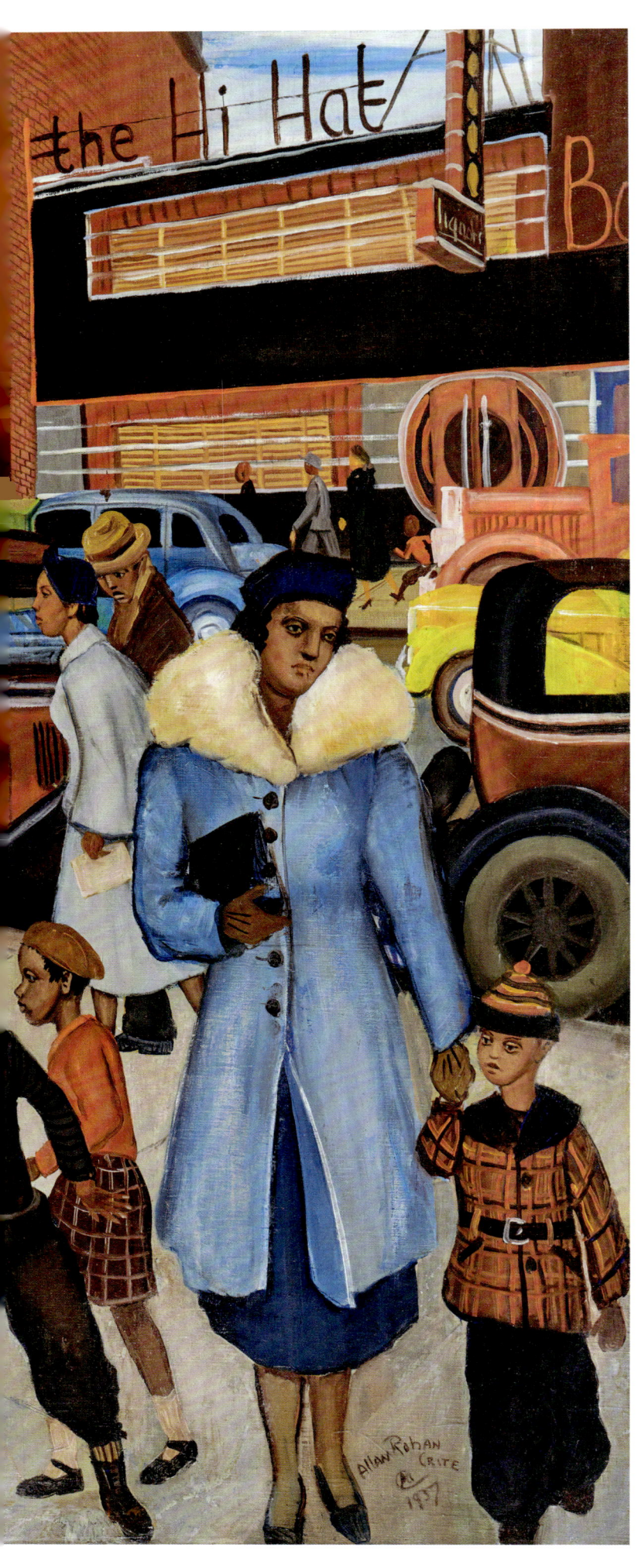

Plate 9. Allan Rohan Crite, *Columbus Avenue,* 1937. Oil on canvas, 87 × 102.2 cm. Courtesy of Museum of African American History Boston | Nantucket

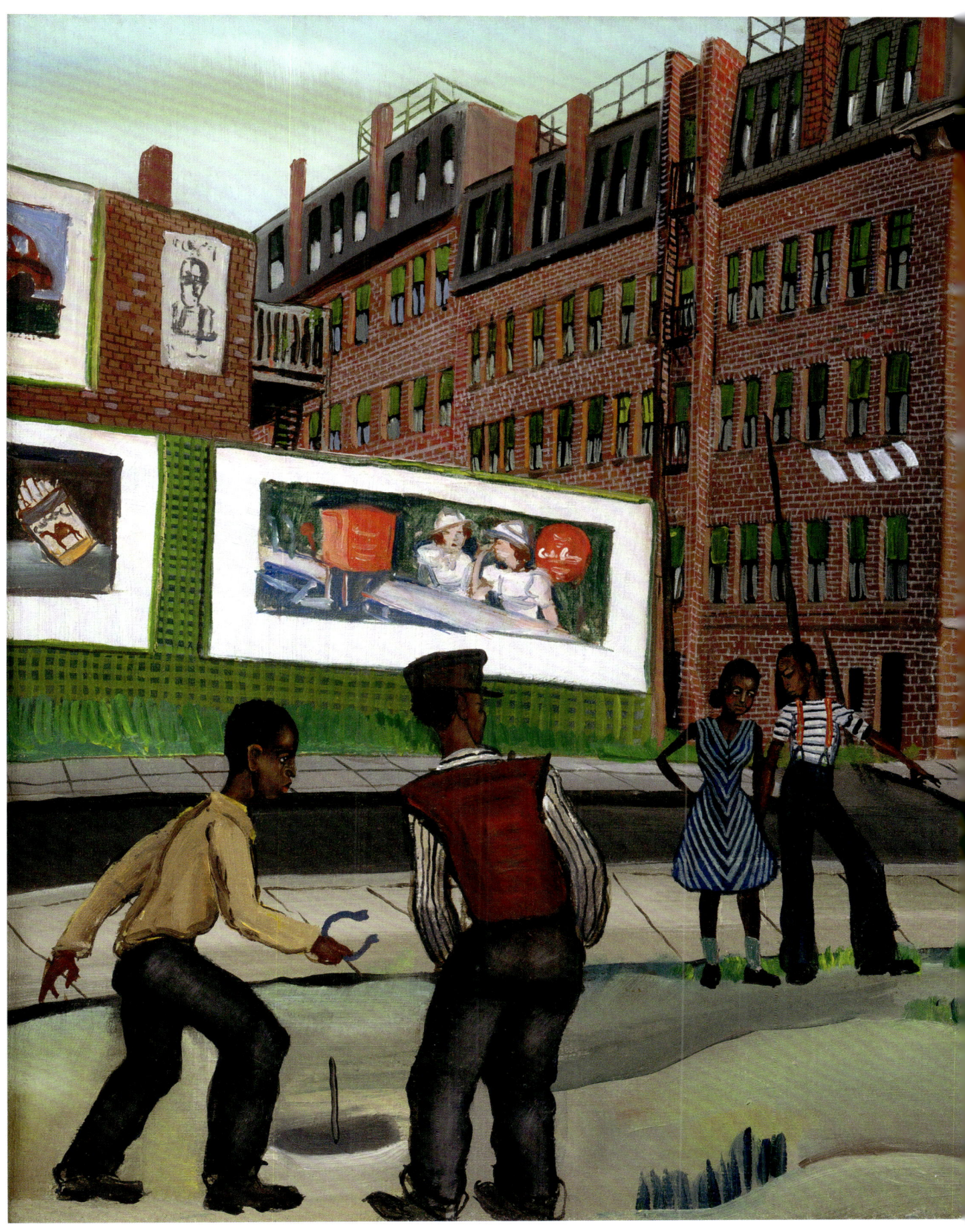

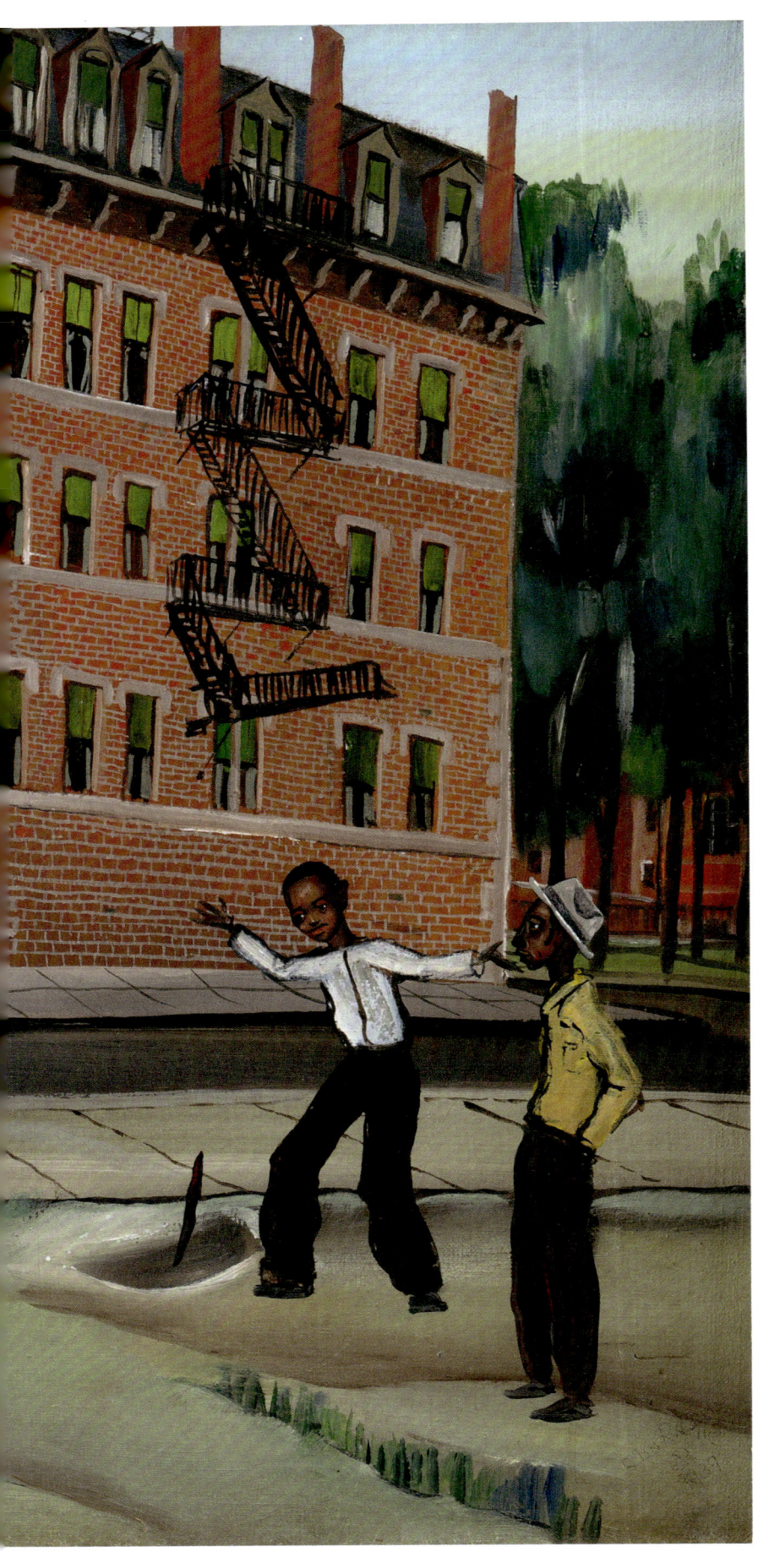

Plate 10. Allan Rohan Crite, *Horseshoe Playing,* 1939. Oil on canvas, 47 × 57.5 cm. Boston Athenaeum

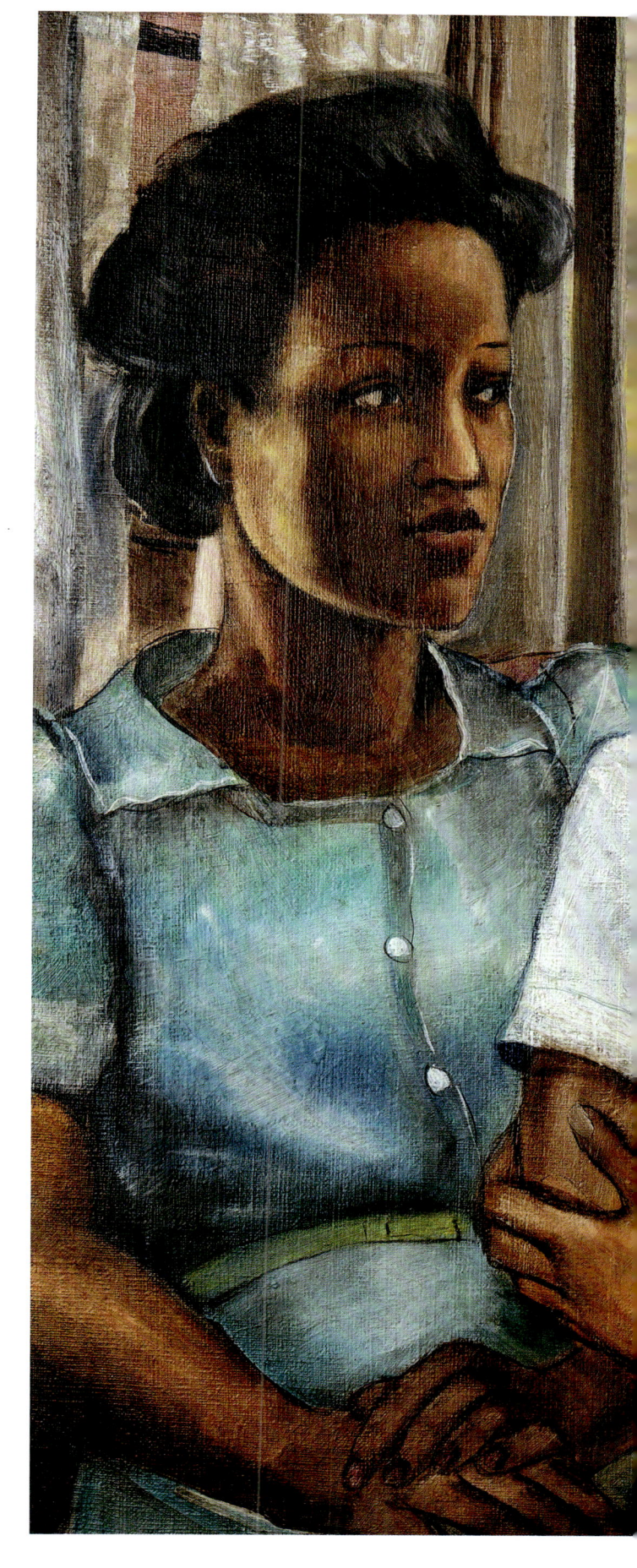

Plate 11. Allan Rohan Crite, *Mrs. Martin's Misses*, 1941. Oil on canvas, 74 × 95.3 cm. Courtesy of The Martin Family Heirs

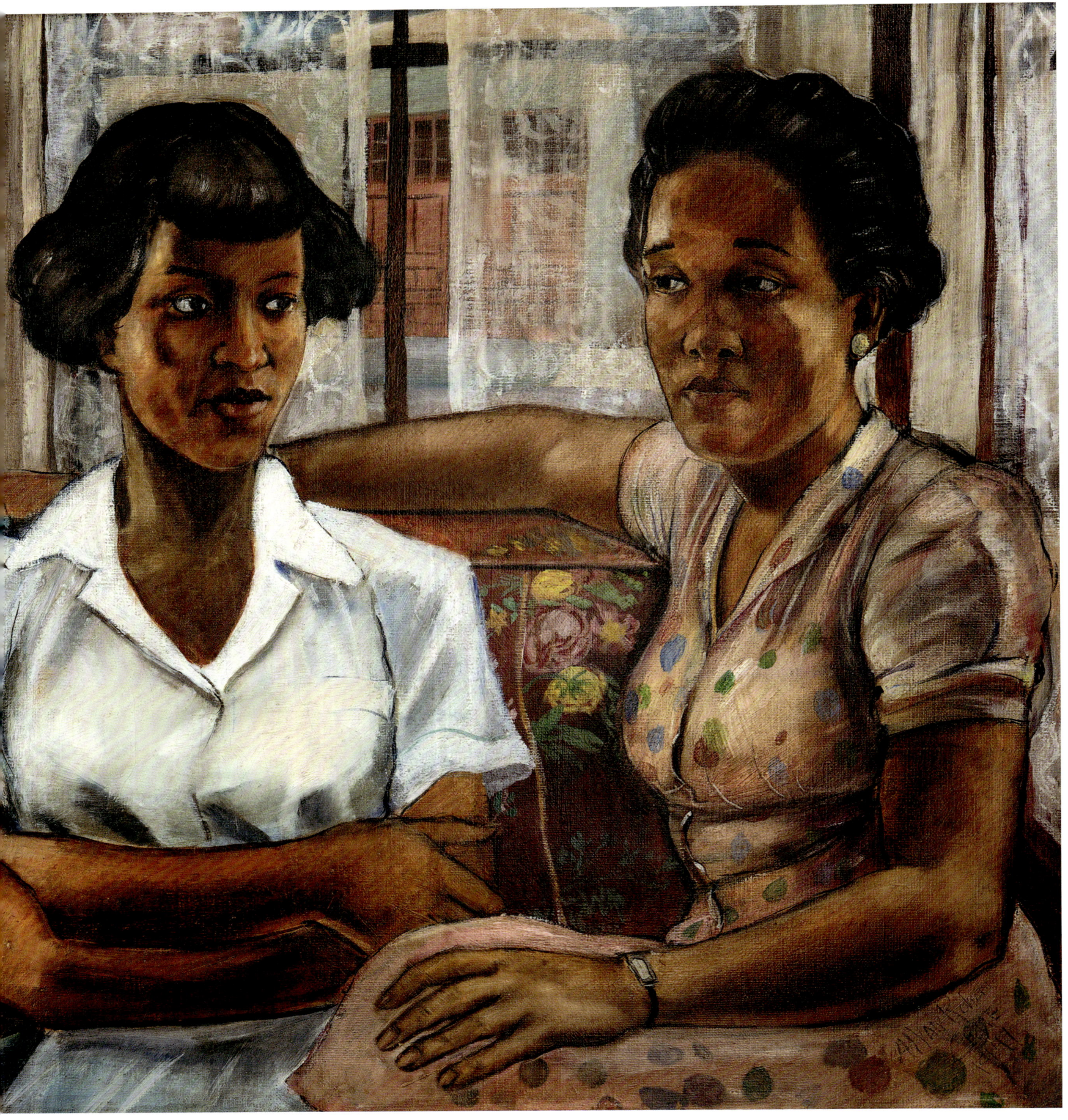

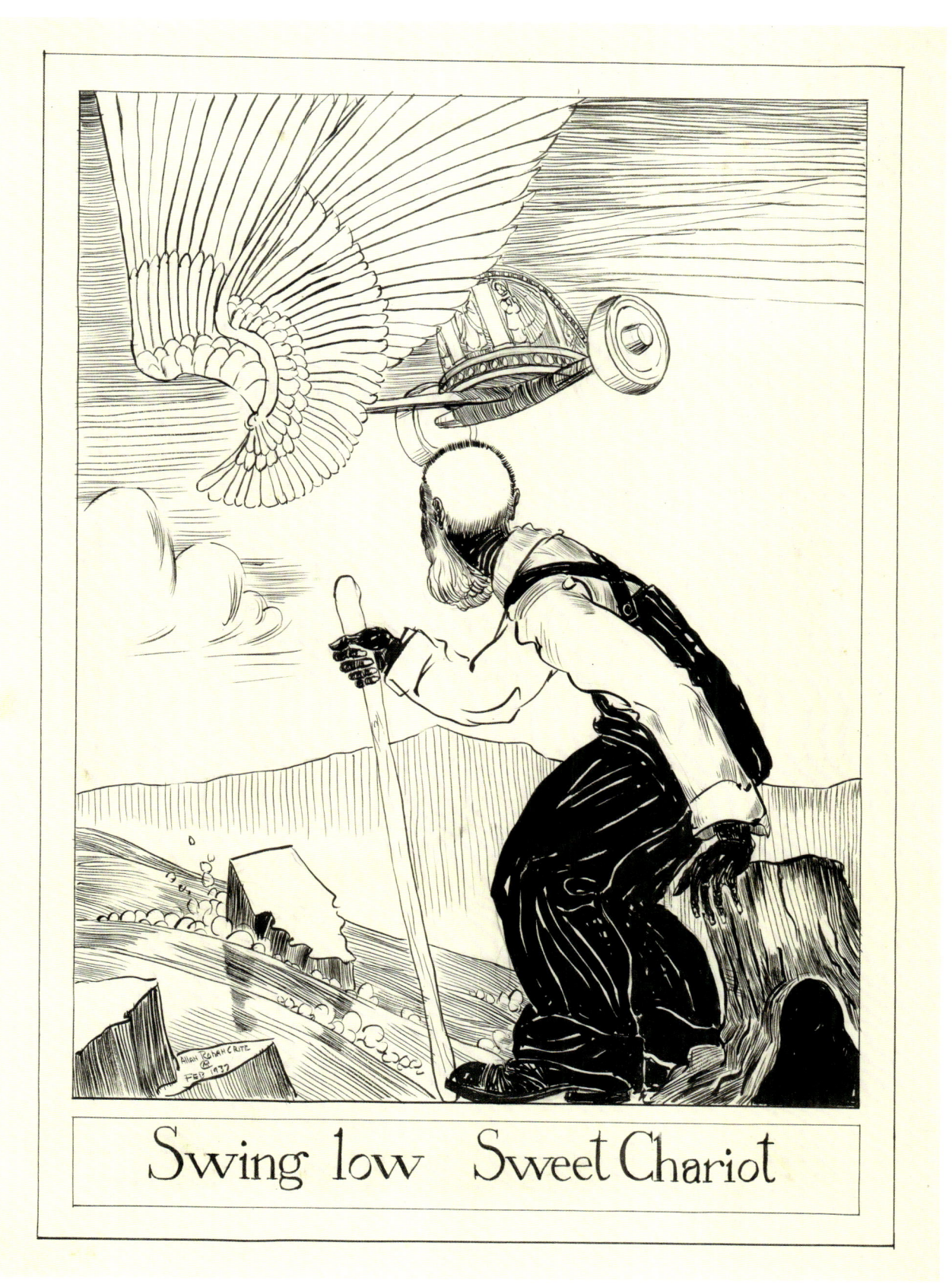

Plate 12. Allan Rohan Crite, *Swing low Sweet Chariot,* illustration for *Three Spirituals from Earth to Heaven* (Cambridge, MA, 1948), 1937. Ink on paper, 51 × 38 cm. Houghton Library, Harvard University

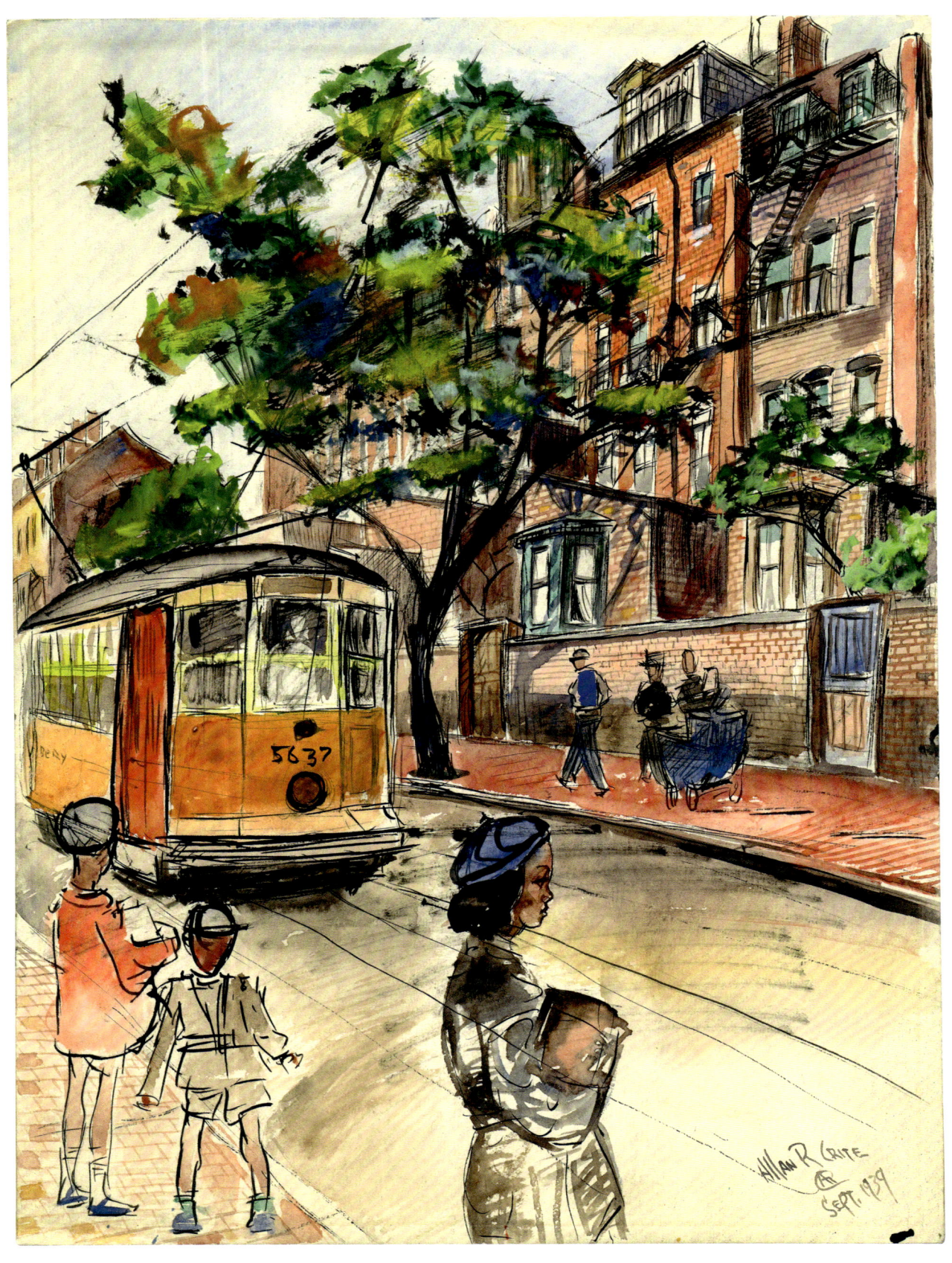

Plate 13. Allan Rohan Crite, *On Old Northampton Street, Boston,* September 1939. Watercolor, black ink, and gouache on paper, 38.1 × 27.9 cm. Boston Athenaeum

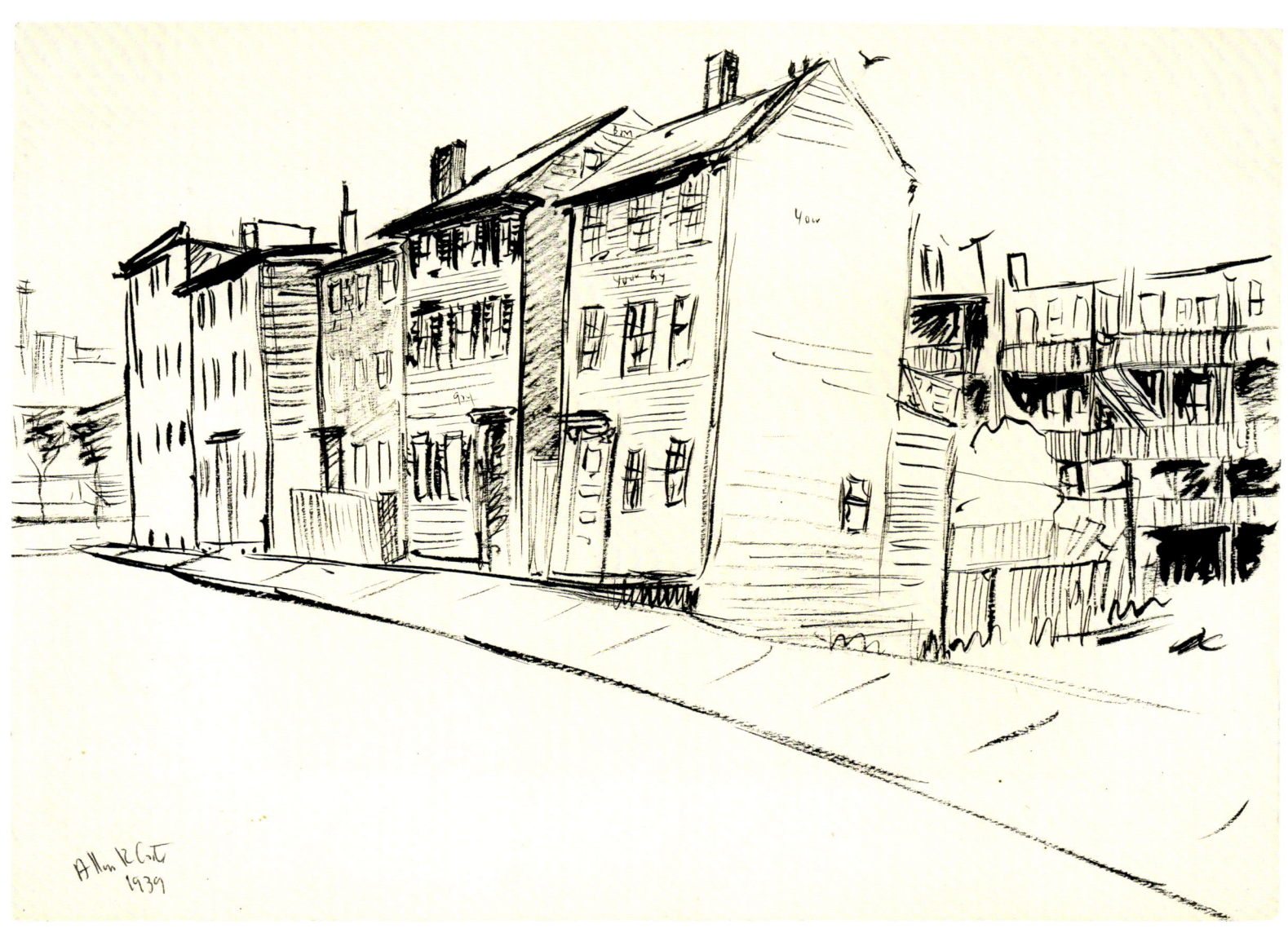

Plate 14. Allan Rohan Crite, *Near Columbus Avenue, Street Next to Davenport,* 1939.
Brush and black ink with graphite notations, 28.1 × 38.2 cm. Boston Athenaeum

Opposite: Plate 15. Allan Rohan Crite, *Come On, Gramps,* 1940. Oil on board,
53.5 × 43.5 cm. Boston Athenaeum

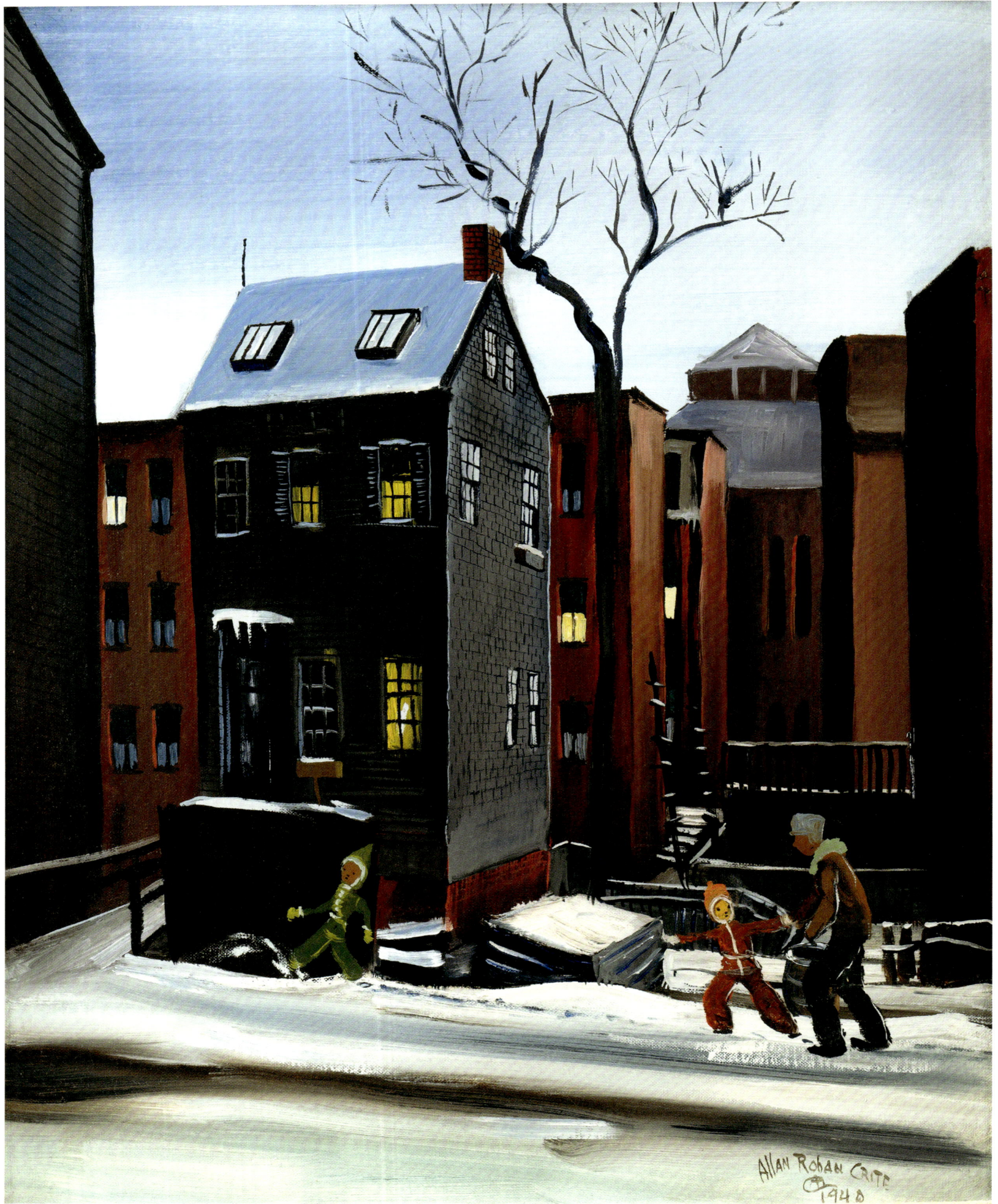

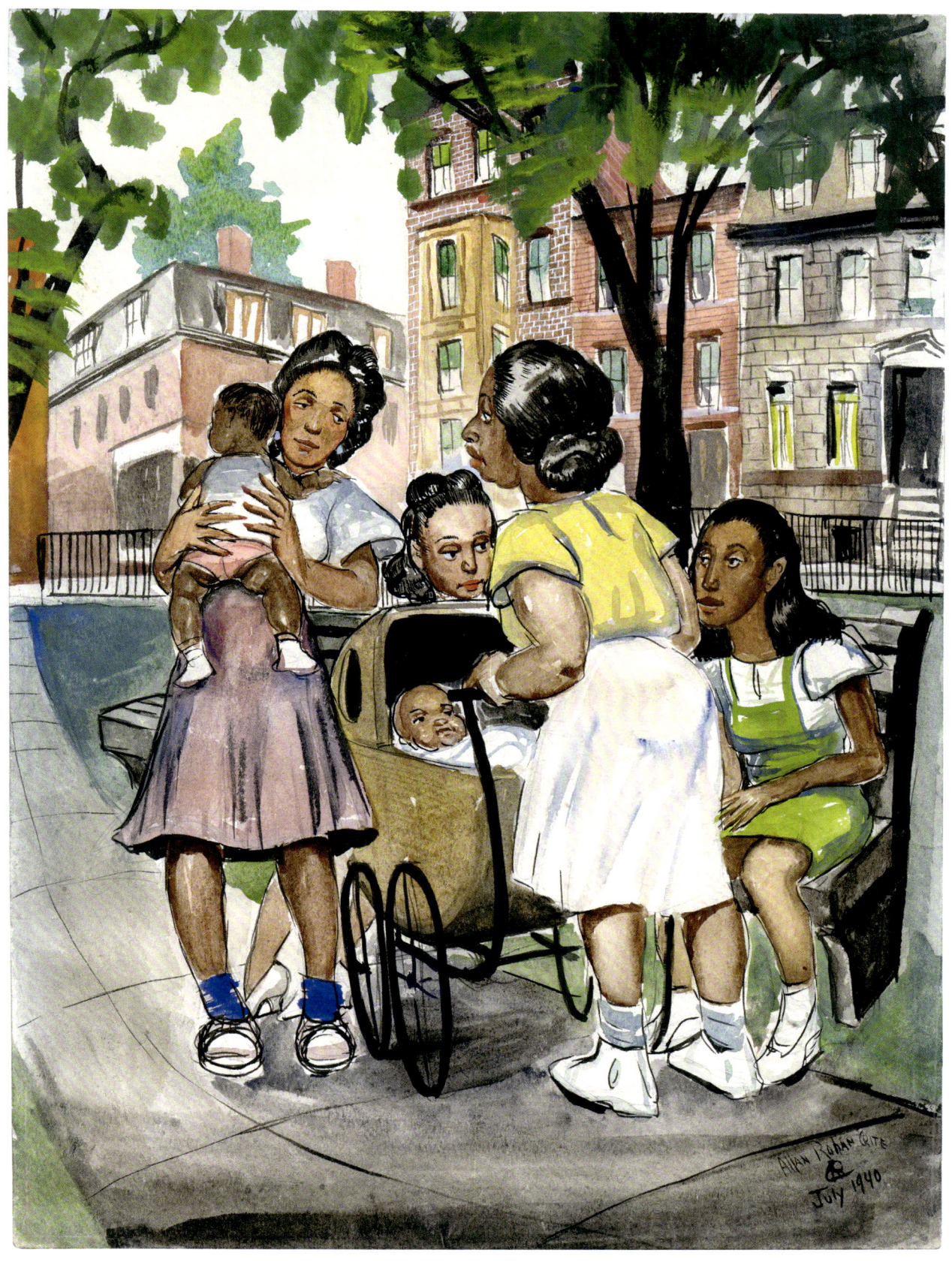

Plate 16. Allan Rohan Crite, *A Maternity Club,* July 1940. Watercolor with black ink and white highlights over graphite on paper, 38 × 28 cm. Boston Athenaeum

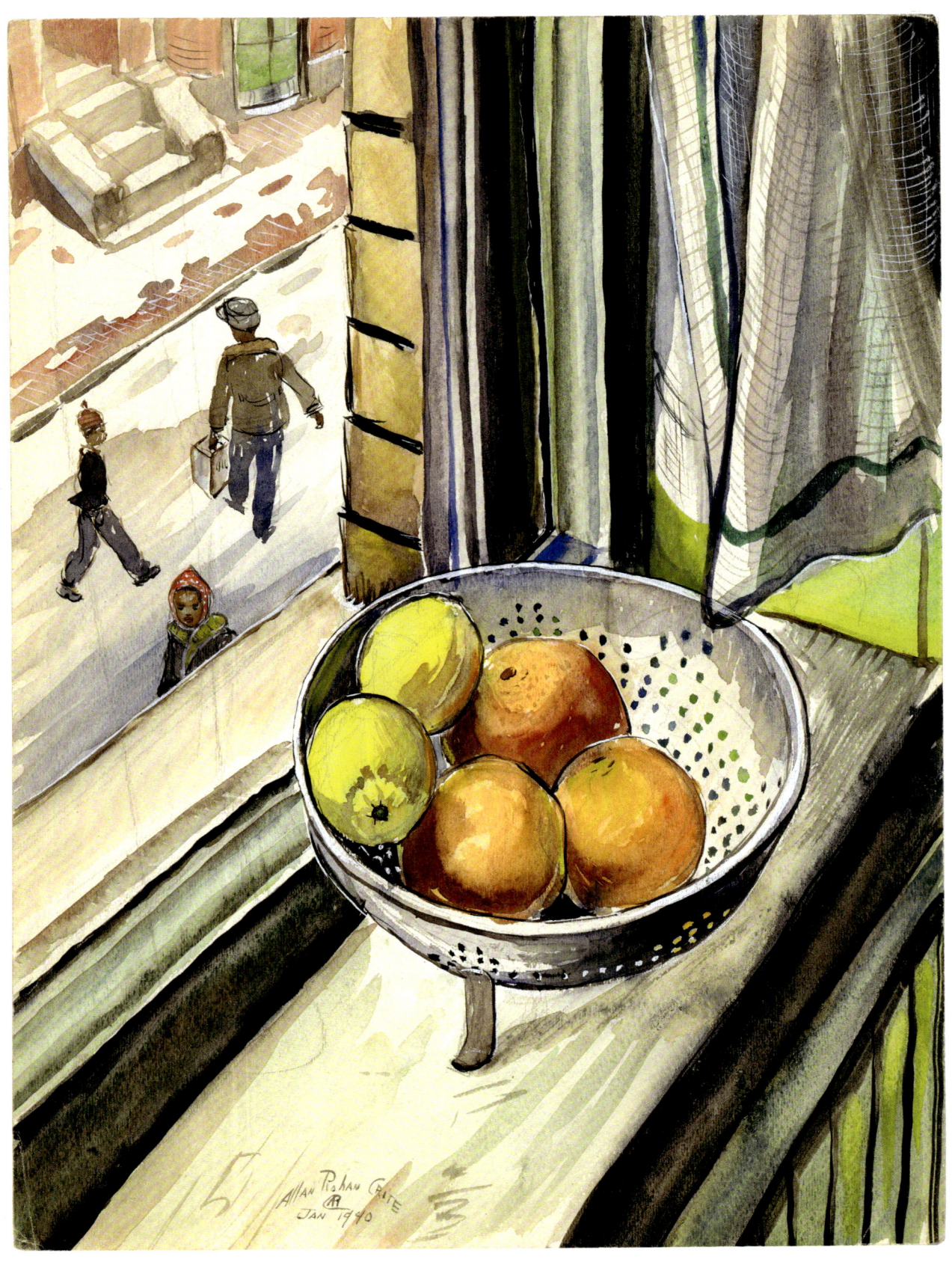

Plate 17. Allan Rohan Crite, *Fruit and Snow: From My Window at 2 Dilworth St.*, January 1940.
Watercolor with ink and white highlights over graphite on paper, 38.1 × 28 cm. Boston Athenaeum

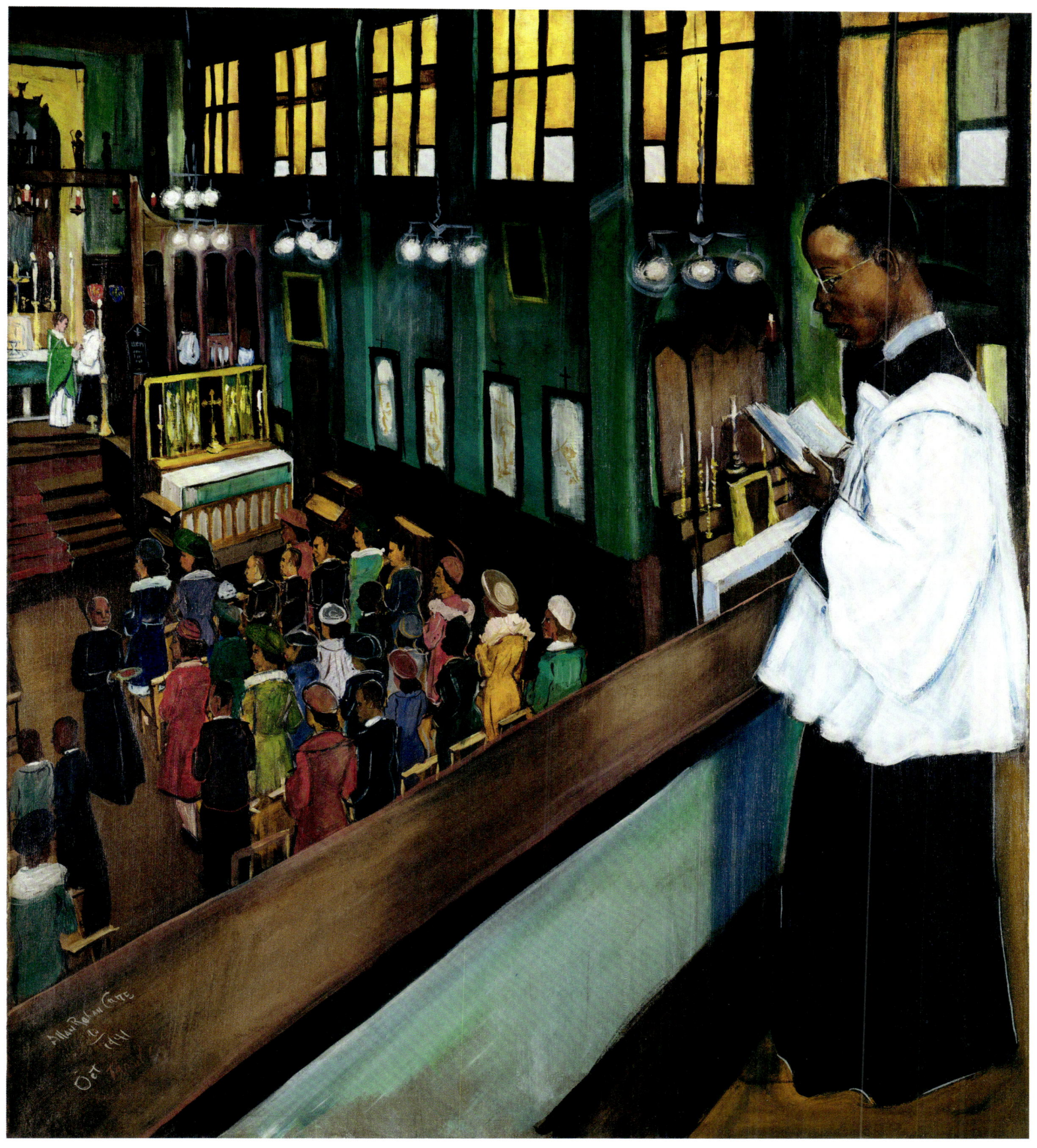

Plate 18. Allan Rohan Crite, *The Choir Singer,* October 1941. Oil on canvas, 101.6 × 88.3 cm.
Church of St. Augustine and St. Martin, Boston

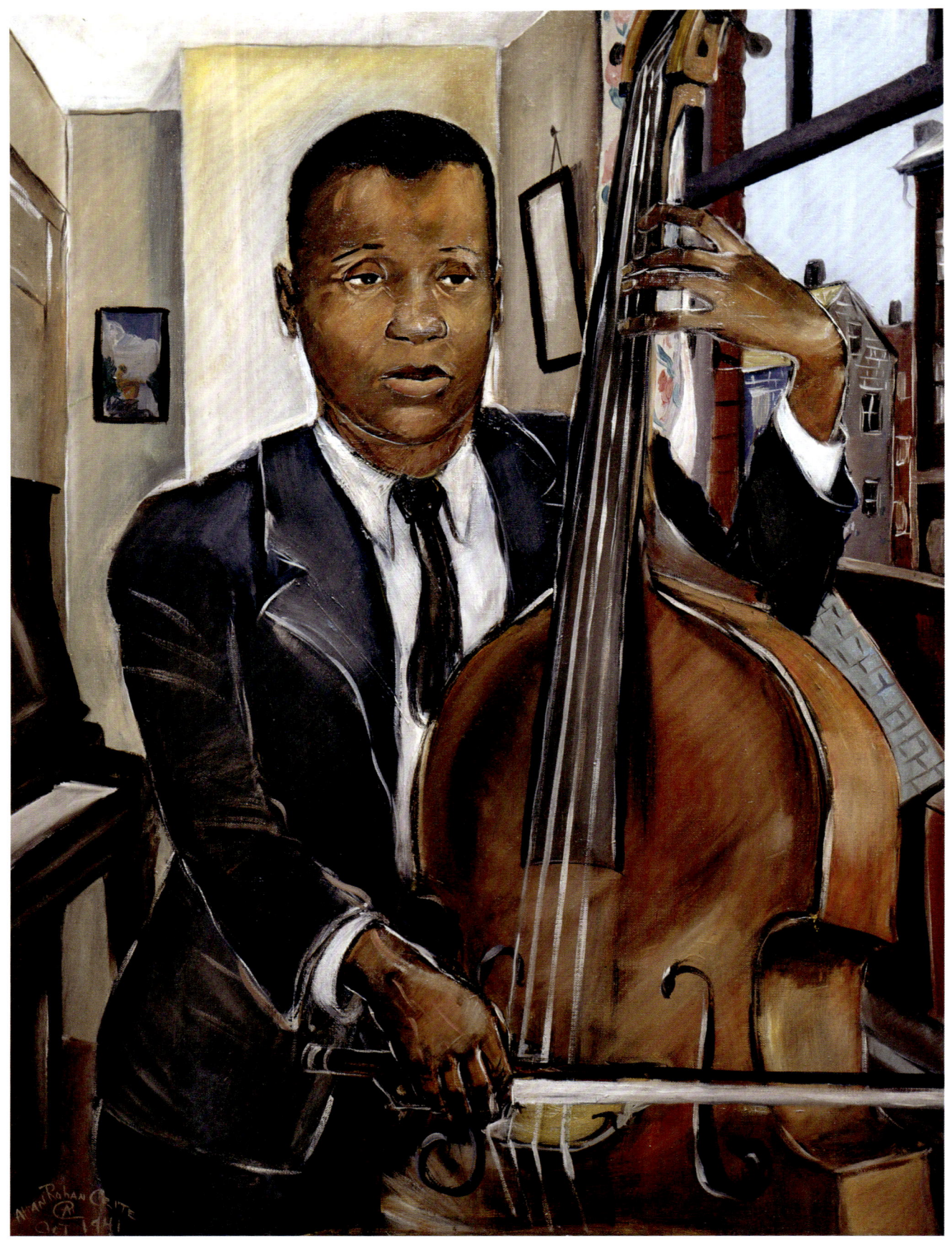

Plate 19. Allan Rohan Crite, *Bass Violin Player,* October 1941. Oil on canvas, 85 × 66.5 cm. Boston Athenaeum

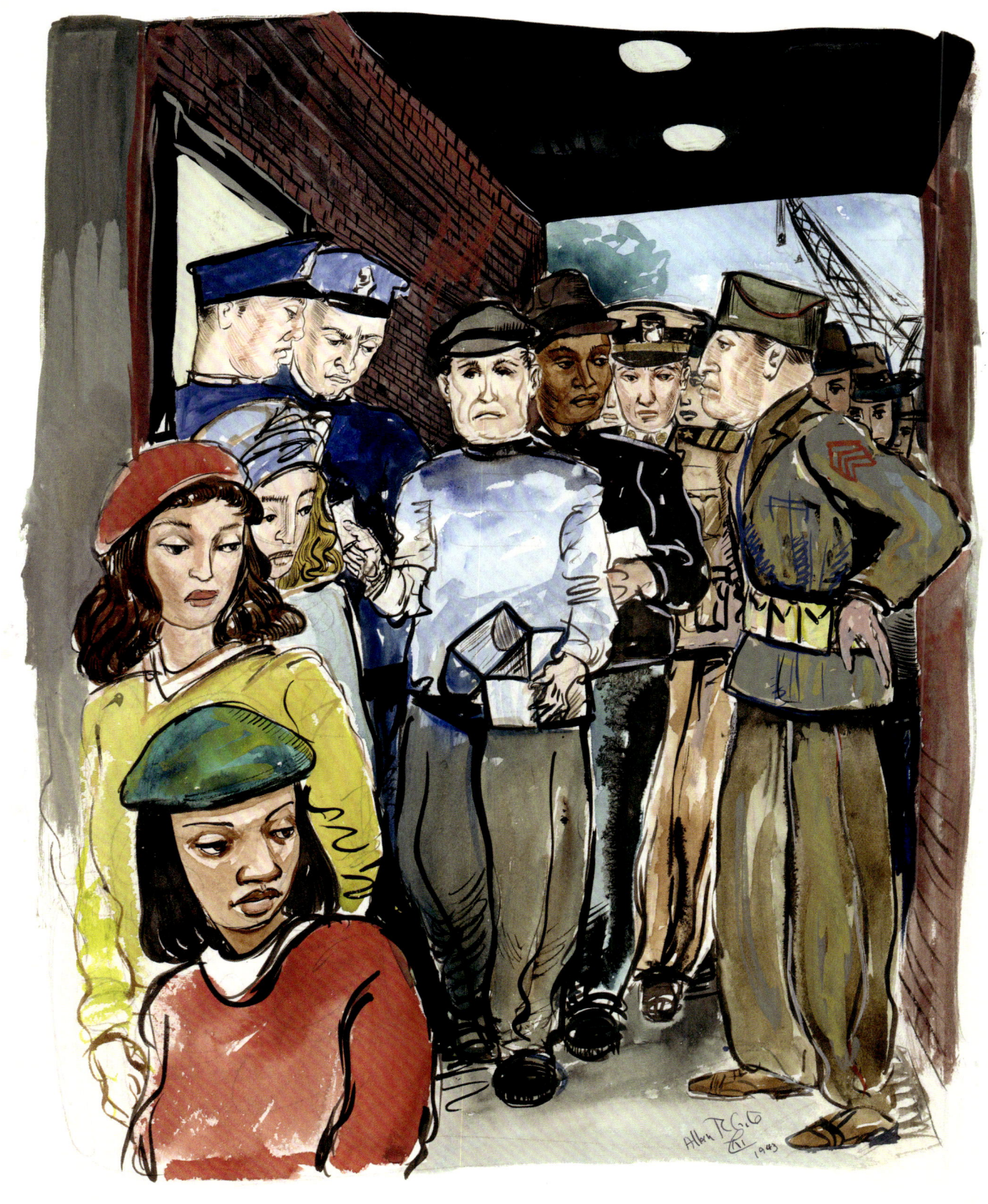

Plate 20. Allan Rohan Crite, *Have Your Pass Ready,* 1943. Watercolor with black ink and gouache over graphite on paper, 36.2 × 28.8 cm. Boston Athenaeum

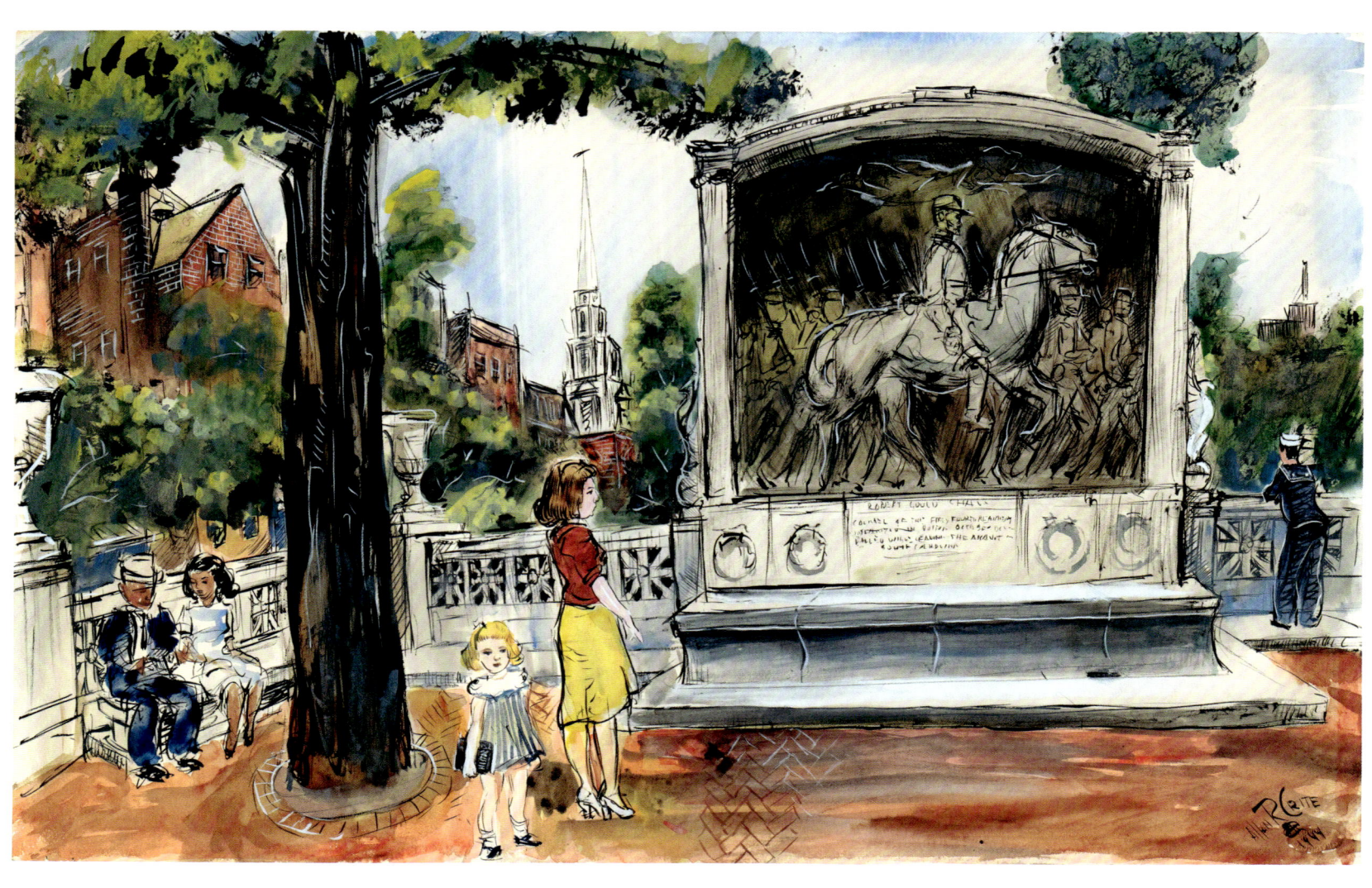

Plate 21. Allan Rohan Crite, *Meeting at St. Gaudens Shaw Memorial,* 1944. Watercolor on paper, 35.6 × 55.2 cm. Addison Gallery of American Art

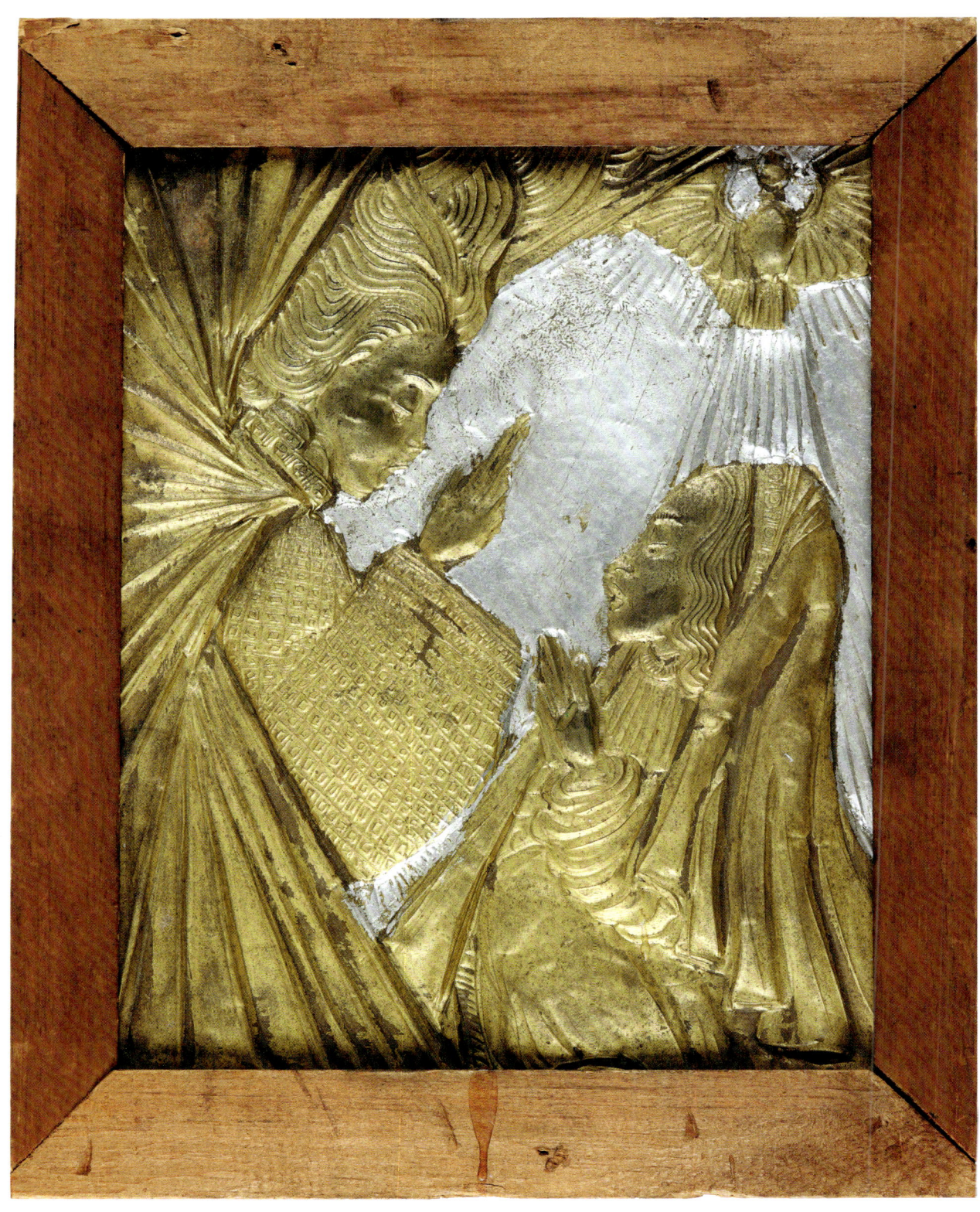

Plates 22 and 23. Allan Rohan Crite, *Untitled (Annunciation Scene)* [front and back], 1945. Pressed gilt copper with paint additions, 20.3 × 16.2 cm. Society of Saint John the Evangelist, Cambridge

To the Rev. Father Wessinger S.S.J.E.
on the occasion of
his final profession
to the service of GOD
in the Society of St. John the Evangelist

Allen Rohan Crite
1945

CRITE AND POLITICS

"Some people refer to him as kind of the silent revolutionary, but it wasn't nothing silent about him. It's just the way he presented it. . . . He didn't present it with the fervor you think of for revolutionar[ies] . . . but his fervor came through his penmanship—you know, his ability to express it on paper."

Aukram Burton

"[Our] conversations would span from just what happened on the street or something with a political event. I'll say, for example, when Mel King was running for mayor, the conversations around that and the works of art that we would create with regard to helping push his image and his program forward." (Fig. 62)

Napoleon Jones-Henderson

"If you went to his house, he gave the downstairs [storefront] area [to] Mel King's Rainbow Coalition. He gave it to him for free."

Kathleen Bitetti

"Allan definitely celebrated women and their contributions to the community. He depicts women as more than worthy of respect. In fact, he honors women throughout his work as leaders in the community, caregivers, family members, and really as pillars within the community who could keep the community spirit moving forward." (Fig. 63)

Ted Landsmark

"He really loved and cherished women and he was a champion of women's rights and a woman's right to own her own body. [He talked about] how males are raised in this society to be macho, to be in charge, to have authority, so they find it necessary to subjugate women and to keep women in their place. So this kind of works itself out in men getting to say what goes on with a woman's body and what they can and cannot do. I wish he was here now to just tell these people off about what a woman can do with her own body. . . . He was a champion of women and women's rights."

Susan Thompson

"He always talked about women and their bodies and how men try to control women's bodies, like what's happening today. He would always say: 'What about male responsibility? You know, women didn't get pregnant by themselves.' . . . Very forward thinking. It's just incredible to think he was born in 1910." (Fig. 64)

Johnetta Tinker

"He did a solo show with us of drawings at the Harbor Gallery and it had some controversy [for being sexually explicit], but even before the controversy, he gave this speech called 'Art Is Public Business.' And it was all about censorship . . . and he typed it up on his typewriter. And this was [a] really important speech . . . in the middle of this whole censorship war and HIV/AIDS war."

Kathleen Bitetti

"He believed in protesting, you know. Yeah, he had a little radicalness in him. He wasn't going to get out there and do it himself; he was not a violent person on any means of this earth. He did not believe in violence any kind of way. But he felt that if something was wrong, he would say, 'Look, this is not right.'"

Johnetta Tinker

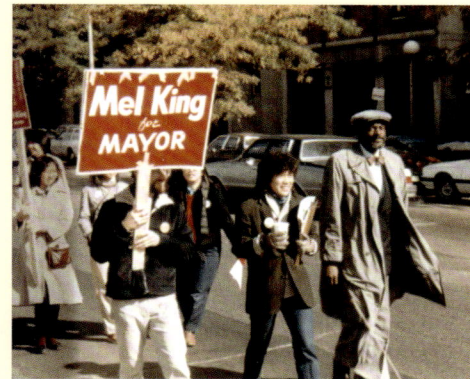

Fig. 62. Mel King campaigning for mayor of Boston, July 1987. Northeastern University Library, Archives and Special Collections

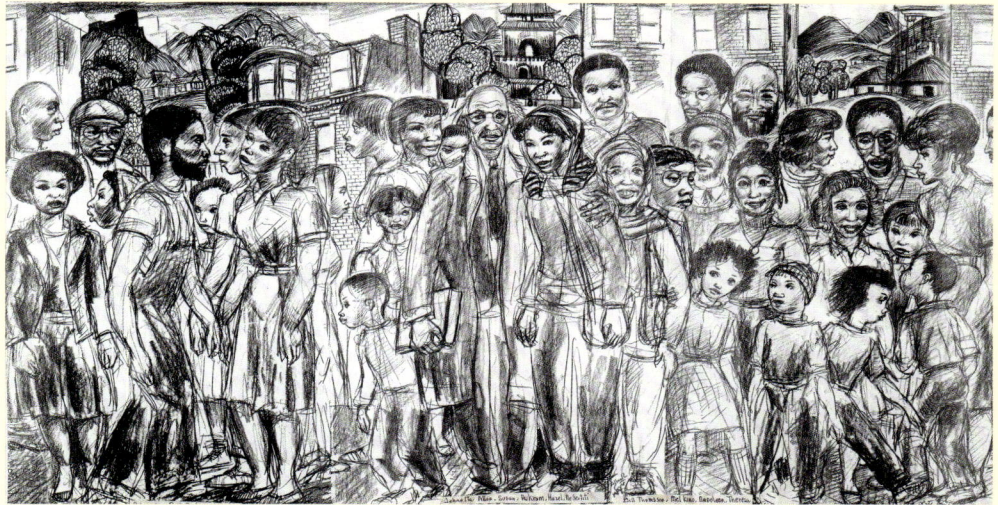

Fig. 63. Detail of *Ancestors and Our Neighborhood,* fig. 39

CRITE'S EROTIC ART

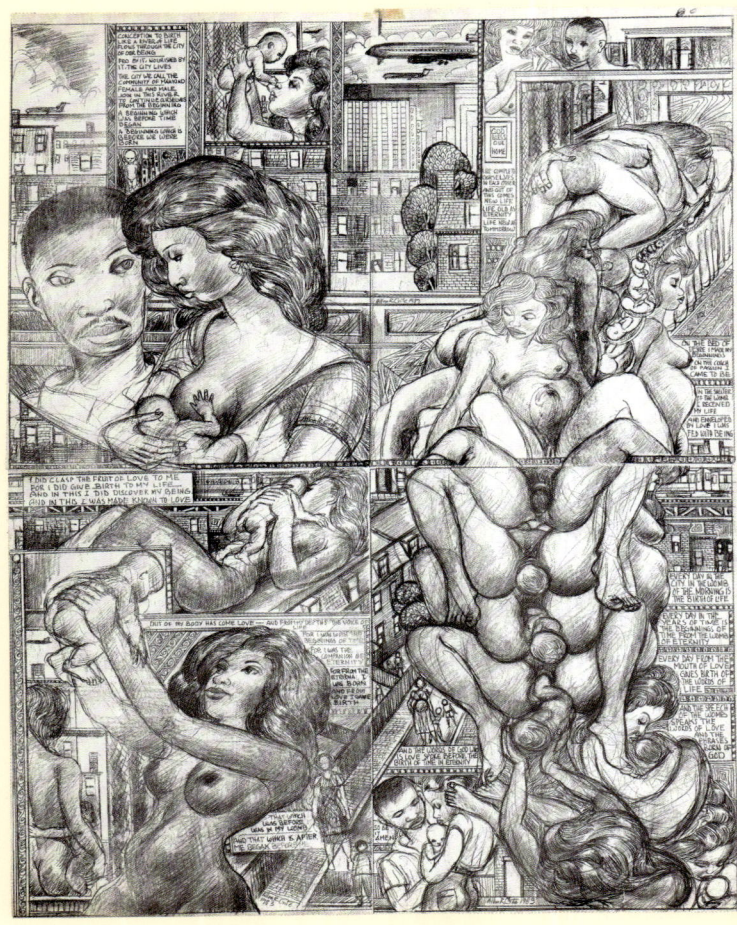

Fig. 64. Allan Rohan Crite, *Untitled (Birth Progression)*, 1983. Multilith print collage, 55.1 × 43 cm. Collection of Susan Thompson

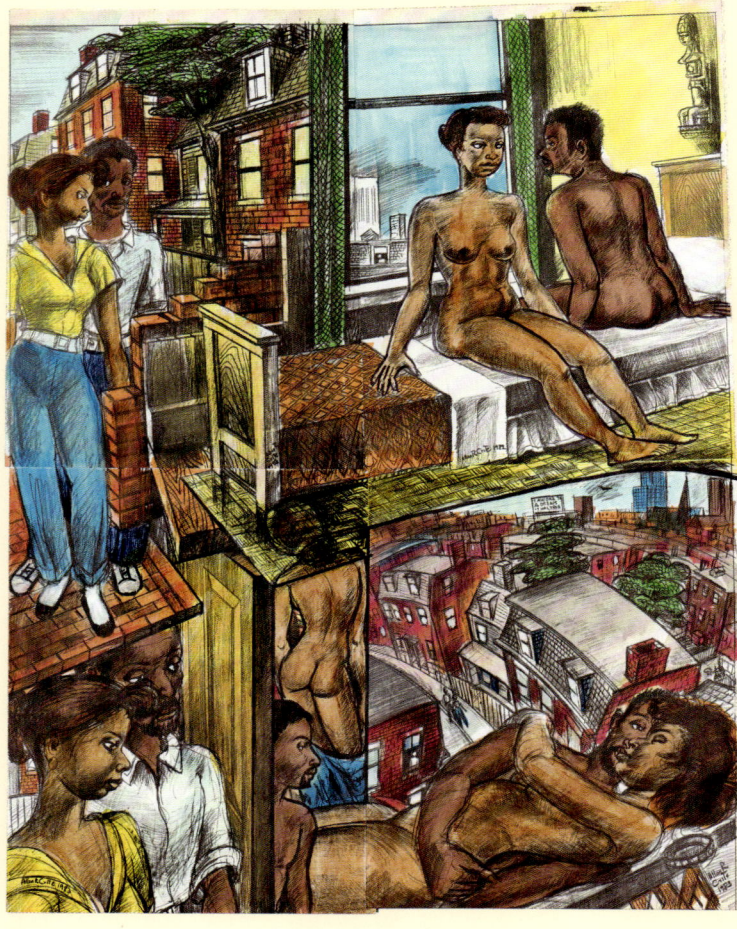

Fig. 65. Allan Rohan Crite, *Untitled (I Awoke to a Dream It Was True—Scenes of a Couple)*, 1982–83. Multilith print collage hand-colored with marker, 54.6 × 41.6 cm. Collection of Susan Thompson

"He always said the human body is our body. Why are we ashamed of the human body? There's something wrong with the human mind if you think there's something wrong with the human body."

Johnetta Tinker

"I was definitely surprised when I saw [his erotic art]. I kind of giggled because he was this straitlaced cool older man who was always with a suit. And then to see this work, I said, 'Oh, he had another, funky side.'" (Fig. 65)

Hakim Raquib

"Allan wasn't one of these New England puritans."

Napoleon Jones-Henderson

"He just felt it was all the same. When you look at religion, the human body is a part of religion. He always talked about Adam and Eve; they were nude in the Garden of Eden."

Johnetta Tinker

"He didn't call it erotic art, he called it human art."

Johnetta Tinker

"Through the story of censorship, we get to the fact that he was creating an incredible array of work that spanned genres and mediums and that he was exploring human sexuality. He would say, 'Go look at the Greek vases—I'm not doing anything new.'"

Kathleen Bitetti

CRITE AND GENTRIFICATION AND URBAN RENEWAL

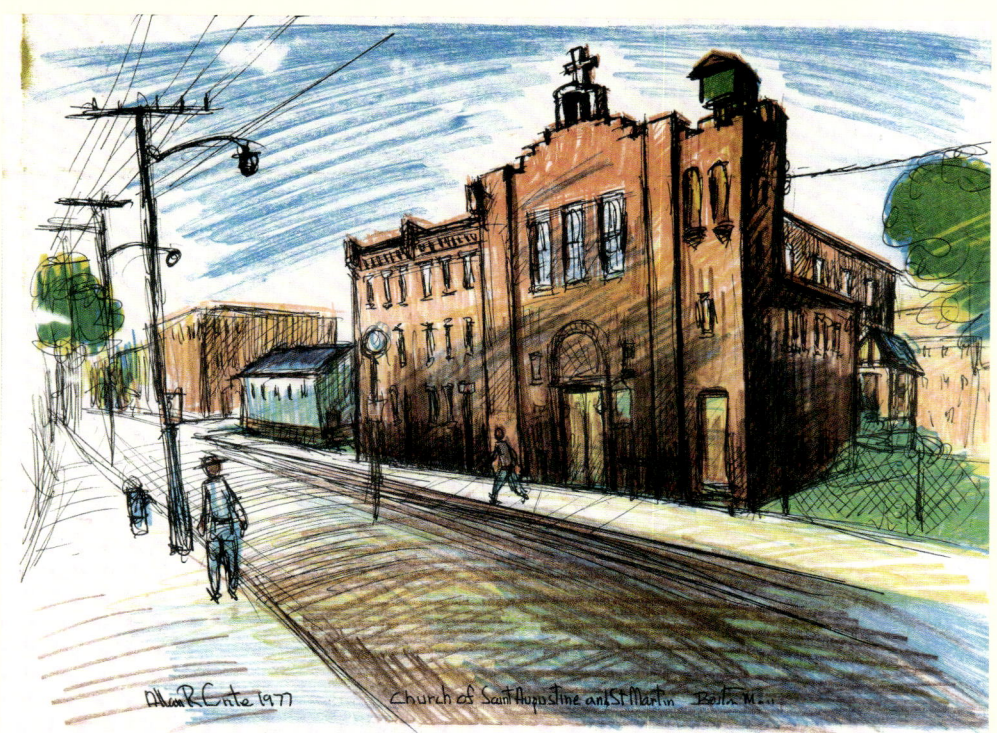

Fig. 66. Allan Rohan Crite, *St. Augustine and St. Martin,* from *An Artist's Sketchbook of the South End: A Walking Tour about Black People,* 1977. Offset color lithograph, 21.7 × 27.9 cm. Boston Athenaeum

"He always talked about urban renewal, [but] he always called it urban removal. You remove all these beautiful communities that have a unique friendship and family together and you disperse them because you're . . . supposed to be doing something better. And it's worse because, he said, there's the whole downtown area [that] was called the West End of Boston that was a diverse community of people . . . it seems like all of a sudden it just went away."

Johnetta Tinker

"He was not a person opposed to change, but he was a person who valued the human need for community, and who saw that a community is where you live, and it is the association with the things that give you a sense of location and involvement. So that was always important to him. It centered very heavily in the church, as I previously noted, but it also was strongly rooted in architecture." (Figs. 66 and 67)

Barry Gaither

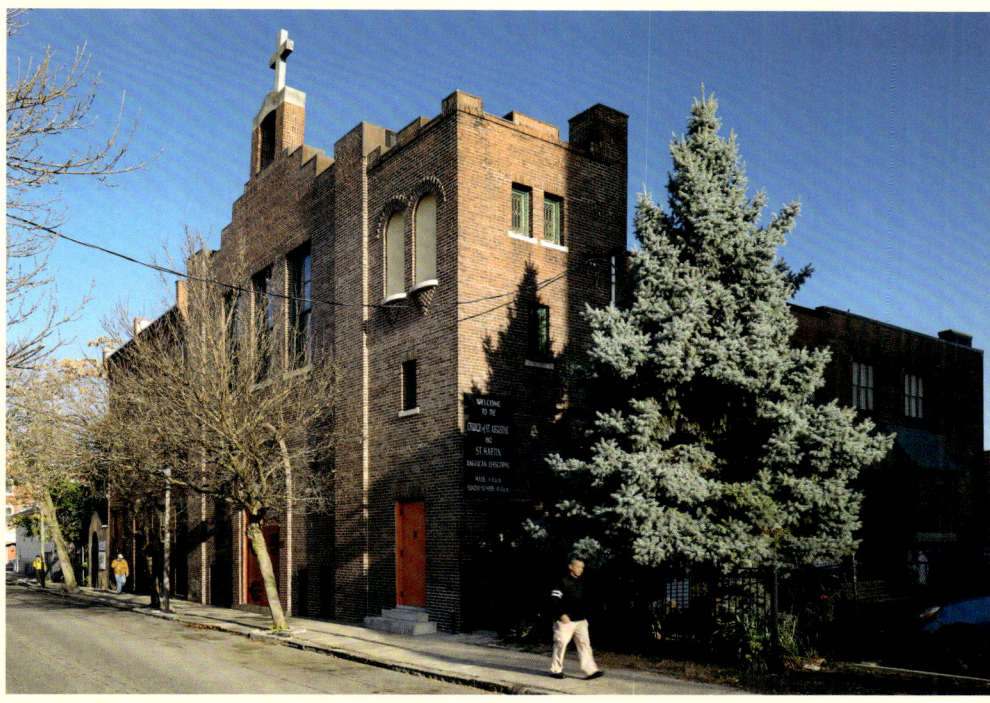

Fig. 67. Church of St. Augustine and St. Martin, Boston, 2024

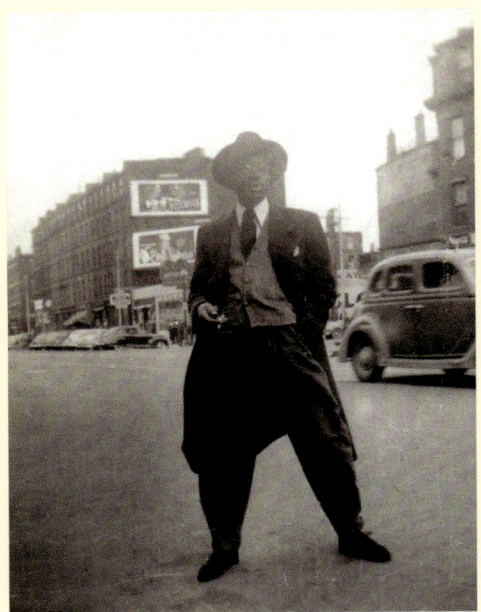

Fig. 68. Winifred Irish Hall (1924–2013), *Russell "Russ" in Frederick Douglass Square (Hammond Street at Tremont Street)*, 1939–40. Northeastern University Library, Archives and Special Collections

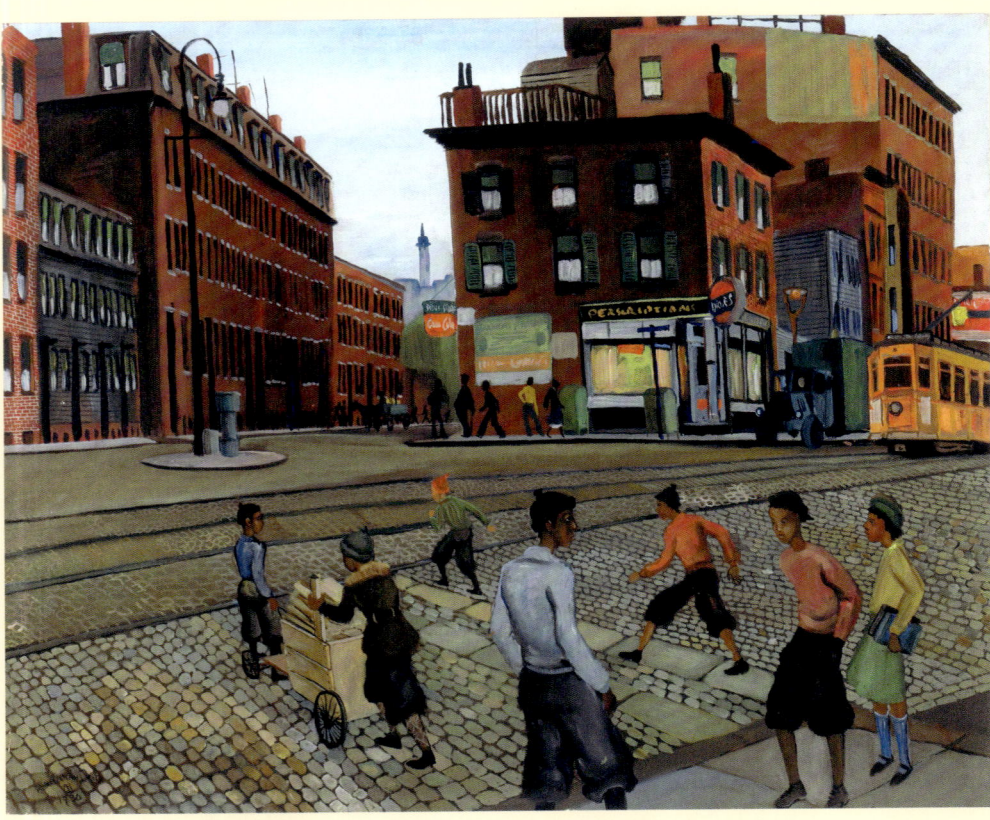

Fig. 69. Allan Rohan Crite, *Douglass Square,* 1936. Oil on canvas-covered artist's board, 59.7 × 68.6 cm. Saint Louis Art Museum

"One of the things that's really striking about his work is that there are a lot of landmarks in his work, like places that you can recognize, but then also places that have been developed and don't really exist anymore in the city." (Figs. 68 and 69)

Ted Landsmark

"Allan . . . recognized that change was inevitable, but he also lamented the fact that that change was diminishing the presence of young families in the community and was having the effect of driving Black and brown people out of the neighborhood into other parts of the city."

Ted Landsmark

"Allan was very concerned that the changes would undermine the strength of the Black artistic community in Boston. . . . Even now I think a lot of artists tend to leave Boston because they can no longer afford to live here . . . because of the substantial prices that they have to pay for studio and workspace and living space. . . . I think that's why it was so, so important that he gave artists space, a studio space in his home. I mean, he really did open up his home as a place of learning and cultural exchange and, yeah, just as a place for artists, Black artists to kind of establish a place of their own."

Ted Landsmark

"Allan would always talk about 'urban removal' because of what happened in the South End to communities of color; they just would up and move folks. The same thing with the West End. So he had a real front-seat perspective on that."

Kathleen Bitetti

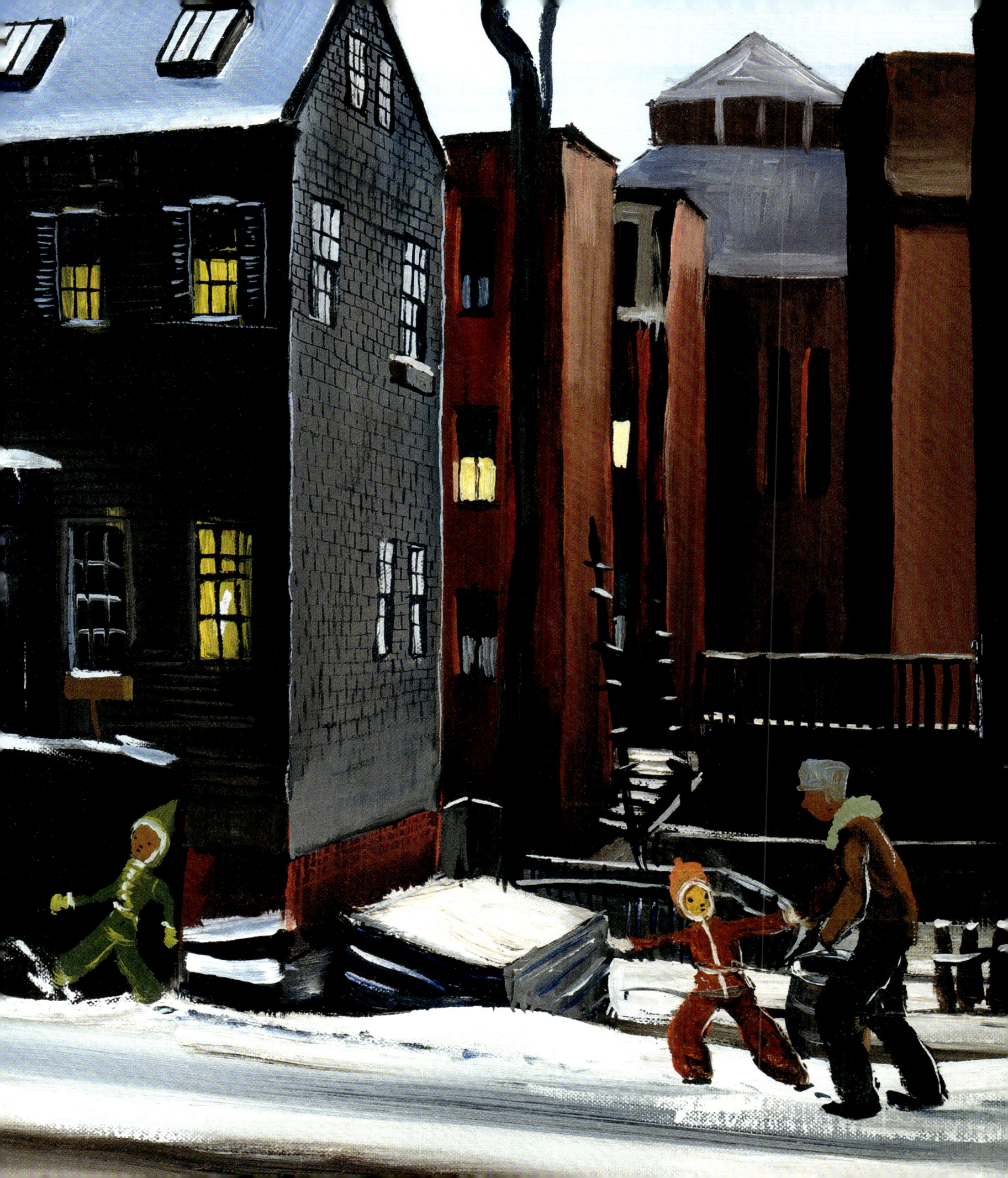

STREET IS A MEMORY

Paula C. Austin

"I am human. Nothing human can be alien to me."
—Terence, enslaved playwright during the Roman Republic,
quoted by Maya Angelou

This sentiment might be the most appropriate way to describe Allan Rohan Crite's approach to his art and his life.[1] In making his art, Crite was a consummate student, engaging in some sort of research for everything he produced. While Crite's visual artworks were not always titled, they were always accompanied by edifying, contextualizing, or historicizing text, sometimes written in a draughtsman's small, neat handwriting. Crite's work from the 1920s through the 1990s serves as a landscape and social history of Black Boston, mapping segregation and urban renewal, Black arts, and the Black Power movement, all of which foregrounded Crite's critical belief in an inclusive human family.

Allan Rohan Crite was born in North Plainfield, New Jersey, in 1910 and moved with his parents, Oscar and Annamae Palmer Crite, to Boston while he was still a baby. Crite lived with his eventually widowed mother until her death, in three locations in the South End: 401 Shawmut Avenue, 2 Dilworth Street, and finally 410 Columbus Avenue, the last of which currently displays a plaque (figs. 70 and 71) celebrating Crite as a "visual artist, painter, printmaker, author, lecturer, historian, and good neighbor."

Crite came up in a diverse, predominantly Black working- and aspiring class neighborhood in the South End that included aspiring migrants and second-generation children who hailed from South Carolina, North Carolina (like his father), Florida, Georgia, and Virginia (like his widowed aunt Eliza, who lived with them for a bit). Early on, his community also included German and Irish immigrants, and then eventually Caribbean immigrants from Jamaica, Cuba, Trinidad, Barbados, and a historic community of Black Nova Scotians. Crite and his parents were members of St. Bartholomew's Episcopal Church in Cambridge, organized by Afro-Caribbean Episcopalians at the turn of the century and ministering to an African American and West Indian congregation. Crite's early community was one of arts and activism, as were many urban Black communities.

Opposite: Detail of *Come On, Gramps*, plate 15

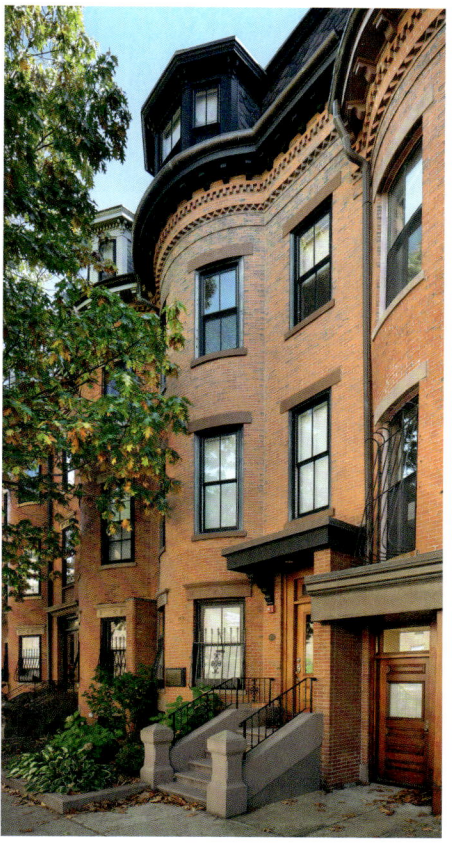

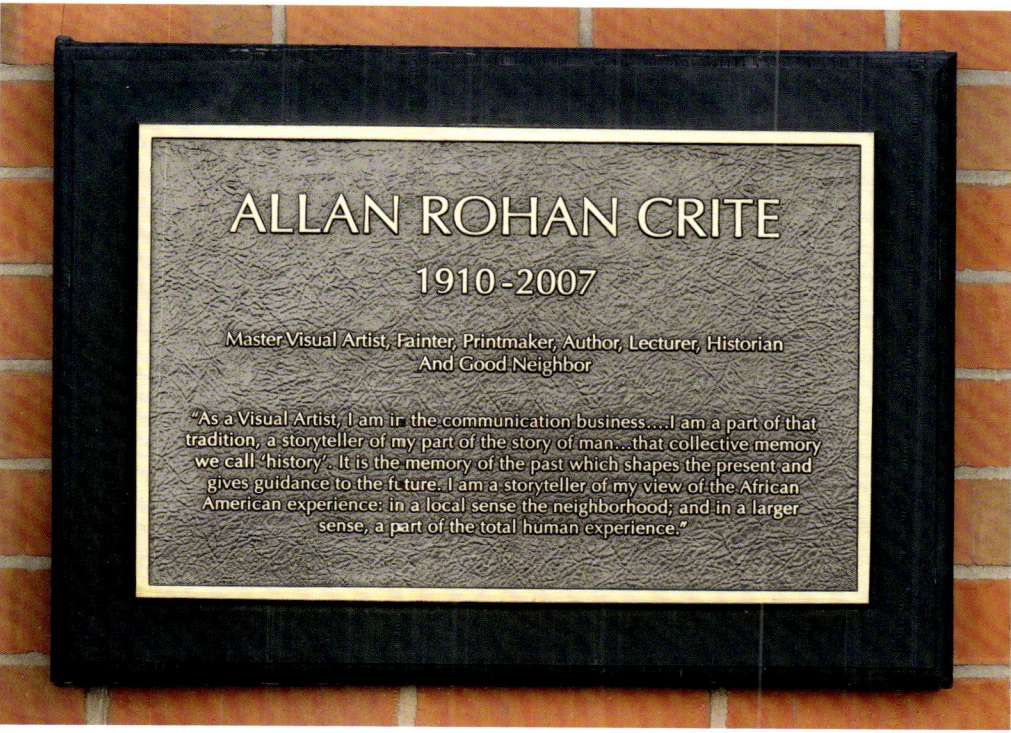

By the time Crite was nine years old, the South End was home to the League of Women for Community Service (LWCS), a Black women's organization that was, in Crite's words, "dedicated towards the cultural and educational advancement of Black women."[2] In addition to providing a lunch program and room and board for Black women students denied housing in segregated Boston, the LWCS also sponsored a vibrant cultural scene, some of which was hosted at the nearby Harriet Tubman House.[3]

During Crite's teenage years, as he sketched scenes from his window and began taking classes as a scholarship student at the School of the Museum of Fine Arts, he accompanied his parents to see the tenor Roland Hayes, one of only two men his father admired, perform at Symphony Hall. Crite recounted that when he was a child, his mother often opened the window so she could hear Hayes practicing with the Fisk Jubilee Singers.[4] Hayes would later write the foreword for Crite's *Three Spirituals from Earth to Heaven.*[5] The LWCS also hosted Black musical groups and exhibited the work of sculptor Meta Warrick Fuller and painter Lois Mailou Jones. Crite and his mother may also have attended lectures by James Weldon Johnson as Johnson worked to raise awareness about and support for the Dyer Anti-Lynching Bill of 1918, and they may have gone to the Tremont Temple Baptist Church to hear W. E. B. Du Bois give a talk.[6]

The house the LWCS purchased at 558 Massachusetts Avenue was a stone's throw from all three of the places Crite lived, and it was certainly on his radar, as it shows up in his 1977 series *An Artist's Sketchbook of the South End: A Walking Tour about Black People,* compiled just a few months after his mother's death (fig. 72). In this sketchbook, Crite traced sites from Lower Roxbury through the South End, mapping Black religious and community spaces and annotating their historical significance to Boston's landscape. Both the LWCS house and the Harriet Tubman House are featured, as is Plymouth Hospital (figs. 73 and 74), a Black hospital that employed Black doctors and trained Black nurses when neither could practice in other, predominantly white Boston hospitals.[7]

Fig. 70. Allan Rohan Crite's home, 410 Columbus Avenue, in Boston's South End, 2024

Fig. 71. Allan Rohan Crite plaque at 410 Columbus Avenue in Boston's South End, 2024

Opposite top: Fig. 72. Allan Rohan Crite, *588 Massachusetts Avenue (League of Women for Community Service),* from *An Artist's Sketchbook of the South End: A Walking Tour about Black People,* 1977. Offset color lithograph, 21.7 × 27.9 cm. Boston Athenaeum

Opposite bottom: Fig. 73. Allan Rohan Crite, *Harriet Tubman House,* from *An Artist's Sketchbook of the South End: A Walking Tour about Black People,* 1977. Offset color lithograph, 21.7 × 27.9 cm. Boston Athenaeum

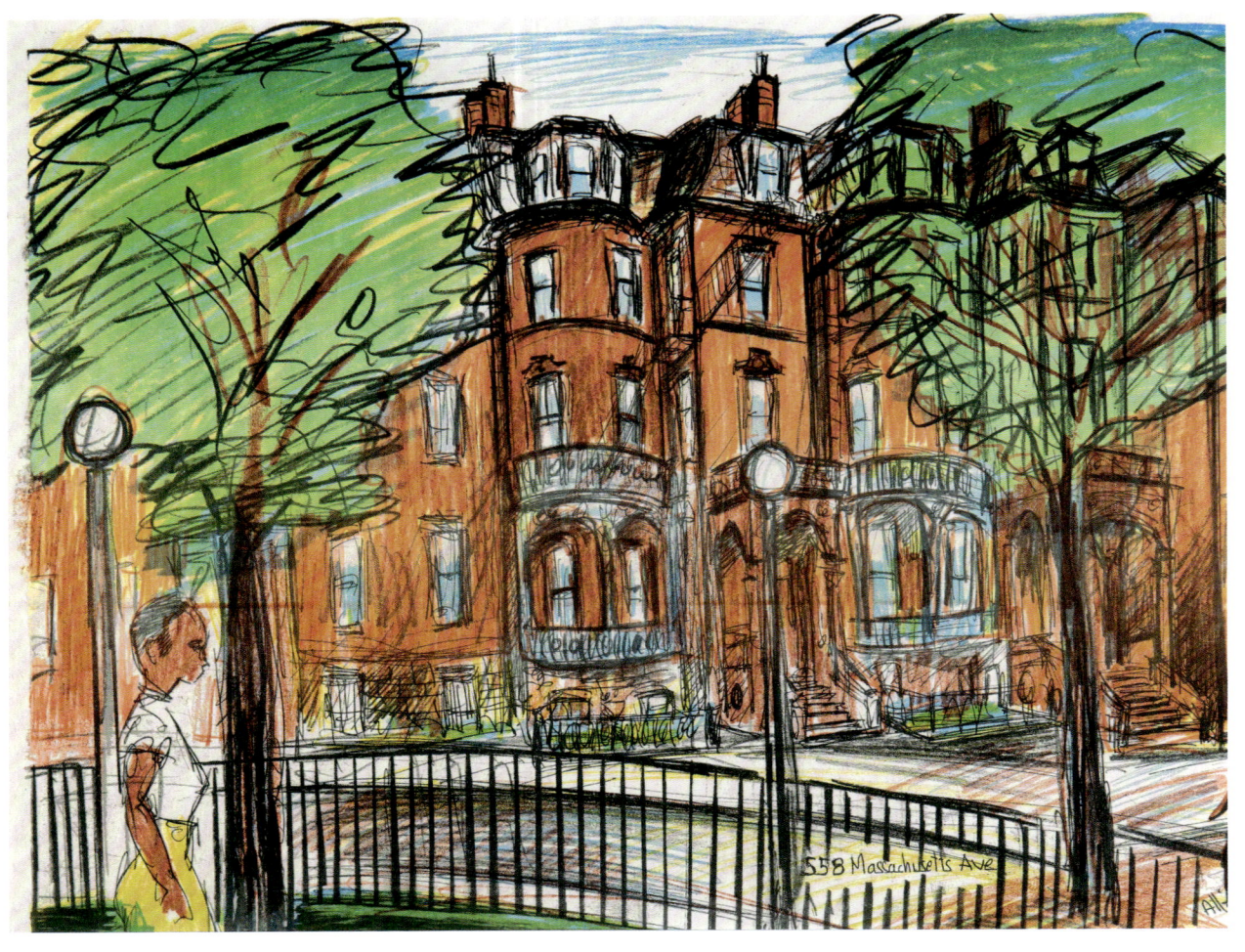

558 Massachusetts Ave.

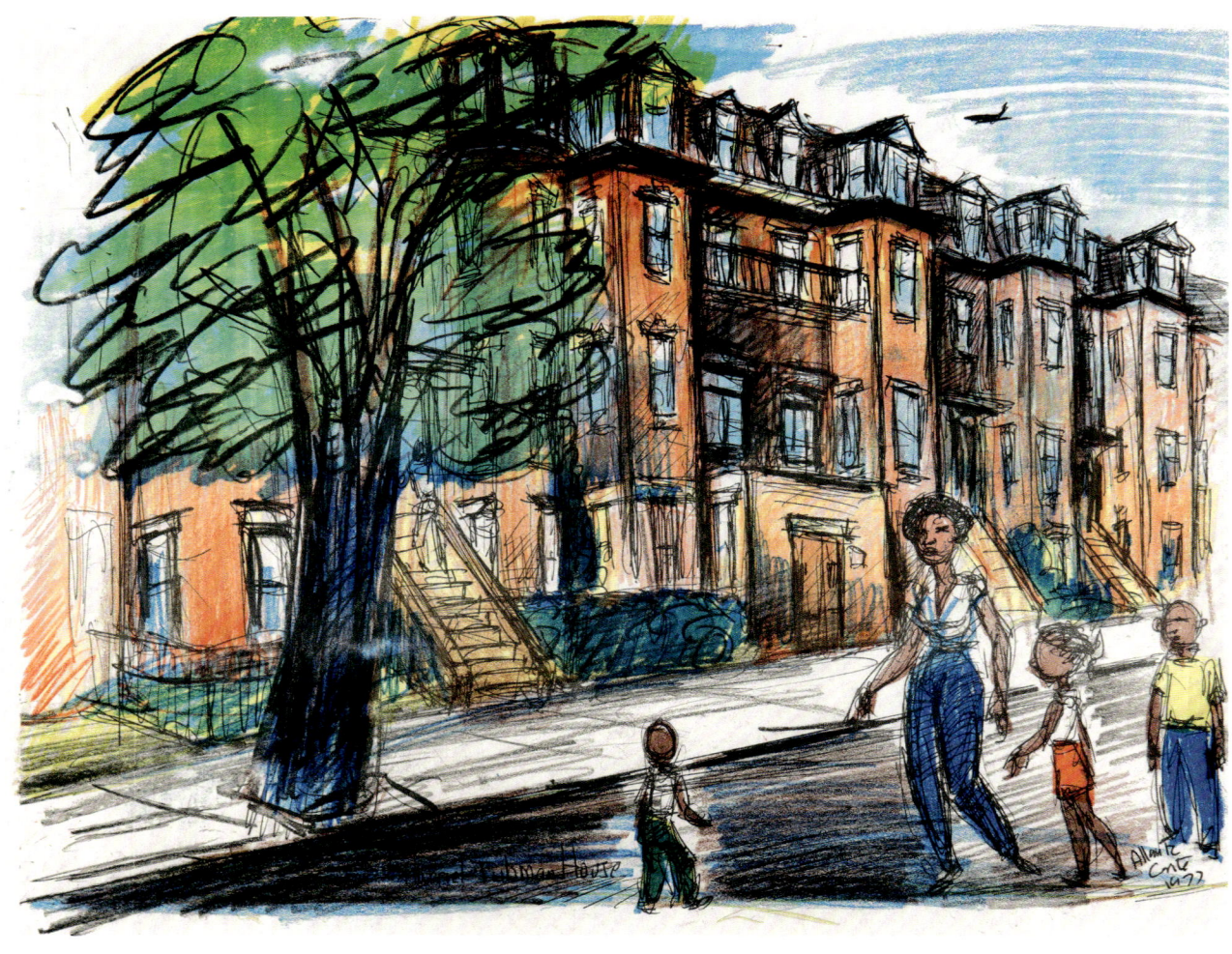

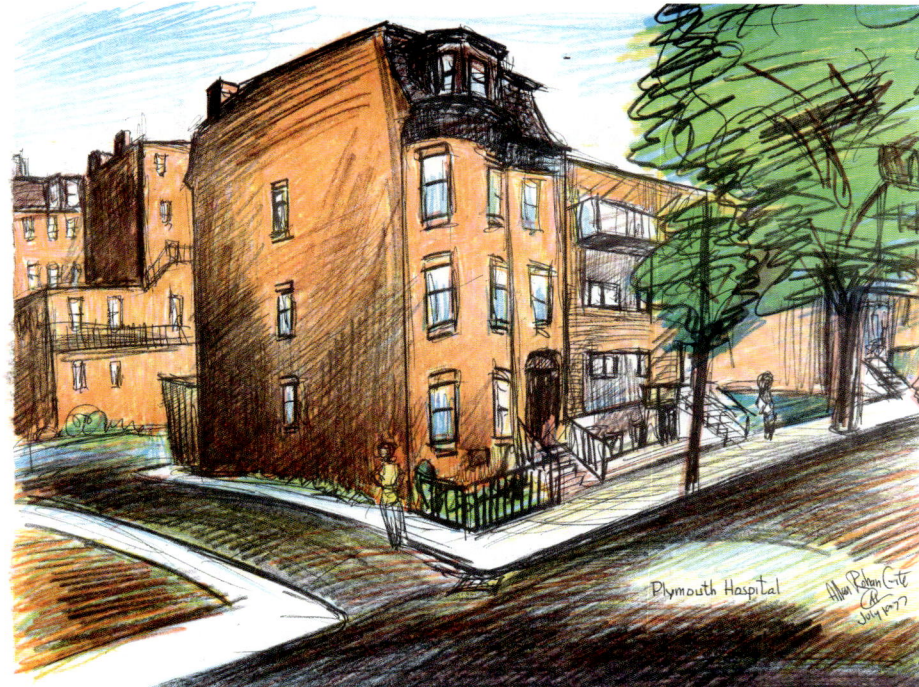

Fig. 74. Allan Rohan Crite, *Plymouth Hospital,* from *An Artist's Sketchbook of the South End: A Walking Tour about Black People,* July 1977. Offset color lithograph, 21.7 × 27.9 cm. Boston Athenaeum

In December 1971, Crite was forced to move with his mother to 410 Columbus Avenue, as his old neighborhood was in the path of Boston's redevelopment plars. In 1960, the Boston Redevelopment Authority assessed parts of Boston, including the South End and Roxbury, as "blighted" and "deteriorated," and aimed to raze these neighborhoods to extend Interstate 95.[8] It was a highly contested plan that, in Crite's words, created "thousands of 'Redevelopment Refugees.'"[9] Crite lamented the loss of the home at Dilworth and Northampton (fig. 75), which his father had purchasec but had lost ownership of during the Depression—a house where Crite had lived for more than forty years, and where his mother, who loved airplanes, could watch them in the sky from their bay window above the corner drycleaners on the ground level of the building.

Crite had seen twenty years of what he called "massive demolition" in his neighborhood, and he documented the loss of buildings (including his first home on Shawmut Avenue) and community spaces in some of his early work, such as his painting of Leon Bailey and Harriet Jackson. In 1976, well after he and his mother had been forced to relocate, Crite reflected that his old street was still just "a vacant lot, . . . a memory, [like] all the other vanished streets of the city." Streets that were "once alive with chi dren and the busy chatter of Black people" had been turned into "acres of desolation" by "hungry bull dozers."[10]

Allan Crite loved his community. When asked in an oral history interview about the Black power phrase "Black Is Beautiful," he joked that he "started that movement . . . in Boston," but much, much earlier.[11] The beautiful Black folks in Crite's South End community, whom he depicted in his several neighborhood series from the Depressior through World War II, were ordinary people: domestics, of whom his mother was one, janitors, porters, clerks, seamstresses, waiters, mechanics, chauffeurs, and military veterans. Some have misconstrued his statement that Black artists were too often associated with "the jazz person up in Harlem" as reflecting Crite's identification with a politics of early twentieth-century Black middle-class respectability, but his point, as he emphasized later, was more about his preference, in his early art, for depicting the quotidian, the beauty of the day to day, and thus the humanity of Black life.[12] In a profile in the *Boston Globe* in 1981, he said his aim was to "give another picture of Black people" that would

Fig. 75. Allan Rohan Crite, *Self-Portrait,* 1975. Pencil and ink on paper, 30.5 × 50.8 cm. Private collection

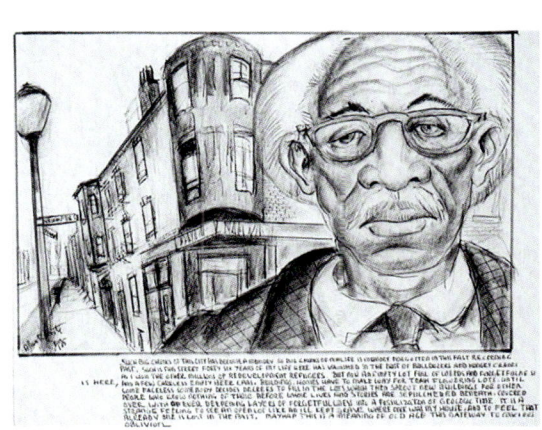

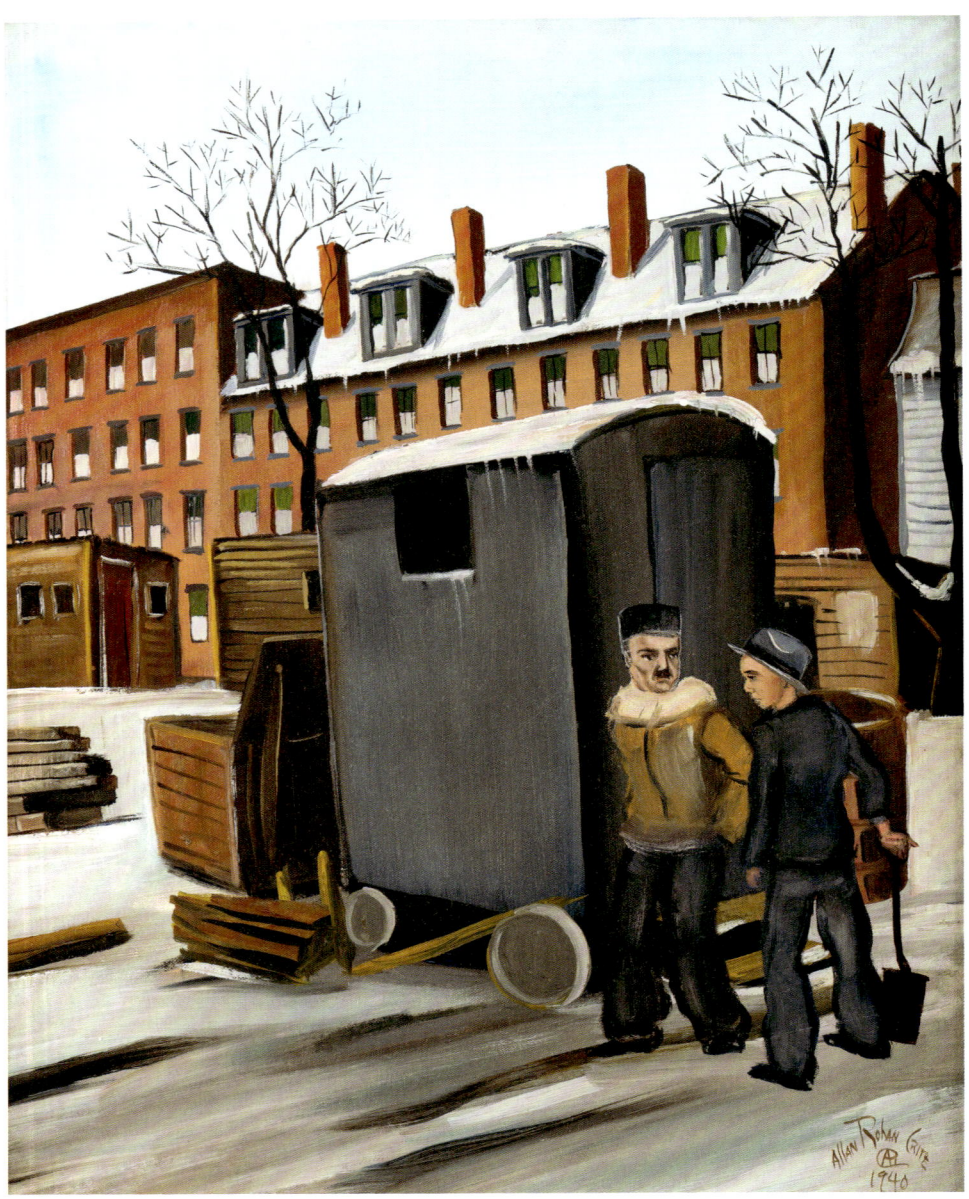

counter what he called "mild distortions." He wanted "to show Black people in their
ordinary life in a northern city . . . BOSTON because I lived here—just going about their
business, walking down the street, talking, gossiping with the ice man the coal man, the
vegetable man, capturing the ebb and flow (fig. 76)."[13]

Less an indictment of a certain kind of Black music or the culture around it,
Crite's work in this early period, and really throughout his career, was more a counternar-
rative to the ways in which pervasive white supremacist thinking and racist imagery
narrowed the possibilities of Black representation in visual arts and culture. His desire
to humanize Black people was part of a political project of vindication widespread in
Black intellectual and artistic circles for much of the twentieth century. Its objective was
to change the minds and policies of segregationists, to end anti-Black violence, and to
uplift Black people themselves, both emotionally and spiritually. His 1941 portrait *Bass
Violin Player* (see plate 19) and his *Parade on Hammond Street* (1935), even his drawing
Holworthy Street, "Sugar Hill," Roxbury (1938) (fig. 77), where a teenage Malcolm X
would soon take up residence in 1940 and where a young Black janitor was killed in his
home by police in 1934, stand in contrast to the predominant ways in which Black people

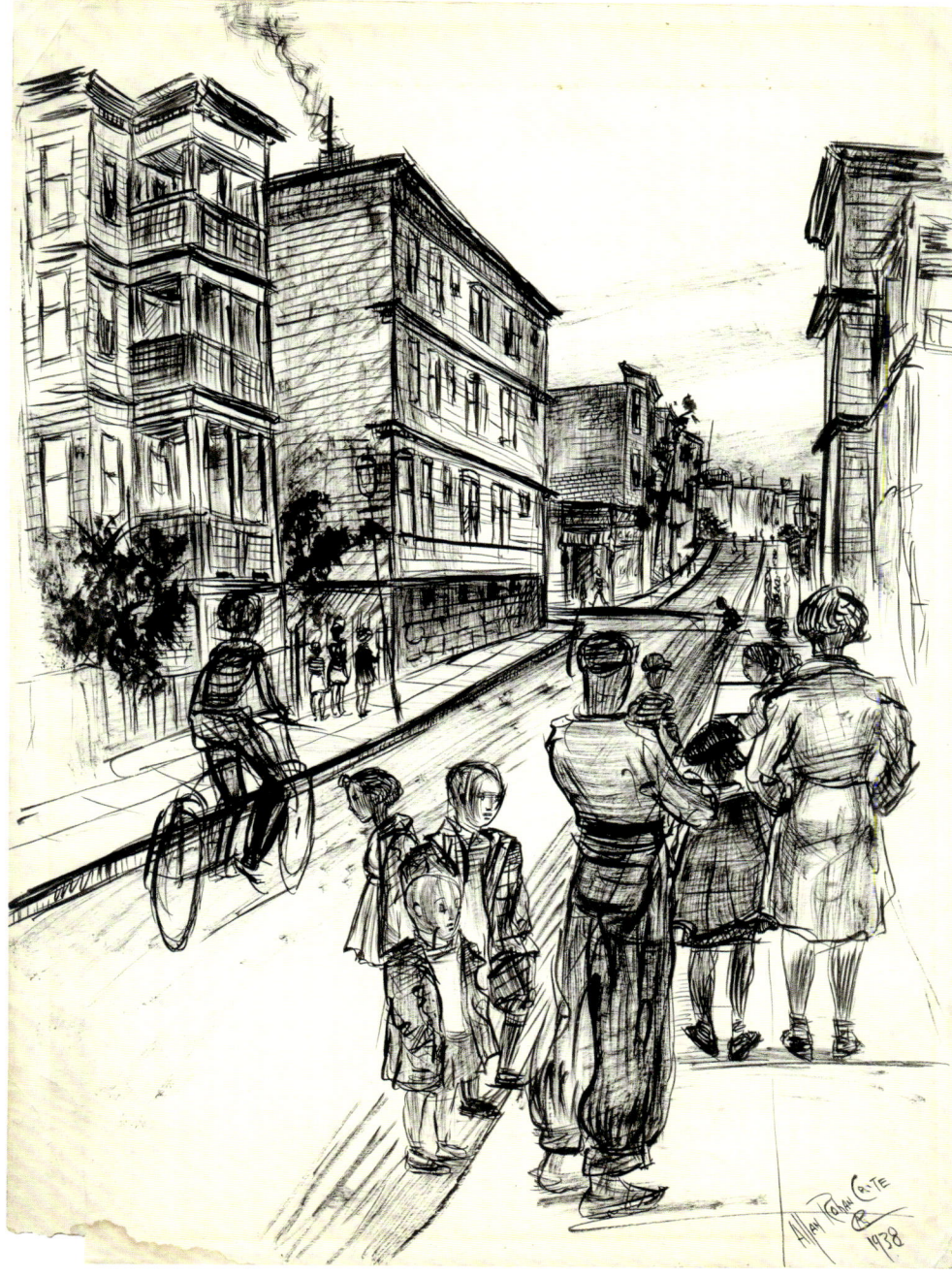

Fig. 77. Allan Rohan Crite, *Holworthy Street, "Sugar Hill," Roxbury,* 1938. Pen, brush, and black and brown ink, 38.2 × 27.9 cm. Boston Athenaeum

were portrayed in art, culture, and the media, as "traumatic figure[s] out of the ghetto" or as "a social problem."[14]

    Crite believed that as long as these pervasive images proliferated, racist ideas about Black people and Black life would continue to influence both white and Black minds and would ultimately inform public policy. He believed that "artists are observers of what they see, but sometimes artists can bring about a change in what they see . . . they can help others to see and thus act as a catalyst for change."[15] So in contrast to the portrayal of Black men, women, and children as potential criminals or as inherently pathological, the street in Crite's Black community was, as he put it, "a meeting place of ideas and lives . . . the ongoing fabric of living . . . La Humanidad."[16] Crite's early work received considerable attention: he was among a small group of young Black artists, supported by the Works Progress Administration's Federal Art Project and private philanthropists who

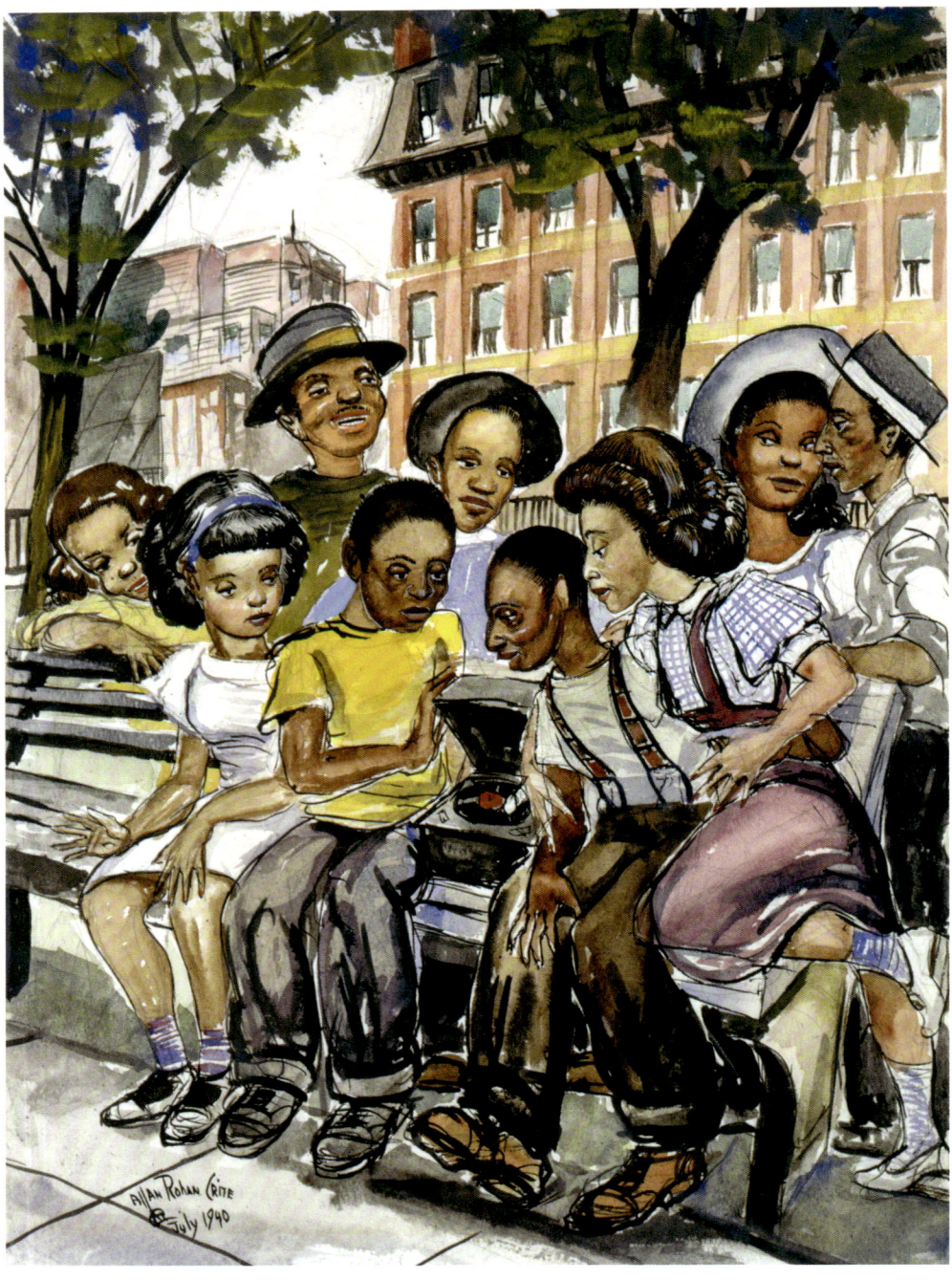

showed their work throughout the country. His contemporaries included Archibald J. Motley Jr., Romare Bearden, and Palmer Hayden.[17]

In Crite's renditions of the mundane—kids at play, people going to and from work and school, a multigenerational group of folks congregated on a sidewalk bench, in deep conversation "settling the world's problems" (as he titled one oil painting), or huddled around a record player (fig. 78)—Crite also sketched divinity. His (Black) Madonna and Child—on public transportation, on a bustling city sidewalk, or hovering above apartment buildings (see plate 24)—were recurring figures in Crite's vast portfolio from the 1930s through the 1980s. Whether she was iconically clad as in his early work, sporting an Afro and a bare belly in the 1970s, or in West African regalia in the 1980s, she and her child were a part both of the fleshy and messy human community and of the ancestors, who were often represented in some way at the top of the frame.

Crite's self-published autobiography, which he wrote in the mid-1970s, interweaves both Boston and national politics into his artistic productions. He was part of the dynamic shifts in Black politics and cultural representation taking place at the time. While Crite credits his mother, Annamae, with encouraging and supporting his interest in art, some of Crite's early political positions and cultural sensibilities were no doubt informed by his father, Oscar, who died in 1937. Crite remembered that Marcus Garvey "was one of the few Black men who was able to capture Dad's interest." Garvey, founder of the Universal Negro Improvement Association (UNIA), "stressed the relationship of Black people with Africa . . . ; he stressed the world wide relationship of Black people with this ancestral home, and he stressed that Black people should be free, and that Black people should have a sense of nationhood." Crite remembered that Reverend George A. McGuire was the "former rector" at his church, St. Bartholomew's, but he was also chaplain-general of Garvey's UNIA and would later found the African Orthodox Church, with a congregation in Roxbury. For Crite, the Garvey movement offered northern Black people some access to education about Black people and Black history, and to Black cultural pride, at a time when very little was "readily available" to the general public. These "intellectual and cultural stirrings" included "significant breakthroughs" in music, theater, and dance. Crite reminisced about attending the production of Eubie Blake's *Shuffle Along* with his father when it came through Boston in 1922–23, describing it as "a dazzling performance of color, rhythm, melody, and high comedy."[18] Crite may have seen a teenage Josephine Baker dance as one of the chorus girls in the 1922 production.[19]

During World War II and for the next thirty years, Crite worked as a draughtsman for the Charlestown Navy Yard, while also taking courses at Harvard Extension School, where after fourteen years of night classes he earned his bachelor of arts in natural sciences.[20] As he said, his "civil service" gave him some financial security and allowed him to "experiment as an artist." He also helped write and edit the *Knot,* a monthly news-letter produced by his parish, St. Bartholomew's Episcopal Church in Cambridge, which was "sent to young people in the Service" during the war.[21] As the Civil Rights Movement ramped up in the postwar years, centered, in Boston, around school desegregation, welfare rights, housing, and police brutality, Crite acquired an offset printing press, which allowed him to "do my own printing, from black and white to color," and worked on his first mural for St. Augustine's Episcopal Church in Brooklyn, New York (the church and the mural were destroyed by fire in 1972), and he made some small metal panels for churches in Roxbury, Cambridge (plate 22), and Washington, DC.[22]

In the summer of 1958, Crite gave a talk before the Episcopal Young Churchmen's Convention at Oberlin College titled "The Religious Artist and This Culture." It was not his first talk on liturgical art; he had lectured in Wisconsin, Evanston, Illinois, New Haven, Connecticut, and Berkeley, California. At Oberlin, Crite critiqued capitalism and its dehu-manizing effects "regarding [man] in terms of function, use, and commodity," a view Crite held as early as the 1940s. Referencing the recent proliferation of nuclear weapons, he denounced technological advances, like "clean bombs" that had resulted in the gen-eral and violent disregard for human life. He lamented urban renewal, which he called urban removal, and the "serious dislocation" it wrought—the demolition of buildings and "forcing lower income bracket people into huge [impersonal] housing projects."[23]

Then, anticipating comments that Reverend Dr. Martin Luther King Jr. would make in response to the urban rebellions of the late 1960s, Crite reframed "youthful gangs" as a reaction to an anti-Christian and antihuman postwar world. "There is no place in society," he said, "for the individual, especially the artist, or any other type of creative being who functions organically rather than mechanically. Human beings revolt against this . . . conformity and uniformity, sometimes violently, . . . flesh and blood arrayed against stone, concrete, and steel and an indifference in airless streets of airless stench laden

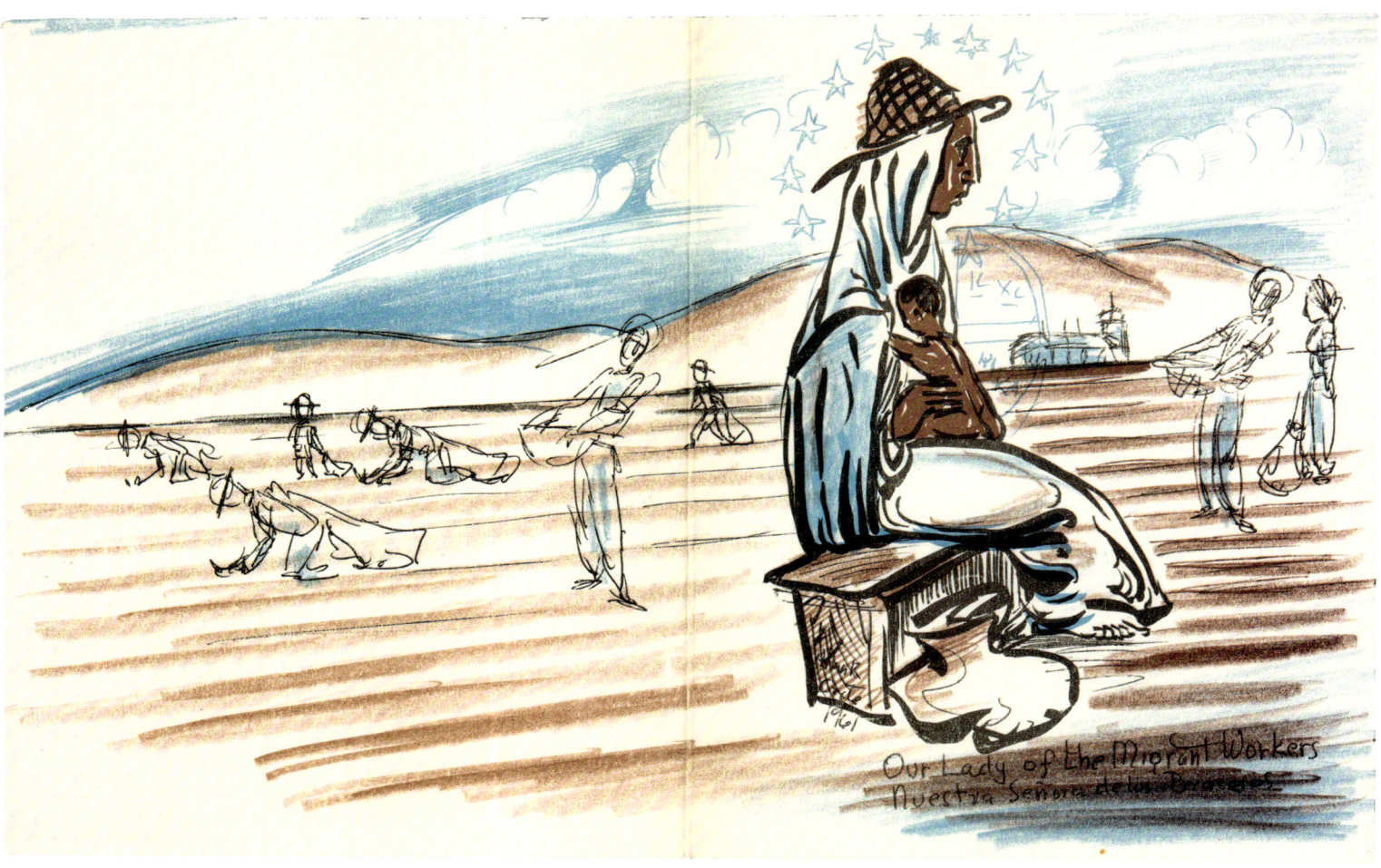

Fig. 79. Allan Rohan Crite, *Our Lady of the Migrant Workers/Nuestra Señora de los Braceros,* 1961. Offset lithograph, 10.9 × 13.8 cm. Boston Athenaeum

houses burdened with the steamy sweat of sorrow and pain." For Christian-identified artists like Crite, in particular, art was not mere "decoration." It must be "proclamation."[24] In an undated essay titled "A Statement: One of the Problems in the United States," Crite made his politics clear: "it is erroneous to think of Civil Rights as being 'Negro Rights.' . . . There is no provision for 'racial rights,' neither should there be. There are only rights of American citizens." To Crite, racial segregation, which the Ford Foundation denounced as "urban apartheid," was "an act of treason against the dignity of American Citizenship and as such ha[d] no rights and no defense."[25]

In the 1960s, Crite made three international trips that further expanded his thinking and art, both culturally and politically. He traveled to France, Denmark, and England as part of an "Ecumenical pilgrimage," and he also visited Puerto Rico and then Mexico. Crite's interest in both Puerto Rico and Mexico emerged from his involvement with the Massachusetts Council of Churches' relief work with local, mostly Puerto Rican migrant workers. Crite visited cranberry bogs on the Cape and orchards and tobacco farms in western and southern Massachusetts, documenting "the conditions under which migrants worked." "It was an education," he said. Crite observed prejudice against migrant workers: "the attitudes of the people of the community," he said, were a "problem." For Crite, citizenship was not a prerequisite for human rights. [26] His 1961 *Our Lady of the Migrant Workers/Nuestra Señora de los Braceros* situated a brown Madonna and Child in a field of so-called guestworkers (fig. 79). The piece appeared just one year before the United Farm Workers union officially formed and organized successful strikes demanding improved wages and working conditions.

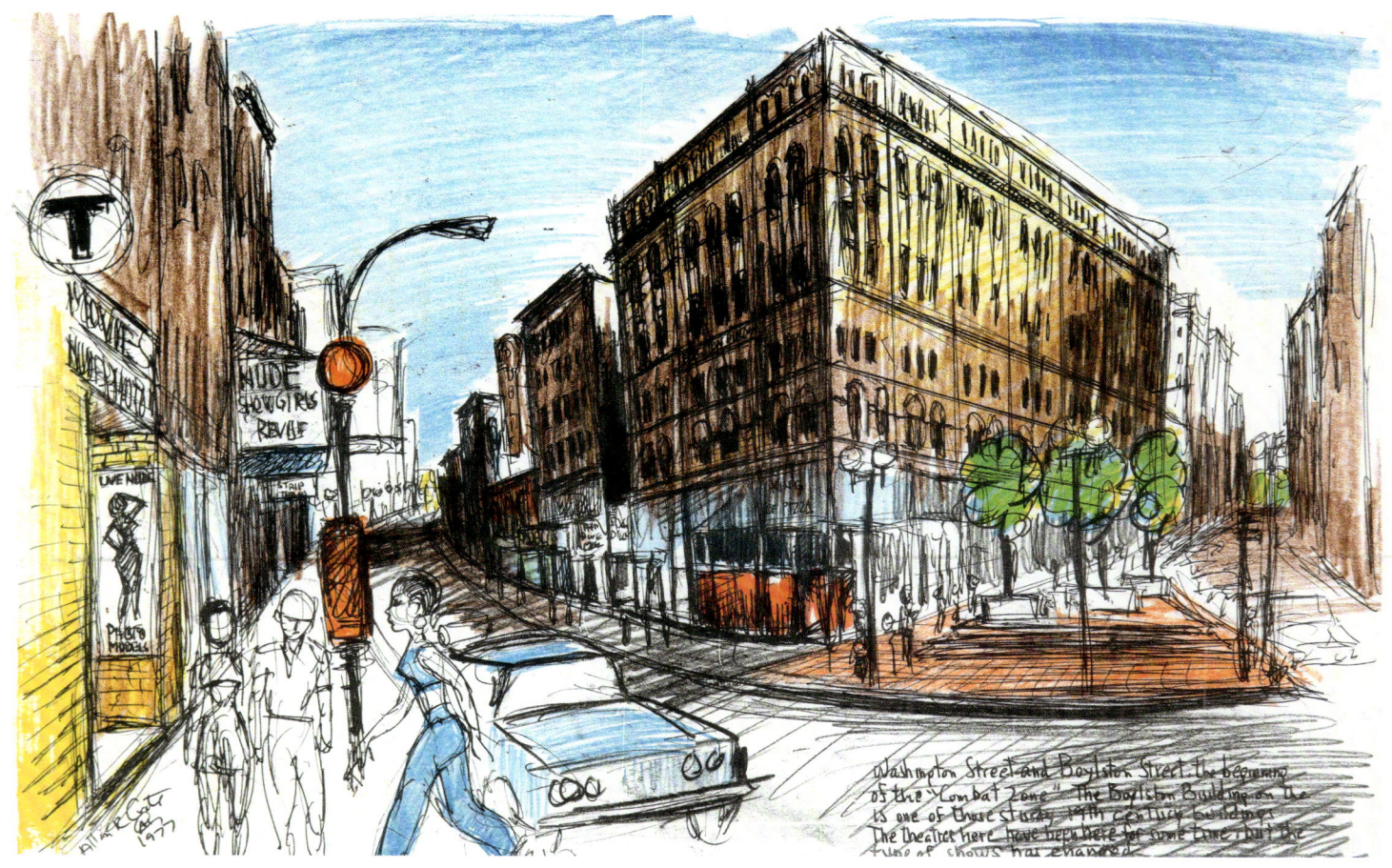

Washington Street and Boylston Street. the beginning of the "Combat Zone". The Boylston Building on the is one of those standing 19th century buildings The Theater here have been there for some time but the type of shows has changed

Fig. 80. Allan Rohan Crite, *Washington Street and Boylston Street,* from the *Combat Zone* portfolio, 1977–78. Offset lithograph, 21.7 × 35.5 cm. Boston Athenaeum

On a cold, drizzly day in April 1965, as Boston's school desegregation conflict heated up, Martin Luther King Jr. led a march from Roxbury to a "Freedom Rally" on Boston Common.[27] Crite referred to King as both an "Apostle of non-violence" and an "Apostle of freedom." Against this backdrop and that of the sit-in by Mothers for Adequate Welfare at the Grove Hall welfare office and march on Beacon Hill, Crite turned to world history.[28] In 1968, in the wake of King's assassination, Crite produced a heavily researched paper, some twenty pages long, on the history of the Western Hemisphere called *Towards a Rediscovery of the Cultural Heritage of the United States.* What Crite called a "position paper" was meant to outline the rationale for an accompanying exhibit. Crite remembered being disappointed in his high school education about other civilizations and cultures, and being told that "the Negro had made no contribution to civilization whatsoever." Crite immersed himself deeply in African and Indigenous cultural histories, dynamically describing South, Central, and North American and West and Central African peoples. Crite's paper highlighted the ways in which, for many non-Western, non-European cultures, "'art' was a part of everyday living and not a separate function." More important, perhaps, the document was an indictment of European settler colonialism and "exploration" and a call for a "better understanding" of the Indigenous cultural foundation of the Americas and the "fusion of [European, African, and Indian] blood and cultures" that is the United States.[29]

As Boston's Black Panther Party offered sickle-cell anemia screenings and health education at its Franklin Lynch Peoples' Free Health Center in a trailer in Roxbury, set up on the contested Boston Redevelopment Authority highway site, Crite took himself on a sketching tour of Boston's "adult entertainment district" (fig. 80), what folks called the Combat Zone.[30] The city had officially zoned this small, four-block area adjacent to

Boston Common in 1974 as a downtown redlight district, complete with the racial restrictions of white business owners who only hired white employees. This relegated already overcriminalized Black women sex workers to the Combat Zone, making them vulnerable to arrest and harassment.[31]

Walking through the Combat Zone with a younger Black woman friend in the late summer of 1977, Crite tried to understand the need for a place like the "Zone." Here, Crite returned to his ideas from more than a decade earlier: that technological advances continued to create an impersonal society, one generally inhospitable to humans, where the person has been "reduced to a commodity" and where people, men in particular, in Crite's estimation, must seek out human connection and love. To Crite, places like the Combat Zone emerged from human loneliness. While on their walk, a white man verbally accosted Crite and his friend, hurling racial slurs at them. In a series of captioned lithographs that read like an illustrated travelogue of his visit to the Combat Zone, Crite reflected that at least he and his friend had escaped physical harm.[32] The desegregation drama may have been unfolding in other parts of the city, but Jim Crow violence was alive and well downtown, perhaps most iconically depicted in the Pulitzer Prize–winning photograph of Ted Landsmark being attacked with the American flag in 1976 at City Hall, just north of the Combat Zone.

When Crite was interviewed in 2001 for the oral history project the HistoryMakers, he was asked whether his work had changed after his mother's death in 1977. He responded that it had not but conceded that some observers might think it had taken on a pornographic tone. Certainly, his written reflections from the time gesture toward his own sexual awakening, albeit late. But, for Crite, the naked body was merely human. Moreover, at a moment when Black women were seen by many government agencies, including the police, as menaces, whether they were sex workers or mothers advocating for a fair welfare system, Crite sketched loving homages to Black women in his "portrait studies," their beatific faces sometimes taking up the whole frame. In other sketches, a bare-chested Black heterosexual couple entwine in a sexy, tender embrace. These works would form the bases of his *River of Human Sexuality* series, the subject of his show in the early 1990s at Boston Center for the Arts (fig. 81).[33]

Fig. 81. Allan Rohan Crite, *The River of Human Sexuality,* 1992. Hand-bound book, 21.6 × 28.3 × 2 cm closed. Courtesy of the private collection of Johnetta Tinker

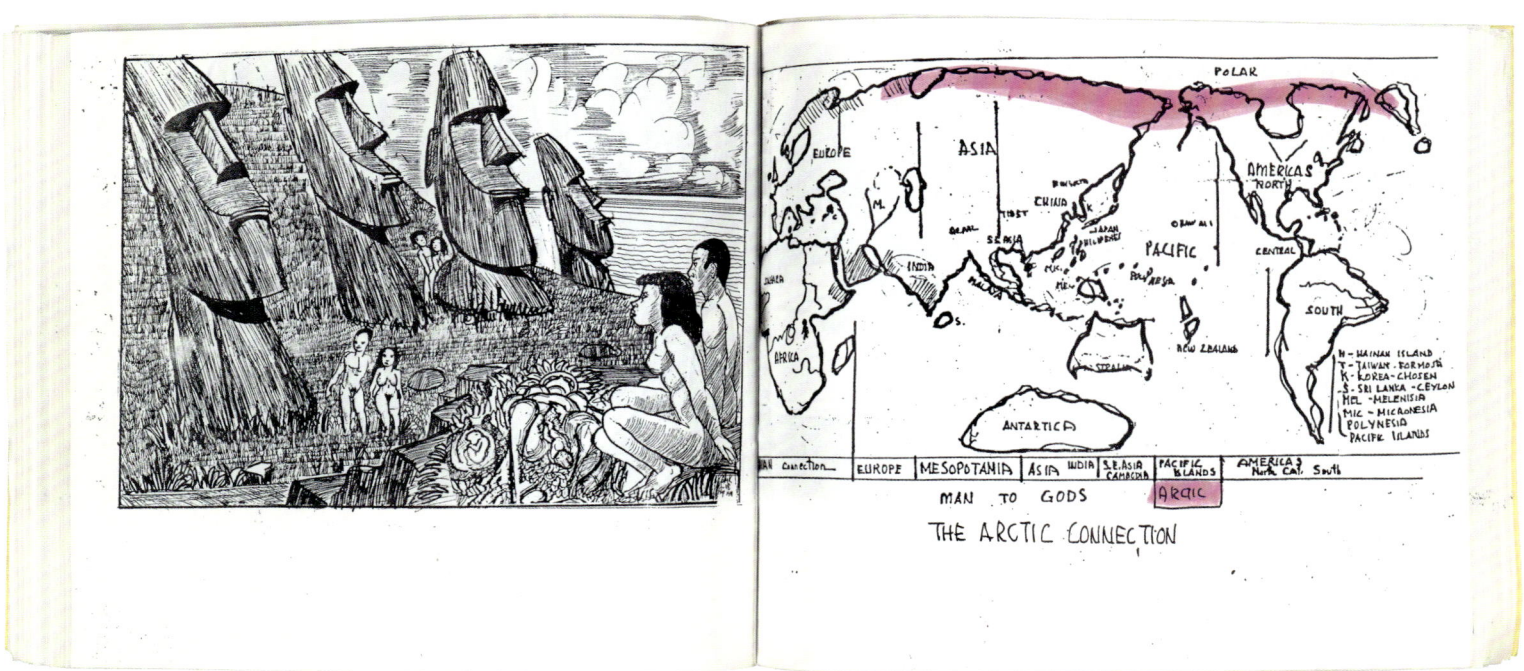

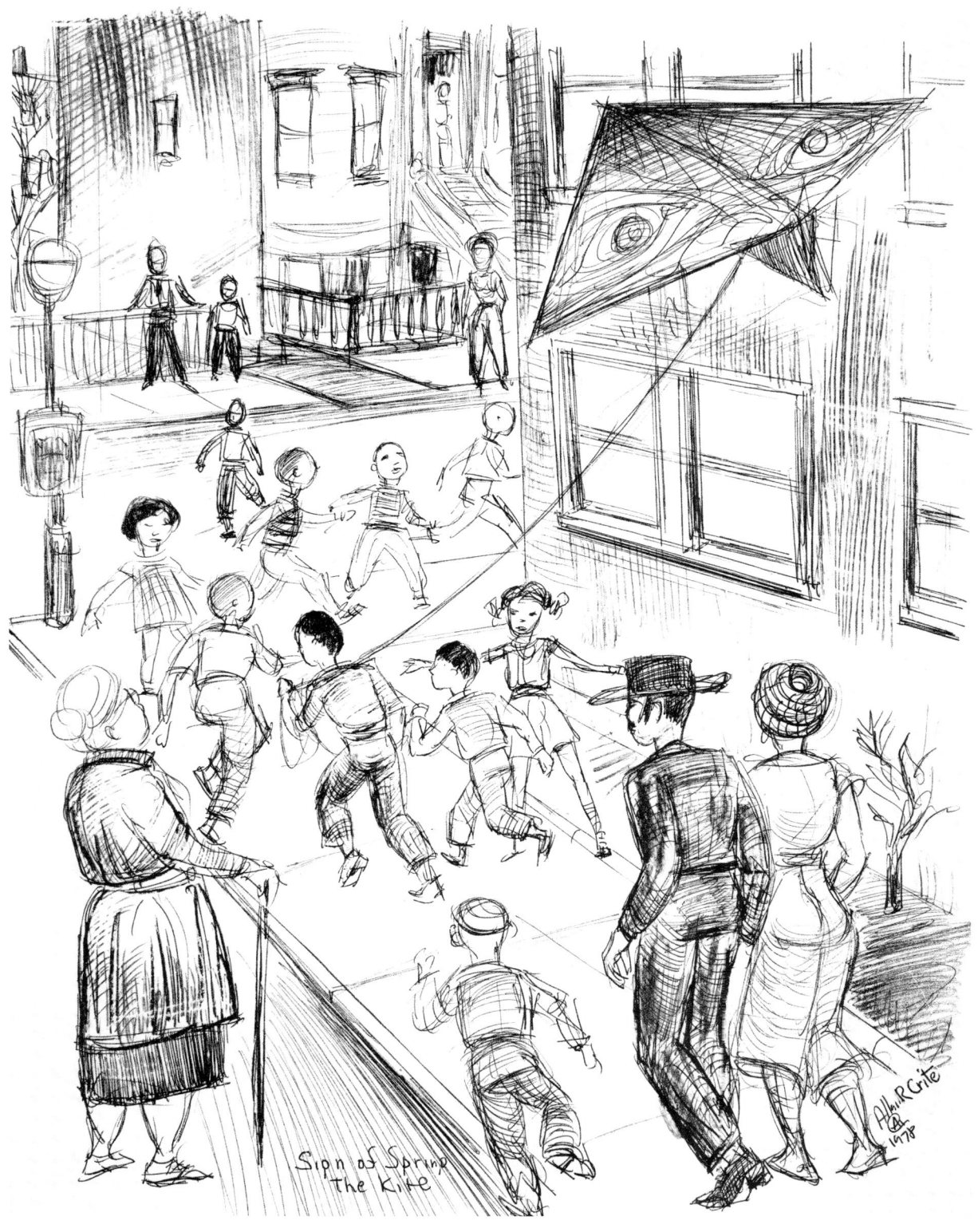

Fig. 82. Allan Rohan Crite, *Signs of Spring,* from *Neighborhood Scenes* [no. 2], 1978. Offset lithograph, 27.9 × 21.7 cm. Boston Athenaeum

In his 1977 and 1978 *Neighborhood Scenes* and *Combat Zone* offset lithograph series, Crite's work documented Boston's fraught and changing landscape, while also representing the ways in which Black people continued to live full lives in their communities. In *Signs of Spring,* for example, kids play and fly kites or follow their teachers on a field trip, parents holding their children's hands (fig. 82). These images stood in contrast to the violence that Black children in Boston experienced in their poor and underresourced schools, and in the generally unsuccessful efforts to integrate Boston-area schools.

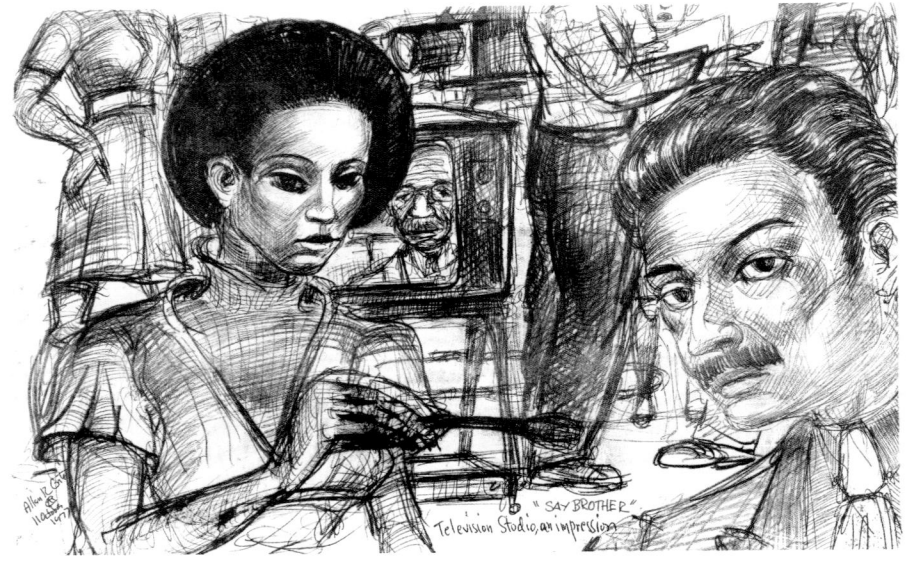

Crite used his appearance on *Say Brother,* Boston's first Black public affairs television program and the media's answer to the racial reckoning that followed Martin Luther King's assassination, to talk about education (fig. 83).[34] In the episode, which aired in the fall of 1977, Crite introduced his fourth- and fifth-grade illustrated curriculum, based on his 1968 publication *Towards a Rediscovery of the Cultural Heritage of the United States.* He hoped that this curricular intervention would disabuse students of a "parochial view" of the United States.[35] Inspired by the Black Power movement and the energy and popularity of Negro History Week, established fifty years earlier and expanded in 1976 to Black History Month, Crite's curriculum also grew out of his own educational experience and his relatively new membership on the board of the Children's Art Centre, a longtime institution in the South End, where Crite had taken classes as a child. Crite was working to create hundreds of watercolor drawings to be made into photographic slides accompanied by recordings of the content from *Towards a Rediscovery* for schools that had agreed to pilot his curriculum, which, according to Crite, were two South End schools, his alma mater, the Bancroft School, and the Blackstone Elementary School, and St. Luke's School in New York City.[36] Crite insisted that his lesson plans were for all children, with the intention of teaching them about the "multi-racial" origins of the United States, what he called an "Afro Eurasian culture on an Indigenous base." It was a curriculum that Crite believed could prepare children for "one world." While Boston was "seeing whirlpools of social change [and] the resistance to change," Crite saw the "rich cultural heritage of the United States, [and] the potential for a cultural renaissance" founded on the "basic diversity of the peoples of the Americas." [37]

As early as the late 1970s, Crite also weighed in on reproductive justice. In a later self-published booklet that gathered a series of short essays he had written on the topic over the years, titled *Men, Abortion, Sex, and Other Essays,* he criticized the high value that capitalist society put on human reproduction and Christian conservativism's tremendous influence on the state, which led to withholding not only contraception but also sex education for young people. Crite's writings bring into relief the rise of the conservative religious Right in the late twentieth century and its impact on daily life. In Crite's estimation, "an industrialized society has a strong anti-life element," and in a "male dominated society . . . [women's] needs are not an area of consideration."[38]

For Crite, this period also served as the backdrop for the formation of a Black arts collective that revolved around him as their "patriarch" and "dean." He was nearly seventy years old when the Boston Collective—a group of young Black artists living and

working in Boston—gathered and exhibited their work together.[39] Crite described it as an informal gathering space where artists who worked in different media found camaraderie and fellowship.[40] Photographer Aukram Burton, visual artist and arts educator Lotus Do, photojournalist Reginald Jackson, dancer Weeta Lopes, textile artist Susan Thompson, painter and graphic artist Johnetta Tinker, painter Paul Goodnight, sculptor Vusumuzi Maduna (Dennis Didley), and textile artist Napoleon Jones-Henderson, who had just come to Boston from Chicago, where he was a member of AfriCOBRA, a Black revolutionary arts organization, made up the membership of the Collective.[41]

Many remember Crite's support and mentorship, and Crite reveled in the role of elder in the group, calling members his "sons and daughters." But Crite's support for younger artists was a consistent element of his life. Sculptor John Wilson, whose bust of Martin Luther King Jr. sits in the U.S. Capitol Rotunda and whose large bronze heads are in the collections of the Museum of Fine Arts and the Museum of the National Center of Afro-American Artists in Roxbury, lauded Crite's early support for him as a teenage artist in the 1930s, when there were few Black artist role models. Crite encouraged Wilson to "keep up the good work" and offered him information and advice for applying to what would be his first prize winning exhibition.[42] But Wilson noted that it was not just Crite's encouragement that inspired other Black artists coming up in Boston; it was also the "sensitivity" with which Crite depicted Black people and his "total disciplined commitment to the perfection of his art."[43]

Crite's interest in world history and the Black diaspora informed the mission of the Boston Collective, and with funding from the Massachusetts Council on the Arts and Humanities, the Massachusetts Office of International Trade and Investment (fig. 84), the Community Fellows Program in the Department of Urban Studies and Planning at MIT, a program started by community activist and state representative Mel King, and the US-China Peoples Friendship Association, the Collective took its work to China and was part of an exhibit at the Guangzhou Academy of Fine Arts in 1986, just three years before the Tiananmen Square protests.[44] In Crite's HistoryMakers interview, he marveled at the size of the square itself, describing it as the "Boston Common and the Public Gardens, extend[ed] down to . . . Massachusetts Avenue."[45]

Crite's work with the Collective also yielded his book *Reflections on the Afro-Asian-American Cultural Heritage of Peoples of Color* in 1985, which begins with an intricately drawn panel featuring Crite at the center, surrounded by members of the Collective, other artists, such as Barbara Ward Armstrong and Theresa-India Young, community leaders like Mel King, former director of the Harriet Tubman Gallery Robin Barlow, Hazel Bright, an administrator at Roxbury Community College, Byron Rushing, then a state representative, and Barry Gaither, director of the newly formed National Center of Afro-American Artists in Roxbury. Situated around the panel, in the fashion of plate-glass windows, are a dense array of "neighborhood and ancestors," "watching over" Crite and his chosen family. A continuation of his 1968 essay, *Reflections* included panels for Arabia, Korea, the Olmecs, and Nubia. Crite traced "the routes of the migrations of Man," undoing the erasure and "denial" of the histories of peoples of color and the misrepresentation of those people as "recipients of Europe's enlightenment." "The recovery of the heritage of Peoples of Color," Crite insisted, "is a recovery for all."[46]

In 2001, Crite reflected on his career as an artist, first, and a Black man, second. Still, he said, the Black community was reflected throughout his work, in every visual story he told. When asked if he had a favorite piece, he responded, "as far as I'm concerned, it's all ONE piece." For Crite, "everything that's ever happened on this earth [was] part of [his] heritage . . . part of everyone's heritage": a human heritage. His interests, he said, took in "the whole planet." He warned that "we better wake up to the fact that we are one people, or wake up to the dubious distinction of being the only civilization that brought about its own extinction."[47]

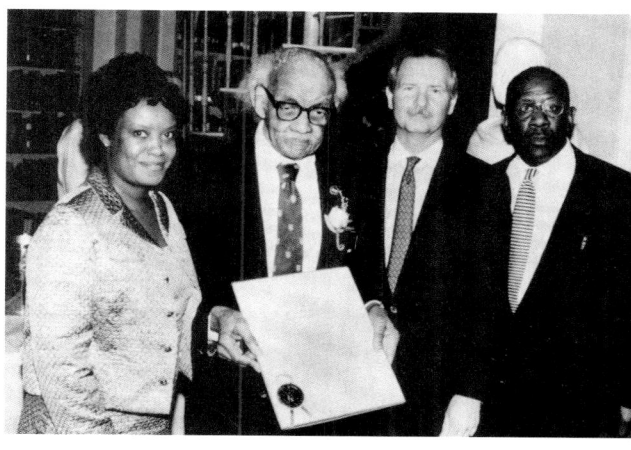

Fig. 84. Allan Rohan Crite receives a proclamation from the Massachusetts secretary of state, 1997. Boston Athenaeum

Notes

1 For Terence's statement, see Angelou 2011.

2 See Crite 1977a, "558 Massachusetts Avenue."

3 See Roses 2017; Greenidge 2019, 216–33, 297–99.

4 See Boston Symphony Orchestra 2023; "Appendix III: An Approach to Non-Western Art and Non-Western Art in Africa—A Pilgrimage," in Crite n.d. [after 1970], 8.

5 See Crite 1948, unpaginated.

6 See Walshin 1997, 17–19; Mellin 1997–98.

7 Gordon 2023.

8 See Boston Redevelopment Authority 1965.

9 Quoted in McLaughlin 1981; see also "List of Boston Residents, 1909–1972" and "Boston, Massachusetts, City Directory" for 1972, both at Boston Public Library; Crite n.d. [after 1970], 54.

10 Crite 1977a, "2 Dilworth Street"; see Walshin 1997, 17–19; Boston Redevelopment Authority 1965; Mellin 1997–98; Crite n.d. [after 1970], 15, 34.

11 See Crite 2001.

12 See Clark 1979.

13 See McLaughlin 1981.

14 See Clark 1979.

15 See Crite n.d. [after 1970], 39.

16 See Allan Rohan Crite, personal statement, 1962–65, in Crite 1927–68, box 2, folder 16.

17 See Chicago Defender 1940.

18 "Appendix III: An Approach to Non-Western Art and Non-Western Art in Africa—A Pilgrimage," in Crite n.d. [after 1970], 3–4; Greenidge 2019, 297–99.

19 Sullivan 2016; Boston Daily Globe 1922.

20 National Park Service 2024.

21 Crite n.d. [after 1970], 18.

22 Ibid., 22.

23 "The Religious Artist and This Culture," included in the self-published booklet The Vocation of Christian Art, n.d., in Crite 1948–2002, MS L757, folder 3, "Lectures."

24 Ibid.

25 "A Statement: One of the Problems in the United States," n.d., in Crite 1927–68, box 2, folder 16.

26 Crite n.d. [after 1970], 32–33; see also Carvalho 2015.

27 See Grimberg and Readdean 2023; Levey 1965a and 1965b.

28 See Fripp 1967; Bay State Banner 1967.

29 Towards a Rediscovery of the Cultural Heritage of the United States, in Crite n.d. [after 1970], 40–41.

30 Bassett 2016; Schorow, 2017.

31 Fischer 2022, 108–13.

32 Crite 1978.

33 Stapen 1992.

34 See Heitner 2009.

35 WGBH 1977.

36 Crite n.d. [after 1970], 41–44.

37 WGBH 1977.

38 Crite 1990, 1–3.

39 See Tanga 2024b.

40 See Crite 2001.

41 See Tanga 2024b.

42 Allan Rohan Crite to John Wilson [1943]; see also John Wilson, notes for a talk on Allan Rohan Crite, n.d., John Wilson Archive, Brookline, MA.

43 John Wilson, notes for a talk on Allan Rohan Crite, n.d., John Wilson Archive, Brookline, MA.

44 Barlow 1986.

45 See Crite 2001.

46 Crite 1985, unpaginated preface.

47 See Crite 2001.

PLATES 1946–1960

Plate 24. Allan Rohan Crite, *Groton Street, South End, Boston,* 1946. Watercolor, gouache, and black ink over graphite on paper, 36.7 × 29.7 cm. Boston Athenaeum

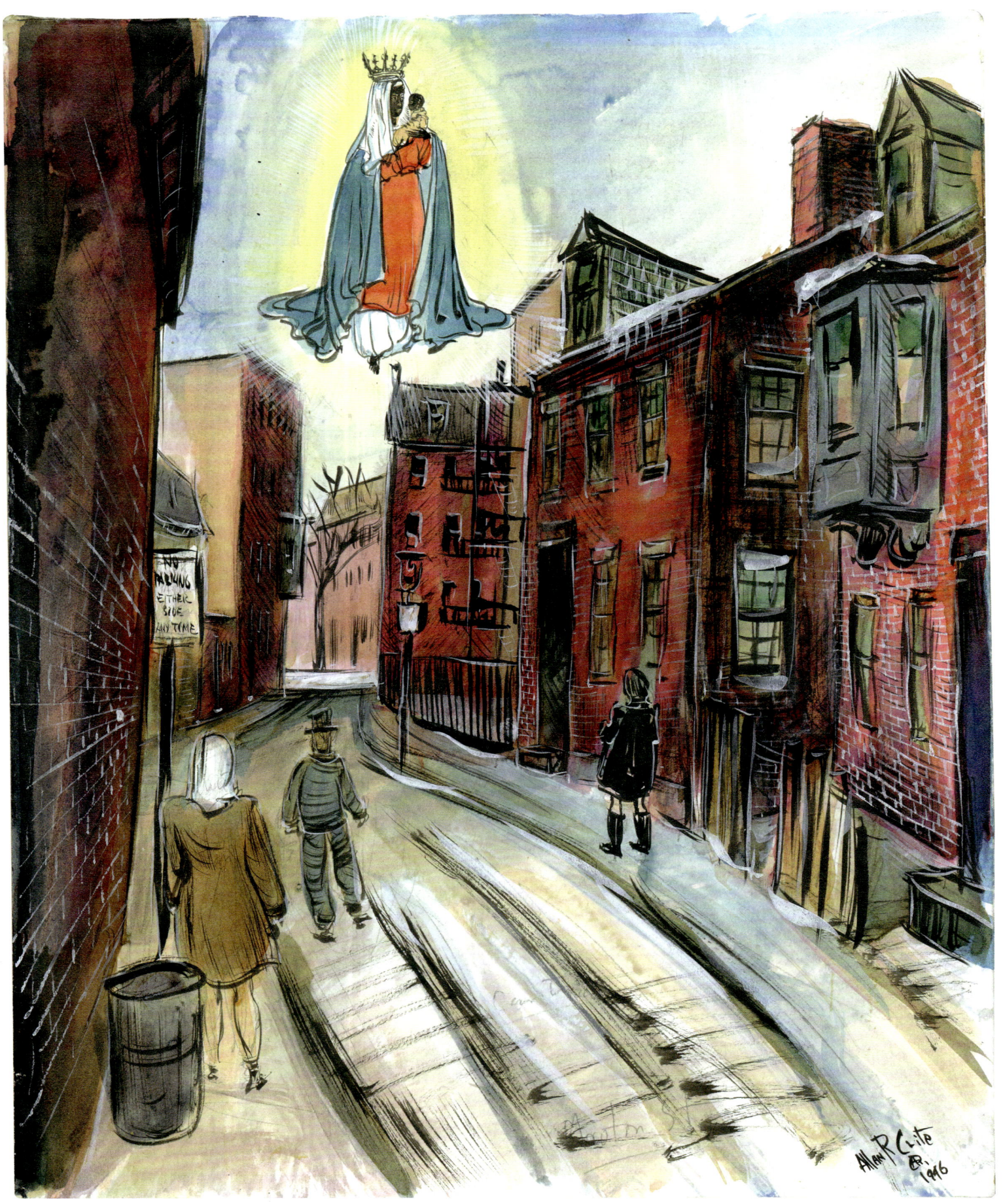

Plate 25. Allan Rohan Crite, *The Stations of the Cross I,* 1947. Linoleum cut with hand-applied watercolor and metal leaf, 42 × 31 cm. Museum of Fine Arts, Boston

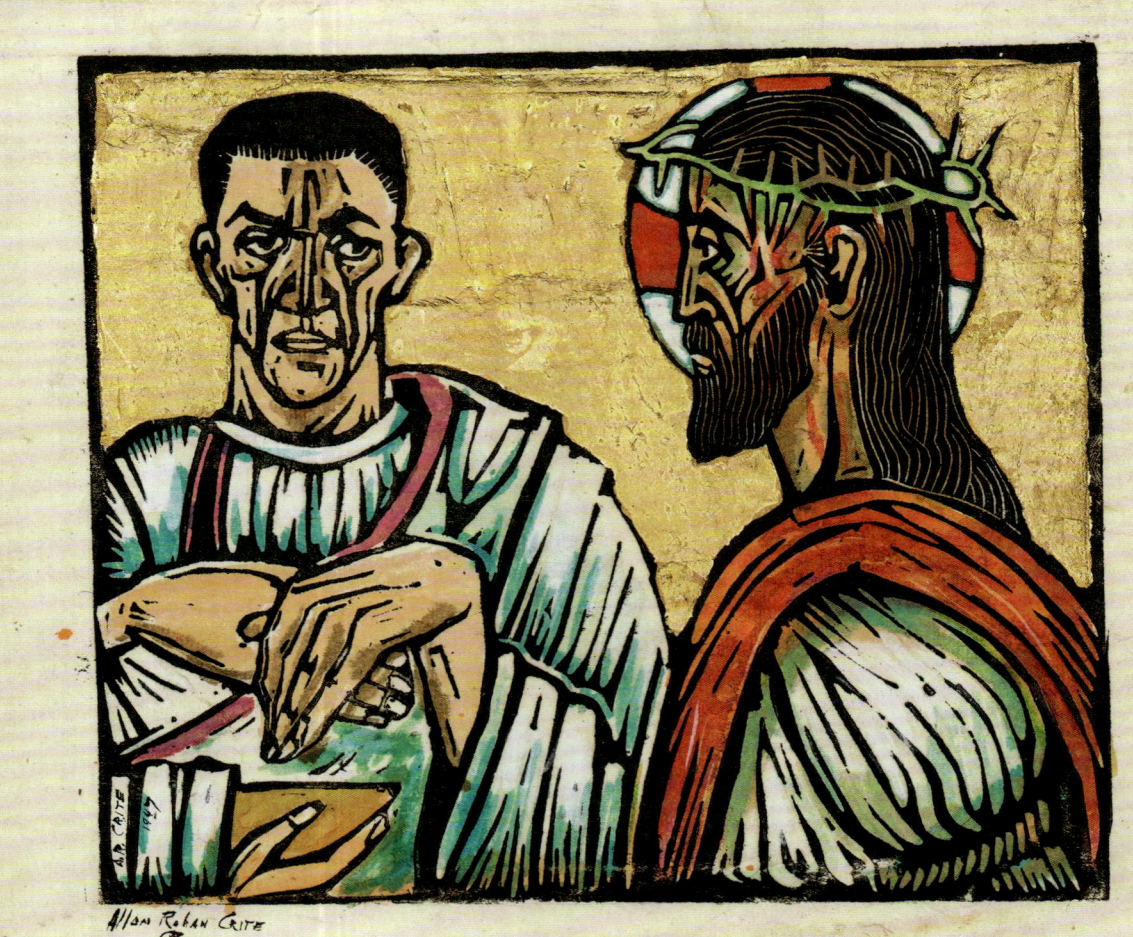

Allan Rohan Crite
1947

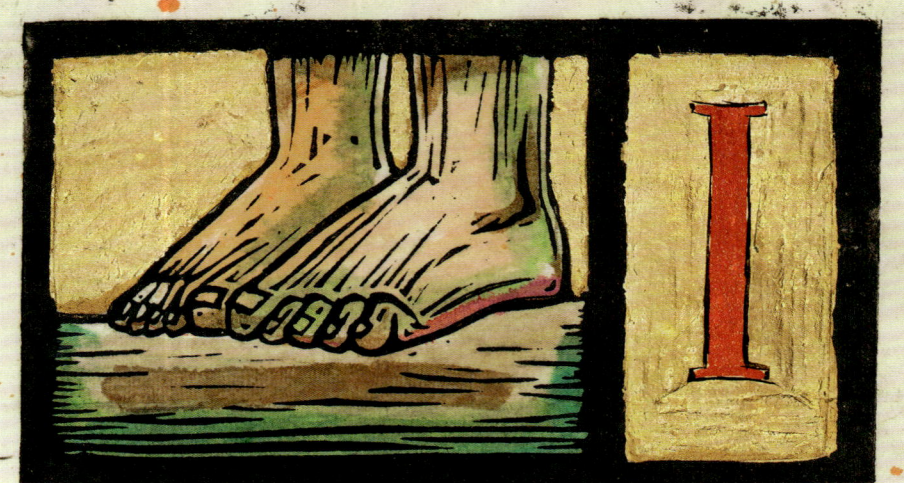

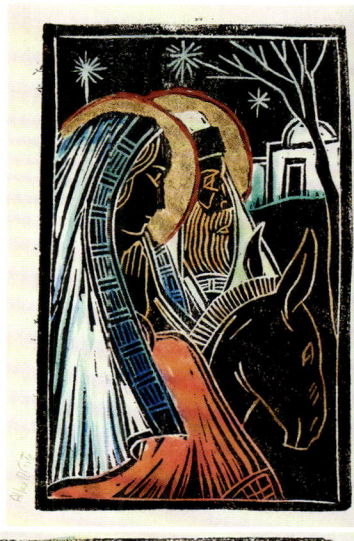

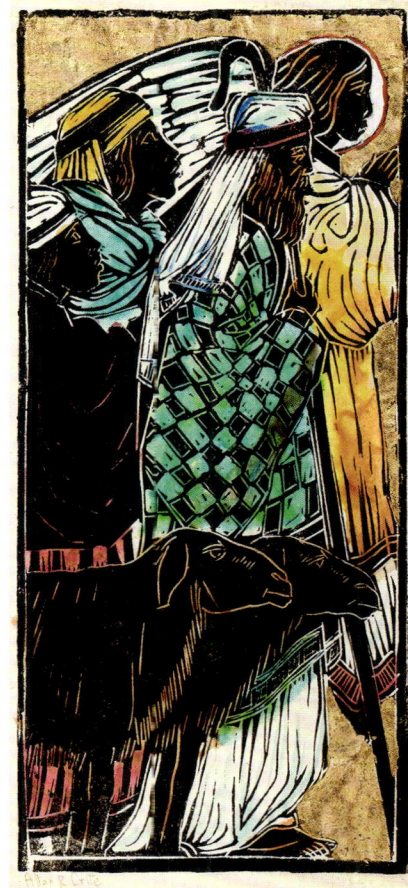

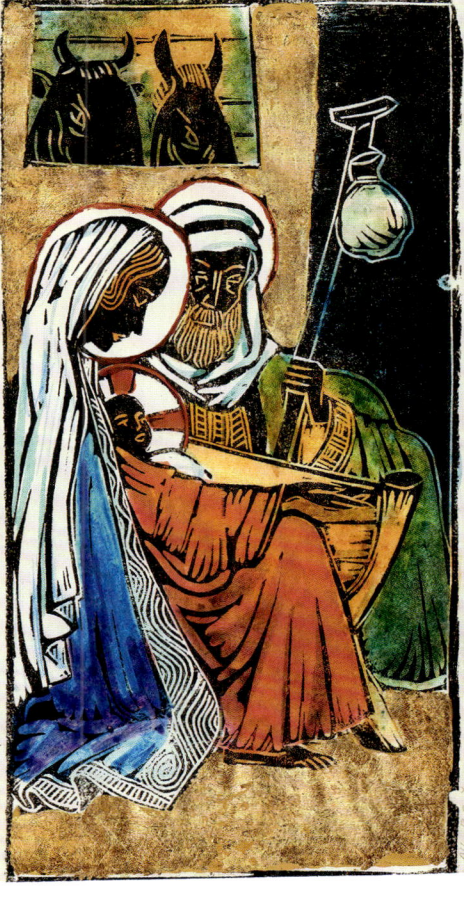

Plate 26. Allan Rohan Crite, *The Nativity According to St. Luke,* about 1947. Linoleum cuts,
with hand-applied transparent and opaque watercolor, metallic paint, and metal leaf on paper
41.3 × 66.7 cm. Museum of Fine Arts, Boston

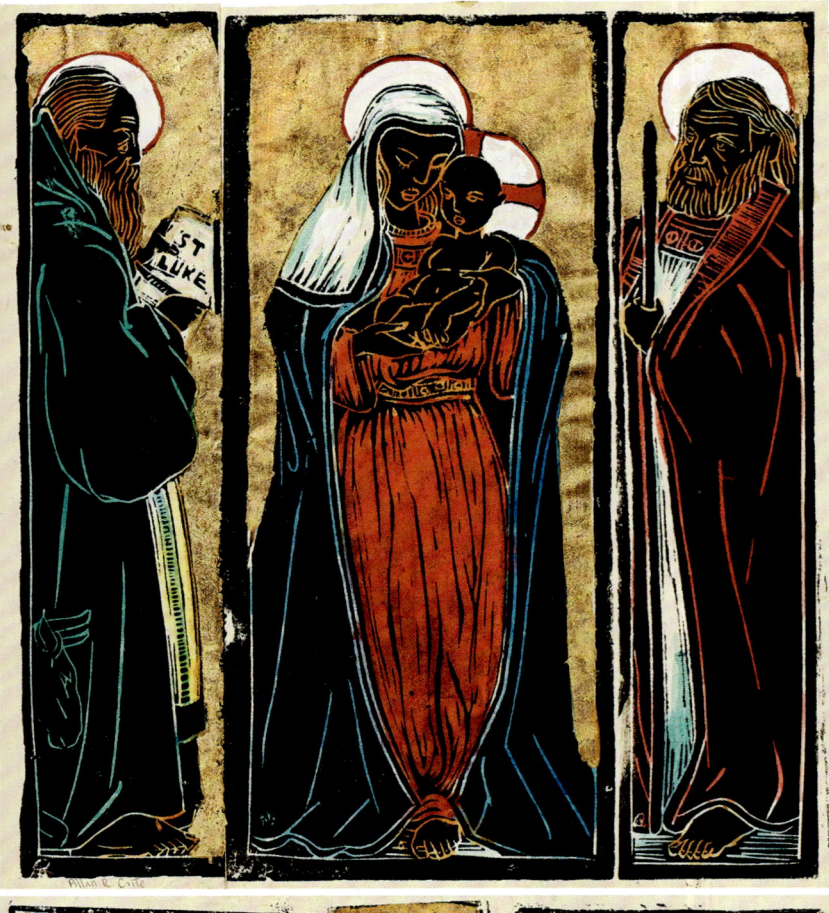
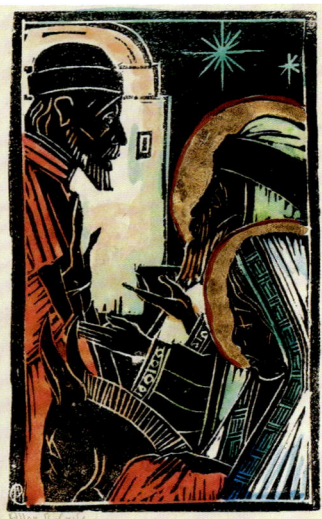
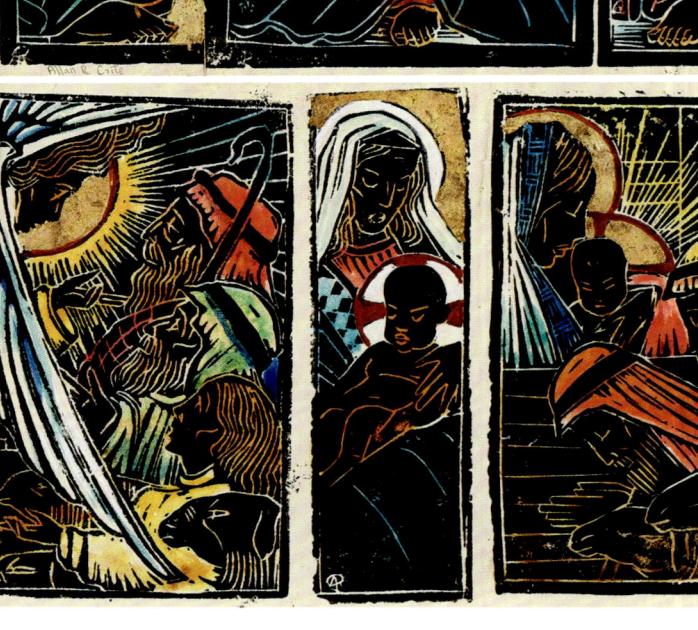
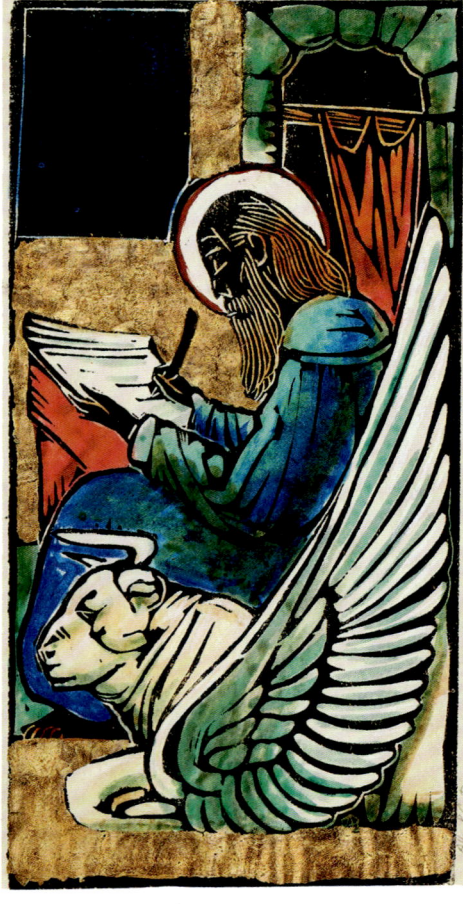
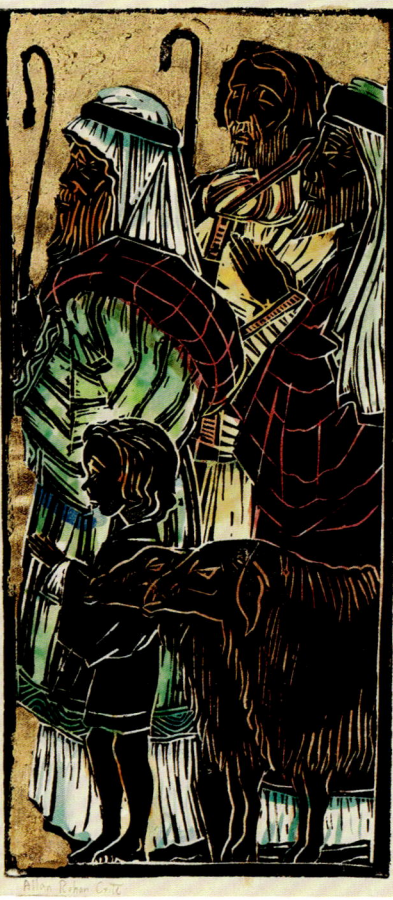

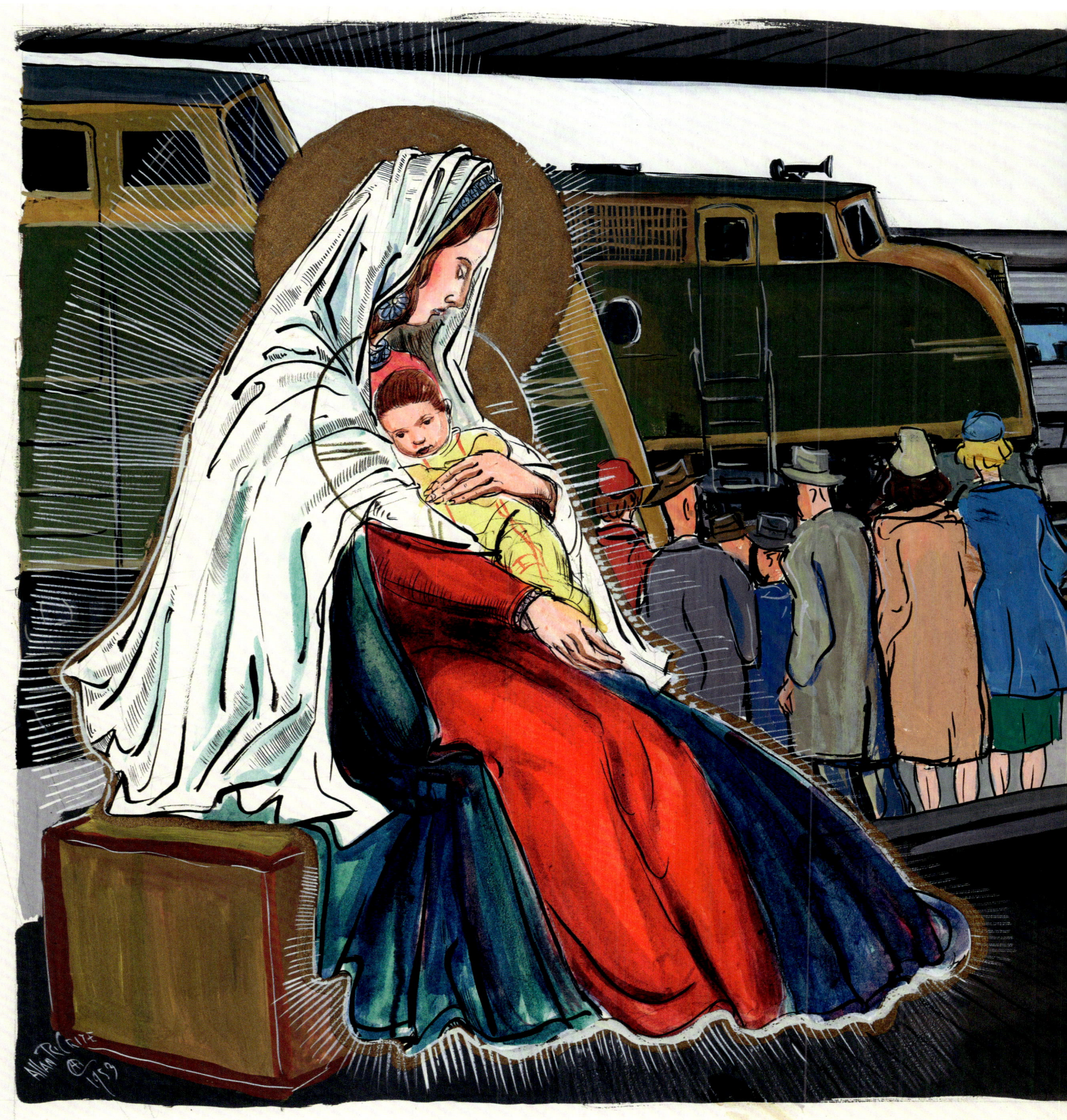

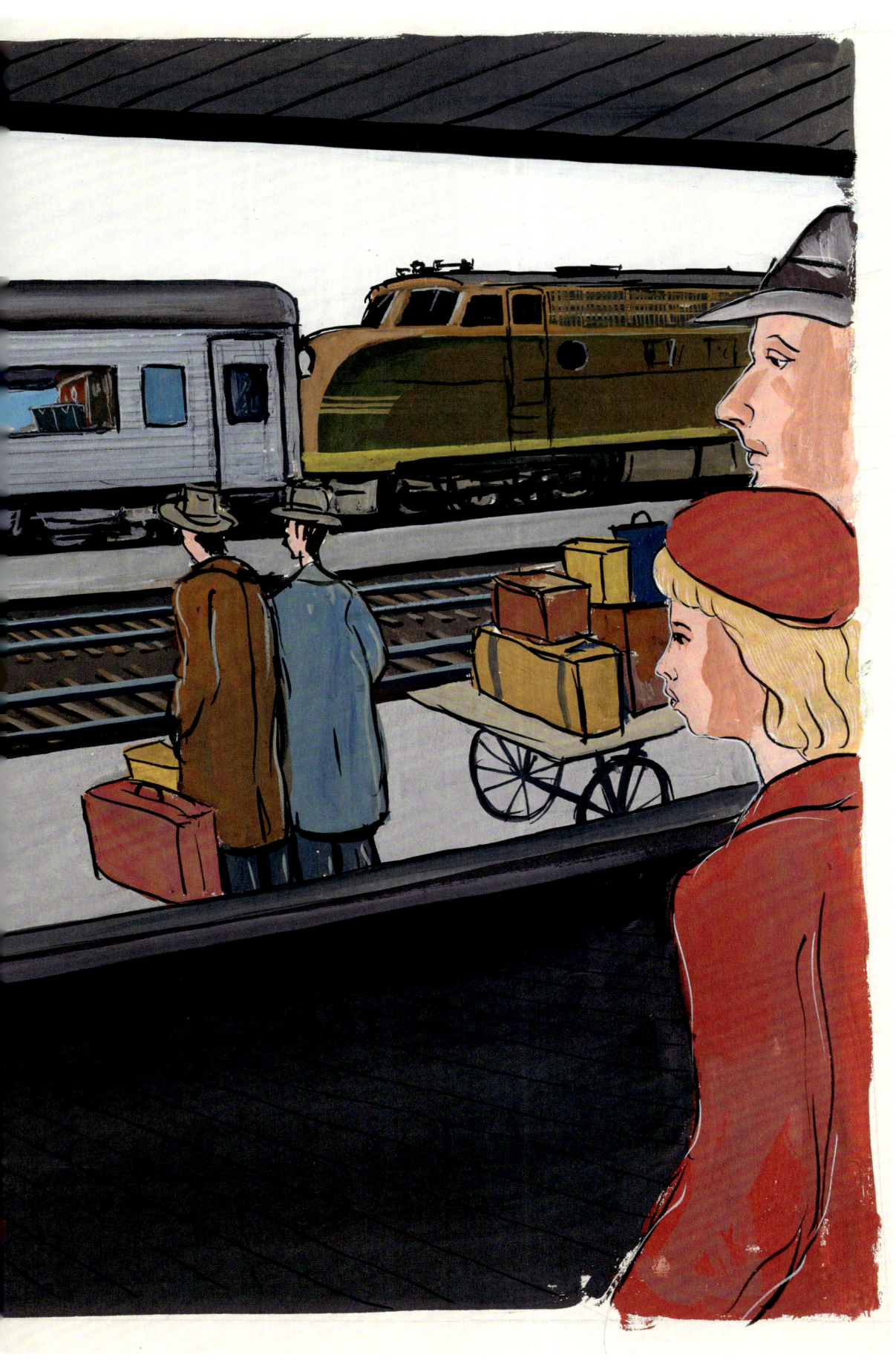

Plate 27. Allan Rohan Crite, *Our Lady of the R. R. [Railroad] Station,* 1953. Gouache on paper, 50.8 × 76.2 cm. Arts Department, Special Collections, Boston Public Library

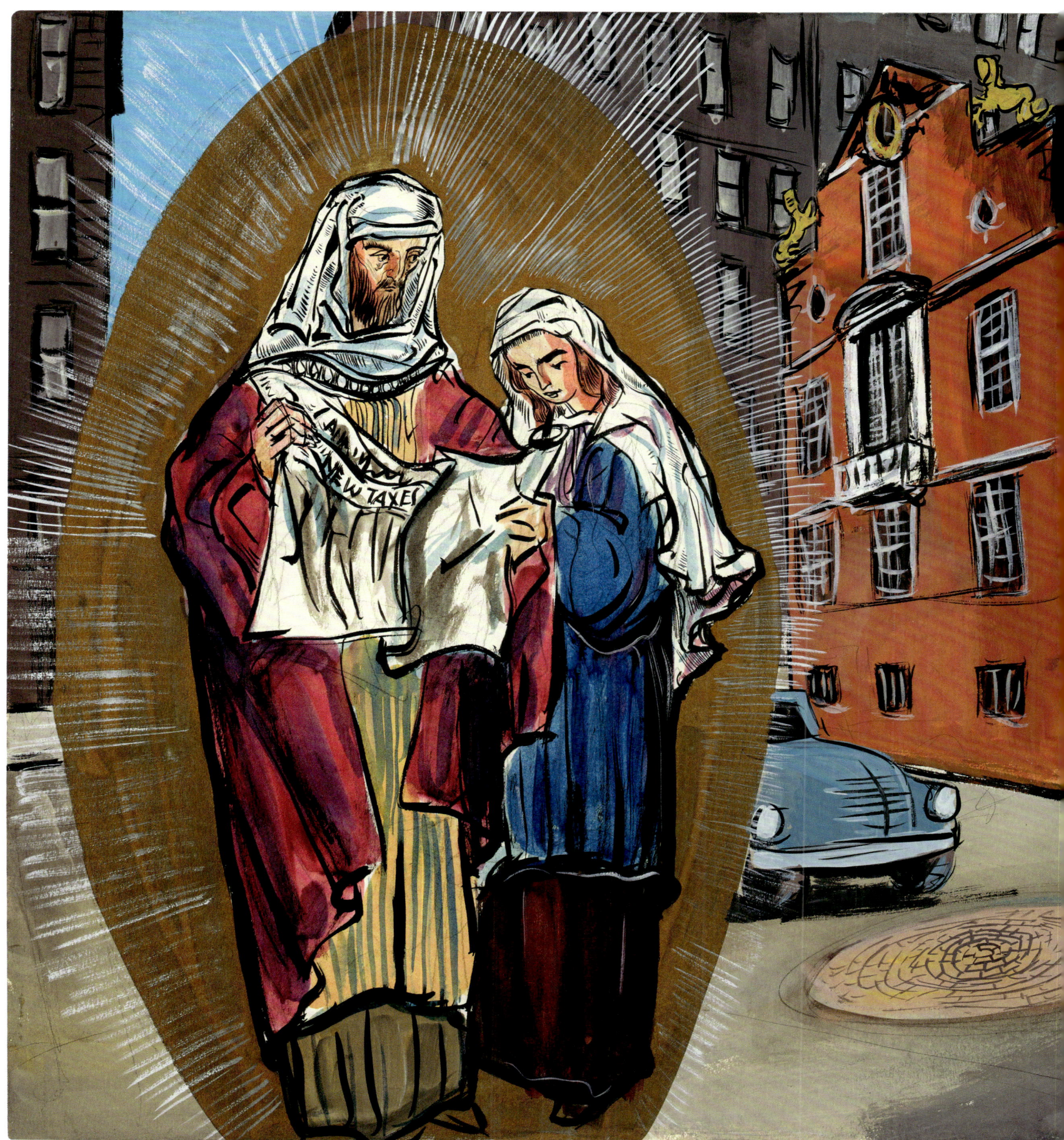

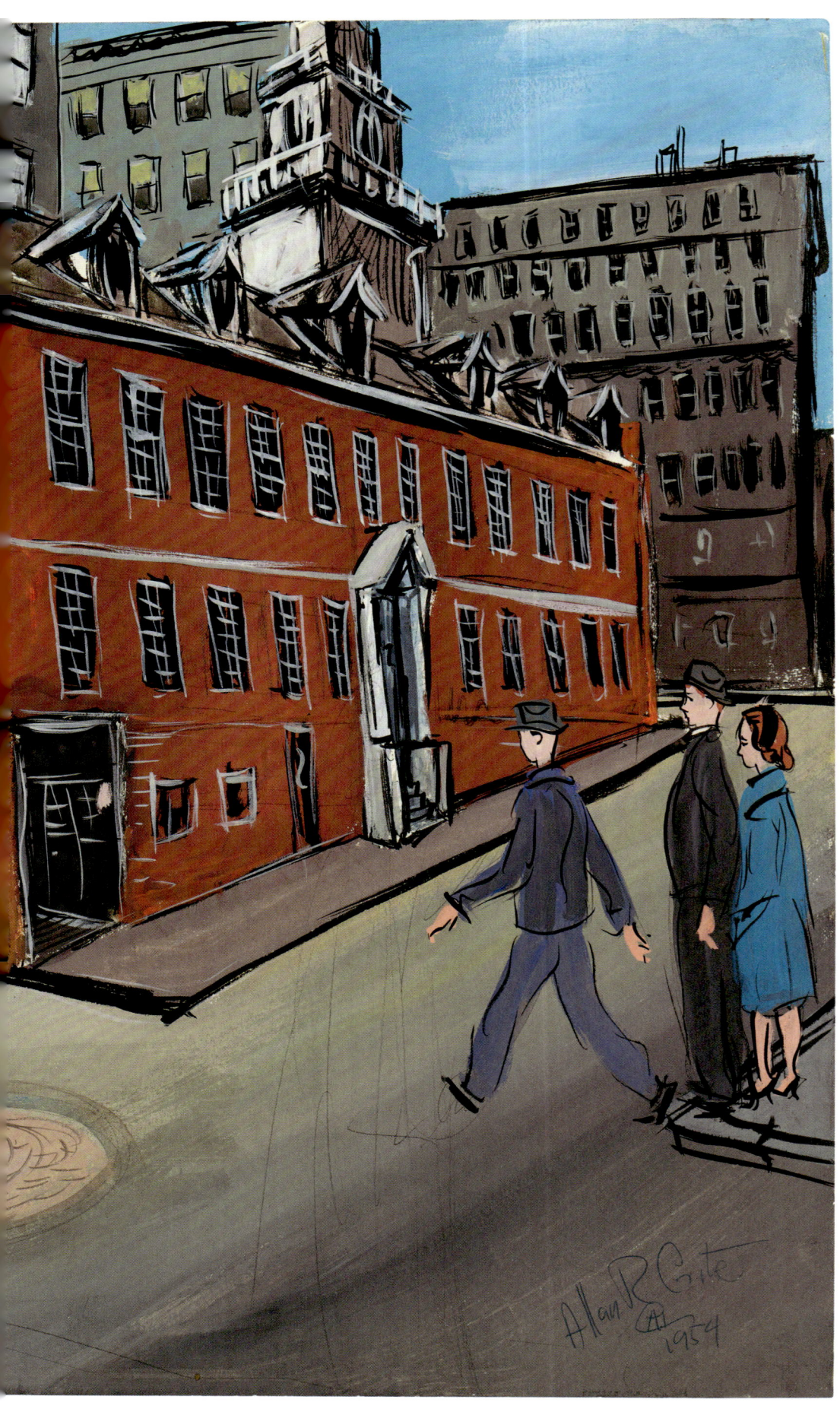

Plate 28. Allan Rohan Crite, *The Tax Announcements (Old State House)*, 1954. Gouache on paper, 50.8 × 76.2 cm. Arts Department, Special Collections, Boston Public Library

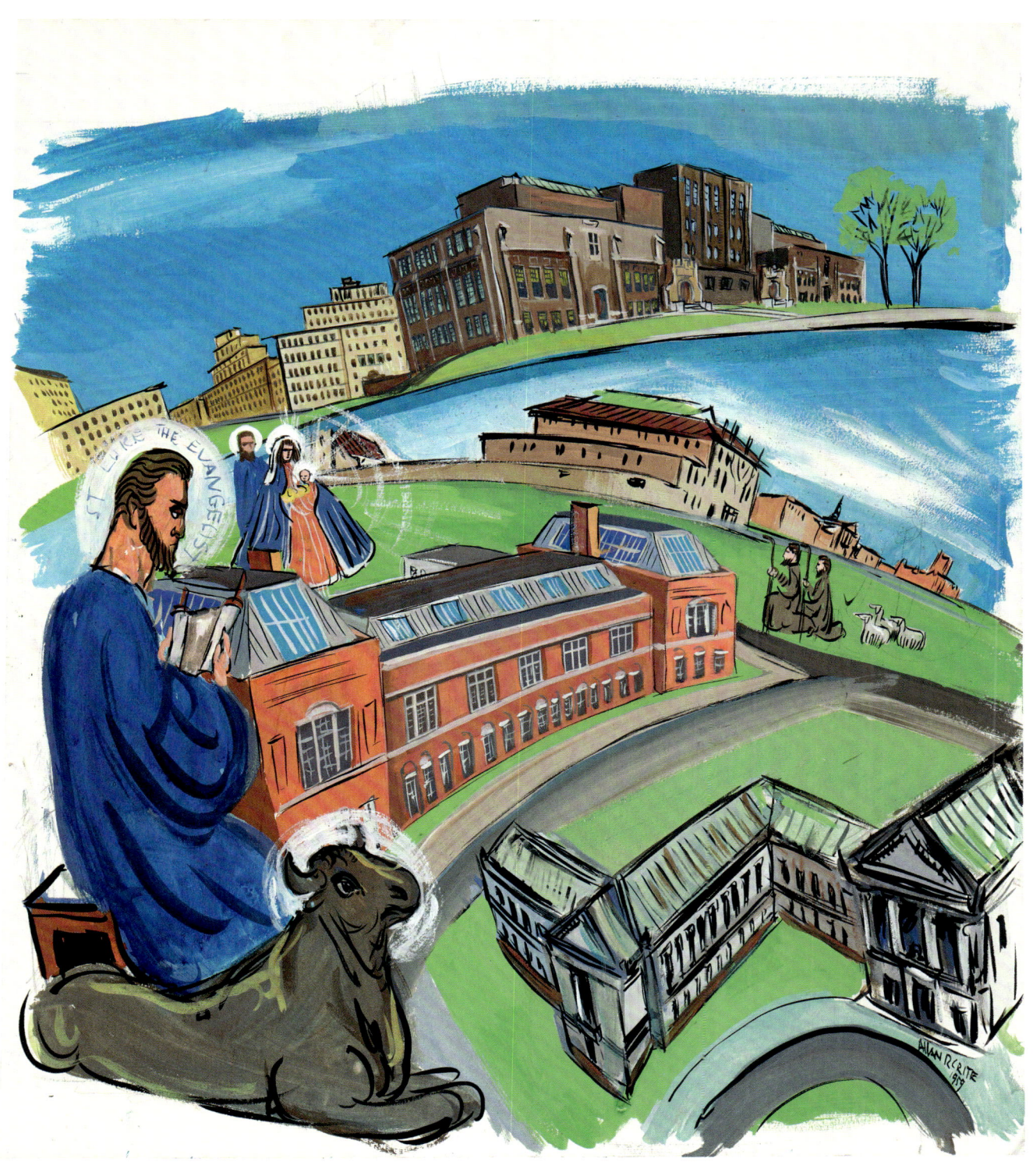

Plate 29. Allan Rohan Crite, *St. Luke the Evangelist,* 1959. Gouache on paper, 48.3 × 45.7 cm
Arts Department, Special Collections, Boston Public Library

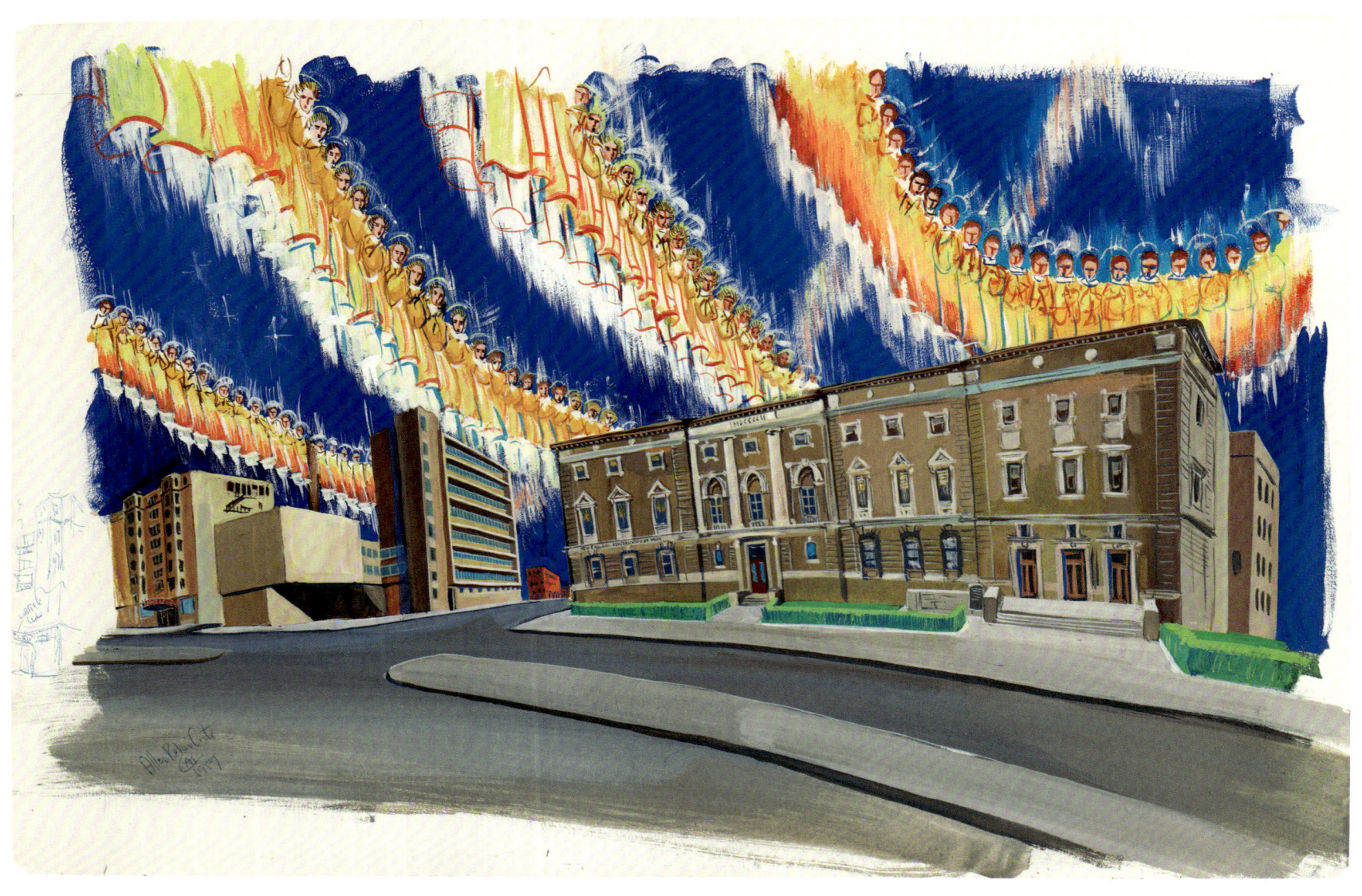

Plate 30. Allan Rohan Crite, *Untitled (Empty College Campus Facing Street, with Choirs of Yellow Robed Angels in the Sky)*, 1959. Gouache on paper, 50.8 × 76.2 cm. Arts Department, Special Collections, Boston Public Library

Overleaf: Plate 31. Allan Rohan Crite, *Untitled (Annunciation Scene with Angel and Mary, Overlaid on Emmanuel Administration Building and Simmons College Academic Building)*, 1959. Gouache on paper, 50.8 × 76.2 cm. Arts Department, Special Collections, Boston Public Library

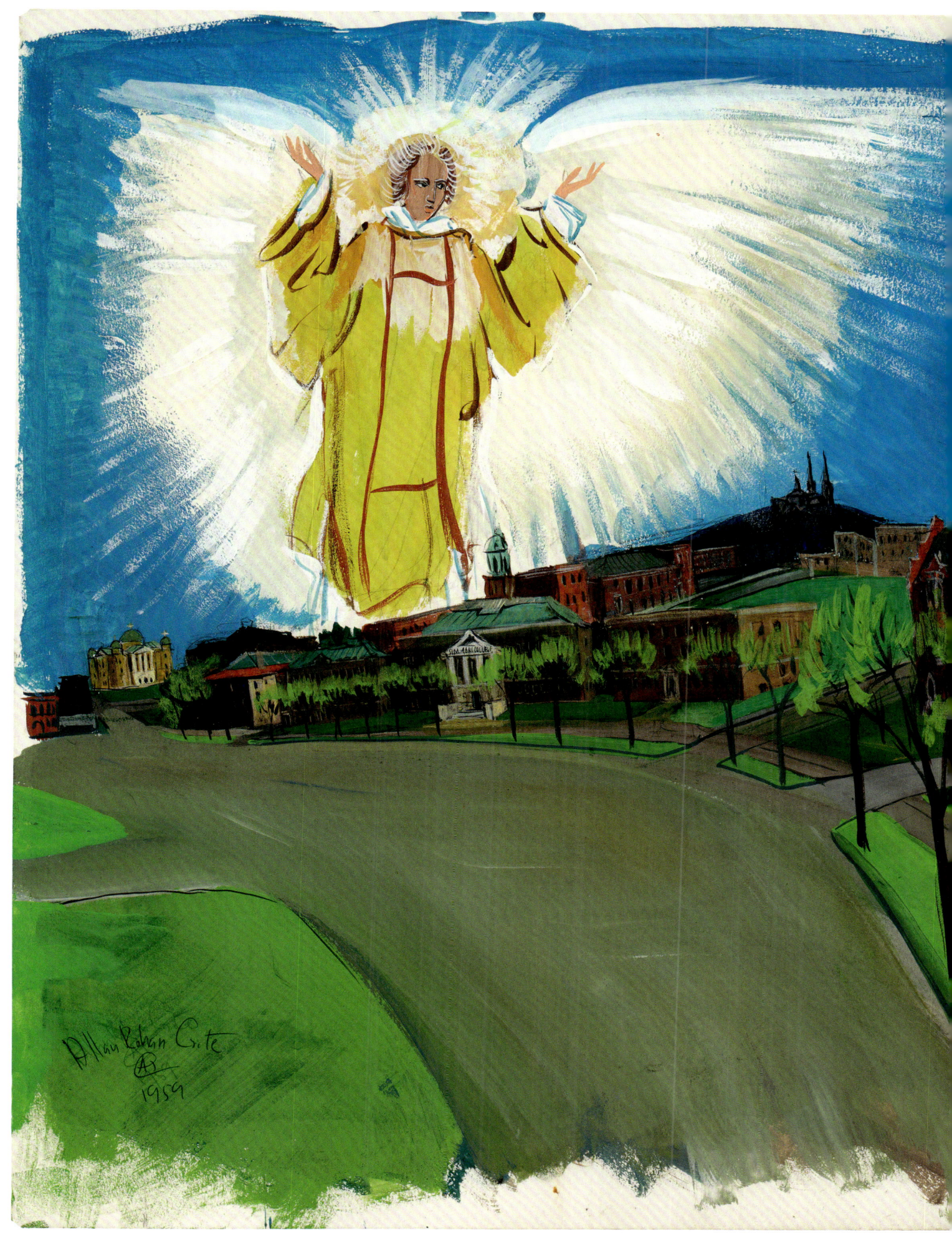

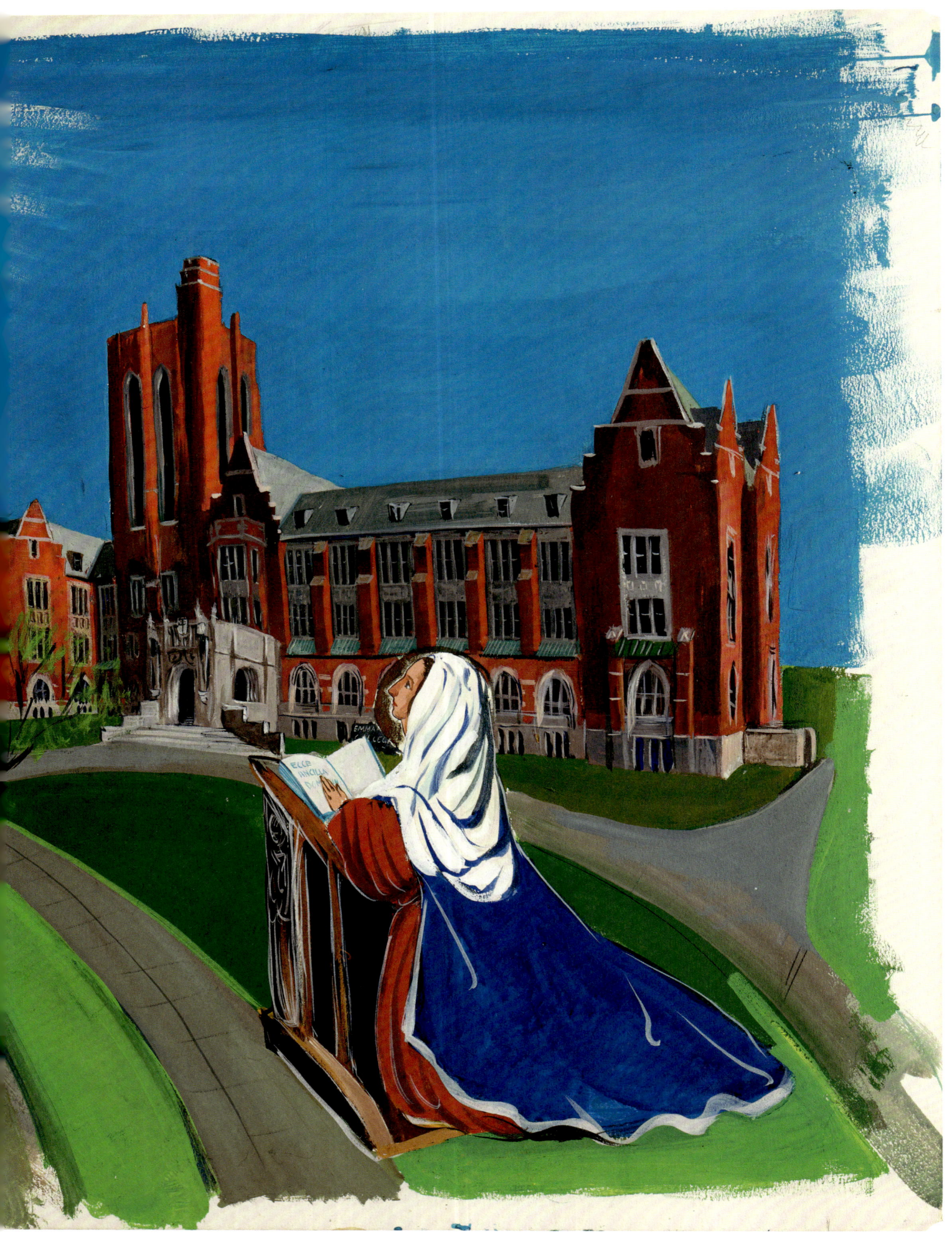

THE IMPORTANCE OF ANNAMAE CRITE

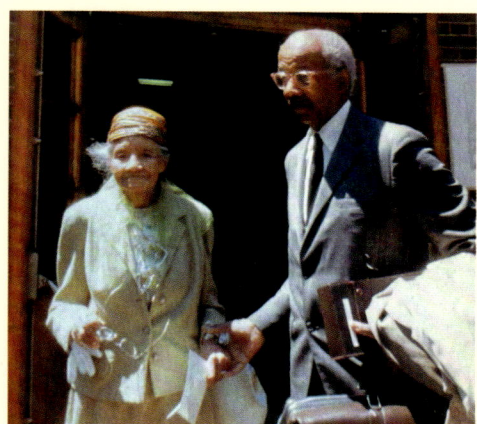

Fig. 85. Allan Rohan Crite and his mother, about 1970

"Visiting in the time of his mother had a protocol. You came in, his mother . . . was bedridden [when I visited], and she would be in place in her receiving room and bedroom on the second floor. So the first thing you did was to go up to the second floor and present yourself essentially at the foot of her bed with greetings, and she sort of stamped your approval and then you got

to see everything else. She was fully the person who you had to be cleared by to get the rest of the tour."

Barry Gaither

"I often say his mother wanted three things for him, and she lived to see them all fulfilled. She wanted him to have a lifelong relationship to the Episcopal Church . . . and he built and sustained that relationship. She wanted him to have a relationship to Harvard University, herself being among the early students of the Extension School. He himself earned a degree from the Extension School, so that Harvard relationship got cemented in place. And the third thing she wanted for him was a career in the arts. From when he was a small boy, she was taking him to museums, to the MFA, to the Isabella Stewart Gardner, those two in particular. And he was already learning and studying art in the South End. So she put him on the path that he was then to build on." (Fig. 85)

Barry Gaither

"[His mother] was so important [in] forming his love of his Blackness at a time when it was just so unique and . . . uncelebrated. He was really against the grain. . . . So where do you get that from? You know, you get that from your family."

Denise Patmon

"[Annamae Crite] was a lovely lady. . . . She had a wealth of ideas and embraced the arts. I think it's sometimes difficult for us in this period of time to appreciate what a sacrifice it was to pay for your child to take, I don't know, piano lessons, and art lessons. . . . It was a sacrifice that she calculated was absolutely the right thing for her son." (Fig. 86)

Denise Patmon

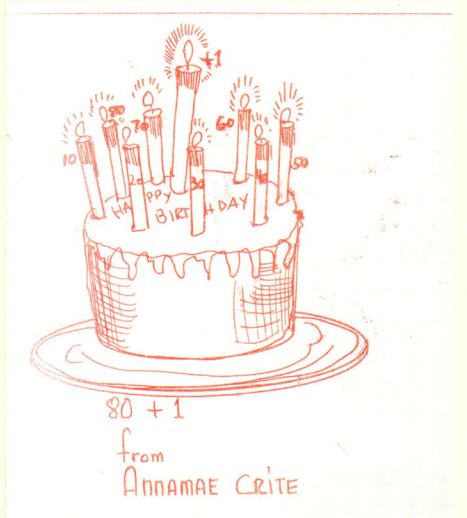

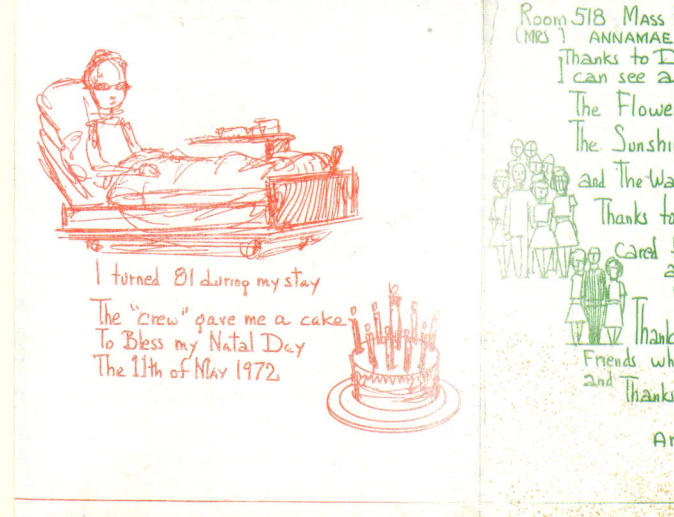

Fig. 86. Allan Rohan Crite, birthday card for Annamae Crite, 1972. Offset color lithograph, 12.9 × 11.1 cm. Collection of Susan Thompson

CRITE AND CHRISTIAN ART

"He showed the sacred personages, the holy figures, and Christ and Mary as Black. And this was not a standard practice. It was actually a daring direction to go. There were very few other artists who had taken that step of representing the holy personages as people of color. And that really struck me. And it continued to be the case throughout the whole body of his work." (Fig. 87)

Barry Gaither

"He would say, 'Denise, I need to get over to the post office,' because he had to post . . . the bulletins . . . for different . . . churches. He had to post at a certain time, and we would go down to the big post office near South Station . . . so that it would get to the church on time. . . . It's always amazing to just see him crank out these church programs on his own printing press." (Fig. 88)

Denise Patmon

"I would drive him to the post office to mail out these bulletins. And I think how it worked, he would do a month's worth of bulletins for every church. And each week would have a different cover. . . . I would see him running off the church bulletins—that was his tithe, really, that was his giving back that, because it wasn't a paid job, but he would do it. It was like a duty to do these church bulletins."

Susan Thompson

"With the liturgical art, he's telling the story through art. He's telling the story of Christ through his art. And the fact that it's not a white Christ, that his Christ is Mexican, his Christ is Black. So people see themselves if you're worshipping the Christ as God (fig. 89). Visually, if he's portrayed as white, then does that mean God is white? Is that what it means when this is what we see in the churches, or how he's portrayed in Europe? Allan broke with that, and he says, 'No, we're all a part of God. We're all a part of this.' And so I think that's where he was stepping out on new territory. These people weren't portraying the Christ as Black.

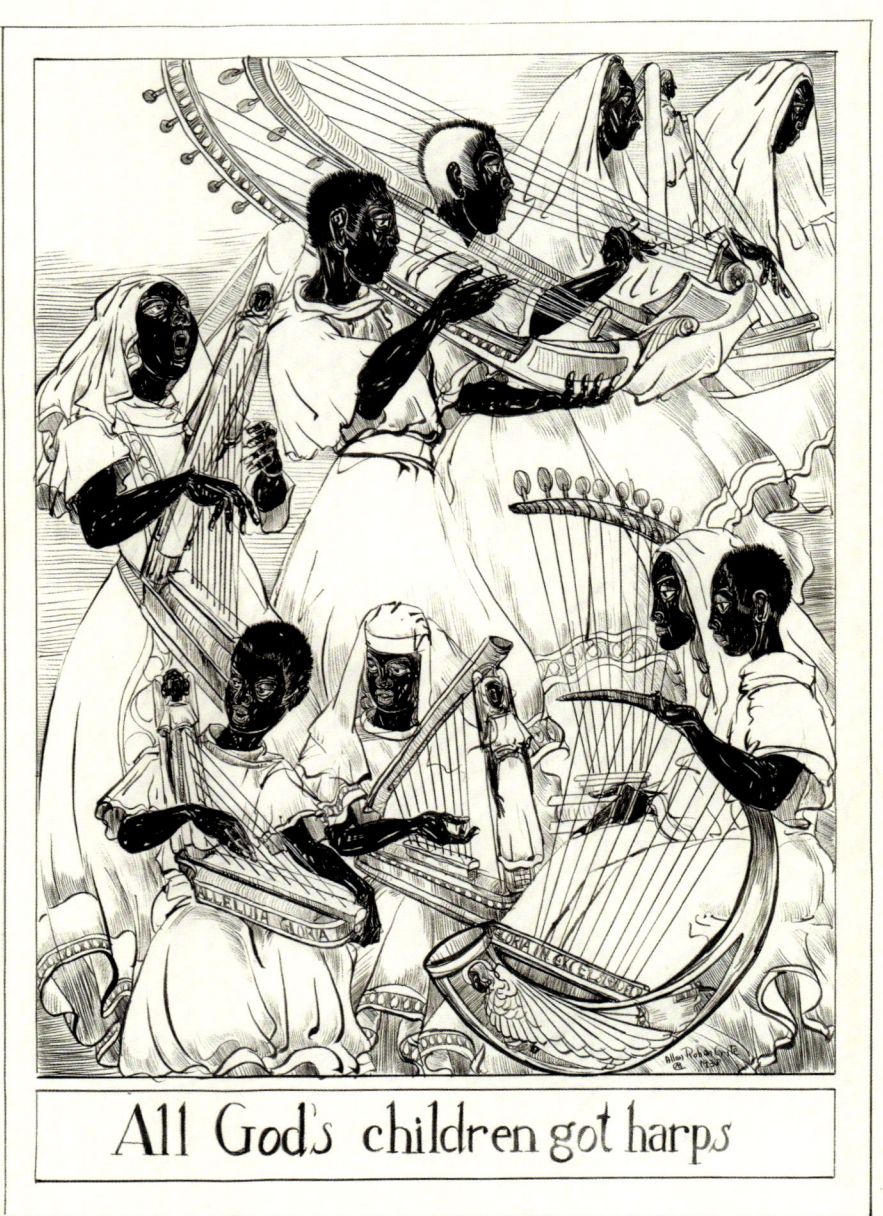

Fig. 87. Allan Rohan Crite, *All God's children got harps,* illustration for *Three Spirituals from Earth to Heaven* (Cambridge, MA, 1948), 1937. Ink on paper, 51 × 38 cm. Houghton Library, Harvard University

He was always this white figure. And he's saying, 'No, let's look at this. Let's think about it.'"

Susan Thompson

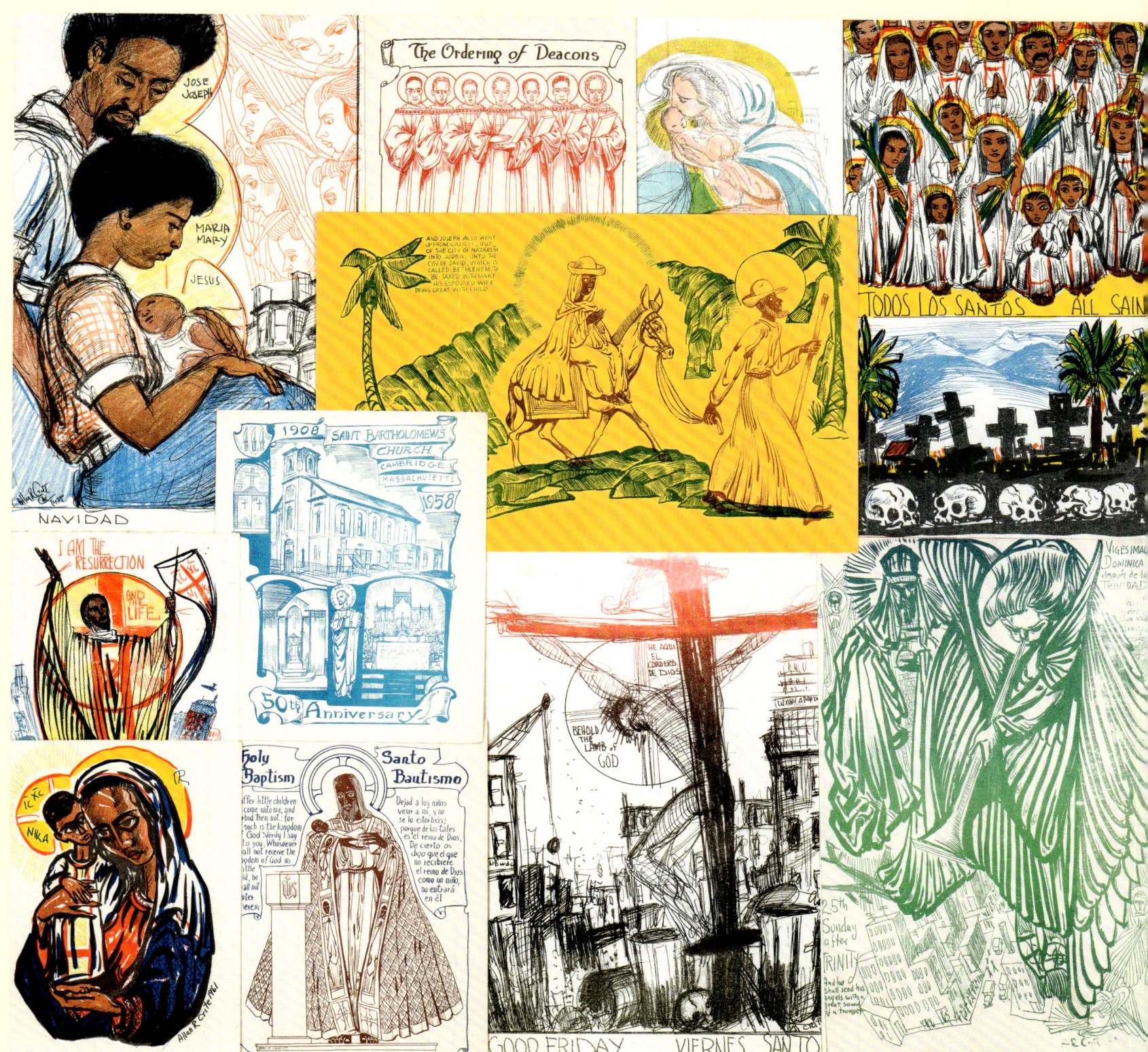

Fig. 88. Allan Rohan Crite, selection of church bulletins, 1957–78. Offset color lithographs and colored Multilith prints. Collection of Susan Thompson

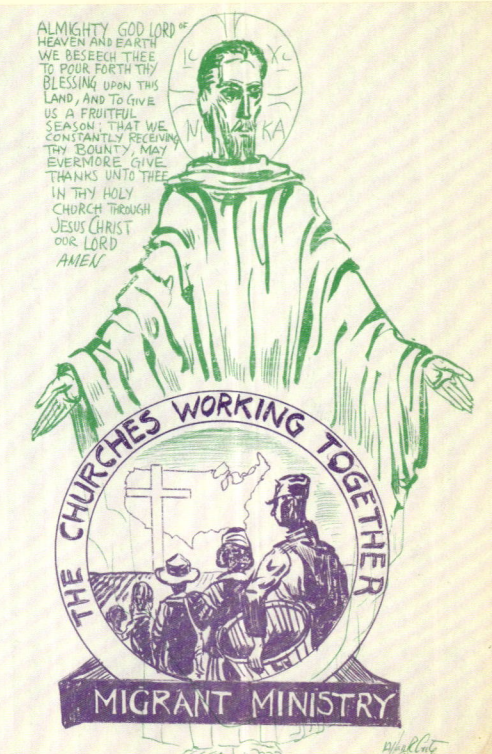

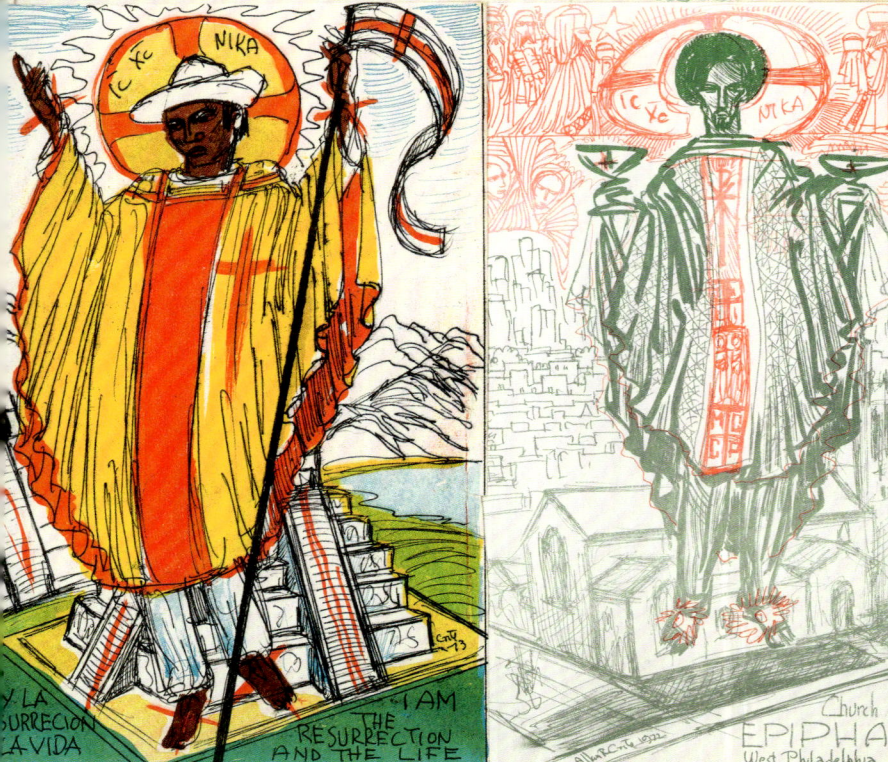

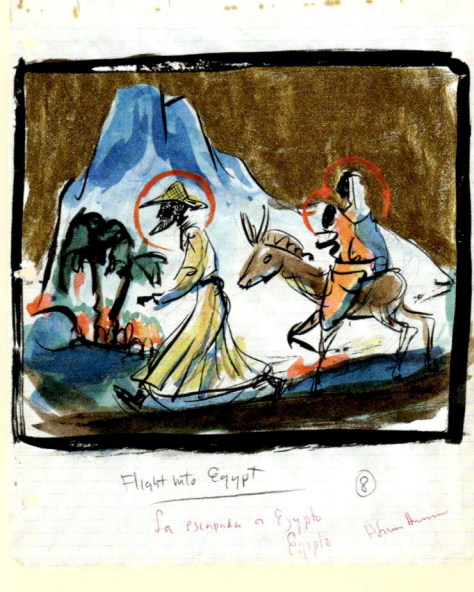

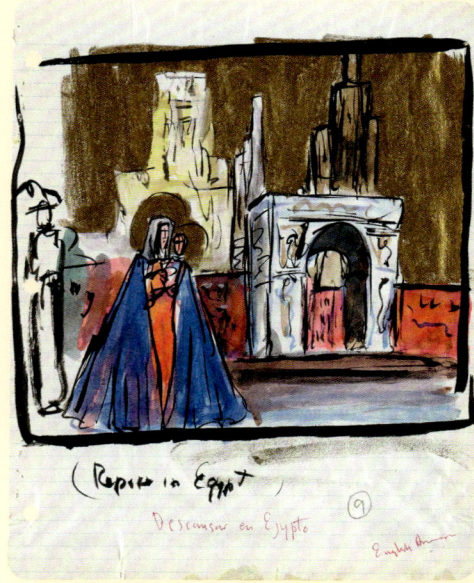

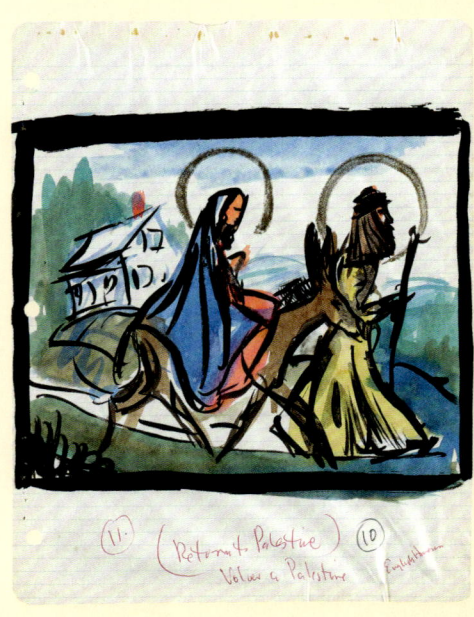

Right top to bottom: Fig. 89. Allan Rohan Crite, *Haitian Background–Flight into Egypt*; *Washington Square NYC Background Repose in Egypt*; *New England Mountains for Background Return to Palestine*, 1950–69. Watercolor, gold paint, marker, pencil, and ink on lined paper, individual works: 24.8 × 19.7 cm; 21.6 × 19.7 cm; 24.8 × 19 cm. Arts Department, Special Collections, Boston Public Library

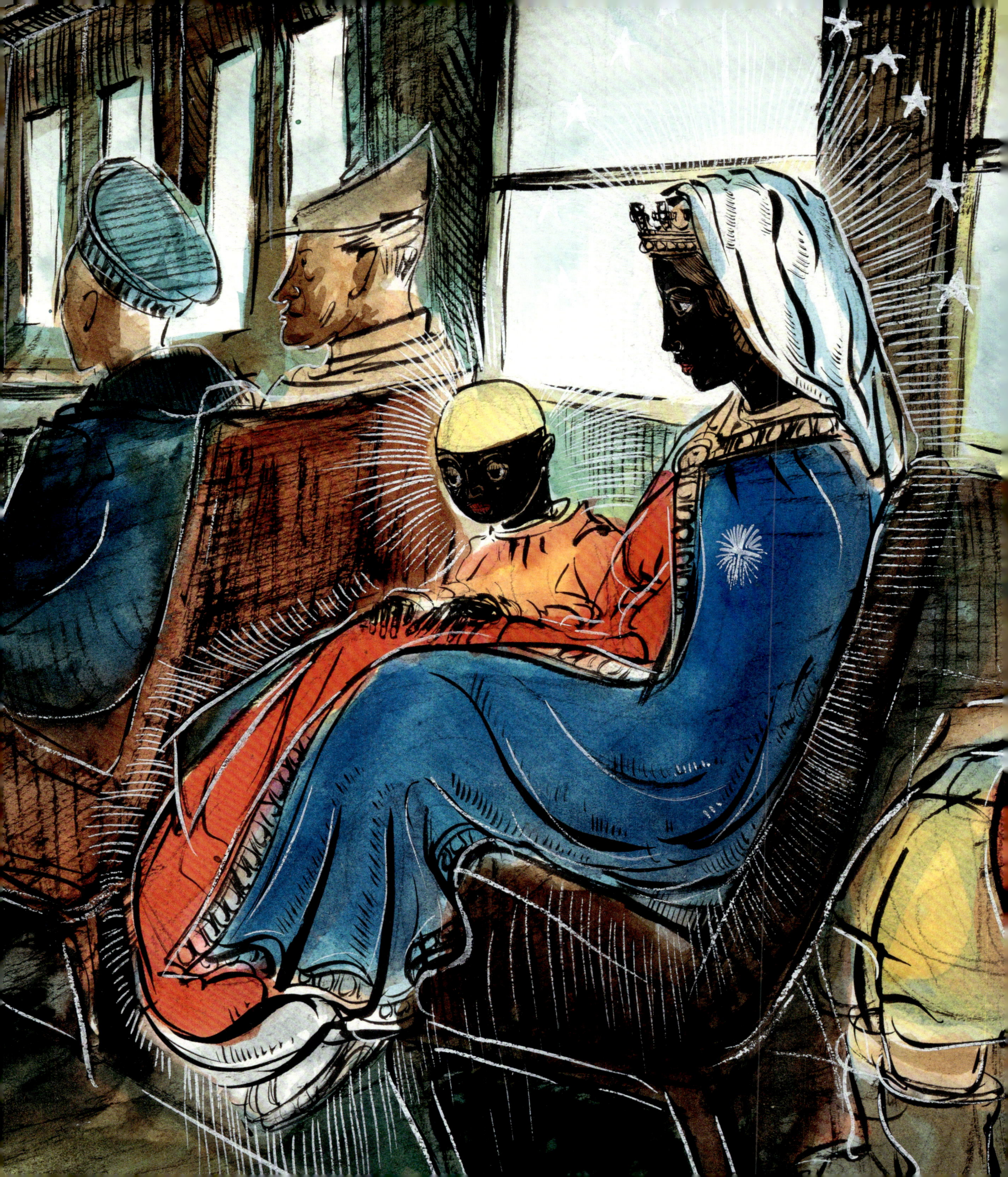

ORDINARY DIVINITY

THE ENDURING APPEAL OF ALLAN ROHAN CRITE'S *STREETCAR MADONNA*

Efeoghene Igor Coleman

A young Black mother and her son sit among commuters in a crowded streetcar. No one seems to be paying attention to the two distinctly different passengers. Only we, the viewers, understand that this is the Virgin Mary and a young Jesus Christ. Artist Allan Rohan Crite's religious works frequently juxtapose iconic Christian imagery with scenes from his contemporary life. In this watercolor painting, *Streetcar Madonna* (1946) (fig. 90), Crite echoes centuries-old representations of the Virgin and Child. Mary wears a red tunic covered by a royal blue mantle, with a white veil and a golden crown, a stark contrast with the modern streetcar, which is busy and populated with other commuters in contemporary dress. She appears demure, her eyes cast downward toward Jesus. A glowing aura surrounds her body, but instead of floating like an apparition, Mary is fully rooted in the scene among the twentieth-century passengers. The same goes for her holy son. He sits beside Mary, wearing a red tunic and a yellow kufi (a brimless short round cap) encircled by bright rays. Although associated with Islam, the kufi symbolized cultural pride among African Americans during the twentieth century. In this case, the cap illustrates the porous nature of Black sartorial nationalism rather than religious affiliation.[1] Crite was just as invested in creating religious art as he was in making work that reflected the Black experience in the United States.

Crite believed that it was the task of the Christian artist, as he defined himself, to contextualize biblical stories in spaces that modern audiences would readily understand.[2] In a lecture he gave at St. Anne's School for Girls in 1959, which he preserved in his self-published booklet *The Vocation of Christian Art* (figs. 91 and 92), Crite explained, "Christian Art is supposed to be the mirror of God / So that in it we may see the Face of Our Lord / And in so looking upon the face of Our Lord in this mirror / We discover our own face / And in that discovery, find that Our Lord's Face is reflected thru us."[3] He believed that it was crucial to create Christian art that reflected the people and the time in which it was made. This, for Crite, renewed the relevance of the Bible's messages for African Americans. He suggested that this has always been true of Christian art, "for as the Gothic villager saw himself present at the Holy events, by means of the Arts of the Church, the altar paintings and all other media of expression, so that he identified himself with Our Lord's life,

Opposite: Detail of *Streetcar Madonna*, fig. 90

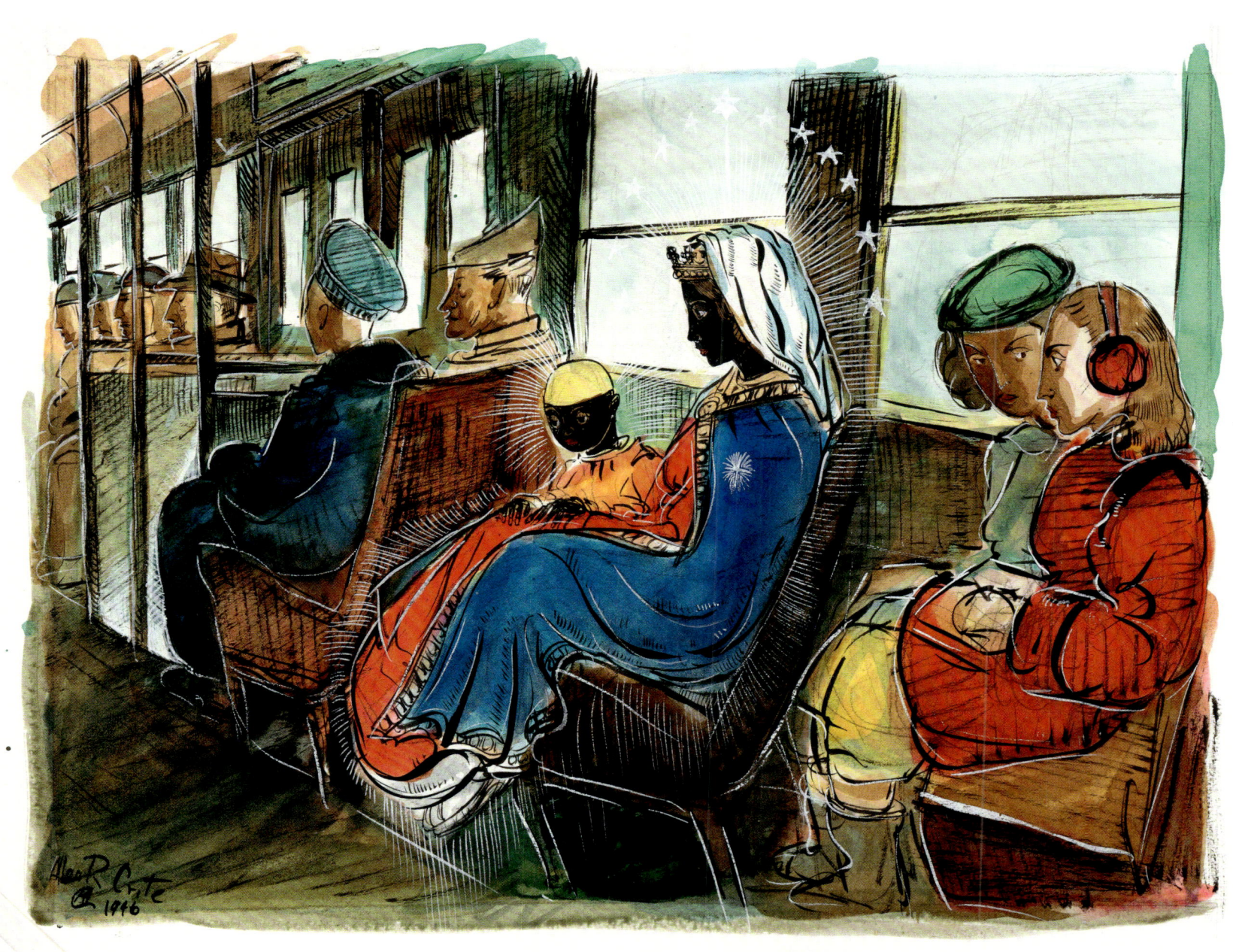

Opposite: Fig. 90. Allan Rohan Crite, *Streetcar Madonna,* 1946. Watercolor with black ink and white gouache over graphite on paper, 29 × 37 cm. Boston Athenaeum

so too, we today need the same type of message, that we may see a Nativity in our hills, a Miracle of Cana in our towns, a Calvary in our cities, and a Resurrection in our gardens and parks."[4] In this painting, the red coat with padded shoulders worn by the white woman seated behind Mary and Jesus brings us into Crite's present moment.[5] The fashion and the form of transportation enabled a contemporary audience to place themselves in the image.

In *Streetcar Madonna,* Crite depicts Mary and Jesus as both sacred and ordinary. He incorporates symbolic elements and allegorical themes, reflecting on his deep engagement with spirituality, history, and social justice. He does this as a deliberate strategy that invites viewers to contemplate the intersection of faith and everyday life. Crite wanted African Americans to see the Bible's relevance in the mid-twentieth century, to extend the life of scripture beyond the past and push it into the present. As a devout Episcopalian, he found art to be an essential expression of his faith.[6] Ultimately, his work entertains difference without an assumed or imposed hierarchy—he made the biblical figures Black so as to open up the interpretive possibilities of Christianity rather than attempting to create a more accurate depiction of the biblical story. His work demonstrated the malleability and relevance of the Christian tradition to modern audiences.

Along with depicting biblical stories in contemporary context, Crite drew from art historical depictions of the Virgin and Christ Child, namely, *Sedes Sapientiae* (Throne of Wisdom), examples of which he could have seen in Boston's museum collections, including the enthroned Virgin on display in the Early Italian Room of the Isabella Stewart Gardner Museum (fig. 93). In this pictorial trope, Mary is literally the throne of Christ; she is the seat, and he represents divine wisdom. As scholar Ilene H. Forsyth explains, "As a

Below left: Fig. 91. Allan Rohan Crite, *The Vocation of Christian Art,* 1959, cover. Booklet, 27.9 × 21.6 cm. Boston Athenaeum

Below right: Fig. 92. Allan Rohan Crite, *The Vocation of Christian Art,* 1959, p. 10. Booklet, 27.9 × 21.6 cm. Boston Athenaeum

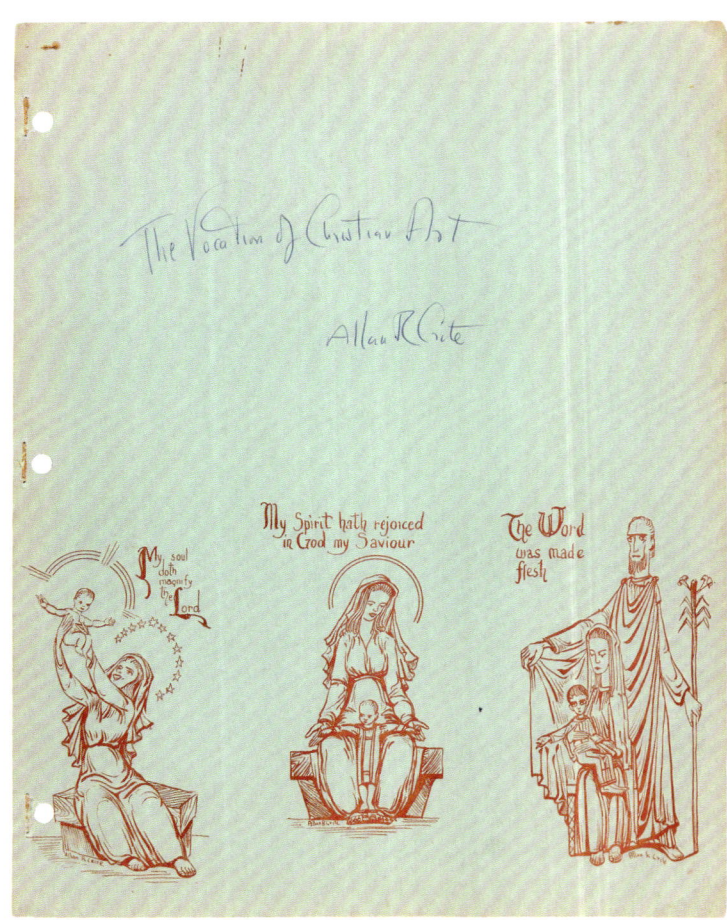

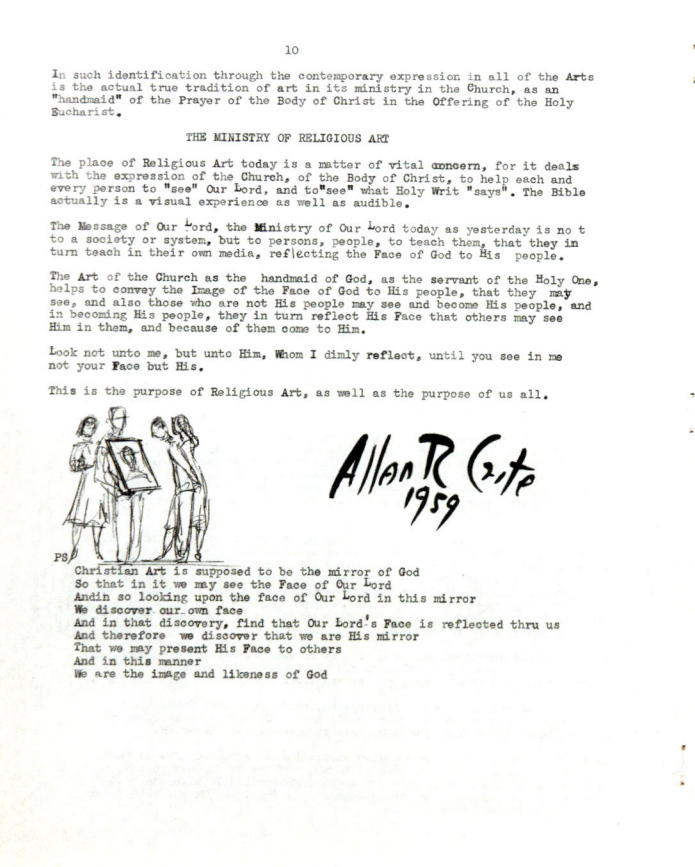

mother, [Mary] supports her son in her lap, yet as the Mother of God she serves as a throne for the incarnation of Divine Wisdom. Thus, Christ's humanity and divinity are equally apparent in the image so that it expresses clearly and simply the profound meaning of the Incarnation."[7] In Crite's depiction of the seated Mary, Christ is seated beside her instead of on her lap. Still, she remains the throne of Christ, as he peers around her to look at the rest of the streetcar. This compositional choice emphasizes Mary's role as a protective shield between Jesus and the world. She is also an important contextual element, like a throne, that signals Jesus's divine status.

In the mid-twentieth century, Crite was in the vanguard of artists who were representing the complexity of modern family life within the Black community. He was best known for his neighborhood scenes—narrative paintings that offered glimpses into Black middle-class life, such as his renowned oil painting *School's Out* (1936) (see fig. 48). He drew inspiration from Dutch and Flemish art, especially the portrayals of social life in sixteenth-century Belgium. He was particularly interested in work by Pieter Bruegel the Elder, whose work was widely reproduced; some of it was acquired by the MFA in Boston in the 1940s (fig. 94).[8] Crite was interested in art history and used historical iconography to make the Christian Gospels applicable to contemporary Black life. However, his less acknowledged contribution involves incorporating Black figures into biblical narratives, as noted above (fig. 95). This was particularly conveyed through his circulating pamphlets. His religious ephemera, along with his paintings, promoted more inclusive interpretations of Christianity, offering new perspectives on familiar narratives. In his religious scenes, Crite wanted to display the ordinary divinity in Black experience, just as sixteenth-century painters working in the Low Countries had discovered the ordinary divinity in the faces and places that surrounded them.

Unlike some of his contemporaries, Crite was devoted to showing middle-class values and upwardly mobile African Americans. He resented the fetishization of Blackness and the conflation of Blackness with poverty. As art historian Julie Levin Caro observes, "Crite regarded the image of the 'jazz Negro' and the 'backwoods Southerner' as two versions of an exoticized stereotype that not only disparaged African Americans but also obscured the 'ordinary' Black life that was his own experience living in the urban north."[9] Crite's work typically portrayed the effects of the Great Migration, the movement of millions of African Americans who left the segregated rural South searching for freedom and opportunity in northern cities. He painted portraits of Black community life and Black people in public.

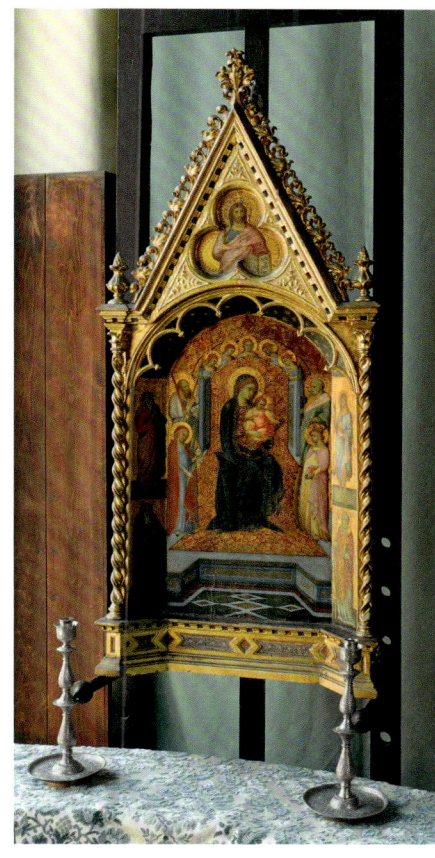

Fig. 93. Bartolomeo Bulgarini, *The Virgin and Child Enthroned with Saints and Angels,* 1355–60. Gold and tempera on panel, 65 × 46 × 10.5 cm. Isabella Stewart Gardner Museum, Boston

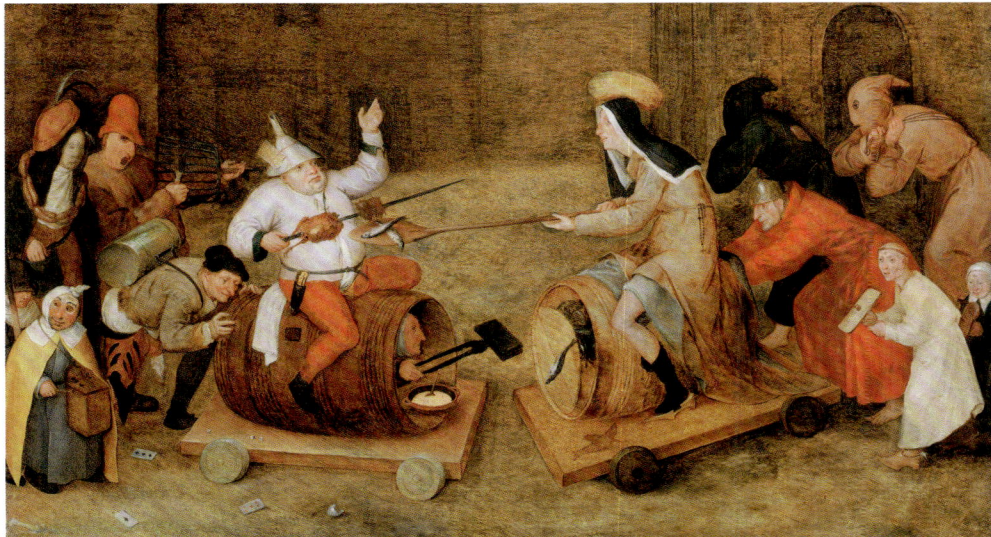

Fig. 94. Workshop of Pieter Bruegel the Elder, *Combat between Carnival and Lent,* 16th century. Oil on panel, 36.5 × 63.5 cm. Museum of Fine Arts, Boston

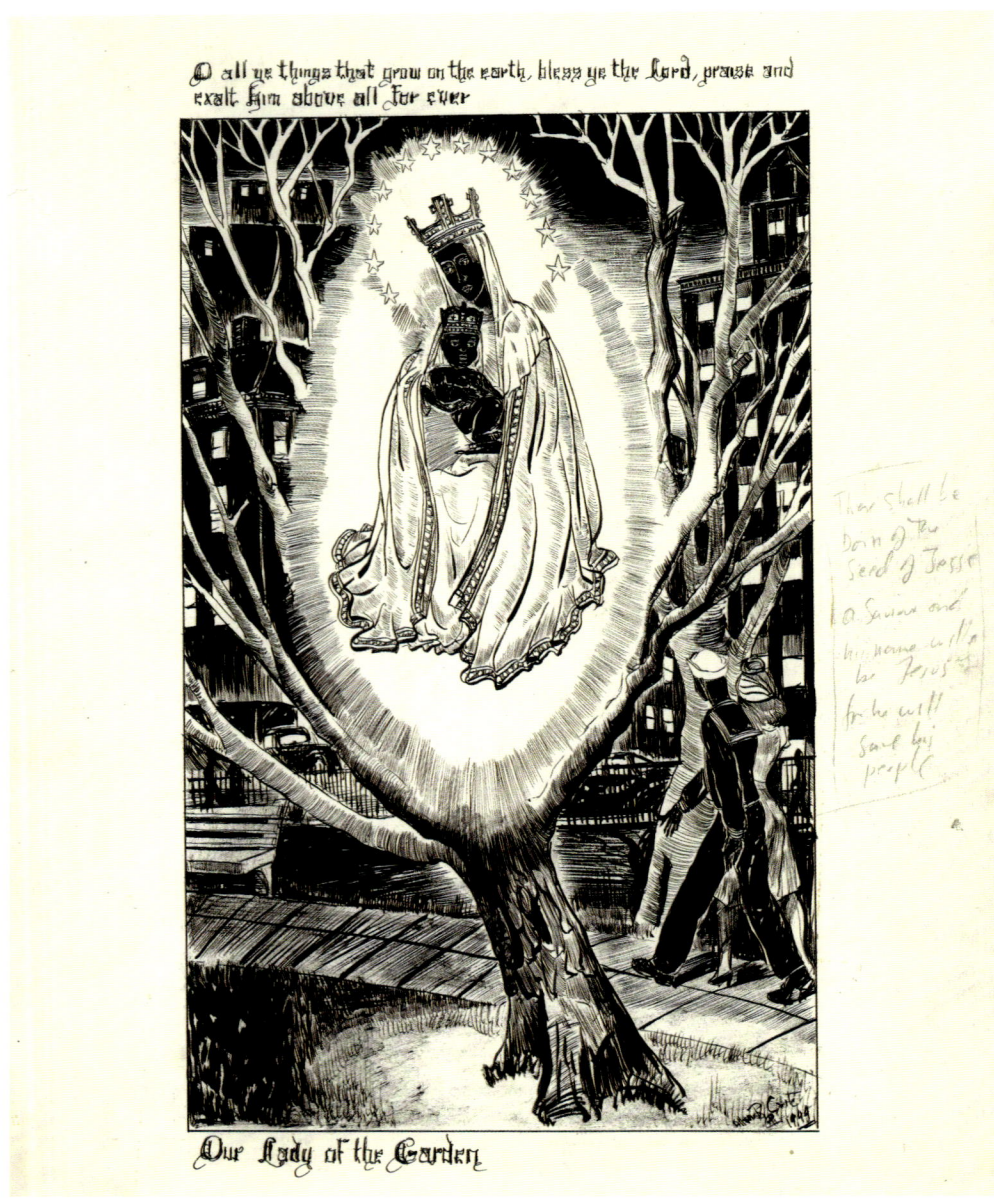

In *Streetcar Madonna,* Mary and Jesus are the only Black people on a predominantly white streetcar—an experience that may have resonated with Black viewers particularly in Boston, which had a smaller Black community than other northern cities, like New York and Chicago, that had been primary destinations during the Great Migration. In addition to making the story of the Madonna and Child relevant to mid-twentieth-century audiences, Crite's painting conjures up past and present anxieties that Black mothers' have about raising Black boys in America. This painting was made not too long after the National Association for the Advancement of Colored People flew the now famous flag that read, "A man was lynched yesterday." The flag would appear outside the headquarters of the NAACP every time a Black person was murdered by mobs around the country between 1920 and 1938 (fig. 96). The Equal Justice Initiative reported that there were an estimated 4,084 lynchings in twelve southern states between the end of Reconstruction in 1877 and 1950.[10] The NAACP stopped flying the flag outside their Fifth Avenue office only when the landlord threatened to evict the organization.[11] In Crite's painting, Christ is protected behind Mary, potentially from the two white women seated behind them, who wear suspicious facial expressions. Their brows are furrowed, their lips pressed together,

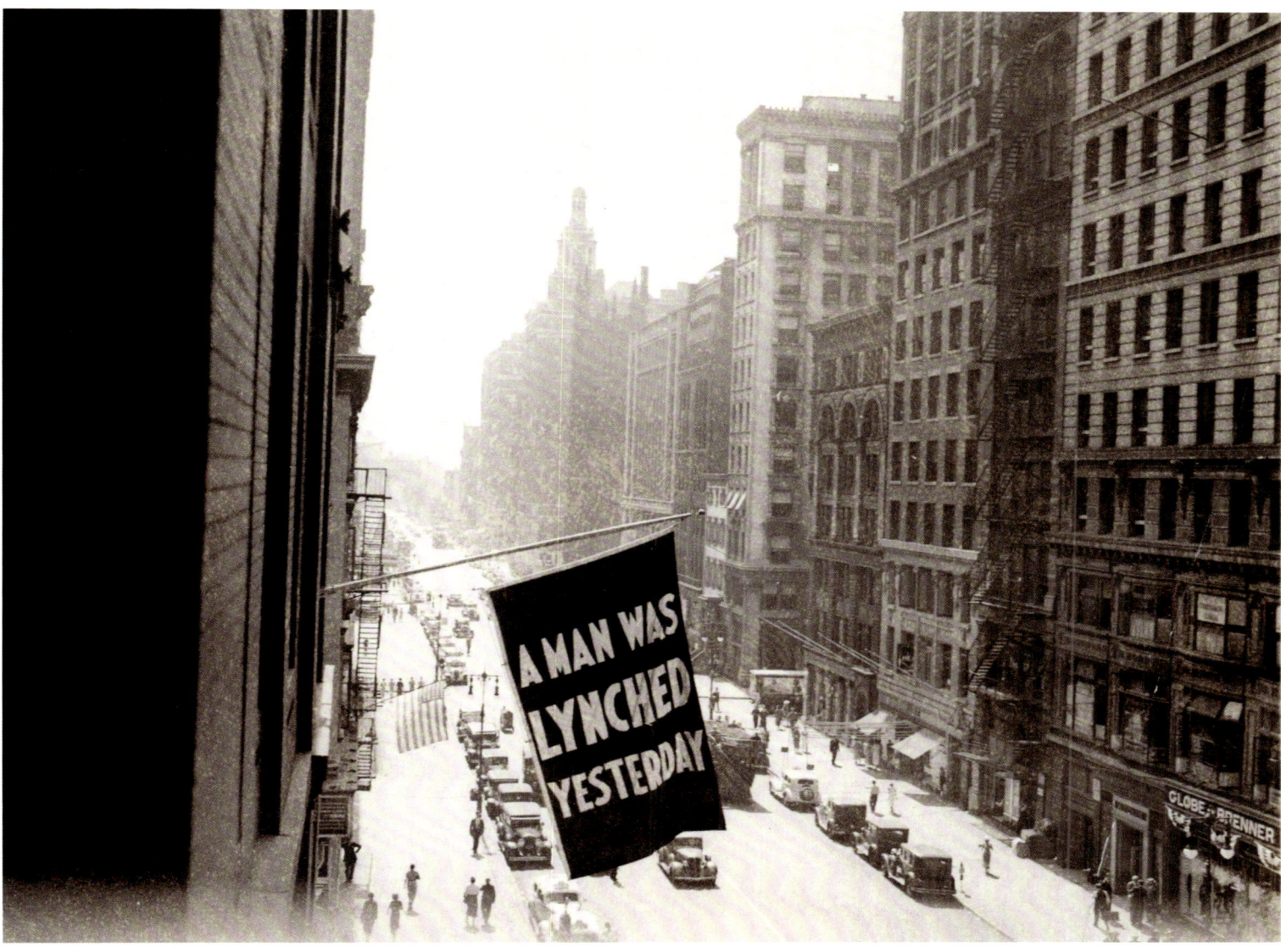

Fig. 96. Flag, announcing lynching, flown from the window of the NAACP headquarters at 69 Fifth Ave., New York City, 1936. Gelatin silver print, 16.8 × 21.5 cm. Library of Congress

and their bodies are upright and tense. It is not lost on this viewer that racial violence against Black people was (and is) often the by-product of racist suspicion and fear.

For today's audience, the worried Mary in this painting is reminiscent of images of mourning Black mothers in national media coverage and social media posts. What stands out for viewers today, in the wake of state-sanctioned deaths like that of George Floyd in 2020, who, in his final breath, called out for his mother, is the fragile innocence of Black boys. In Elizabeth Alexander's retelling of Floyd's murder, she writes, *"I can't breathe, again. Eight minutes and forty-six seconds of a knee and full weight on his neck. 'I can't breathe' and, then, 'Mama!' George Floyd cried. George Floyd cried, 'Mama . . . I'm through!'"* Crite's prophetic voice also points us to the enduring grief that Black mothers face when, again and again, their children are haunted by the specter of violence and death. In this poignant watercolor, Mary is deep in thought—her eyes are focused on a single spot, her head slightly tilted. Absorbed, she could be concerned for her son. As Alexander declares, "Let's be clear about what motherhood is. A being comes onto this earth and you are charged with keeping it alive. It dies if you do not tend it. It is as simple as that. No matter how intellectual and multicolored motherhood becomes as children grow older, the part that says *My purpose on earth is to keep you alive* has never totally dissipated. Magical thinking on all sides."[12] The troubling reality is that depicting Mary as

Black associates her with a group of mothers who are, tragically, more likely than parents of any other race to lose a child to state violence in America. Consequently, the knowledge that Jesus will die at the hands of the state echoes contemporary issues surrounding police brutality in our times.

Although Crite preferred to see himself as a Christian artist retelling an ancient holy story in his context, just as European artists did centuries ago, his work reflects racial realities in the United States. Embedded in this painting is Crite's admiration for Mary and Jesus and a sense of racial pride that identifies the Black experience as part of a deep religious tradition. When we see Crite as a Christian artist who contributed signifi-cantly to American aesthetic traditions and social realities, he and his artistic practice come more fully into view. Remembering that the story of Christ is the original narrative of state-sponsored death, sacrifice, and martyrdom, we cannot help but see how it con-nects with the story of African Americans living in the United States, then and now.

In the past decade, we have come to know Tamir Rice (2002–2014), Michael Brown (1996–2014), Elijah McClain (1996–2019), and Tyre Nichols (1993–2023). These are but a few of the well-known boys and young men killed at the hands of the police, their deaths drawing national and international attention to racial injustice and police brutality in America. For this contemporary viewer, Jesus's innocence and Mary's contemplative expression speak to the universal anguish of mothers in charge of vulnerable children. Crite's deliberate decision to depict Jesus and Mary as Black not only subverts Eurocentric representations of biblical figures; it also makes meaningful connections between faith, race, and social justice in the mid-twentieth century and beyond.

Notes

1   See Brooks-Key 2023.
2   See Crite 1959, on the occasion of judging an exhibition of students' work.
3   Ibid., 10.
4   Crite 1958, 5.
5   See Reddy 2019.
6   For more on Crite's religious background, see Greenwald and Michelon's essay in this volume, 29–34.
7   Forsyth 2019, 2.
8   Jenkins 2021, 17.
9   Caro 2008, 1.
10 Equal Justice Initiative 2017.
11 Segal 2016.
12 Alexander 2020.

PLATES 1961–1978

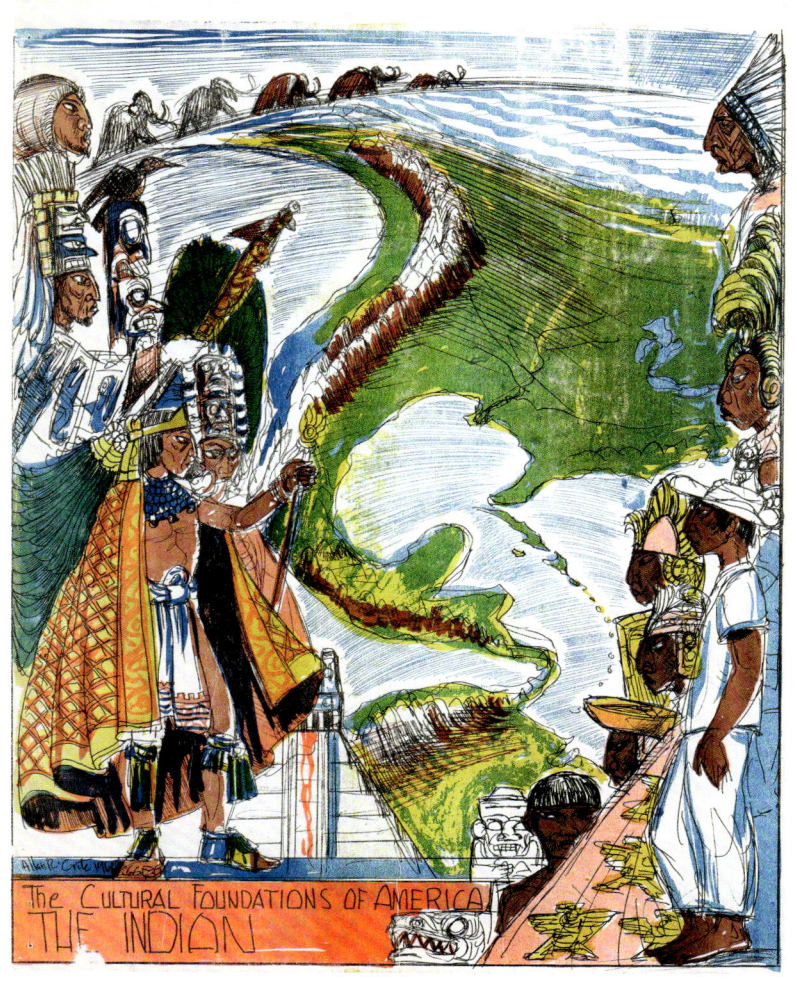

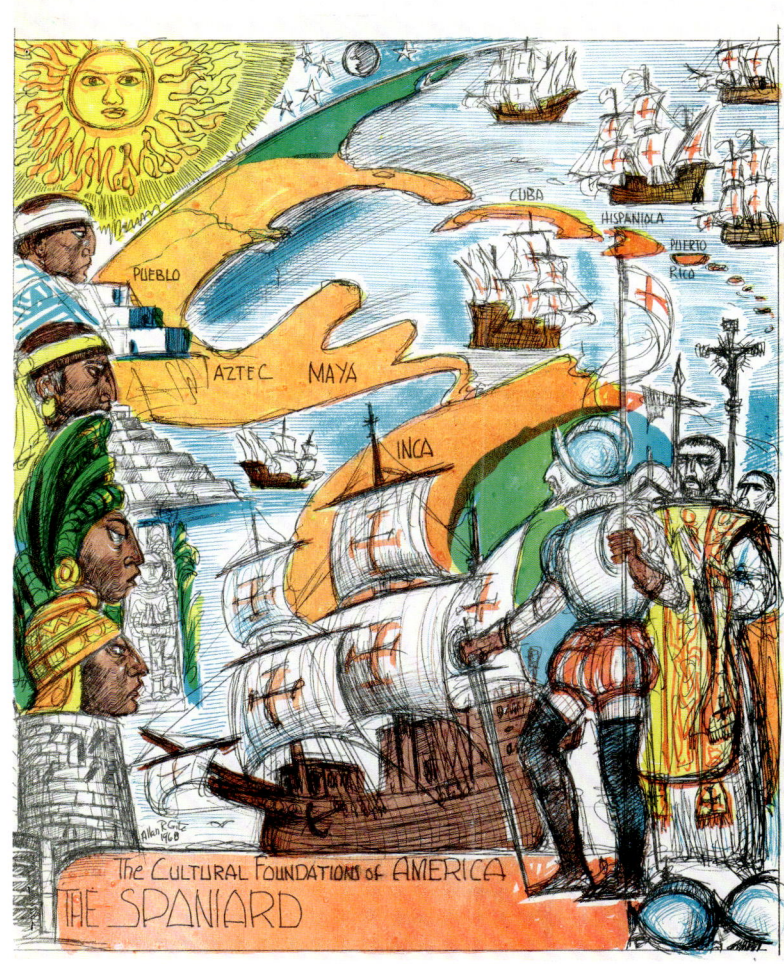

Plate 32. Allan Rohan Crite, *The Cultural Foundations of America: The Indian,* 1968. Photomechanically printed booklet, 27.9 × 21.6 cm. Arts Department, Special Collections, Boston Public Library

Plate 33. Allan Rohan Crite, *The Cultural Foundations of America: The Spaniard,* 1968. Photomechanically printed booklet, 27.9 × 21.6 cm. Arts Department, Special Collections, Boston Public Library

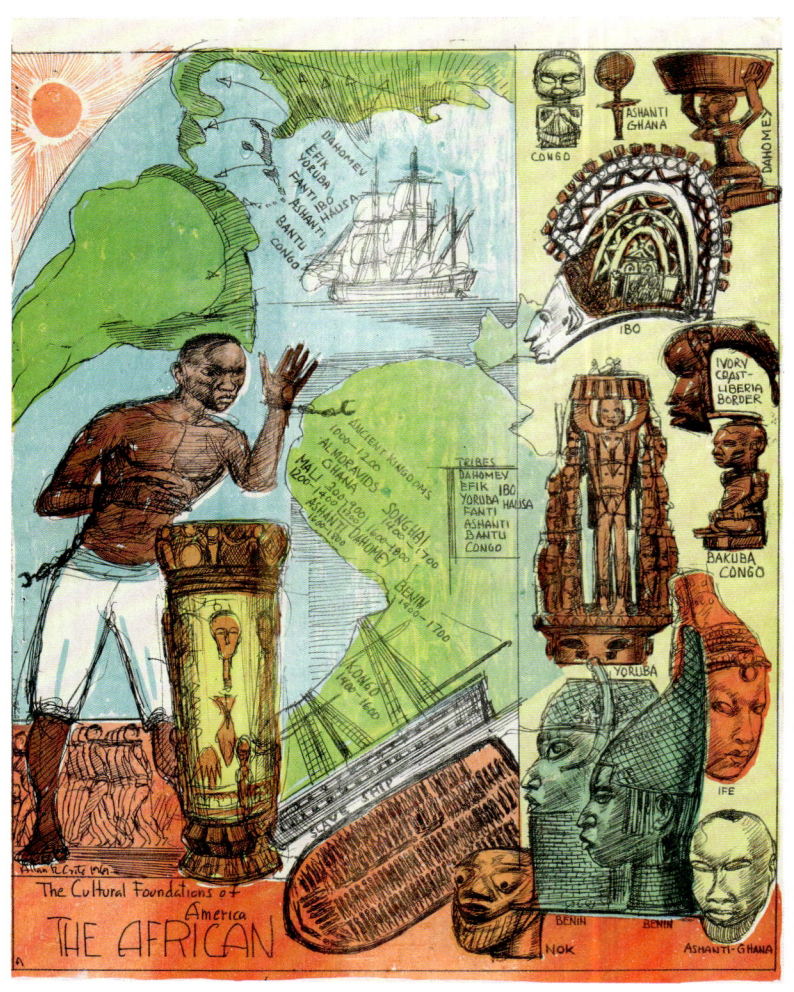

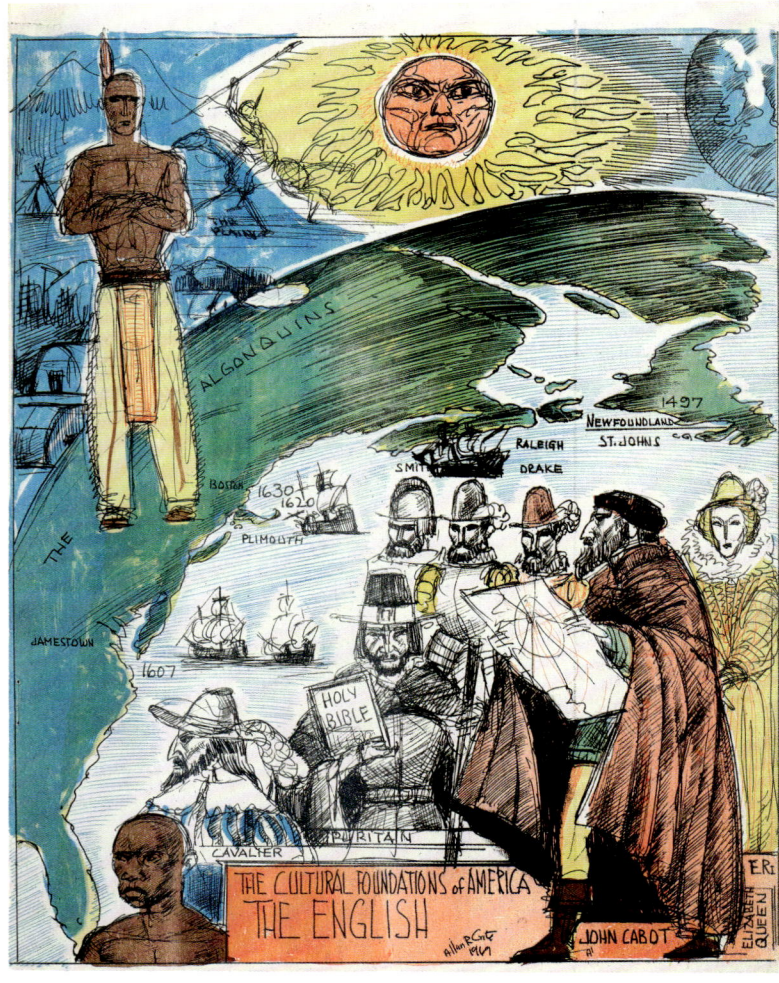

Plate 34. Allan Rohan Crite, *The Cultural Foundations of America: The African,* 1969. Photomechanically printed booklet, 27.9 × 21.6 cm. Arts Department, Special Collections, Boston Public Library

Plate 35. Allan Rohan Crite, *The Cultural Foundations of America: The English,* 1969. Photomechanically printed booklet, 27.9 × 21.6 cm. Arts Department, Special Collections, Boston Public Library

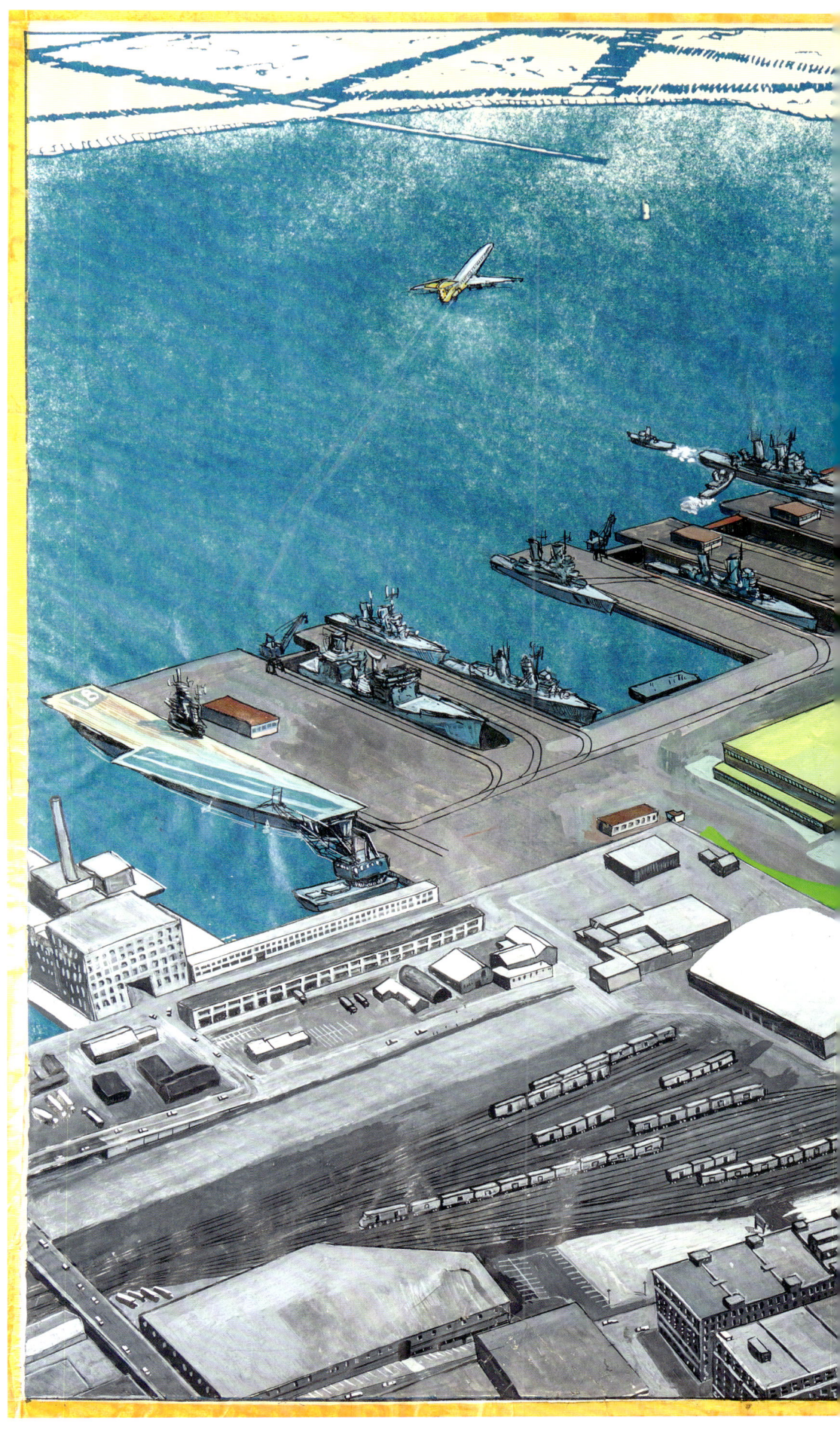

Plate 36. Allan Rohan Crite, *Boston Naval Yard, Aerial Perspective*, 1970–71. Diazo print with gouache, 78.7 × 106.5 cm. National Park Service, National Parks of Boston, Charlestown Navy Yard

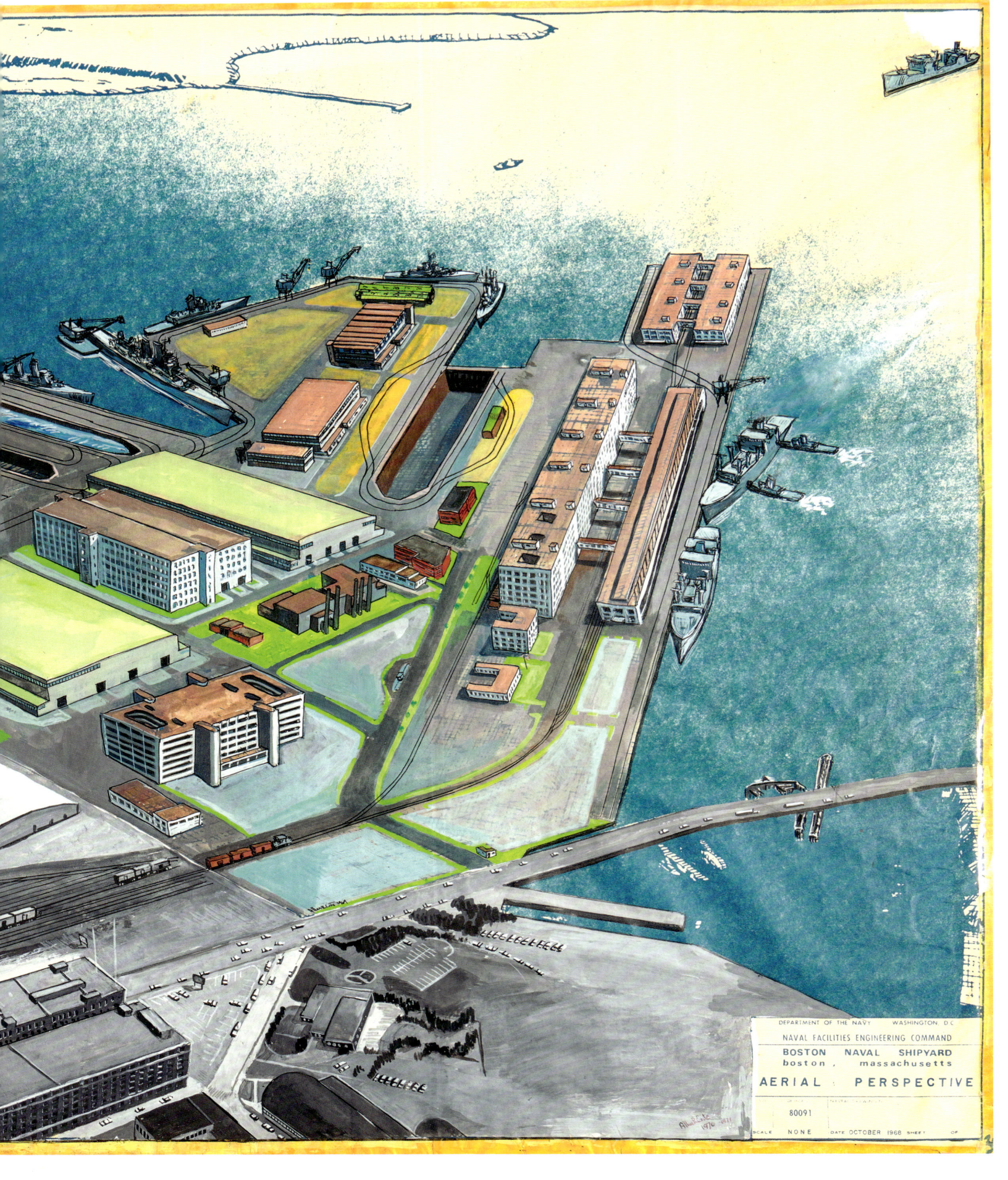

DEPARTMENT OF THE NAVY   WASHINGTON, D.C.

NAVAL FACILITIES ENGINEERING COMMAND

BOSTON   NAVAL   SHIPYARD
boston ,   massachusetts

AERIAL   PERSPECTIVE

80091	
SCALE NONE	DATE OCTOBER 1968 SHEET OF

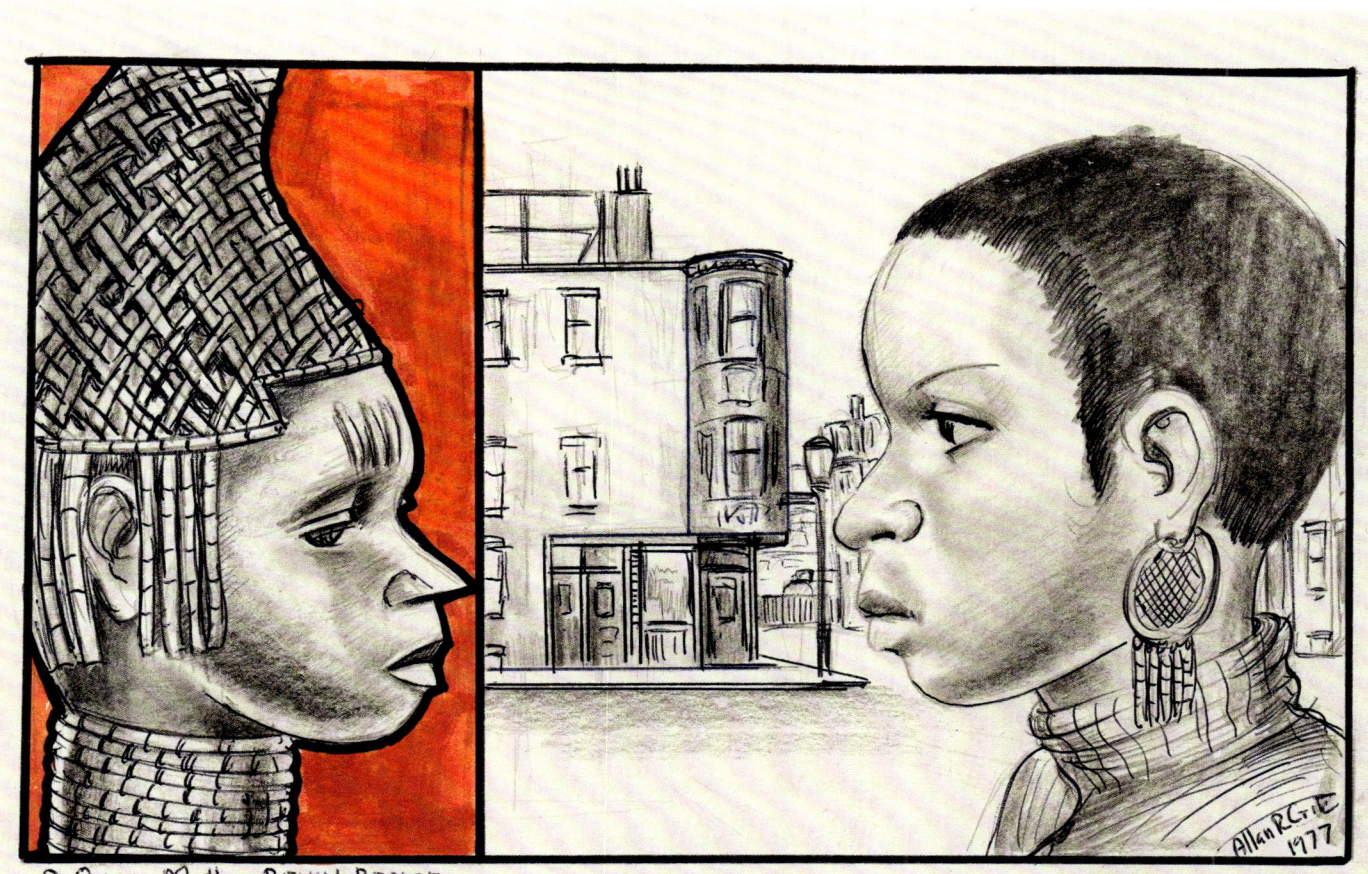

Plate 37. Allan Rohan Crite, *A Queen Mother, Benin Bronze, 16th Century, Ancient Nigeria,*
1977. Graphite, pen and ink, and felt-tip pens on paper, 20.2 × 25.2 cm. Museum of Fine
Arts, Boston

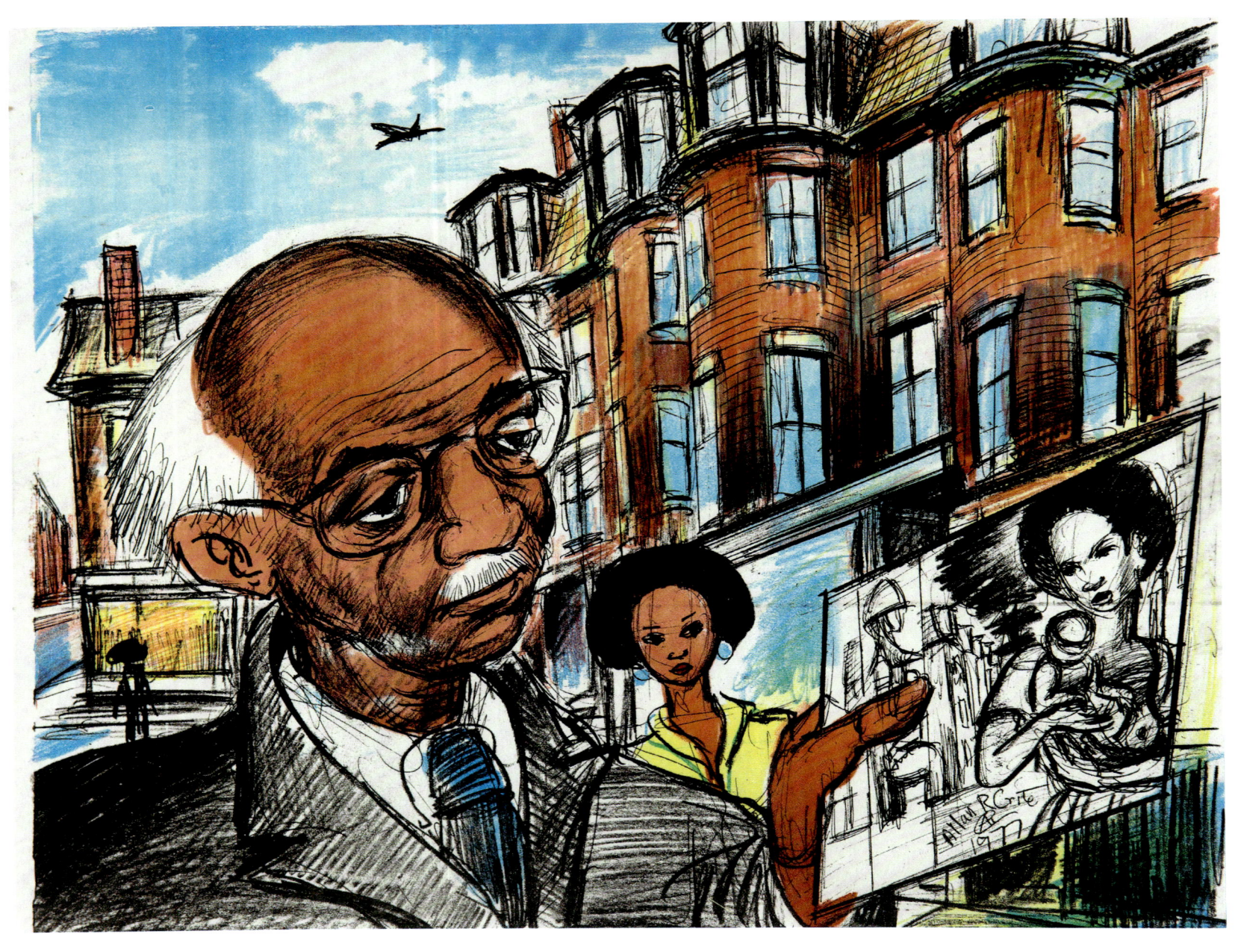

Plate 38. Allan Rohan Crite, *410 Columbus Avenue,* from *An Artist's Sketchbook of the South End: A Walking Tour about Black People,* 1977. Offset color lithograph, 21.7 × 27.9 cm. Boston Athenaeum

Plate 39. Allan Rohan Crite, *Ekua Holmes,* from *Portrait Studies,* 21 May 1978.
Offset lithograph, 28 × 21.7 cm. Boston Athenaeum

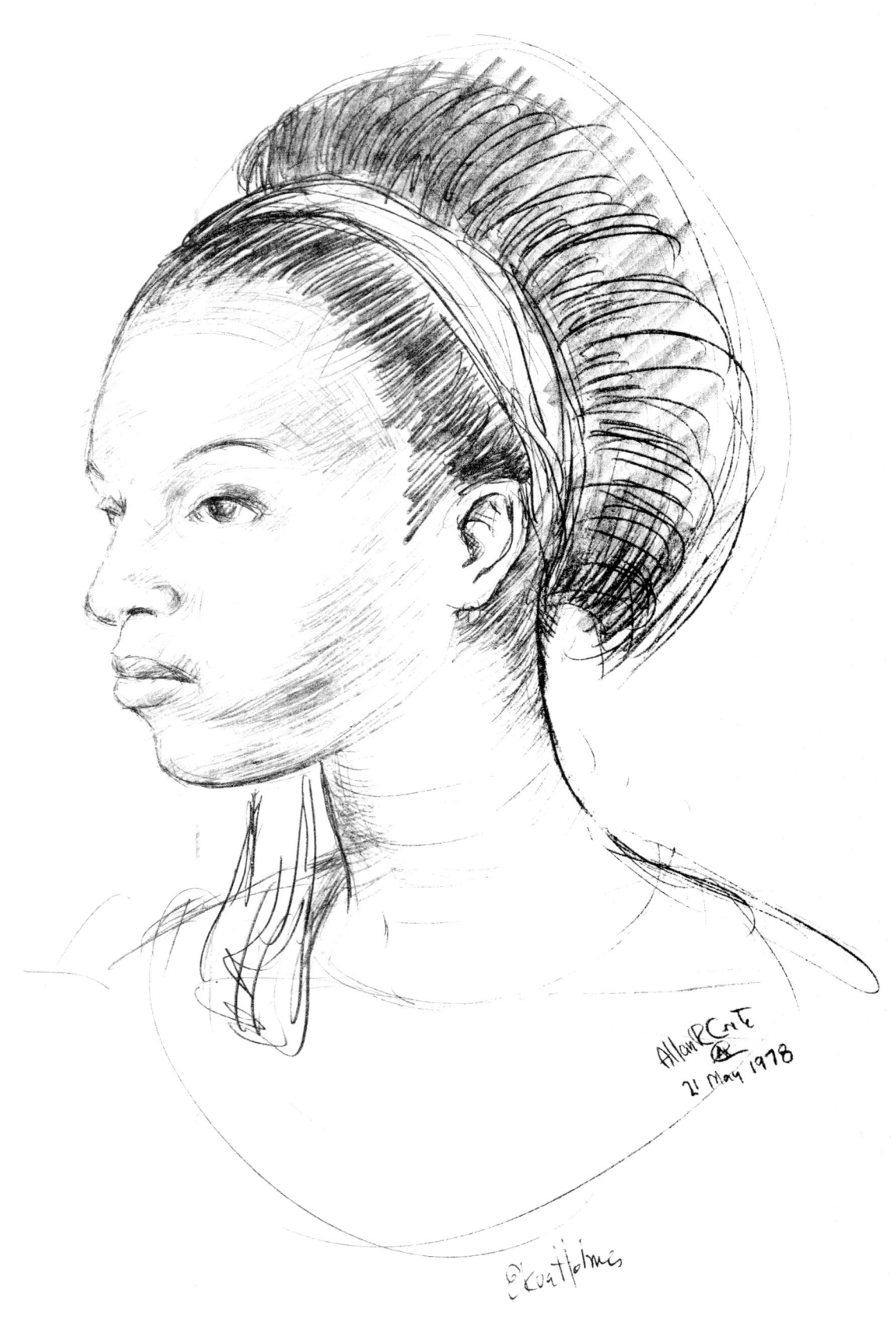

AllanRCat
21 May 1978

@CurtHolmes

CRITE AS MENTOR

"He felt that it was his supreme duty to support younger artists."

Susan Thompson

"He was [a] grandfatherly type to me. He . . . was my surrogate grandfather . . . because he was lovable. He, you know, he always wanted to help somebody. He loved Black people, and he loved Black people at a time when maybe it wasn't even cool." (Fig. 97)

Denise Patmon

"After a show at AAMARP that was called *Four Women*—it was Lotus Do, Weeta Lopes, me, and Susan Thompson—and when Allan Crite saw our work together, he said, 'You guys, your work blended so well together.' . . . So we all became a part of What in the World, our own little female art group. But [later] we were, you know, ushered in by him to be a part of the Boston Collective, because he didn't want Susan to be the only female in the group. Very forward-thinking." (Fig. 98)

Johnetta Tinker

"[The Collective] was influenced by the Black Arts Movement of the '60s, and the Black Arts Movement was influenced by the Harlem Renaissance . . . and the Harlem Renaissance was influenced by people like [Lois] Mailou Jones and Allan Crite and all these other artists. And why is that? Because we realized as a people that our image was being disparaged. And so we had the image warriors like Allan and others who would get it correct in terms of who we were at the time and who we were aspiring to be. . . . And this is what the Collective was about, too. I mean, if you look at the work that was depicted in our exhibition, it was about Black beauty."

Aukram Burton

"I showed him [all my art]. And he decided right then and there that I was an artist and that all I had to do was [make] more. My living situation at the time wasn't conducive to doing a lot of art because I lived in a dormitory for married students at Harvard. . . . We had a little small [bed] room, a little small kitchen, and a little small living room, and there was not much space in there for art. So [Allan] cleared out space on his top floor of his house and he said I could use that to work. So I got a sewing machine, moved it up there, and started making art." (see fig. 102)

Susan Thompson

"He was very lonely after his mother died. And then Susan came into his life and the Boston Collective came into his life. And there he felt as though he had his children. We were his children."

Johnetta Tinker

"He never had children. So he kind of adopted us. Right. And that's how, pretty much, the Collective was formed. It was formed through Allan."

Aukram Burton

"When we did Allan's 75th birthday, *Say Brother* did a showcase. It was an art showcase, but it was celebrating Allan's 75th birthday. So they dedicated the whole program [to him]. It was like they staged a big reception . . . [with] the Who's Who in the Black arts community. I have that video." (Fig. 99)

Aukram Burton

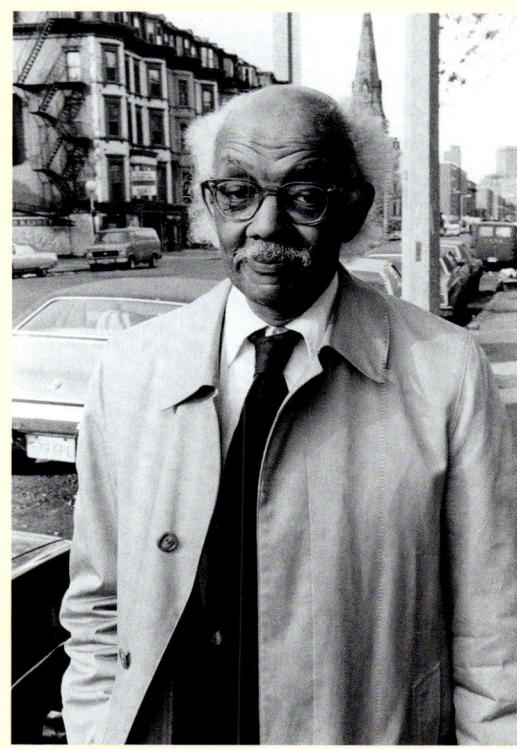

Fig. 97. Allan Rohan Crite on Columbus Avenue in front of the Harriet Tubman House in Boston's South End during the *East Meets West* exhibition, 18 April 1981. Photograph by Aukram Burton

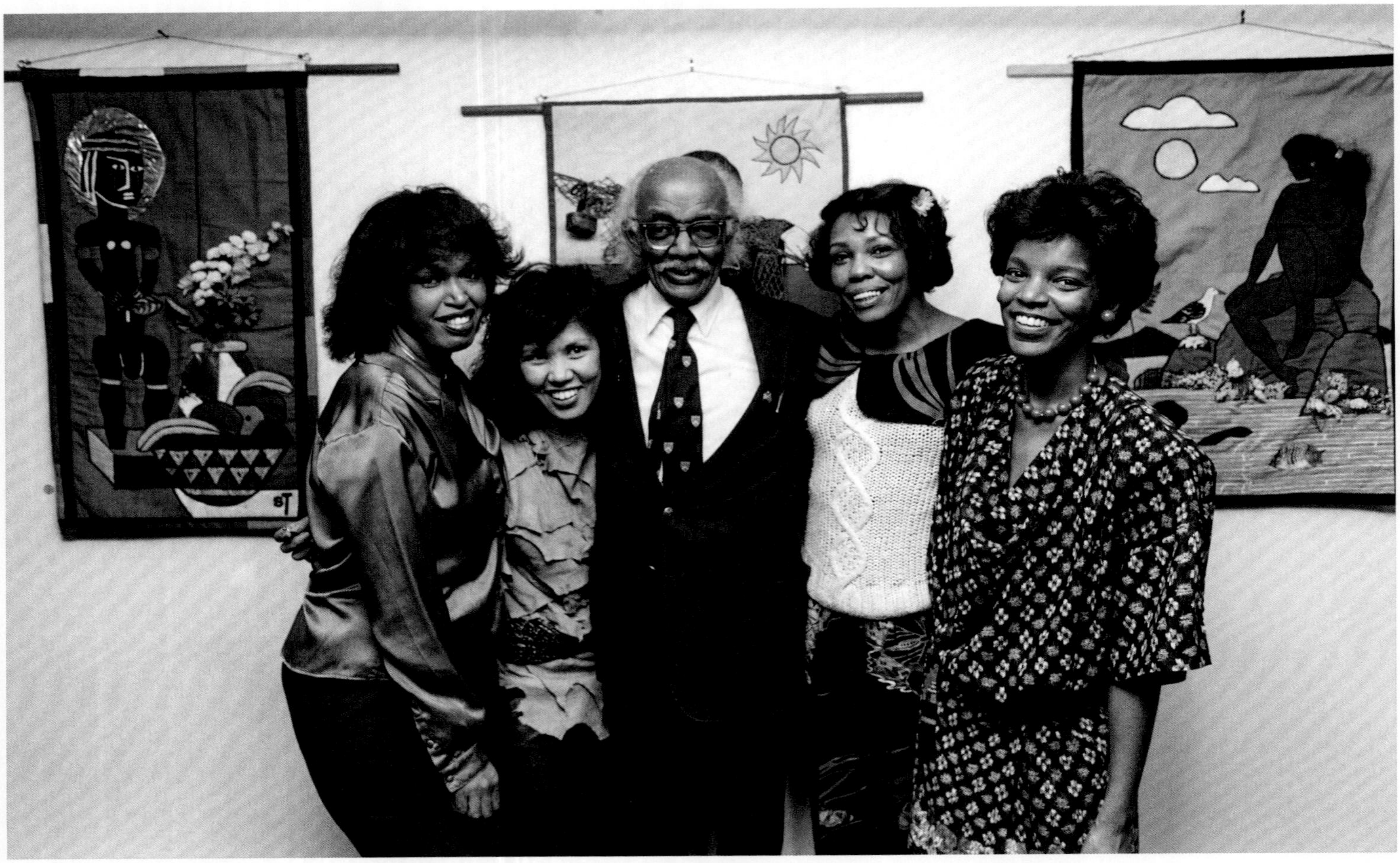

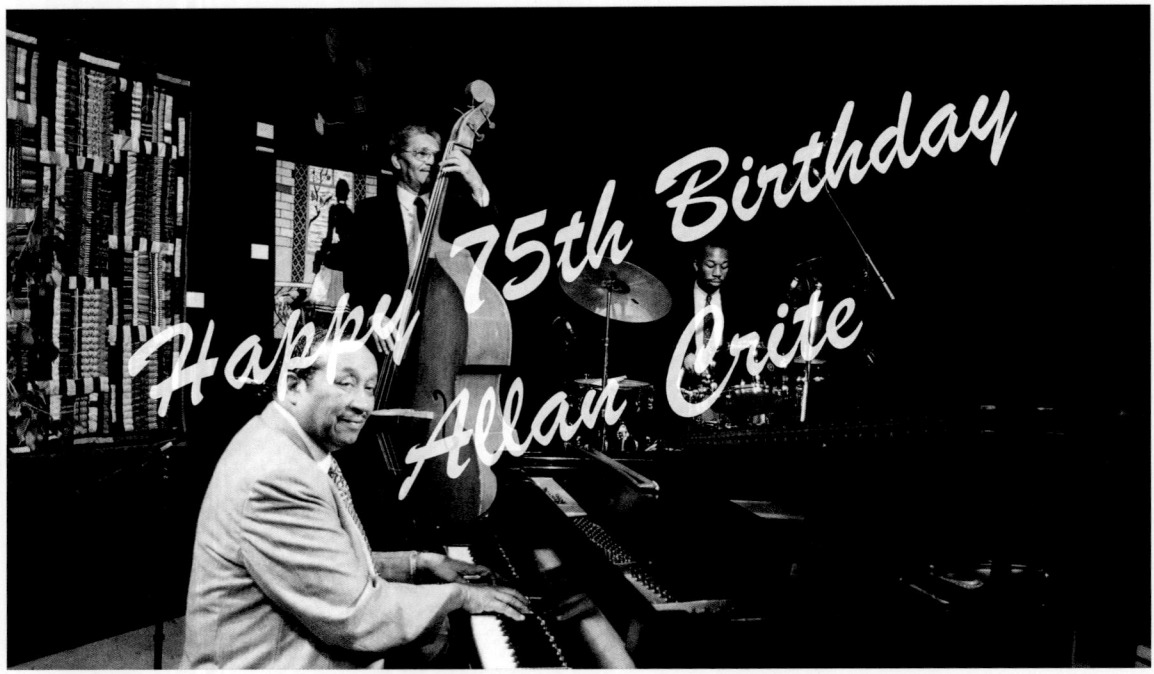

Fig. 98. *Left to right:* Weeta Lopes, Lotus Do, Allan Rohan Crite, Susan Thompson, and Johnetta Tinker during the Boston Collective and What in the World premiere exhibition at the Piano Craft Gallery during African American History Month, February 1980. Photograph by Aukram Burton

Fig. 99. The Sabby Lewis Trio performs during a live *Say Brother* broadcast celebrating Allan Rohan Crite's seventy-fifth birthday at the WGBH studio in Cambridge, Massachusetts, 20 March 1985. Photograph by Aukram Burton

"[When I] ran into Mr. Crite, the things were aligned in the universe . . . that's what happened. But I didn't meet him. What happened was that my father died, and I was supposed to be in an exhibition at AAMARP [African American Master Artists-in-Residence Program]. . . . I said, I can't do it, this is too much . . . and Allan Crite found out that I was thinking about backing out of the exhibition, so he wrote me this letter, and I have it framed." (Fig. 100)

Johnetta Tinker

"That's what he used to call us at the Boston Collective, his recalcitrant family. He'd always have to pull our coattails about one thing or the other, and that relationship really blossomed for all of us. It was really something very sacred and very special for all of us, and we took it extremely seriously, [his] allowing us to be in his presence." (Fig. 101)

Napoleon Jones-Henderson

"Everybody knew who he was. Everybody protected him. Because he would walk around the neighborhood all times of night and day. He walked everywhere . . . unless we picked him up and drove him somewhere. And I would say, 'You shouldn't walk around at nighttime.' And people would say, 'Oh, we're watching out for him.' So it was that type of neighborhood, coming together and really understanding who he was and protecting him, you know, and making sure he got food. . . . They invited him out for Christmas and Thanksgiving dinners, and they would drop things off at his house. He was very protected in the neighborhood, and everybody knew who he was. He was the Dean of Boston."

Johnetta Tinker

Allan Rohan Crite
410 Columbus Avenue
Boston Massachusetts 02116
28 February 1982

Ms Johnetta Tinker
791 Tremont Street
Boston Massachusetts 02118

Johnetta Tinker:-
          I don't believe that we have ever met, though it may
be possible, as I do meet a lot of people, but at any rate the burden
of this letter is just a few words of whatever comfort they may be. Lotus
Do was talking to me about your taking part at the exhibition at AAMARP
but alsothe sharp pain you had because of your father's death. Susan
Thompson, another artist taking part in this exhibition had a similar
experience, not in the violence of her father being shot,but rather
through cancer. At the time of our exhibition, a joint affair, that is
Susan and myself, in Atlanta,her father was dying in New York and she
went to see him and she knew that it would be the last time she would
see him alive, and she had to make the decision as to whether she should
go to Atlanta to scheduled receptions and other activity, which had been
months to a year in preparation or not. I talked with her from Boston
and we decided to go ahead, leaving a telephone availability should her
father die. It was a difficult decision to make. Her father did die, but
Susan did what her father would want her to do, to go ahead with her work
But the pain of her father's death was real.I made a promise to her
mother that I would try to be to Susan as a father. I only cite this to
you, so that in your group of this present exhibition you will know
some one who to a degree knows your pain.
You may at times feel a sense of frustration, and does this all matter
what you are doing, your work and so forth. I had something of that when
I lost my mother just a few years ago in 1977, and I was alone for the
first time. I never married. For a while I had a question as to what was
my work worth, it all seemed so meaningless in the face of death. But
this is not true, for your work, my work and the work of artists has
meaning for other people in their lives in all kinds of ways.

The void caused by death is real, and it has a pain all of its own and
we are helped through it by hands stretched towards us, hands of love,
of affection, of friendship. Susan's hand was stretched towards me when
in my mother's death I was alone for the first time in my life, and my
hand was stretched towards her when she lost her father, and my hand is
stretched towards you to help even a little, for you to walk through
this bit of life

Allan Rohan Crite
artist/historian

Fig. 100. Letter from Allan Rohan Crite to Johnetta Tinker, 28 February 1982. Courtesy of the private collection of Johnetta Tinker

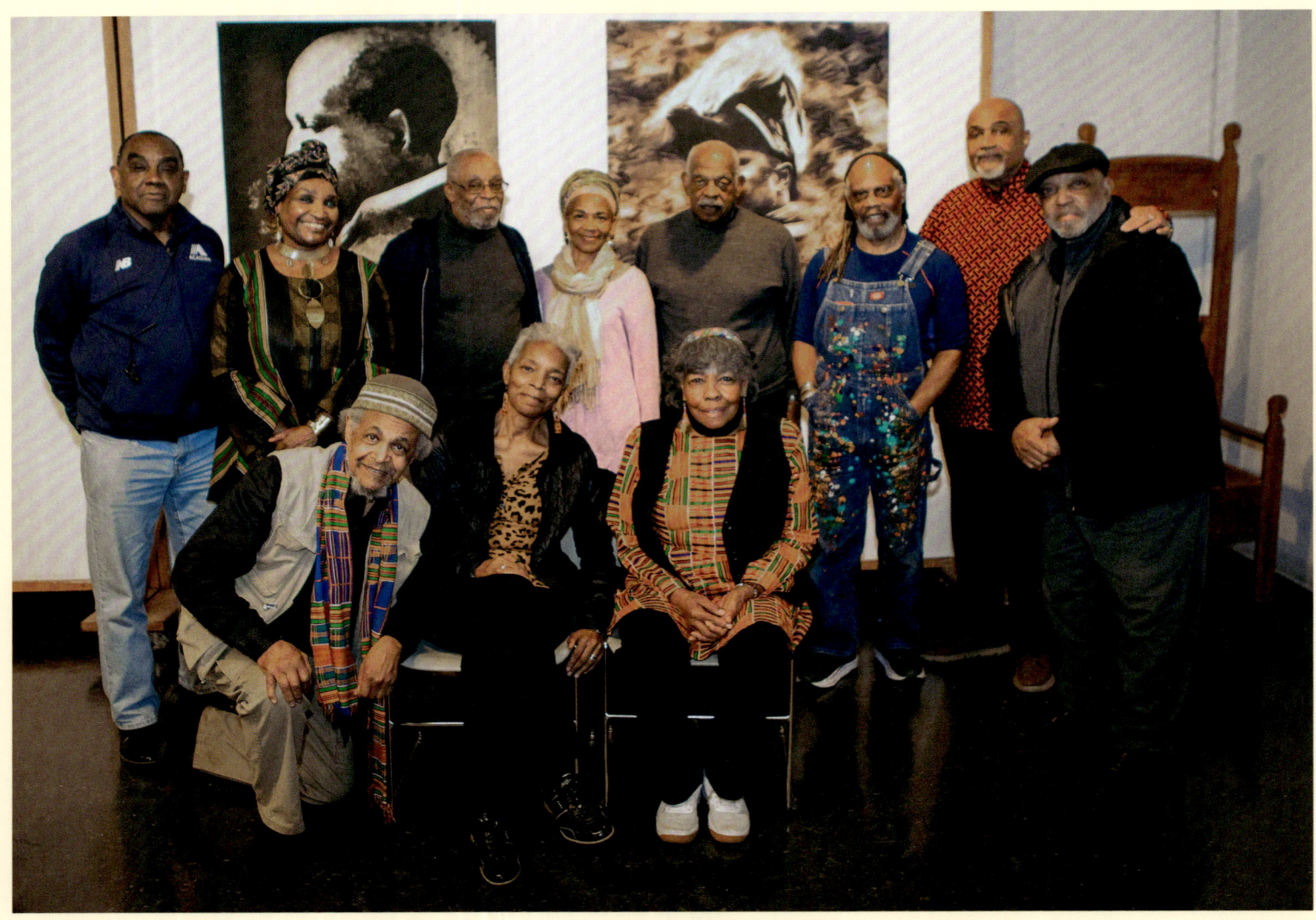

Fig. 101. Boston's Black arts community members, including the Boston Collective and What in the World, meet at the African American Master Artists-in-Residence Program (AAMARP). *Front row, left to right:* Napoleon Jones-Henderson, Johnetta Tinker, and Susan Thompson; *back row, left to right:* Tony Van Der Meer, Gloretta Baynes, Reginald Jackson, Nefertiti Burton, Barry Gaither, Paul Goodnight, Aukram Burton, and Laurence Pierce, 15 March 2024. Photograph by Aukram Burton

"By the time I would leave him, my head would be swimming because he had laid so much information on me, but it was good. So the next week, I came back, and I think I had brought him a dinner, which he really appreciated. And so it became kind of like a thing we had that I would bring him down a dinner on Saturdays and we [would] have dinner together."

Susan Thompson

"He was the glue. He was the visionary. He was the grandfather. He was the father."

Denise Patmon

THE CRITE HOUSE MUSEUM

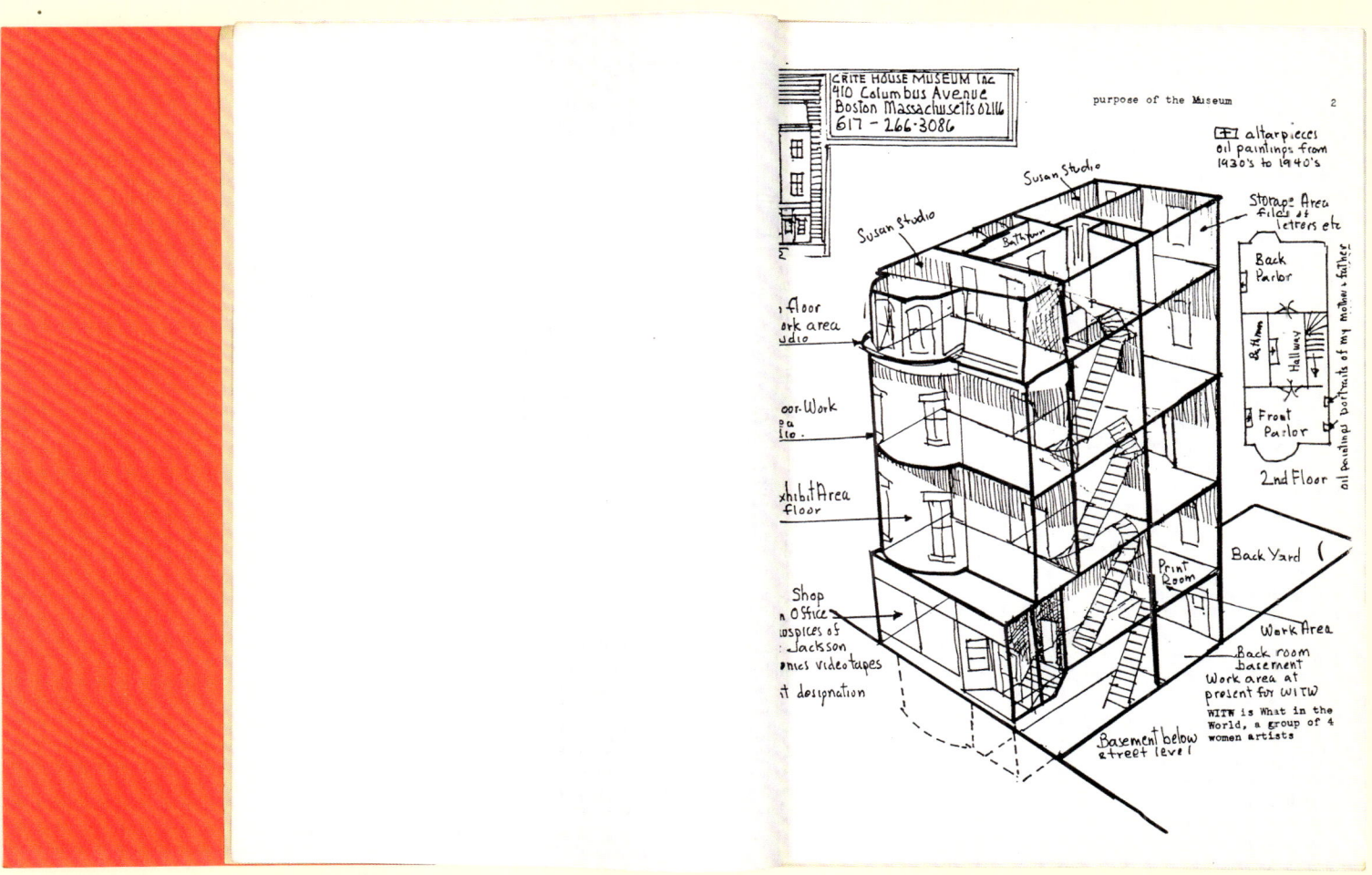

Fig. 102. Allan Rohan Crite, *The Museum Project and Organization of the Crite House Museum,* about 1986. Hand-bound book. Collection of Susan Thompson

"His house was a studio, a living studio."

Napoleon Jones-Henderson

"You just go into a different orbit in his house."

Denise Patmon

"Now, the house itself was like many in the South End. It had multiple floors. I think there were four floors in all, and there was a narrow central stair[case] that you had to climb to all of those spaces. And Allan had studios on multiple floors. On his first floor, he had a copy machine from which he could generate copies similar to what we would call mimeograph. It's always a little effort to explain these because they're way before Xerox and all of that electronic copying. This was done on, like, an offset machine with a crank that turns (fig. 102). So he had a studio on the first level where he could do that kind of work, and every level was full of work previously done. When you ascended that first stair[case] in his house and you came to the second landing, there was a huge altarpiece on the wall there, and hardly any vacant space anywhere to be spotted. In the mix of that, there was a portrait of his mother and other references to Roxbury, because he made his subject the community where he lived, extending it to pick up some of Cambridge because he was involved at Harvard and church life [across the river]."

Barry Gaither

"Allan and I bonded very quickly . . . in part because I was doing legal work for artists. And at the time [the 1980s], he was very interested in converting his home in the South End into a nonprofit museum where people could see his work and sit with him and learn from him as a teacher and mentor." (Fig. 103)

Ted Landsmark

"The Crite House Museum was a very interesting challenge because at that point in time there really weren't any other living artists in Boston who were interested in opening their homes and studios on a full-time basis to young and emerging artists in the community. And Allan was really in the leadership of a group of artists who were beginning to think about how their work could be transmitted to the community and to other emerging artists by creating house museums and galleries. . . . Entering the house gave one a sense that he was incredibly prolific. . . . He collected the work of other artists in the Greater Boston area, but his own work filled the house. Every drawer, every wall, every crevice had some drawing or book that he had produced. And so walking into the house was like walking into a culture that he had created . . . his vision of what Boston was."

Ted Landsmark

"It was very difficult to turn a studio space into a living museum of the work of a living artist. The tax code, the city's building codes, and regulations that existed that limited the way you could work. . . . In fact, when you look around the city, you find that there are relatively few house museums that are dedicated to the work of a single artist. Turning a personal home into a museum, particularly when that home is not designed for large crowds . . . structure, access, and financial management [are] . . . a real challenge."

Ted Landsmark

"Oh, he had guestbooks. Oh, Lord. Allan Rohan Crite had guestbooks. I mean, he was just naturally a chronicler, a collector of important information, and that was his way of honoring all the people who had come through his life."

Napoleon Jones-Henderson

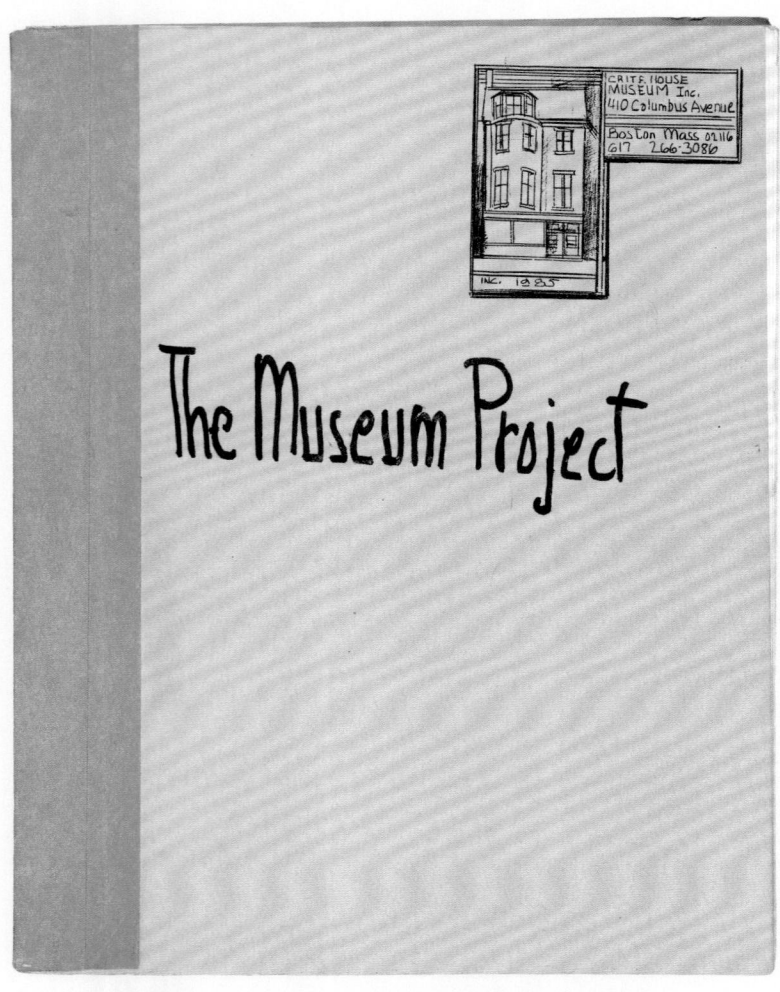

Fig. 103. Allan Rohan Crite, *The Museum Project and Organization of the Crite House Museum,* about 1986. Hand-bound book, 27.9 × 21.6 cm. Collection of Susan Thompson

"It was sort of like being in a Renaissance or Baroque-period European museum with his use of sacred images, gold leaf, and the Christian iconic symbolism that European artists utilize, and taking that all the way back beyond European artists to ancient Ethiopia. . . . His house was actually an art university."

Napoleon Jones-Henderson

"I got tired of going to his house and taking still pictures. And I started going with my movie camera so I could get it all right. Every time I was there . . . I saw something different. It was literally a museum. And I'm so heartbroken about the current situation." (Fig. 104)

Aukram Burton

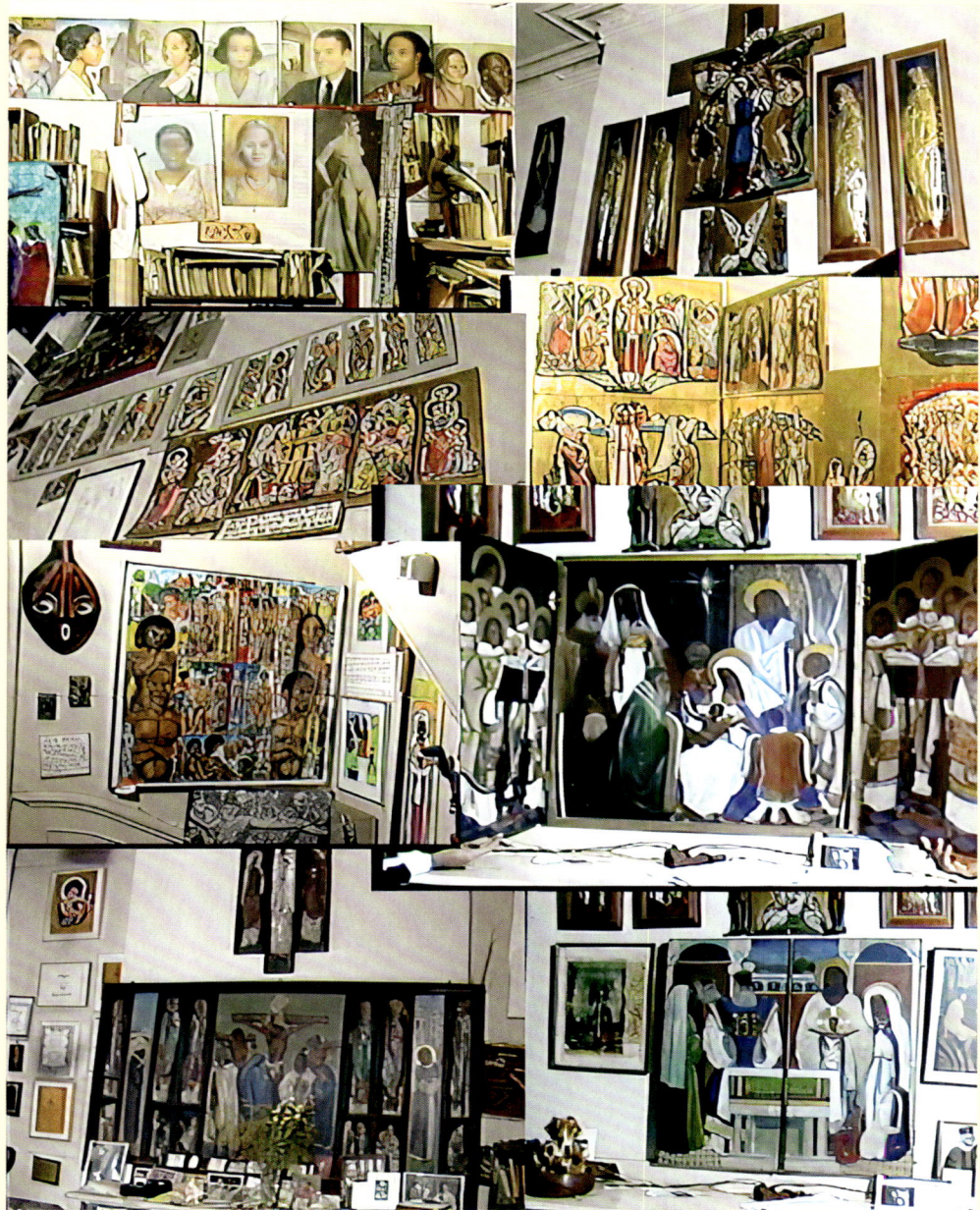

Fig. 104. Allan Rohan Crite House Studio, 1980s. Many people believed that the Allan Rohan Crite House Studio was like visiting a museum. Every wall was covered with art. This collage gives the viewer a vicarious experience of its interior. Photograph by Aukram Burton

"When you walked into that house, it was like, where am I? You're transported to another world because the whole place was plastered with art from floor to ceiling, and three floors of it. So there was art everywhere. There was no resting place for your eye. And these [prints] were just, like, all over. And it was the most amazing experience. I think anybody who's visited him in his house, they were in for a treat."

Susan Thompson

"That's when he invited me over to his house for the first time, and I was so amazed. I was like, 'How can somebody do so much work?' I mean, it was so much that it was almost overwhelming. . . . Then all the artists from the Boston Collective and everything, they donated work; we all gave him work, too. So, with the combination of people giving him work, his staircase going up—[it] was just so much work, it was layered one over the other. He made sure you could see everything." (Fig. 105)

Johnetta Tinker

"It was a gathering place of ideas, laughter, fun, messing with each other, looking at each other's work, critiquing each other's work, inspiring one another, finding out more information about what's going on in the community and if there's some way we could help. . . . We would bring food together. . . . You know, it's like, oh, I'll make something and bring it because I'm going to Mr. Crite's house. I'll make something and Susan will show up with something. And we didn't even know we were all coming there. . . . Then we [would] wind up eating and, you know, having fun."

Johnetta Tinker

"I went to his place and it was a museum. It was a shrine. It was the most magnificent array of someone's life experience and psyche in their environment that I've ever seen."

Arthur Dion

Opposite: Fig. 105. This collage represents a snapshot of the continual flow of people, young and elderly, who had the privilege of visiting the Allan Rohan Crite House Studio, 1980s. Photograph by Aukram Burton

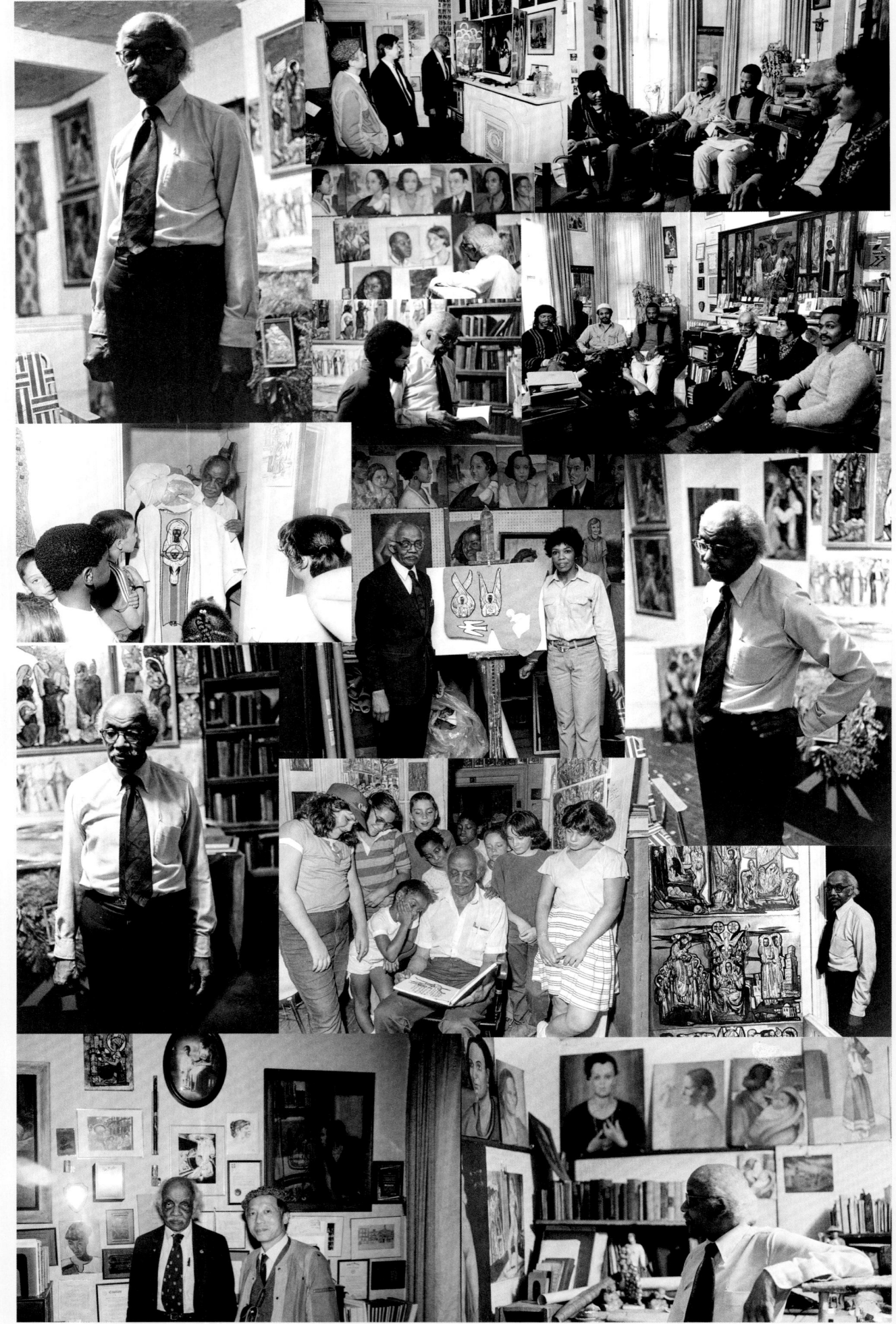

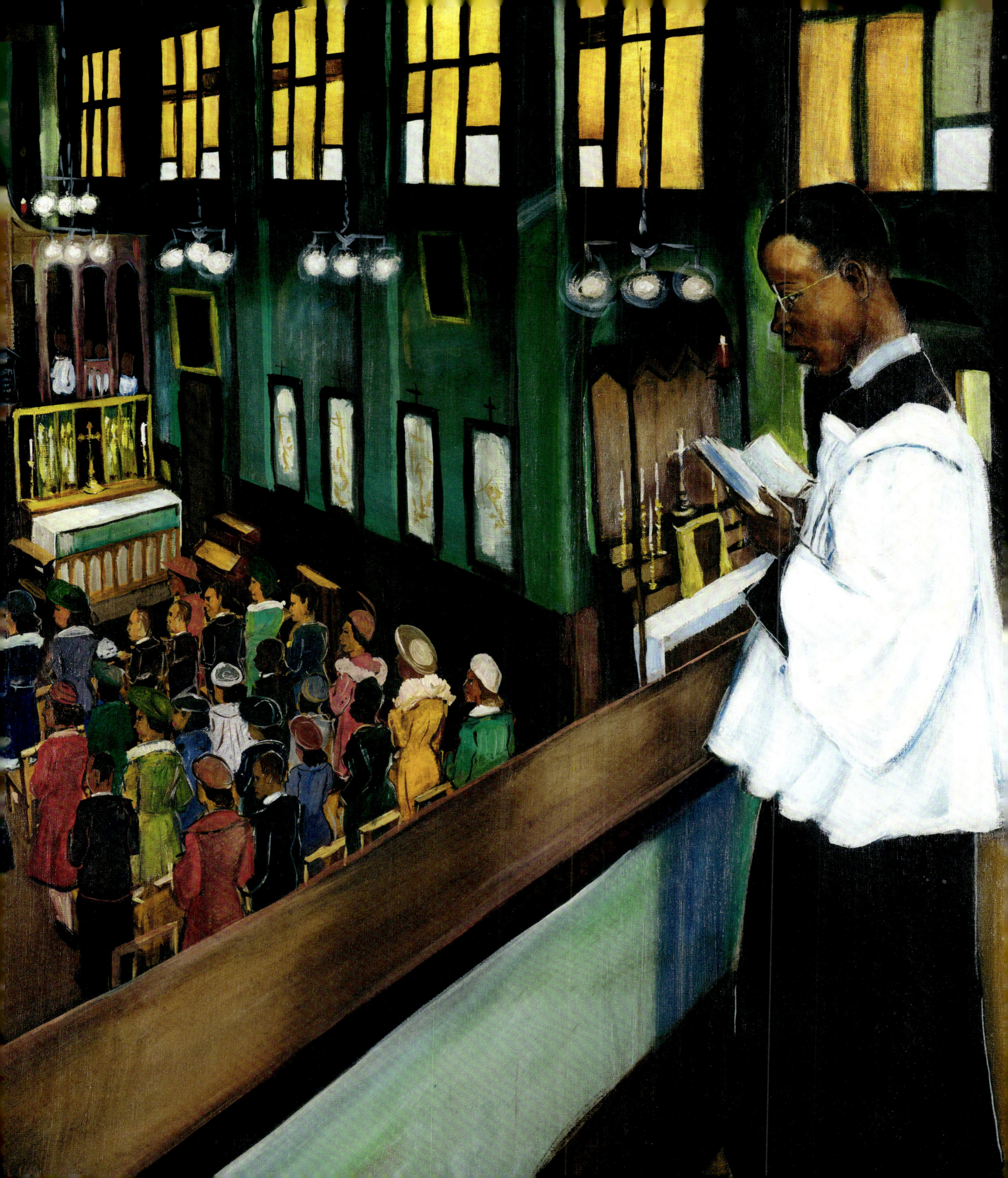

CHRONOLOGY

Compiled by Julie Levin Caro

1910
Allan Rohan Crite is born on 20 March, in North Plainfield, New Jersey, to parents Oscar William Crite (1875–1937) and Annamae Palmer Crite (1891–1977).

The Crite family relocates to Boston, residing at 401 Shawmut Avenue in the South End. Oscar Crite works as an engineer
and Annamae as a homemaker. Mother and son begin attending services at St. Bartholomew's Episcopal Church in Cambridge, and Annamae becomes a prominent member of the Altar Guild and the first African American to enroll in classes at Harvard Extension School. Beginning in the 1940s, she encourages her son to study there as well.[1]

1915
Crite begins education in the Boston Public Schools, first at George C. Bancroft Elementary and later at Rice Middle School.

1918–1925
Attends the Children's Art Centre in the South End and studies drawing with Elizabeth Ward Perkins and Charles H. Woodbury, producing a series of action stick-figure drawings, two of which are reproduced in Woodbury and Perkins's *The Art of Seeing* (1925) (see. fig. 9).

about 1919
Allan visits the Isabella Stewart Gardner Museum on a field trip with students from the Children's Art Centre. Annamae and some of the other mothers are invited to have tea with Mrs. Gardner.[2]

1924
Enrolls in Boston English High School and takes vocational classes at the School of the Museum of Fine Arts, Boston.

1925
Crite family moves to 2 Dilworth Street in the Lower Roxbury neighborhood of Boston; lives there for forty-six years, until the street is demolished as part of an urban renewal project.

1928
Crite is invited by Jane and Walter Kilham to spend the summer working and painting in the artists' colony they had established at their estate in Tamworth, New Hampshire.[3]

1929
Allan graduates from Boston English High School and enrolls at the School of the Museum of Fine Arts, Boston, where he is awarded a tuition scholarship and studies industrial design and a traditional academic art curriculum with teachers Philip Leslie Hale, a leading member of the Boston School of painters, and Russian émigré artist Alexandre Iacovleff, who exposes Crite to non-Western art and ethnographic portraiture (plate 2).[4]

In his first semester at art school, he writes to sociologist and activist W. E. B. Du Bois asking for "a list of books dealing with the Negro in the world of art," and receives an immediate response; Du Bois recommends "'New Negro,' Alain Locke, 'The Negro in Literature and Art,' [Benjamin] Brawley, and 'The Complete Works of Leo Frobenius.'"[5]

Crite joins the Boston Society of Independent Artists and participates in its annual exhibitions through the 1950s.[6]

Oscar is incapacitated by a massive stroke caused by a workplace accident. This event creates financial hardship for the

Crite family. Annamae goes to work cleaning apartments and office buildings, allowing her son to remain in art school.[7]

Also in the 1920s
Crite designs sets and acts with the Allied Arts Players, an African American theater group in Boston. Sings spirituals on the radio with the Clef Choir.

1930
His watercolors and drawings are included in the Harmon Foundation's annual exhibition of African American artists. Participates in subsequent exhibitions in 1931 and 1933.[8]

Illustration *Depth* is published in the May issue of *Opportunity: A Journal of Negro Life.*

Crite plays the part of Petou, a schemer, in the Allied Arts Players' 1930 production of *Dessalines, Black Emperor of Haiti,* by William E. Easton, directed by Maud Cuney Hare.[9]

1933
Brush-and-ink drawing *Down with the Walls Black Boy!* is published in *Crisis Magazine.*

1934
In his review of the Seventh Annual Exhibition of the Boston Society of Independent Artists in the *Boston Evening Transcript,* art critic Albert Cochrane comments favorably and illustrates Crite's oil painting *Settling the World's Problems* (1933) (plate 3). The review formally introduces Crite to the Boston art world and leads to his being added to the roster of artists represented by the Grace Horne Gallery on Newbury Street in Boston.[10]

Opposite: Detail of *The Choir Singer*, plate 18

From February to May, Crite is one of a small group of African American artists included in the short-lived experimental government art program, the Public Works of Art Project (PWAP).[11]

A painting is included in a group exhibition of PWAP artists at the Corcoran Gallery of Art, Washington, DC.

Crite has his first one-person show at the Grace Horne Gallery. He continues to show his work at the Grace Horne Gallery and, after 1945, at its successor, the Margaret Brown Gallery, until the late 1950s.[12]

1935
Crite creates his first set of *Stations of the Cross* (three-by-five-inch linoleum block prints). Examples of these works are in the collections of the Metropolitan Museum of Art, the Boston Public Library, and the National Center of Afro-American Artists, Boston.[13]

1936
He graduates from the School of the Museum of Fine Arts, Boston, and receives the Boit Prize for Painting.[14]

In February, Crite joins the Easel Division of the Federal Art Project (FAP), part of President Roosevelt's New Deal. Resigns from the FAP in December, when funding cuts would have required that he apply for relief assistance to continue in the program.[15]

Participates in a government-sponsored artist workshop at the Fogg Art Museum at Harvard, learning about fresco, encaustic, and mosaic techniques, some of which he would use in large-scale religious art commissions completed for the Rambusch Decorating Company in the late 1940s.[16]

Crite's oil painting *School's Out* (1936) is included in the exhibition *New Horizons in American Art* at the Museum of Modern Art, New York.[17]

Another painting is included in the Texas Centennial Exhibition, Hall of Negro Life, Dallas.

1937
Crite's father, Oscar William Crite, dies at home.

Crite begins creating his series of brush-and-ink illustrated spirituals, which he develops from serial brush-and-ink illustrations of the Passion of Christ and other New Testament scenes begun in the 1920s.[18]

1939
He exhibits for the first time at the Boston Museum of Modern Art (renamed the Institute of Contemporary Art in 1948) and continues to exhibit there regularly through the 1960s.[19]

Also in the 1930s
Crite takes evening courses in business and psychology at Boston University.[20]

He participates in the restoration and renovation of the artworks inside Boston's Trinity Church.[21]

1940
He begins working full-time as an engineering draughtsman and technical illustrator at the Charlestown Navy Yard in Boston.[22]

Crite's work is included in the exhibitions *35 under 35* at the Museum of Modern Art in New York and *The Face of America,* an exhibit in the Contemporary Art Building at the New York World's Fair.

Crite's oil paintings *Douglass Square* (1936) (St. Louis Art Museum) (see fig. 69) and *Last Game at Dusk* (1939) (Boston Athenaeum) are published in Alain Locke's *The Negro in Art: A Pictorial Record of the Negro Artist and of the Negro Theme in Art.*[23]

His oil paintings *The Handy Street Bridge* (1939) (see fig. 53) and *Last Game at Dusk* (1939) are included in the *Exhibition of*

the Art of the American Negro (1851 to 1940), curated by Alain Locke and presented at the American Negro Exposition at the Tanner Art Galleries in Chicago from 4 July to 2 September.[24]

1941
The oil painting *Parade on Hammond Street* (1935) (see fig. 49) is included in the historic exhibition *American Negro Art* at Edith Halpert's Downtown Gallery in New York, alongside works by Henry Ossawa Tanner, Romare Bearden, Augusta Savage, and Jacob Lawrence. Duncan Phillips purchases *Parade on Hammond Street* from the exhibition for his growing collection of American art in Washington, DC.[25]

1943
Crite's oil painting *Shawmut Avenue* is included in the *Exhibition of the Work of 37 Negro Artists* at the Mountain View Officers' Club, Fort Huachuca, Arizona.[26]

1944
Harvard University Press publishes *Were You There When They Crucified My Lord: A Negro Spiritual in Illustrations.*[27]

A two-person show of works by Crite and Hale Woodruff is mounted at Grace Horne Gallery, Boston.[28]

1947
The Society of St. John the Evangelist in Cambridge, Massachusetts, publishes *All Glory: Brush Drawing Meditations on the Prayer of Consecration.*[29]

1948
Harvard University Press publishes *Three Spirituals from Earth to Heaven* ("Nobody Knows the Trouble I See," "Swing Low, Sweet Chariot," (plate 12) and "Heaven") with a foreword by Roland Hayes.[30]

The Boston Department of Social Services and the Episcopal Diocese of Massachusetts publish the pamphlet *Is It Nothing to You?*, a series of pen-and-ink drawings showing a Black Crucifixion against the backdrop of the modern city.[31]

An exhibition is held at the Boston Athenaeum of Crite's religious works on paper, including original illustrations for *Three Spirituals* and *Is It Nothing to You?*[32]

1949–1950
While employed by the Rambusch Decorating Company, Crite completes several large-scale liturgical artworks, including an altar mural for St. Augustine's Episcopal Church in Brooklyn, New York (destroyed by fire in 1972), paints the Baldachin at the Franciscan Monastery in Washington, DC, and completes a set of *Stations of the Cross* and five other sanctuary paintings in the Convent of the Oblate Sisters of Providence, Detroit, Michigan.[33]

Also in the 1940s
Produces additional series of illustrated spirituals: *Joshua Fit the Battle of Jericho* (incomplete) (1940), *O Lord, Have Mercy on Me* (1940), *Go Tell It on the Mountain* (1941), *Ride on King Jesus* (1941), *O Mary, Where Is Your Baby* (1942), *I Know the Lord He Laid His Hands on Me* (1943).[34]

1950
The Department of Religion and the School of Painting and Sculpture at Columbia University in New York host an exhibit of Crite's religious artworks.[35]

1951
Exhibition of Christmas wood engravings at the Boston Athenaeum, overlapping with an exhibition of paintings by Crite's former teacher, Charles H. Woodbury.[36]

about 1955
Crite purchases an offset lithography press and uses it to make multiple reproductions of his liturgical drawings and to create the weekly church bulletin covers that he sold to Episcopal congregations in Boston and other places in the United States and Mexico from the mid-1950s to the early 1990s. Crite also used his lithography press to self-publish illustrated texts, such as *An Autobiographical Sketch*

(1977), *Recollections of My Childhood* (1978), and *Reflections on the Afro-Asian-American Cultural Heritage of Peoples of Color* (1985), which he distributed to libraries, public schools, and archives in Boston and elsewhere.[37]

1957
He delivers a lecture at the School of Theology at the University of the South in Sewanee, Tennessee.[38]

1957–1959
Paints mural in youth room at Grace Church in Vineyard Haven, Martha's Vineyard[39] (see fig. 21).

1961
Crite participates in an international exhibition of religious art in Trieste, Italy.[40]

1965
Crite travels on a three-week ecumenical pilgrimage to Europe.

1966
He travels to Puerto Rico and subsequently depicts the Nativity, Stations of the Cross, and other biblical narratives featuring Black and Latino figures.

1968
He earns a bachelor's degree from the Harvard University Extension School.[41]

Crite creates accordion books printed on his press, among them *Reflections on the Afro-Asian-American Cultural Heritage of Peoples of Color*. The Boston Athenaeum publishes his essay *Towards a Rediscovery of the Cultural Heritage of the United States*, and hosts an exhibition of Crite's paintings, drawings, and carvings in celebration of his Harvard degree (plates 32–35).[42]

Elma Lewis founds the National Center of Afro-American Artists, which will collect work by Crite under the direction of curator, and later director, Edmund Barry Gaither.

1969
Crite travels to Mexico and produces sets of *Stations of the Cross* on his printing press.

Second edition of *Were You There When They Crucified My Lord* is published by the McGrath Publishing Company, College Park, Maryland.

1970
Crite's work is included in the exhibition *Afro-American Artists: New York and Boston,* curated by Edmund Barry Gaither for the Museum of Fine Arts, Boston.

1971
Our Elders: Crite & Dames, an exhibition of works by Crite and Chester A. Dames, is organized by the National Center of Afro-American Artists, Boston.

Crite gifts sixteen oils, thirty-nine watercolors, and fifteen ink drawings to the Boston Athenaeum, accompanied by an exhibition.

The Crites' home at 2 Dilworth Street is torn down as part of Boston's redevelopment program. Crite moves with his mother to 410 Columbus Avenue in the South End (see fig. 70).

1972
Crite supplements his Boston Athenaeum gift with an additional thirty-seven childhood drawings.

1974
He retires from the Charlestown Navy Yard.

Begins work at Harvard University Extension School's Grossman Library as a part-time librarian, a post he holds until 1989.[43]

1975
Crite's work is included in the exhibition *Jubilee: Afro-American Artists on Afro-America,* Museum of Fine Arts, Boston.

1977

Annamae Crite dies at home.

Crite self-publishes *An Autobiographical Sketch*.[44]

He creates the series *An Artist's Sketchbook of the South End: A Walking Tour about Black People* as part of an artist's residency at the Museum of African American History in Boston. He gifts this portfolio and other prints to the Boston Athenaeum.

Artist Dana Chandler founds the African American Master Artists-in-Residence Program (AAMARP) at Northeastern University (plate 98).

about 1979

Crite organizes the Boston Collective, a group of younger Black Boston artists, including Paul Goodnight, Vusumuzi Maduna (Dennis Didley), Reginald Jackson, Aukram Burton, Napoleon Jones-Henderson, and Susan Gilliam Thompson. Later other artists will join, like Johnetta Tinker, Weeta Lopes, and Lotus Do.[45]

1979

Receives Honorary Doctorate of Humanities, Suffolk University, Boston.

Crite exhibits at the Boston Athenaeum with "The Group," including Calvin Burnett, Dana Chandler, John Wilson, Richard Yarde, and others.[46]

The Harriet Tubman House Art Gallery opens at the United South End Settlements.

1982

The exhibition *The Lost and Found Paintings of Allan Rohan Crite,* at the Museum of Afro-American History, Boston, organized by Byron Rushing, includes ten of Crite's early *Neighborhood Series* oils, including *Settling the World's Problems* (1933), which were found by William Greenbaum in a Boston warehouse in the late 1960s and then purchased and gifted to the Museum of Afro-American History, now the Museum of African American History.[47]

1983

Crite travels to China with Aukram Burton and Susan Thompson, members of the Boston Collective, as part of the Community Fellows Program in the Department of Urban Studies and Planning at Massachusetts Institute of Technology, a program started by Mel King.[48]

In an MIT newsletter about the Community Fellows Program, Crite first discusses establishing the Allan Rohan Crite House Museum, saying, "Hundreds of people have toured my house and viewed the art and history displayed there. . . . I would love to establish my home [as] a house museum to permanently exhibit the artistic history of people of color in New England."[49]

1985

Institutions across Boston celebrate Crite's work on the occasion of his seventy-fifth birthday, with exhibitions, programs, and performances at the Boston Athenaeum, Boston Public Library, Museum of Fine Arts, National Center of Afro-American Artists, African American Master Artists-in-Residence Program, Harriet Tubman House Art Gallery, and Children's Art Centre.[50]

1986

Crite receives the 350th Harvard University Anniversary Medal.[51]

The Harvard University Extension School and the Harvard Extension Alumni Association establish the Annamae and Allan R. Crite Prize, awarded annually to Extension School degree recipients who demonstrate "singular dedication to learning and the arts."[52]

Crite travels to China with members of the Boston Collective for an art exchange and exhibition at the Guangzhou Academy of Fine Arts.[53]

Allan Rohan Crite Square (now Crite Park) is named at the corner of Columbus Avenue and West Canton Street in Boston's South End.[54]

1988

He receives an Honorary Doctor of Fine Arts degree, Massachusetts College of Fine Arts, Boston.

1989

Crite's work is included in the major touring exhibition *Against the Odds: African-American Artists and the Harmon Foundation.*[55]

1990

The exhibition *Allan Rohan Crite: A Retrospective, 1924–1989* is mounted at the National Center of Afro-American Artists.

1992

The oil paintings *School's Out* (1936) and *Sunlight and Shadow* (1941) (fig. 51) are included in the exhibition and catalogue *Free within Ourselves: African-American Artists in the Collection of the National Museum of American Art.*[56]

1993

Crite marries Jacquelyn Cleveland Cox.

Crite delivers an Eye of the Beholder lecture at the Isabella Stewart Gardner Museum and recalls his first visit to the museum as a child and the importance of house museums for understanding the culture of the time.[57]

about 1993–1997

The artist's work is included in the traveling exhibition *Alone in a Crowd: Prints of the 1930s–40s by African-American Artists from the Collection of Reba and Dave Williams.*[58]

1994

Crite receives an Honorary Doctorate of Divinity from the General Theological Seminary of the Episcopal Church, New York City.

1995

The Limited Editions Club, New York, publishes a set of the artist's original etchings illustrating *The Revelation of Saint John the Divine.*[59]

1997

The exhibition *Allan Crite's Boston* is held from 15 September through 29 November at the Boston Athenaeum. Crite receives a proclamation from the Massachusetts secretary of state at the opening of this exhibition (see fig. 84).

2001

The exhibition *Allan Rohan Crite: Artist-Reporter of the African American Community* is staged at the Frye Art Museum in Seattle.[60]

2007

Crite dies on 6 September at age ninety-seven at his home in Boston's South End.[61]

2008

Memorial exhibitions are held at the National Center of Afro-American Artists, Boston, the Boston Athenaeum, and the Boston Public Library.

2019

A campaign begins to redesign and rebuild Allan Rohan Crite Square as Crite Park.[62]

2020

Words and Images: Allan Rohan Crite, 1910–2007: A Virtual Visit to St. Botolph Club Exhibition.[63]

2022

The exhibition *Unchained: Allan Rohan Crite, Spirituality, and Black Activism* is mounted by the Munson Art Museum, Utica, New York.[64]

Notes

1   The major sources of biographical information that inform this chronology are Crite 1977b, which includes a decade-by-decade account of the events of the artist's life and artistic career, along with excerpts from his diaries with copious images of his artworks; Crite 1930–79; and two extensive interviews: Crite 1979–80 and Clark 1979. While these sources rely heavily on the artist's own memories, which can be unreliable, we have attempted to provide a total picture based on numerous primary and secondary sources.

2   In a lecture Crite delivered on 22 September 1993, as part of the Isabella Stewart Gardner Museum's Eye of the Beholder series, the artist offered the following recollection of visiting the Gardner Museum with his mother on this field trip: "I was astonished, amazed and overwhelmed by the beauty of the place. Later I made some drawings from memory, and as I understand, the drawings were very well received. Somehow [Mrs. Gardner] asked my mother and the other mothers to come up and have a cup of tea with her. And my mother's impression of Mrs. Gardner was a very gracious and kind person. . . . So I do have a kind of personal relationship." Crite quoted in Medvedow 1994, 14. The date of this encounter and the drawing of the Gardner's courtyard—which only survives in reproduction; the original is unlocated—is unclear. Gardner suffered a stroke in late 1919 that caused her largely to withdraw from public life. This suggests that the drawing was made very early in Crite's life—possibly in 1919, when he was eight or nine years old.

3   Crite explained in the Robert F. Brown interview that Walter Kilham encouraged him to join the Society of Independent Artists, and at this time artists Charles Hovey Pepper and Charles Hopkinson also took an interest in his work. Crite 1979–80.

4   A large group of Crite's early works on paper—drawings and watercolors from the artist's childhood and student work from the Museum School and the MFA's high school vocational art program—are in the collection of the National Center of Afro-American Artists, Boston.

5   W. E. B. Du Bois to Allan R. Crite, 14 November 1929, W. E. B. Du Bois Papers, MS 312, Special Collections and University Archives, University of Massachusetts Amherst Libraries, http://credo.library.umass.edu/view/full/mums312-b048-i050.

6   Documentation of Crite's early exhibitions in Boston can be found in the scrapbooks of the Boston Society of Independent Artists and in Crite's artist's file, both located in the Boston Art Archives/New England Art Information File, Fine Arts Department, Boston Public Library (BPL). Additional reviews are in the Dorothy Adlow Archives, Schlesinger Library, Radcliffe Institute for Advanced Study, Harvard University. Adlow, who was the art critic for the *Christian Science Monitor,* a national newspaper based in Boston, wrote the majority of the reviews of Crite's exhibitions in the 1930s and 1940s.

7   Crite 1979–80, 45. Crite also discusses this in Clark 1979.

8   Crite showed watercolors and pencil drawings in the Harmon Foundation's annual exhibitions in 1930, 1931, and 1933. See Reynolds and Wright 1989, 166–71, 284. Another valuable resource is Crite's artist file in the Harmon Foundation Papers at the Library of Congress, Washington, DC.

9   Play program copied from the artist's file at the BPL. Crite also recalled that Harlem Renaissance leader Alain Locke came to Boston in the 1930s to lecture on a national Black theater movement. Allan Rohan Crite, interview by Beryl Wright, audiotape, Allan Rohan Crite Research Institute, Boston.

10 In his review, Cochrane described *Settling the World's Problems* as "an interesting composition, one of the most ambitious and successful present." Cochrane 1934. As Crite explained to Robert Brown, "As a matter of fact, [the Grace Horne Gallery] became my semi-patrons. Back in those days, for an artist to be on Newbury Street, where the Grace Horn [*sic*] Galleries [*sic*] was, was unusual, and I think I was probably the only Black artist who had any gallery working for him at that time. They gave me several one-man shows." Crite 1979–80, 12–13. It is worth noting the important role of independent artists' societies in Boston and other American cities in providing artists of color and women artists with opportunities to show their work to the public.

11 Crite described his involvement in the PWAP and FAP in Crite 1977b, "Appendix I: The Works Progress Administration."

12 Crite 1979–80.

13 Crite also produced pen-and-ink drawings of the Stations of the Cross in the mid-1930s. One example, *Last Station: Suggestion for the Station of the Cross* (1935, Collection of David C. Driskell), is discussed and illustrated in Holland et al. 1998.

14 During his Museum School tenure, Crite also completed a degree in industrial design. According to the *Bulletin of the Museum of Fine Arts,* the courses offered in this program included book decoration, pen-and-ink illustration, Japanese brush drawing, stage set and costume design, metalwork, and stained-glass design. Although Crite's primary practice as a professional artist was as an illustrator and painter, he utilized various aspects of his design training during his early career to create his brush-and-ink illustrations for the spirituals, liturgical objects created in hammered metal, church murals, and designs for vestments, stained-glass windows, and church bulletin covers.

15 According to the artist, "when the money ran out on that particular section [of the FAP], they wanted me to continue, but

I'd have to continue as a relief artist. . . . My mother and I, we didn't quite like that connotation. So we took the painful decision to not continue in the program." Crite 1979–80, 31. Several lost FAP works by Crite are documented in black-and-white photographs in the "Final Report of the Massachusetts Division of the Federal Art Project," located in the Prints and Drawings Department at the BPL.

16 Crite 1979–80, 18–22, 61–62.

17 See MoMA 1936.

18 Examples of the liturgical drawings are in the collection of the National Center of Afro-American Artists, Boston.

19 Crite recalled his participation with this museum in Crite 1977b. Copies of notices, opening invitations, and catalogues for these exhibitions are in the artist's file at the BPL.

20 Crite 1979–80.

21 Allan Rohan Crite, "Religious Art of the 1950s," Allan Rohan Crite Vertical File, Smithsonian American Art Museum, Washington, DC.

22 Although Crite's career at the Navy Yard meant that he could not devote himself full-time to his artistic career, he viewed his work as a draughtsman as integral to his pursuit of art. As he explained to Robert Brown, "I've earned my living by drawing. As an illustrator in the Navy Department of course, I had to use all the skills that I had learned in school. I looked upon my work in the Navy Department as a means towards an end of promoting myself as an artist. It gave me a more secure financial basis, in a way. It really helped me a great deal." Crite 1979–80, 10. See also National Park Service 2024.

23 This volume was reprinted by Martino Fine Books in 2021.

24 See American Negro Exposition 1940.

25 A letter from Duncan Phillips to Edith Halpert dated 23 February 1942 describes the sale of Parade along with several other important works of African American art, including half of the forty panels of Jacob Lawrence's Migration Series (1940–41). Allan Rohan Crite curatorial file, Phillips Collection, Washington, DC. See also Rubenfeld 1999, 496.

26 Schacht et al. 2023.

27 Crite 1944. The set of original larger-scale brush-and-ink drawings are housed at the National Cathedral in Washington, DC. Crite wrote extensively on the spirituals and on the connections between religion and art. See, for example, Crite 1938, 1949, and 1954. In addition, the Allan Rohan Crite Papers include transcripts of his early lectures on religion, art, and the spirituals.

28 It is notable that Crite was shown alongside Woodruff, an artist based in New York and associated with the Harlem Renaissance. While he was a professor of art at Atlanta University from 1931 to 1946, Woodruff established the Atlanta Annuals, an exhibition featuring the work of African American artists, in which Crite participated.

29 Original drawings are, as of now, unlocated.

30 The set of original larger-scale brush-and-ink drawings are housed at the Houghton Library, Harvard University.

31 Copies of this pamphlet are in the artist's file at the Boston Athenaeum. See http://catalog.bostonathenaeum.org/vwebv/holdingsInfo?bibId=249882.

32 Athenaeum Items 1948.

33 The artist includes descriptions and photographs of these works in Allan Rohan Crite, "Religious Art of the 1950s," Allan Rohan Crite Vertical File, Smithsonian American Art Museum, Washington, DC.

34 The original brush-and-ink drawings are all in the collection of the artist's estate (Allan Rohan Crite Research Institute), except for O Lord, Have Mercy on Me (location unknown) and O Mary, Where Is Your Baby (Montclair Art Museum, Montclair, NJ).

35 "Reminiscences of Allan Rohan Crite," interview by Linda Chisholm for the Columbia University Oral History Project, 1977, https://clio.columbia.edu/catalog/4074333.

36 The exhibition is described in Athenaeum Items: A Library Letter from the Boston Athenaeum 53 (1951): 2.

37 In "Appendix III: An Approach to Non-Western Art and Non-Western Art in Africa—A Pilgrimage," in Crite 1977b, Crite related how his early interest in Asian and African art was the beginning of his conscious "move out of the confines of a Greco-Roman-Euro-American outlook." In addition to Reflections, many of his religious artworks that portray Christian subjects in relation to non-Western cultures reflect this shift in outlook.

38 Crite described the experience of confronting segregation in the South for the first time in Crite 1979–80.

39 Allan Rohan Crite to Rev. Tom Lehman, 23 November 1957, in which Crite says he hopes to get to the preliminary sketch for the altar painting in December; and Crite to Lehman, 21 September 1959, in which he refers to having visited the church that month and photographing the completed mural, both in Crite 1948–2002.

40 New York Times 1961.

41 Harvard was very important to the artist, as evidenced by the prominence in his home of his Harvard chairs and framed diploma. See also Queen 1998.

42 Boston Athenaeum: Reports for 1968, 10, https://cdm.bostonathenaeum.org/digital/collection/p16057coll17/id/5417/rec/4.

43 Harvard Gazette 2007.

44 Crite printed An Autobiographical Sketch on his litho press and deposited copies in various libraries around Boston, including the South End Branch of the BPL. Each one was slightly different and thus unique.

45 See Tanga 2024a and 2024b.

46 See Boston Athenaeum: Reports for 1980, https://cdm.bostonathenaeum.org/digital/collection/p16057coll17/id/5429/rec/15.

47 The exhibition catalogue by Byron Rushing, with comments on the paintings by Crite, is available at https://dc.suffolk.edu/afam/1/.

48 Tanga 2024a and 2024b. See also "Community Leaders Tour to China, November 9–25, 1983," Susan Thompson Archive, Boston.

49 Quoted in Duran 1983.

50 "Plans for 75th Birthday: January 1985 Update," Susan Thompson Archive, Boston.

51 "Crite, Allan Rohan," in Matney 1978, 201.

52 Harvard Gazette 2007.

53 Tanga 2024a and 2024b.

54 Ball 1986.

55 Reynolds and Wright 1989, 166–72.

56 Perry 1992, 51–54. This text and other exhibition catalogues and reference books contain some factual errors, which have led to misunderstandings about the artist and his early career.

57 Medvedow 1994, 14–15.

58 King-Hammond et al. 1993.

59 Three hundred copies of fifteen of Crite's etchings were printed on Kitakata paper at Wild Carrot Letterpress in Hadley, Massachusetts, and published by Limited Editions Club, New York.

60 See Caro et al. 2001.

61 Jacquelyn Cleveland Cox establishes the Allan Rohan Crite Research Institute in the wake of her husband's death to preserve her husband's legacy and work with institutions that want to exhibit and celebrate his work.

62 An overview of this project is described and illustrated at https://critepark.org/.

63 This exhibition was canceled because of the Covid pandemic, but a virtual exhibition is available online at https://berkshirefinearts.com/04-08-2020_words-and-images-allan-rohan-crite-1910-2007.htm

64 An overview of the exhibition and some installation photographs are available at https://www.munson.art/product/29756?v=30184.

Opposite: Detail of Mrs. Martin's Misses, plate 11

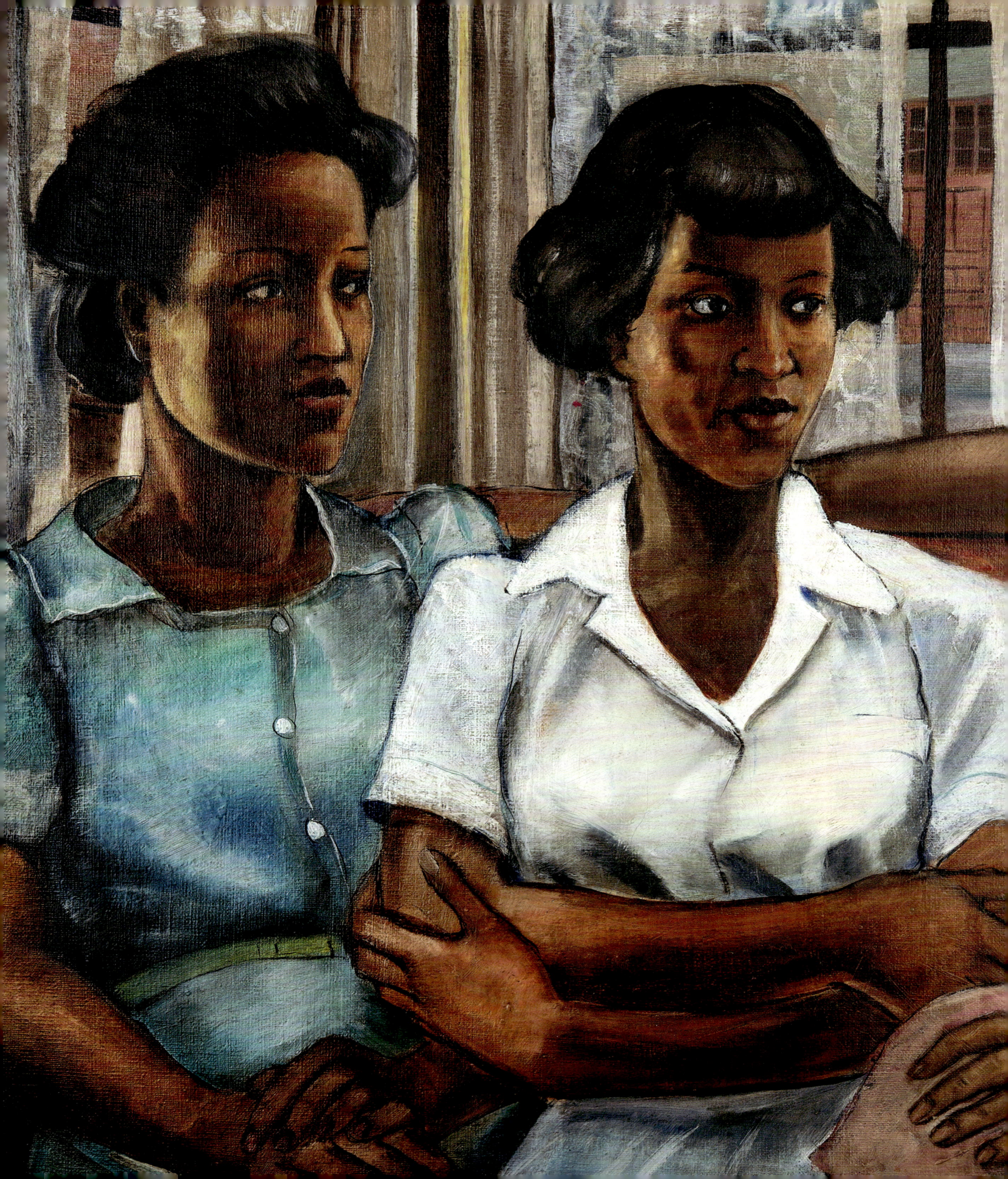

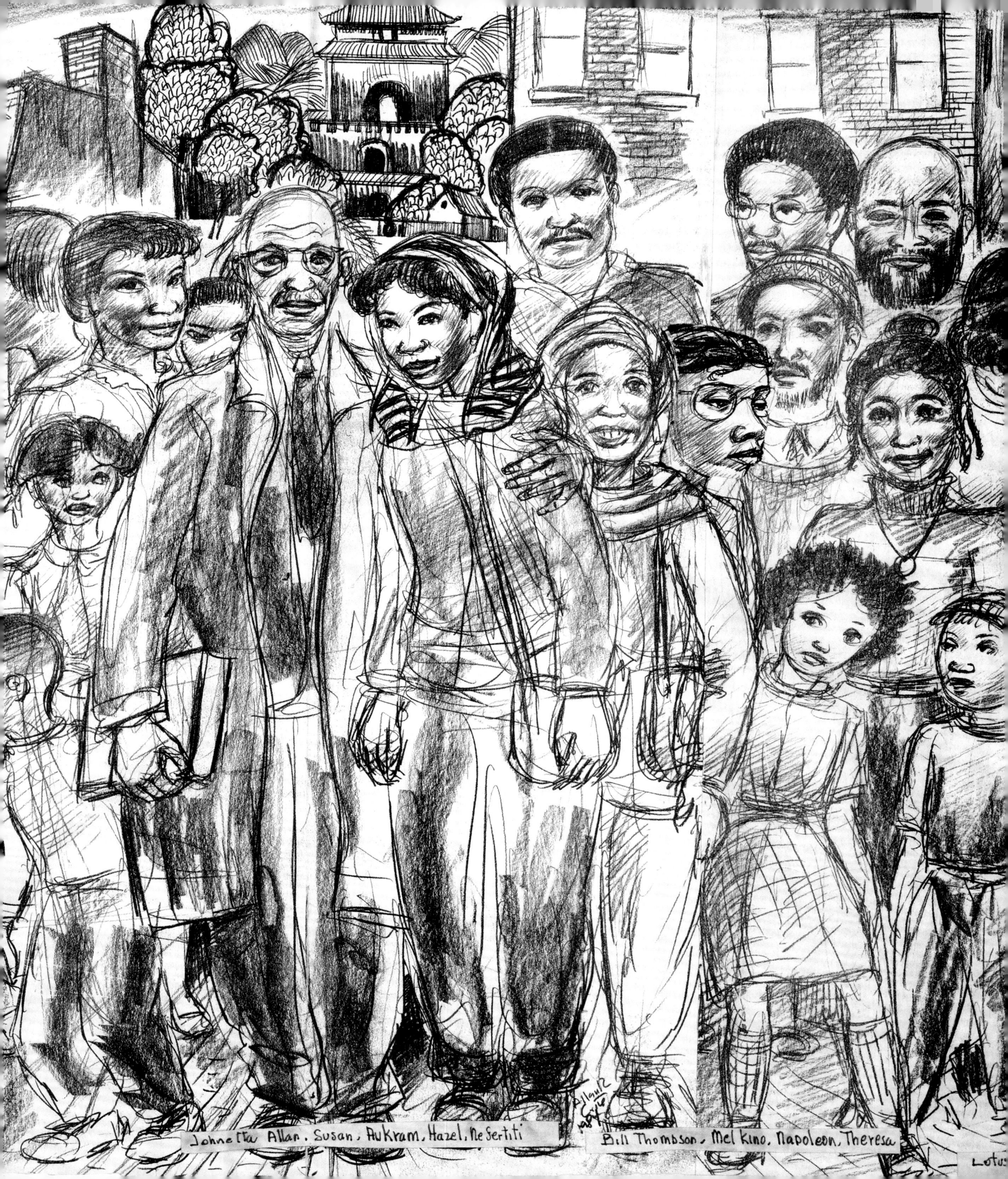

Johnetta, Allan, Susan, Aukram, Hazel, Nefertiti   Bill Thompson, Mel Kino, Napoleon, Theresa

CRITE THE HUMAN

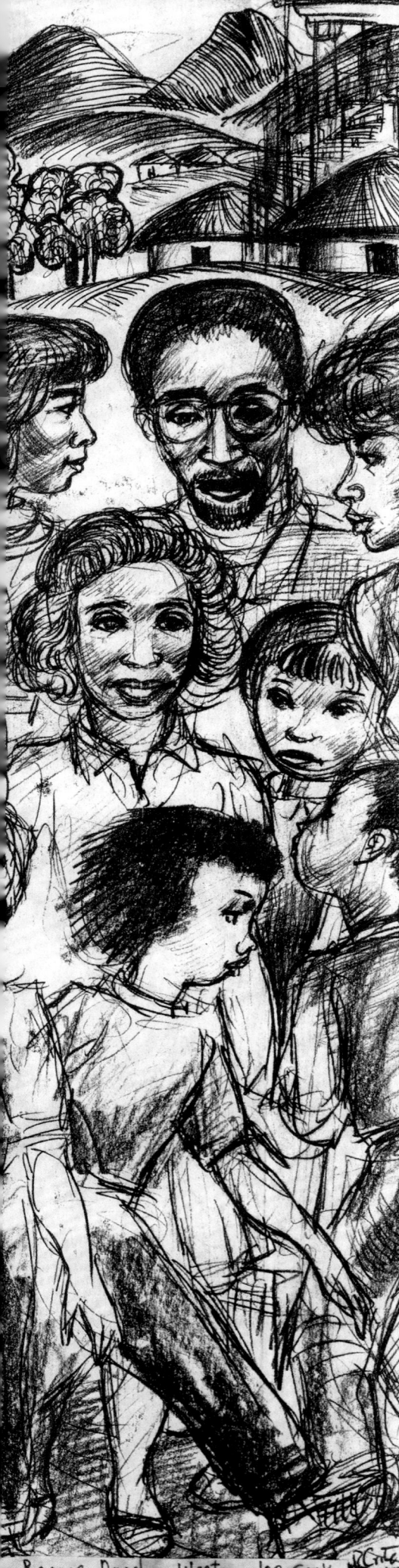

Reggie, Angela, Weeta, Joe Cook

"He was a fair and very calming person to be around. He had a lot of excitement when he saw art. His eyes would get wide and he would nod. But he didn't say very much. But when he did say something, it was very succinct and to the point."

Hakim Raquib

"He liked Moxie sodas. He loved syrup on everything. On his toast. On his chicken. On french fries. . . . He had a sweet tooth."

Denise Patmon

"Allan had a dry sense of humor that enabled people to really reflect on what he was saying and to reflect on themselves."

Ted Landsmark

"Oh, that trench coat, that's something you need to find: that trench coat along with that press, 'cause those two items were Allan Rohan Crite: his printing press and that trench coat."

Napoleon Jones-Henderson

"Very rarely did you see him without a black suit and a tie. He was definitely kind of a gentleman's gentleman."

Aukram Burton

"That little park [Crite Park]. He always tickled me about that park because he said, 'Everybody got a square, and I got a triangle.' I said, 'Well, you know, you use a lot of triangles in your artwork.'"

Johnetta Tinker

"He was very loving, caring, supportive. And he was like that with everybody. . . . [A family] had a fire. . . . The house didn't burn down to the ground, but it was very bad. And on hearing this, the first thing Allan did was give them money so they could cover the roof with tarping so you can keep the elements out of the house while they're figuring out what to do or while it's being fixed up. He always did what he could do. I mean, he couldn't rebuild their house, but he could see that they got tarp to put over the roof so the elements wouldn't get in."

Susan Thompson

"Mr. Crite was just one of those people who was always there, and he was such a quiet and demure gentleman that you almost didn't notice him, but you couldn't help but notice him. He was just so ever present."

Napoleon Jones-Henderson

"His humanity. Just that one word. His loving humanity. . . . Of course, he was talented and all that, but his humanity, his love of people, of human people."

Johnetta Tinker

Detail of *Ancestors and Our Neighborhood*, fig. 39

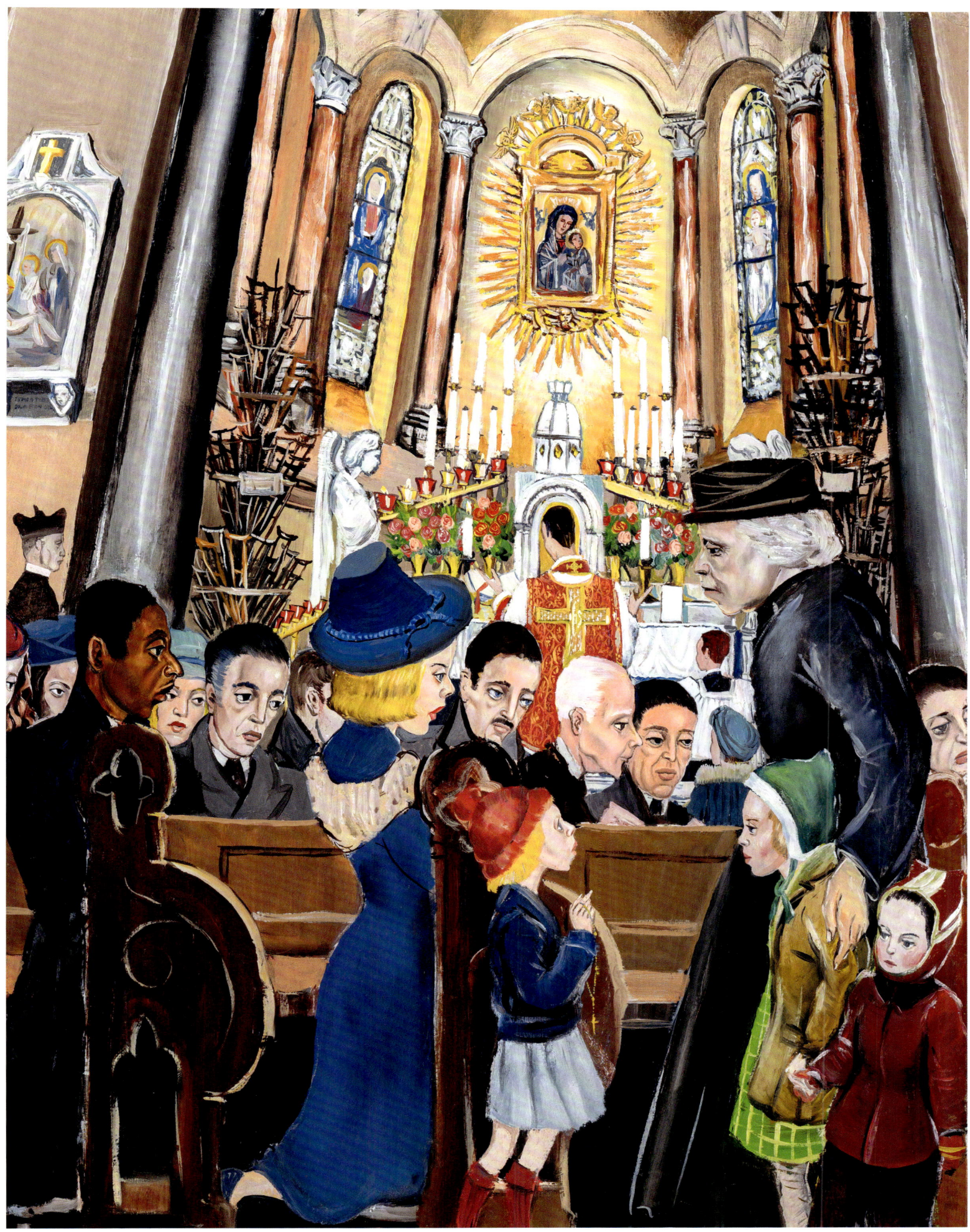

CHECKLIST

Key
* Exhibited in *Allan Rohan Crite: Griot of Boston*, Boston Athenaeum, 15 October 2025–24 January 2026
† Exhibited in *Allan Rohan Crite: Urban Glory* or *Visions of Black Madonnas*, Isabella Stewart Gardner Museum, 23 October 2025–11 January 2026

Addison Gallery of American Art[1]

Meeting at St. Gaudens Shaw Memorial, 1944*
Watercolor on paper
Gift of Lois and Jim Champy
(2024.13)
Plate 21

Boston Athenaeum

Personal Sketchbook of Allan Rohan Crite, about 1932*
Sketchbook with drawings in pen, ink, watercolor, and pencil
Purchase; Howe Fund; 12 April 2021
(UT.9 U9 Cri.a. 1932)

Why I Illustrate the Spirituals, 1938*
Self-published illustrated pamphlet
Offprint, Welles Publication Co., Concord, NH
Gift of Jackie Crite, 14 May 2019
(Bro. 3 .252)

The Handy Street Bridge, 1939†
Oil on board
Gift of Allan Rohan Crite, 1971
(UR80)
Fig. 53

On Old Fort Hill, 1939*
Watercolor with black ink on paper
Gift of Allan Rohan Crite, February 1971 (A U9 Cri.a. 1939.o)

After the Shower, 1939*
Watercolor and black ink on paper
Gift of Allan Rohan Crite, February 1971 (A U9 Cri.a. 1939.a)

Shawmut Ave. Stables, 1939*
Watercolor, black ink, and white gouache over graphite on paper
Gift of Allan Rohan Crite, February 1971 (A U9 Cri.a. 1939.s)

On Old Northampton Street, Boston, 1939*
Watercolor, black ink, and gouache on paper
Gift of Allan Rohan Crite, February 1971 (A U9 Cri.a. 1939.on)
Plate 13

Come On, Gramps, 1940†
Oil on board
Gift of Allan Rohan Crite, 1971
(UR82)
Plate 15

Loading the Truck with Clay, 1940*
Watercolor, black ink, and white highlights on paper
Gift of Allan Rohan Crite, February 1971 (A U9 Cri.a. 1940.lo)

Fruit and Snow: From My Window at 2 Dilworth St., 1940*
Watercolor with ink and white highlights over graphite on paper
Gift of Allan Rohan Crite, February 1971 (A U9 Cri.a. 1940)
Plate 17

Wrecking Old Houses, 1940*
Watercolor and black ink on paper
Gift of Allan Rohan Crite, February 1971 (A U9 Cri.a. 1940.wr)

A Course in Music Appreciation, 1940*
Watercolor with black ink and white highlights over graphite on paper
Gift of Allan Rohan Crite, February 1971 (A U9 Cri.a. 1940.co)
Fig. 78

A Maternity Club, 1940*
Watercolor with black ink and white highlights over graphite on paper
Gift of Allan Rohan Crite, February 1971 (A U9 Cri.a. 1940.m)
Plate 16

33B in Action, 1940*
Watercolor with black ink and white highlights over graphite on paper
Gift of Allan Rohan Crite, February 1971 (A U9 Cri.a. 1940.t)

Burning and Digging: South End Housing Project, January 1940†
Watercolor with ink and white highlights
Gift of Allan Rohan Crite, February 1971 (A U9 Cri.a. 1940.b)
Fig. 26

Harriet and Leon, 1941†
Oil on canvas
Gift of Allan Rohan Crite, 1971
(UR235)
Fig. 56

Old South Church [i.e., Park Street Church] *from the Old Granary Buryial* [sic] *Ground,* 1941*
Watercolor, gouache, and ink on paper
Purchase; Fine Arts Acquisition Fund; 17 May 2021 (B U9 Cri.a.1941.o)

Along Tremont Street, 1941*
Watercolor, black ink, and white gouache on paper
Gift of Allan Rohan Crite, February 1971 (B U9 Cri.a. 1941)

Consultation in the Drafting Room, 1943*
Watercolor with black ink and white highlights over graphite on paper
Gift of Allan Rohan Crite, February 1971 (A U9 Cri.a. 1943.c)
Fig. 17

Morning Train, 1943*
Watercolor with black ink and white highlights over graphite on paper
Gift of Allan Rohan Crite, February 1971 (A U9 Cri.a. 1943.m)

Have Your Pass Ready, 1943*
Watercolor with black ink and gouache over graphite on paper
Gift of Allan Rohan Crite, February 1971 (A U9 Cri.a. 1943.h)
Plate 20

7 a.m. Car, 1943*
Watercolor and black ink over graphite on paper
Gift of Allan Rohan Crite, February 1971 (A U9 Cri.a. 1943.s)

The News, 1945*
Oil on canvas
Gift of the artist, February 1971
(UR73)
Fig. 22

7:45 a.m., 1945†
Watercolor and black ink over graphite on paper
Gift of Allan Rohan Crite, February 1971 (A U9 Cri.a. 1945)
Fig. 3

Groton Street, South End, Boston, 1946*
Watercolor, gouache, and black ink over graphite on paper
Gift of Allan Rohan Crite, February 1971 (A U9 Cri.a. 1946.g)
Plate 24

Streetcar Madonna, 1946†
Watercolor with black ink and white gouache over graphite on paper
Gift of Allan Rohan Crite, February 1971 (A U9 Cri.a. 1946)
Fig. 90

All Glory: Brush Drawing Meditations on the Prayer of Consecration, 1947*
Illustrated book
Cambridge: Society of Saint John the Evangelist
Boston Athenaeum purchase, Henry Harris Fund, 1948 (TBMR U9.C8591.a)

Opposite: Fig. 106. Allan Rohan Crite, *Faith of Our Fathers,* 1940. Oil on canvas board, 78.7 × 58.4 cm. Courtesy of Museum of African American History, Boston | Nantucket

View from an Airplane Window, 1948*
Watercolor with black ink and gouache over graphite on paper
Gift of Allan Rohan Crite, February 1971 (C U9 Cri.a. 1948)
Fig. 19

Three Spirituals from Earth to Heaven, 1948*
Illustrated book
Cambridge: Harvard University Press
Boston Athenaeum purchase, George Francis Parkman Fund, 1948 (TBMR U9 +C8652 +t)

Is It Nothing to You?, 1948*
Illustrated book
Boston: Department of Social Service, Episcopal Diocese of Massachusetts
Gift of Joseph B. Berry, 1948 (TBMR U9 .C8591 .i)

The Cultural Foundations of America, 1968*
Illustrated pamphlet
Preliminary draft, Children's Art Centre, Boston
Anonymous Gift, 1998 (+ D22 .C74 1968)

Towards a Rediscovery of the Cultural Heritage of the United States, 1968*
Illustrated with offset lithographs
Boston: Boston Athenaeum
Publication supported by a gift to the Boston Athenaeum in memory of Senator Robert F. Kennedy by Mrs. Jane Blaffer Owen, 1968 (F109 no. 1)

Selections from *Neighborhood Madonnas,* 1977*
6 offset color lithographs
Gift of Allan Rohan Crite, 1977 (UT.9 U9 Cri.a. 1977.n)

Selections from *An Artist's Sketchbook of the South End: A Walking Tour about Black People,* 1977*
14 offset color lithographs with map and text
Gift of Allan Rohan Crite, 1977 (UT.9 U9 Cri.a. 1977)
Figs. 33, 72, 73, and 74

St. Augustine and St. Martin (from *An Artist's Sketchbook of the South End: A Walking Tour about Black People*), 1977†
Offset color lithograph
Gift of Allan Rohan Crite, 1977 (UT.9 U9 CRi.a. 1977)
Fig. 66

Selections from *Neighborhood Scenes* (nos. 1 and 2), 1978*
16 offset lithographs
Gift of Allan Rohan Crite, September 1978 (UT.9 U9 Cri.a. 1978.n. [no. 2])
Fig. 82

Selections from *Portrait Studies,* 1978*
44 offset lithographs
Gift of Allan Rohan Crite, September 1978 (UT.9 U9 Cri.a. 1978)
Plate 39

A Journal of Community Leaders' Tour to China, 1983*
Self-published, illustrated with offset lithographs
Gift of Allan R. Crite, 1985 (MS L412)
Figs. 32 and 37

The Revelation of Saint John the Divine, 1995*
Fifteen relief engravings
Gift; Proprietors: Howe, Perera, Jr., Perera, Wheatland, Wick; 12 May 1998 (Flat Folio BS2823 1994)

Selection of archival material from the Boston Athenaeum's collection*

Arts Department, Special Collections, Boston Public Library

Mrs. John Gardner's Court from Memory, 1921†[2]
Photocopy
Fig. 44

Our Lady of the R. R. [Railroad] Station, 1953†
Gouache on paper
Plate 27

The Tax Announcements (Old State House), 1954†
Gouache on paper
Plate 28

Untitled (Mary and Older Woman Embracing in Halo of Gold with Capitol Building in Boston in Background), 1956*
Gouache

The Annunciation—Preliminary Studies, 1957†
Pencil, photograph, print

Untitled (Empty College Campus Facing Street, with Choirs of Yellow Robed Angels in the Sky), 1959†
Gouache on paper
Plate 30

St. Luke the Evangelist, 1959†
Gouache on paper
Plate 29

Untitled (Annunciation Scene with Angel and Mary, Overlaid on Emmanuel Administration Building and Simmons College Academic Building), 1959†
Gouache on paper
Plate 31

The Cultural Foundations of America: The Indian, 1968†[3]
Photomechanically printed booklet
Plate 32

The Cultural Foundations of America: The Spaniard, 1968†
Photomechanically printed booklet
Plate 33

The Cultural Foundations of America: The African, 1969†
Photomechanically printed booklet
Plate 34

The Cultural Foundations of America: The English, 1969†
Photomechanically printed booklet
Plate 35

Madonna and Child; 4 Evangelists Saints Luke, Matthew, Mark, and John; Adam and Eve, about 1934†
Linoleum block print hand-colored with marker and gold leaf
Plate 5

Three-part matted demonstration of *Washington Square NYC Background Repose in Egypt; Haitian Background—Flight into Egypt; New England Mountains for Background Return to Palestine,*†
Watercolor, gold paint, marker, pencil, and ink on lined paper
Fig. 89

Charlestown Navy Yard

Boston Naval Yard, Aerial Perspective, 1970–1971*
Diazo print with gouache
BOSTS 4967
Plate 36

Church of St. Augustine and St. Martin

The Children's Mass, 1936†
Oil on canvas
Fig. 15

The Choir Singer, October 1941†
Oil on canvas
Plate 18

Houghton Library, Harvard University

Everybody's talking about heaven, 1937†
Ink on paper
MS Am 1757–1757.1, box 3, folder 11
Fig. 16

All God's children got harps, 1937†
Ink on paper
MS Am 1757–1757.1, box 2, folder 15
Fig. 87

Sometimes I'm Up, 1937†
Ink on paper
MS Am 1757–1757.1, box 1, folder 18

Sometimes I'm Down, 1937†
Ink on paper
MS Am 1757–1757.1, box 1, folder 19

Swing low Sweet Chariot, 1937†
Ink on paper
MS Am 1757–1757.1, box 1, folder 16
Plate 12

The Martin Family

Mrs. Martin's Misses, 1941*
Oil on canvas
Plate 11

Museum of African American History Boston | Nantucket

And the Lord Said, 1934†
Oil on canvas
Fig. 13

Thus Saith the Lord, 1935†
Oil on canvas
Fig. 2

Columbus Avenue, 1937†
Oil on canvas
Plate 9

Faith of Our Fathers, January 1940†
Oil on canvas board
Fig. 106

Untitled (Mother and Children), 1940†
Oil on canvas board
Fig. 1

Ice, May 1939†
Oil on canvas board
Fig. 12

Settling the World's Problems, 1933*
Oil on canvas
Plate 3

Museum of Fine Arts, Boston

A Queen Mother, Benin Bronze, 16th Century, Ancient Nigeria, 1977†
Graphite, pen and ink, and felt-tip pens on paper
Gift of Jo-Ann Edinburg Pinkowitz and Richard Pinkowitz in honor of Patrick Murphy (2019.100)
Plate 37

Ancestor Figure, Bambara, Mali, Wood, 1974*
Black pen and ink, brush-applied red ink, and graphite with porous-tipped black pen on paper
Gift of Martha Richardson and Avrum Belzer (2019.1941)
Fig. 31

The Stations of the Cross: I–XIV, 1947†
Linoleum cuts with hand-applied watercolor and metal leaf
Fund in memory of Horatio Greenough Curtis
(47.1381–47.1394)
Plate 25

The Nativity According to St. Luke, about 1947†
Linoleum cuts, with hand-applied transparent and opaque watercolor, metallic paint, and metal leaf on paper
Fund in memory of Horatio Greenough Curtis (47.1402, 47.1403, 47.1405, 47.1406, 47.1395)
Plate 26

410 Columbus Avenue (from *An Artist's Sketchbook of the South End: A Walking Tour about Black People*), 1977†
Offset color lithograph
The Living New England Artist Purchase Fund, created by The Stephen and Sybil Stone Foundation (2002.331)
Plate 38

National Center of Afro-American Artists (NCAAA)

Self-Portrait, about 1932†
Charcoal and pencil on paper
Fig. 43

Study of African Image, Goddess of Thunder "Shango," 1933†
Watercolor and pencil on paper
Plate 2

Drawing for And the Lord Said, about 1934†
Graphite on paper

The Phillips Collection

Parade on Hammond Street, June 1935†
Oil on canvas board
The Phillips Collection, Washington, DC, Acquired 1942 (0351)
Fig. 49

Smithsonian American Art Museum

School's Out, 1936†
Oil on canvas
Transfer from General Services Administration (1971.447.18)
Fig. 48

Sunlight and Shadow, 1941†
Oil on board
Museum purchase (1977.45)
Fig. 51

Society of Saint John the Evangelist

Untitled (Annunciation Scene), 1956†
Pressed gilt copper with paint additions
Plates 22 and 23

Collection of Susan Thompson

Selections from nearly one hundred prints, drawings, and watercolors, gifted to Ms. Thompson by Mr. Crite, were used in the Gardner exhibition to conjure his home.+
Figs. 9, 40, 88

Our Lady of the Elevated Station, 1946+
Watercolor and gouache on paper

Ancestors and Our Neighborhood, 1984+
Multilith print collage
Fig. 39

Untitled (Madonna and Child), 1984+
Hand-colored and gilded Multilith print
Fig. 35

The Museum Project and Organization of the Crite House Museum, about 1986+
Hand-bound book
Figs. 102 and 103

Madonna of Dudley Station (Curve in the Tracks), No. 4, from the series *Madonnas of Transportation*, March 1987+
Multilith print

Collection of Johnetta Tinker

Untitled (Embracing Couple), 1977+
Colored Multilith print
Fig. 30

Letter from Allan Rohan Crite to Johnetta Tinker, 28 February 1982+
Typewritten letter
Fig. 100

Men, Abortion, Sex, and Other Essays, 1990+
Handmade booklet bound in a manila folder

The River of Human Sexuality, 1992+
Hand-bound book
Fig. 81

Notes

1   The Addison Gallery of American Art at Andover has extensive holdings of childhood drawings by Crite showing both fantastical and biblical scenes. These were all given by Elizabeth Ward Perkins. See https://addison.andover.edu /search-the-collection/.

2   The current location of the original drawing of the Courtyard is unknown, despite its being much reproduced in Crite's own publications.

3   This series of pamphlets was part of a self-published project that Crite created linked to a project for the Children's Art Centre in the South End. Multiple versions of these pamphlets exist in multiple institutions, including the Boston Athenaeum. Later, the Athenaeum also published a synthesis of these pamphlets in a more subdued form.

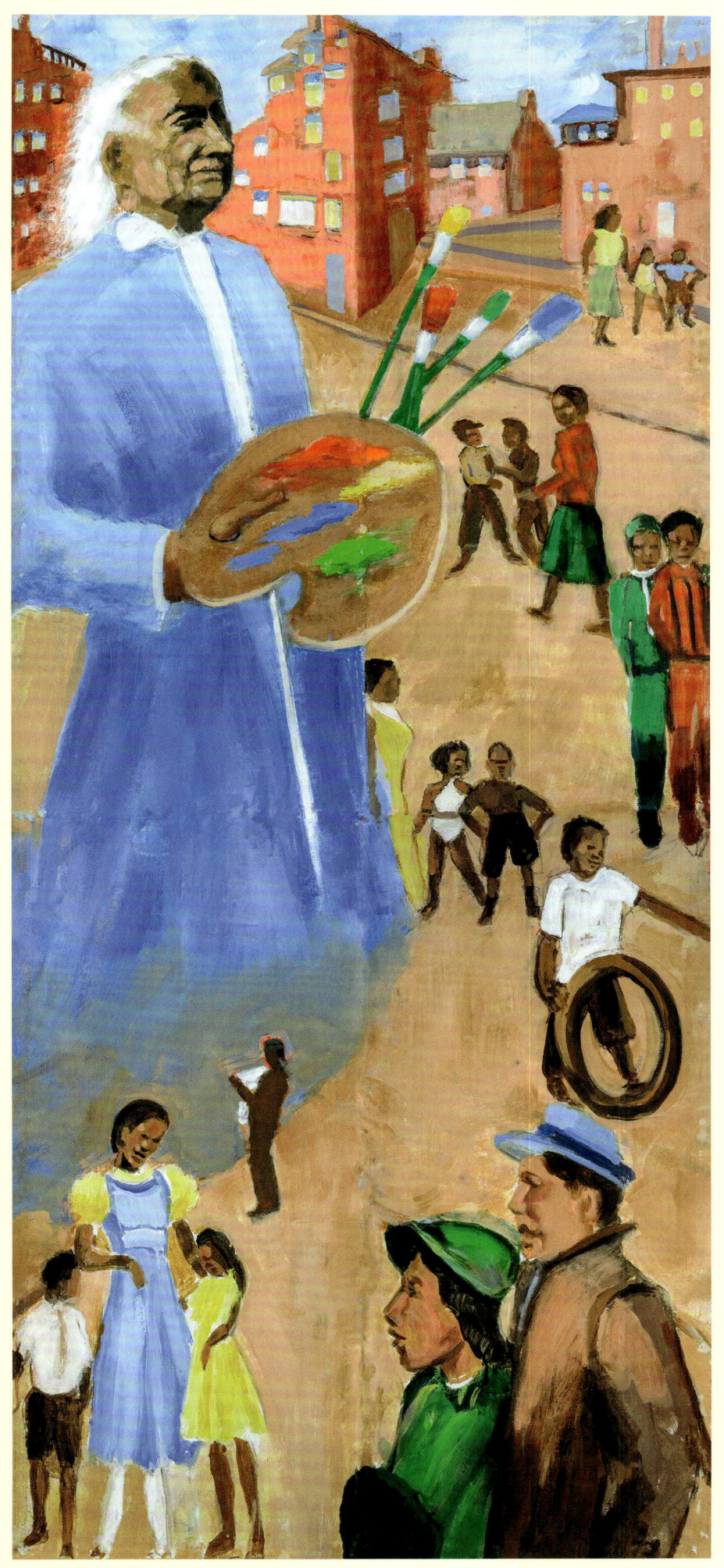

Robert Freeman, *Allan Crite - American Griot*, 2025. Acrylic on canvas, 218.4 × 97.5 cm. Collection of the artist. This image honoring Allan Rohan Crite was shown on the Gardner Museum's Anne H. Fitzpatrick Façade during the run of *Allan Rohan Crite: Urban Glory*.

ALLAN ROHAN CRITE

NEIGHBORHOOD LITURGY

Edited by
Diana Seave Greenwald
and Christina Michelon

with contributions by
Paula C. Austin, Julie Levin Caro,
Efeoghene Igor Coleman,
and Theodore C. Landsmark

Boston Athenaeum

Isabella Stewart Gardner Museum, Boston

Distributed by Princeton University Press,
Princeton and Oxford

CONTENTS

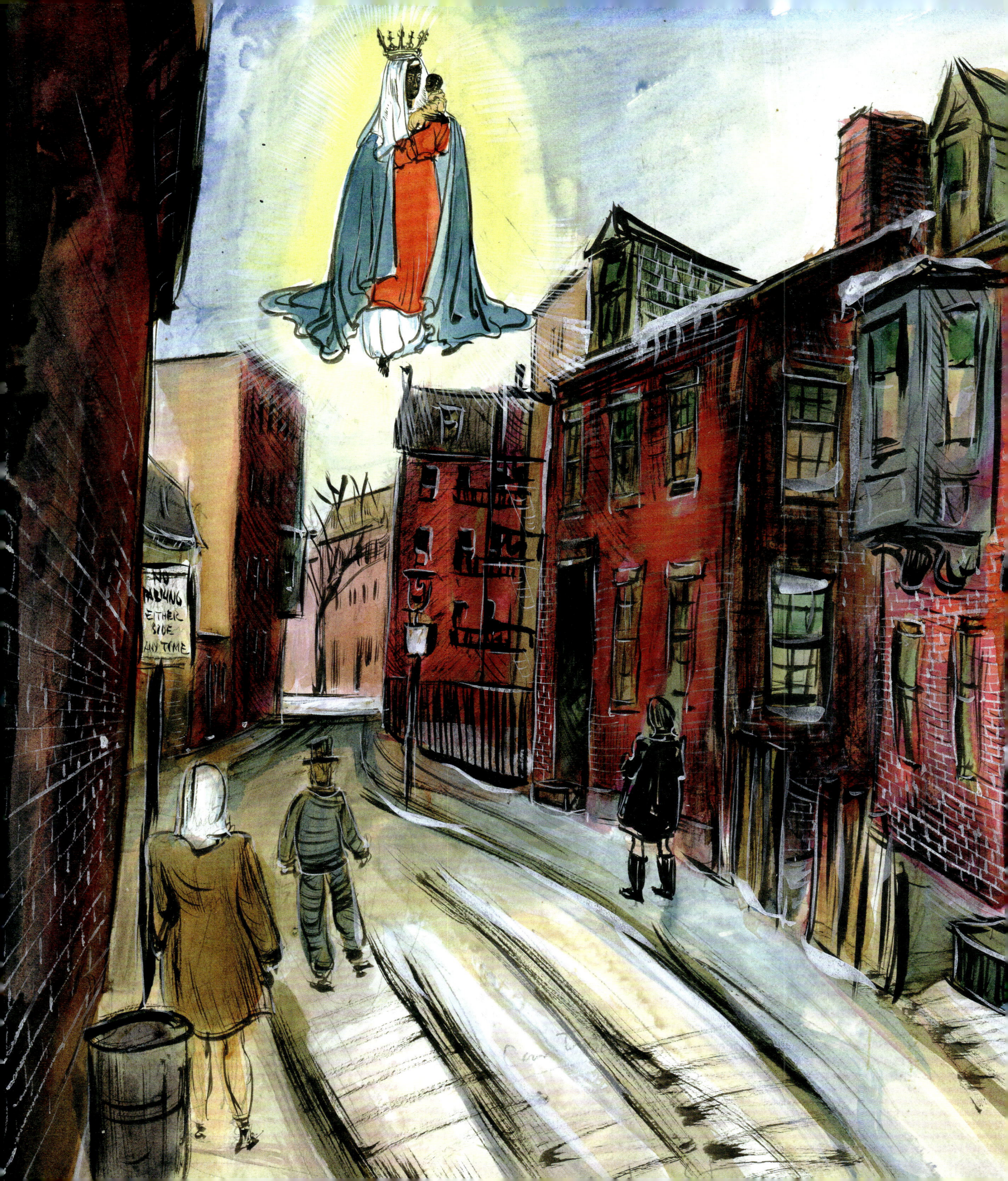

DIRECTORS' FOREWORD

To the artist Allan Rohan Crite (1910–2007), community was sacred. For eight decades, he religiously documented and nurtured the many groups of which he was a part. From the Black arts community to the Episcopal Church, from Boston's South End and Roxbury neighborhoods to the Charlestown Navy Yard, Crite devoted himself to preserving the stories of those around him. With a career spanning most of the twentieth century, encompassing periods of immense change throughout the city and the world, he maintained an intellectually curious and artistically experimental practice. Crite later embodied the role of community elder and remained a generous citizen of Boston, a multifaceted city for which he cared deeply. It is, therefore, fitting that many constituencies of that same city have come together to study and commemorate Crite's legacy. This catalogue and the exhibitions it accompanies represent a triumph of community and collaboration.

First and foremost, two places that Crite loved—the Boston Athenaeum and the Isabella Stewart Gardner Museum—are coordinating to present a crosstown, comprehensive celebration of his art. Crite exhibited at the Athenaeum frequently throughout the twentieth century and ultimately, through gifts and sales, made it the most important repository of his work. At the Gardner, he sought lifelong art historical inspiration—it is where he indulged his appreciation both for the art of the past and for house museums.

The cooperation of these two institutions represents the first level of collaboration that has distinguished this project. But it is just the beginning. Many, many hands and voices have contributed to the shaping of this book and these two exhibitions. The co-editors of this volume—Dr. Diana Seave Greenwald, William and Lia Poorvu Curator of the Collection at the Isabella Stewart Gardner Museum, and Dr. Christina Michelon, formerly Associate Curator at the Boston Athenaeum and now Pamela and Peter Voss Curator of Prints and Drawings at the Museum of Fine Arts, Boston—have worked with a diverse roster of contributors to shape this project. Many are Crite's former mentees and considered him family. At the Gardner, the exhibition has been co-curated with Crite's friend and collaborator Professor Theodore C. Landsmark. Other contributors are new to engaging with Crite's artwork and have a unique take on what he means to our present moment, both in Boston and beyond. This process demonstrates Crite's influence well beyond his own period.

With a chorus of contributors, this volume includes Crite's friends' and collaborators' recollections about the artist—his working methods, his progressive politics, his ever-present sketchbook, his trench coat, and his sweet tooth. Combining scholarly essays with community voices is both an innovative approach and a fitting tribute to Crite's own commitment to elevating his community, whose memory of him is now recorded here for posterity. Also recorded here is the extent to which Crite's artworks have permeated institutions in and beyond Boston—the exhibition's checklist shows the vast range of museums, libraries, churches, and individuals who steward his work. They have all generously lent their objects to reunite works that were not shown together even in Crite's own lifetime.

It is also appropriate that the Boston Athenaeum and the Gardner Museum have co-published the first richly illustrated and extensively researched book about Crite; he himself was an author of illustrated books that featured deep historical research. From books produced by Harvard University Press to dozens of self-published, hand-bound volumes made on his home printing press, he loved the printed word as much as he loved exhibitions of visual art. We celebrate him not just on museum walls, but also within these pages.

Finally, in a moment of national polarization and division, Crite's focus on community—and notably a multicultural, multiracial, multigenerational community—is particularly important to share. In an oral history from the 1980s, he responded to the concept of America as a "melting pot," saying, "A melting pot assumes that everybody is sort of made alike, becomes alike. But that doesn't happen. And it probably never will happen. It would be better if you looked at the thing as like a salad. . . . There's a certain individuality in each element in that particular salad, yet the salad as a whole represents a unit." The optimism that while each person is their own individual, distinct people can come together to form a greater whole, represents an important message that carries across Crite's dynamic oeuvre—from oil paintings to watercolors to graphic-novel-style books. We are thrilled to honor Allan Rohan Crite and share his art and legacy with new audiences at a time when insights like his are more vital than ever.

Peggy Fogelman, Norma Jean Calderwood Director,
Isabella Stewart Gardner Museum

Leah Rosovsky, Stanford Calderwood Director,
Boston Athenaeum

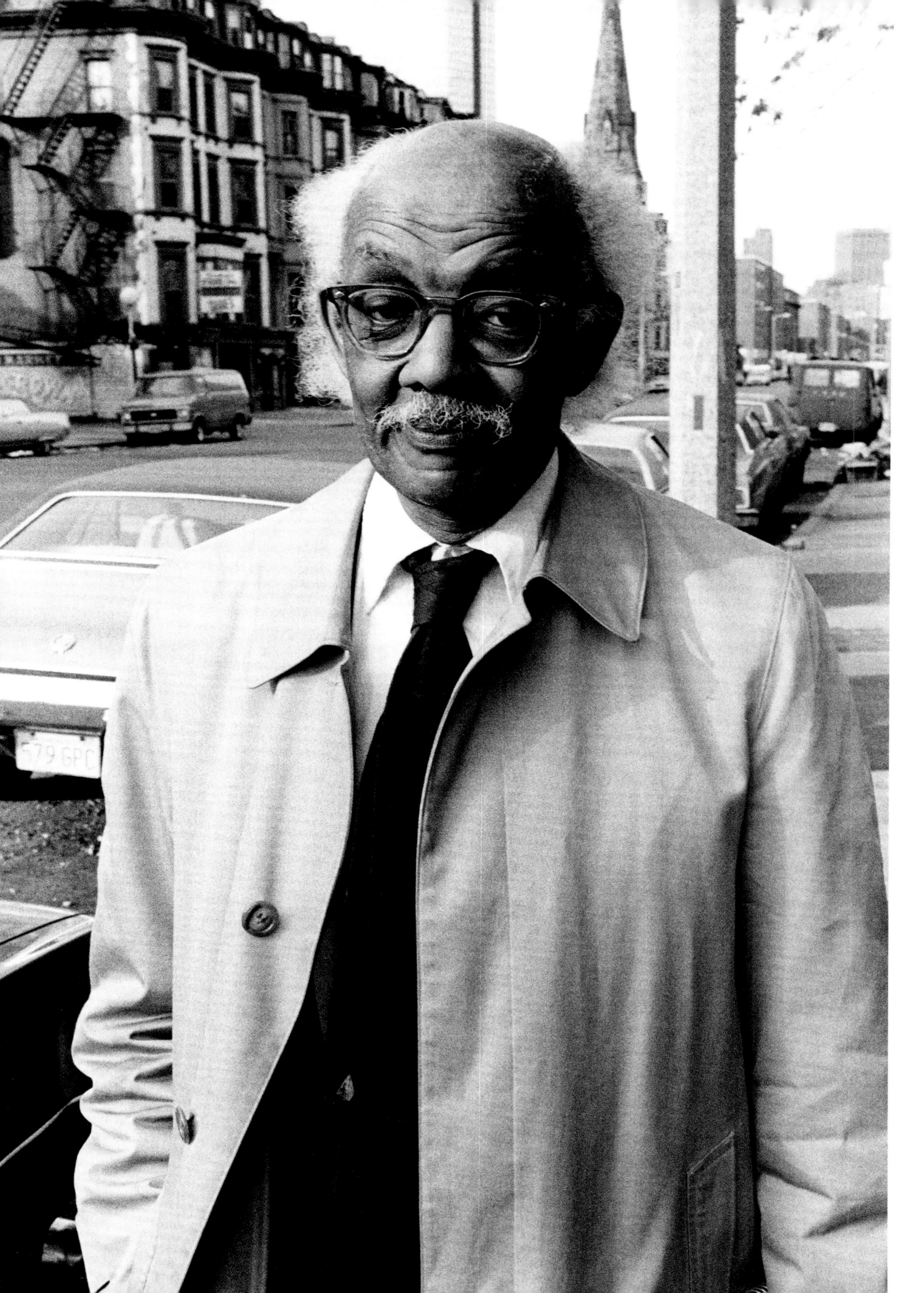

PREFACE

How does one connect art and cultural narrative with community identification, preservation, and empowerment? Who through creative insight and spiritual grounding builds bridges across social differences? What role does the artist play in establishing common ground for transforming cultures? In what ways does an artist provide insights into a vanishing urban community? Behold, Allan Crite.

Allan Rohan Crite's work shows a fine eye for human forms in urban environments, and an affection and empathy for depicting African American families and spiritual values. He was optimistic, wry, open, conversant, spiritually grounded, and precise in his critiques of exploitive forces within our communities. He was ubiquitous in Boston's art world—always appearing at openings and other cultural events around the South End and Roxbury. He was essentially the godfather of Boston's African American arts community—a *griot*, historian, mentor, and spiritual guide who depicted his subjects in everyday joyful, spiritual, and viscerally intimate terms. He facilitated conversations in his South End home of emerging Black artists who discussed how their work could engage, unite, and celebrate Boston's underserved communities. Artists who participated in those conversations became insightful educators in Boston's museums and schools.

Our paths first crossed in the 1980s, when I was running a small non-profit art gallery. We became fast friends. We bonded more deeply and became colleagues when he asked me for legal advice about how to convert his combination home and studio in the South End into a living museum. He sought to formalize what to that point had been an open but informal space where people could both see his art and spend time talking to and learning from him. The bureaucratic, legal, and financial hurdles to converting a historic brownstone into a public museum were immense, and ultimately we were not able to preserve Allan's home and fulfill his goal. Though not a substitute for successfully creating a Crite House Museum, it has been exciting to co-curate the Gardner exhibition, contribute to this catalogue, and help ensure that this cross-city celebration of Crite's work is true to his wishes. It feels like a tribute to my friend and a partial fulfillment of our shared mission.

What I hope readers of this book and visitors to this exhibition take away is what visitors to Crite's home in his own time would have recognized. He was an incredible artist who was enormously prolific. He was also enormously generous—with his works, his thoughts, his time, his informal joy-filled salons for emerging artists, and his mentorship. His often-impromptu gatherings generated ideas about Black history and culture, spirituality, fine art, and the role of artists in advocating for education, family, and supportive communities.

Allan's generosity was infused with a fundamental optimism and joy about the world. Children appear everywhere in his work and are an implicit nod to the promise of the future. Whether it was as a believer in technology, God, equality, or the ability of people to live in a successful multicultural society, Allan believed that the future could be made bright by good people living together in community. This did not mean he was naïve—his voluptuous forms suggest that "he knew a thing or two." His forceful writings in support of women's reproductive rights and about the ills of urban renewal, what he called "urban removal," show that he was realistic about political challenges facing Bostonians, Black people, and Americans more broadly in the twentieth century. But these challenges neither dimmed his hope nor hampered his incredibly rich and evocative work, which celebrated and fostered thriving communities. As an activist role model, his humility, empathetic eye, spiritual core, and sensitivity to change brought diverse communities together.

The great polyglot that is Boston is constantly morphing and changing. This is not an inherently bad thing, but it means that communities that were once in a given place may no longer be there. The joy of Allan's work is that over his long life he recorded the many lives of the diverse neighborhoods he inhabited—the South End and Lower Roxbury. His art is like a pulsing record of urban life that reverberates across almost a century. I want visitors to these exhibitions and readers of this catalogue to look around them and ask who is recording their community, and how they can support those informal narrators and curators of evolving community cultures. Beyond appreciating Allan and his legacy, I want people to be inspired by this exhibition to identify and appreciate the Crites in their midst. Maybe some visitors *are* the Crites of their neighborhoods and communities, preserving their cultural identities through visual art, quilting and crafts, intergenerational music, foodways, fashion, gardening, design, and language. I believe that while Allan would have been happy his work was featured in multiple museum exhibitions across his hometown, it would be most important to him that the show inspired budding artists, writers, artisans, spiritual devotees, and community advocates like him to be interpreters and preservers of the communities within which we live.

Theodore C. Landsmark, Distinguished Professor of Public Policy and Urban Affairs and Director, Kitty and Michael Dukakis Center for Urban and Regional Policy at Northeastern University; Co-curator, *Allan Rohan Crite: Urban Glory*, Isabella Stewart Gardner Museum, Boston

ACKNOWLEDGMENTS

For any exhibition, there are many contributors and thought partners. For two simultaneous shows and a book about an artist like Allan Rohan Crite, there are exponentially more people to thank than usual. Crite touched so many lives, and his work resonates with so many people, that it is no surprise the thank-yous will be long.

From the outset of this project, we as curators knew we needed to consult both scholars and community members about how to study and present Crite's art. This process started with a roundtable and object study session held at the Gardner and the Athenaeum in November 2023. A range of brilliant people came together to talk about Crite: Julie Caro, Barry Gaither, Kerri Greenidge, Ekua Holmes, Theodore Landsmark, Kymberly Pinder, Danny Rivera, Aziza Robinson-Goodnight, Byron Rushing, Susan Thompson, and Johnetta Tinker. Over the course of three days, their insights and feedback made clear that any exhibition and book about Crite needed to be ambitious in both its scope and its intellectual goals. One of the questions that resonated throughout those early gatherings has remained a North Star for this project: how can you create an exhibition that is as generous as Mr. Crite was?

Several attendees at that initial gathering have since deepened their connection and contributions to this project. Ted Landsmark became co-curator at the Gardner, and he has been an essential thought partner in this journey and is a complete joy to spend time and reflect with. He also contributed a moving foreword to this catalogue. Danny, Susan, and Johnetta have all joined the Gardner's exhibition working group and supported the show with both their own art and, in the case of Susan and Johnetta, with loans to that show of their own pieces and of Crite works. We have, in getting to know them, come to admire them all deeply as artists and wonderful, generous people. Byron Rushing generously shared time, insights, and archival resources with Athenaeum staff and was the first to join the Athenaeum's advisory committee. Julie—the scholarly expert on Crite—has written a fantastic essay for this catalogue. Barry Gaither, in his capacity as the director of the National Center of Afro-American Artists (NCAAA), kindly hosted staff from the Gardner and the Athenaeum for a study day in the NCAAA's collection and has agreed to lend works to the Gardner's exhibition. We are enormously grateful for all of their contributions, and for their commitment to this project over the past two years.

Along the way, other collaborators and colleagues have joined this endeavor. First, our two additional, brilliant essay writers:

Paula Austin and Efeoghene Igor Coleman. We are grateful for their words and insights. Dr. Austin also became a valued member of the Athenaeum's advisory committee. Lolita Parker Jr., a key member of the Gardner's working group, facilitated a collaboration with the United Neighbors of Lower Roxbury Community Garden to present images of Crite's work in the very neighborhood he painted so evocatively. She also provided deep knowledge of photographic images of Boston in the same era. Other members of the Gardner's working group include Rob Gibbs, Crystal Bi, Johnette Marie Ellis—who has been a longtime partner of the Gardner's—and Brother James Koester, who for years has celebrated the annual Anglican Mass held at the museum per Isabella's will. It has been wonderful to work with each of them. The final member of the Gardner working group is also a critical contributor to this catalogue: Arielle Gray, reporter at WBUR. Ari spent months gathering the recollections of people who knew Crite—excerpts of which are reproduced here—and spearheaded a collaboration between the Gardner and WBUR to amplify Crite's story. We are grateful for her amazing ability as an interviewer and the insight she has brought to this endeavor.

The Athenaeum's advisory committee was further strengthened by Denise Patmon, a close friend of Crite's and a longtime supporter of "the Ath," and Frieda Garcia, another close friend of the artist's, supporter of his work, and pillar of the South End community. In addition to the advisory committee, the Athenaeum is grateful to a number of interlocutors who shared their recollections of Crite and his work over the years and during the development of this project, or contributed in other ways, particularly Kathleen Bitetti, Aukram Burton, Ted Chaloner, Sari Edelstein, Jean Gibran, Reggie Jackson, Maceo Remy, Martha Richardson, Martina Tanga, Jack Tripp, and Hannah Weisman.

Many staff members across our institutions have contributed their valuable time and expertise to the Crite project. At the Gardner, Jocelyn Edens, Director of Interpretation, was a critical facilitator and thought partner throughout the process—from collaborating with the Crite working group, to exhibition design, to label writing. She was assisted by Danay Vera, Education Associate, and joined by the inimitable Caitlin Lowrie, Director of Exhibitions, who managed timelines, budgets, and the rest. Pieranna Cavalchini facilitated collaboration with artists like Johnetta and Susan, and also commissioned and shepherded Bob Freeman's beautiful façade, *Allan Crite - American Griot*. Sylvia Hickman, Curatorial Associate, and Elizabeth Reluga, Head of Collections Access, were essential partners who managed the

many elements of this catalogue—including beautiful new photography by Gardner photographer Amanda Guerra. Sylvia has also been an organized, cheerful partner throughout the preparation of the Gardner exhibition. Part of the reason why our initial gathering was so successful—and why the relationships with participants were deepened—was the work of Damaris Calderon, then the Community Engagement Manager at the Gardner.

Chenoa Baker contributed early editorial support for this catalogue. This show and catalogue could not, of course, have happened without the support of a range of senior leaders at the Isabella Stewart Gardner Museum, including Peggy Fogelman, Norma Jean Calderwood Director; Nathaniel Silver, Associate Director and Chief Curator; Donna Hardwick, Director of Marketing; and Rebecca Ehrhardt, Chief Development Officer.

At the Athenaeum, Michelle LeBlanc, Director of Education, was an invaluable part of this collaborative effort, stewarding community conversations and creating opportunities to connect audiences with Crite's work through these two exhibitions and beyond. Lily Sterling-Thompson, Special Collections Registrar and Exhibitions Manager, provided critical administrative support for this catalogue and exhibition from their earliest days. G McFarland, Exhibition Assistant, seamlessly joined the team and offered critical insights, research assistance, and infectious enthusiasm. Leah Rosovsky, Stanford Calderwood Director, and Bridget Keane, Chief of External Affairs, were tireless supporters of this project and our vision of celebrating Crite's work across institutions. Special thanks are also due to key Athenaeum staff members who contributed to this project: Autumn Brown, John Buchtel, Will Evans, Lauren Graves, Terra Huber, Carolle Morini, Graham Patten, and Kristina Wilson.

Caring for the Crite works displayed at the Gardner was a group effort led by John L. and Susan K. Gardner Director of Conservation Holly Salmon. Lucia Bay, Associate Paintings Conservator, and Katrina Wilson, Technician, completed six amazing treatments on Crite works belonging to the Museum of African American History (MAAH). An intrepid effort spearheaded by Associate Textile Conservator Anna Rose Keefe helped rehouse hundreds of Crite works from a private collection. Thank you to lenders who trusted the Gardner to care for their works, and to the Gardner conservators who were excited by the challenge.

Speaking of lenders, we are grateful to Angela Tate, Dr. Noelle Trent, and Cara Liasson for supporting these exhibitions with loans from MAAH to both venues. Dr. Gaither generously lent from the NCAAA, and Kristin Parker was instrumental in facilitating loans from the Boston Public Library. Edward Saywell and the Museum of Fine Arts, Boston (MFA) were generous beyond our expectations. Houghton Library, similarly, lent the maximum number of pen-and-ink drawings that they could to the Gardner. Two lenders from DC—the Phillips Collection and the Smithsonian American Art Museum—helped bring two of Crite's masterpieces to Boston to show at the Gardner. Susan Thompson and Johnetta Tinker parted with works from their personal collections. The Church of Saint Augustine and Saint Martin as well as the Society of Saint John the Evangelist generously lent their works. Gordon Wilkins and the Addison Gallery of American Art kindly lent a key watercolor to the Athenaeum and also supported research into Crite's early work. David Vecchioli of the Charlestown Navy Yard and National Park Service generously facilitated research visits and a critical loan to the Athenaeum. The Massachusetts Historical Society lent archival material demonstrating Crite's close connection to the Athenaeum, and Ken Turino made a generous and exciting gift of Crite-related archival material.

This project would not have been possible without the support of Jackie Cox-Crite, who long conceived of a major, multi-institution celebration of her late husband's life and work. With the help of the exceptional theo tyson, Curator of Fashion Arts at the MFA, we were able to make sure that this project sourced images of Crite's works responsibly. We are grateful to them both for their time and effort.

The Athenaeum is grateful to the Terra Foundation for American Art, the Henry Luce Foundation, The 'Quin Impact Fund and The Gladys Krieble Delmas Foundation for their financial support. The Gardner Museum is thankful for exhibition and catalogue support from Barbara and Amos Hostetter, the Barr Foundation, the Henry Luce Foundation, the Ford Foundation, the Wyeth Foundation for American Art, Fredericka and Howard Stevenson, The Tom and Katherine Stemberg Fund for Exhibitions and Programs, and for an endowment grant from the Mellon Foundation and the National Endowment for the Humanities.

Diana Seave Greenwald, William and Lia Poorvu Curator of the Collection, Isabella Stewart Gardner Museum, Boston

Christina Michelon, Pamela and Peter Voss Curator of Prints and Drawings, Museum of Fine Arts, Boston

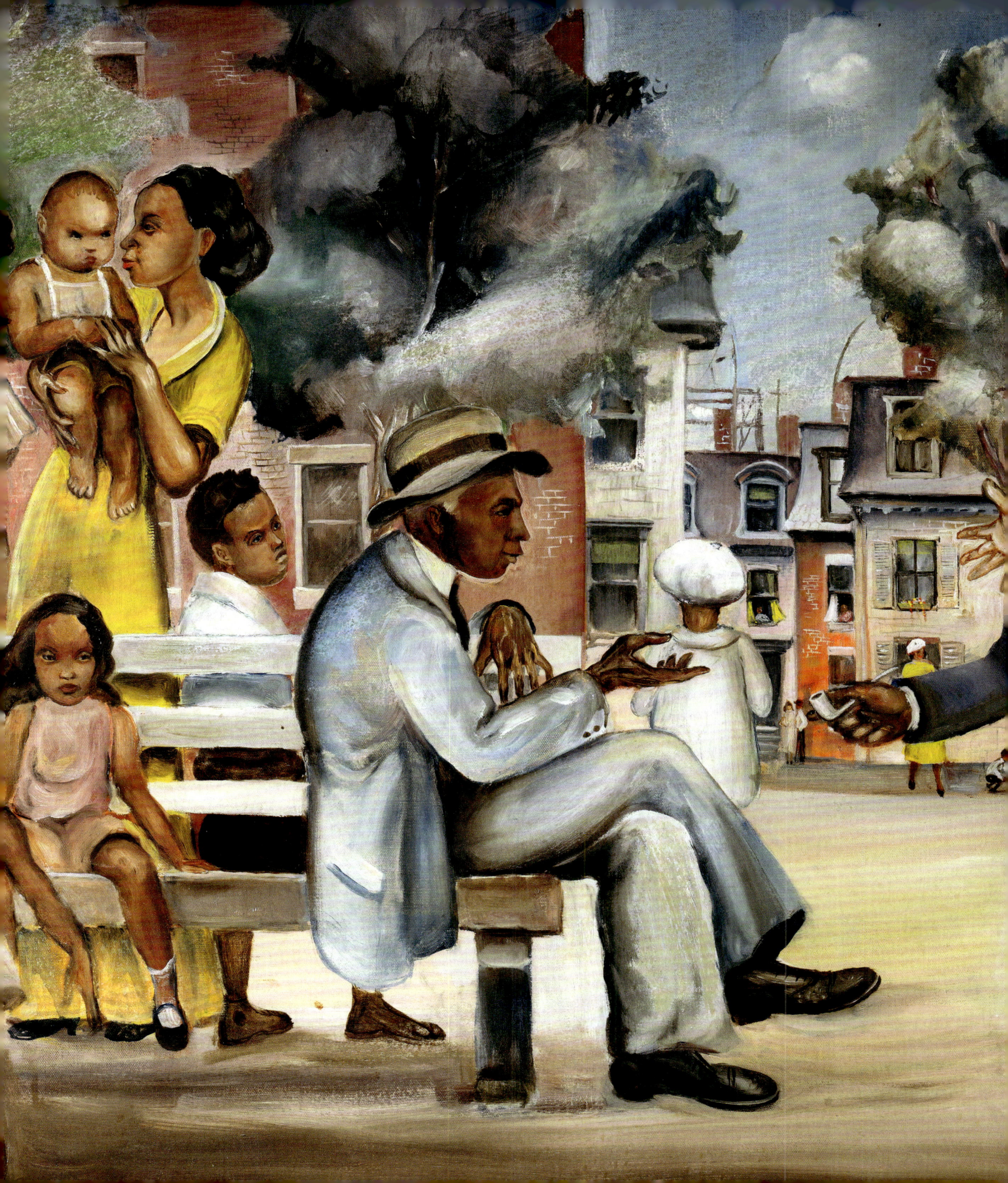

CRITE'S LEGACY

"In many ways there was lack of appropriate attention to Allan's estate since his passing, and there is an assortment of reasons and circumstances as to why . . . but I will say that his legacy is strong, and [that the lack of attention is] just some small little spots in there that—I use a textile term: it's like a woolen garment that the moths have got to; every so often you find a hole here and a hole there, but when you look at the whole fabric, and if you go back and delicately mend those openings that have been created by the moths over the course of time, you still have a full garment. But it's just a garment with a few little small repairs in it. And those repairs don't diminish the integrity and the value of the garment. It just simply lets you know that the garment has passed through a certain period of time. And certain kinds of things are inevitable in the life of any garment. And I use the metaphor of a garment in the sense of our life that we live as an individual. That's our garment because we wear it. And Allan Crite definitely wore his garment very well."

Napoleon Jones-Henderson

"When I was working for the Museum of Fine Arts, I worked in the community program. And they would send different artists out to locations like the Boys and Girls Clubs, and I was assigned to the Vine Street Community Center in Roxbury. Instead of doing just different art activities every week with them, I wanted to do a whole curriculum on Allan Crite. So I wrote this whole curriculum on Allan Crite. And once a week, when I went to do my classes with the children, it would be something Allan Crite. For instance, one week we would work on architecture. . . . So the children would draw buildings and churches, and I had all kinds of examples of [Crite's] architecture. The next week we might do portraits and look at how he did portraits. . . . At the end of the year, we had a big exhibition of the children's work, and one of the interns scripted a play about Allan Crite and the children performed the play. It was very, very beautiful."

Susan Thompson

"Susan [Thompson] and I did a mural together [called *Deeply Rooted in the NeighborHOOD*]. And it's still up in Roxbury at the Breezes Laundromat. So when we were working on the mural . . . I wanted to do a woman sitting on a bench, feeding the pigeons and the squirrels. . . . I had the woman on the bench and I wanted to put, like, a paper bag in her hand. So I just put a little black piece of black paint and I said, 'I'll come back down and put it on, deal with it in the morning, and I'll put a paper bag and paint the pigeons and squirrels around her.' (Fig. 107 and 108)

"I came back downstairs, and I looked at that black square [and] I called Susan up, and I said, 'Susan, guess what? That black square looks like a black book. I'm not messing with that black book . . . Mr. Crite is in here.' You know, it looked like a Bible, and it still does. . . . Everything we did was so connected to his interpretation of the community . . . it was like, his spirit was there guiding us all the way. And when I saw the woman sitting on the bench with a Bible in her hand, [I said,] 'We're gonna leave that alone.'"

Johnetta Tinker

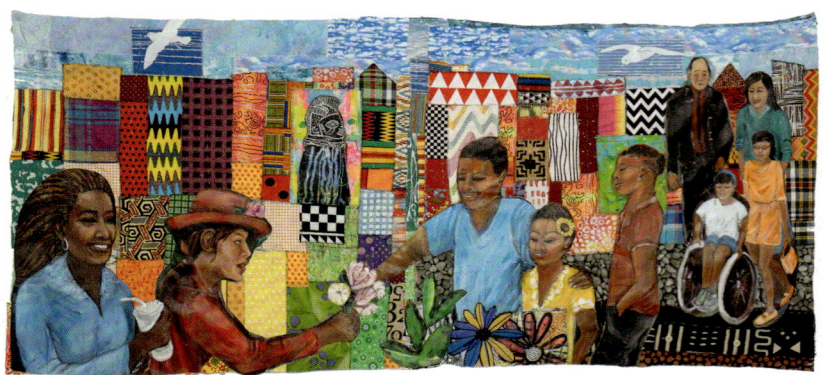 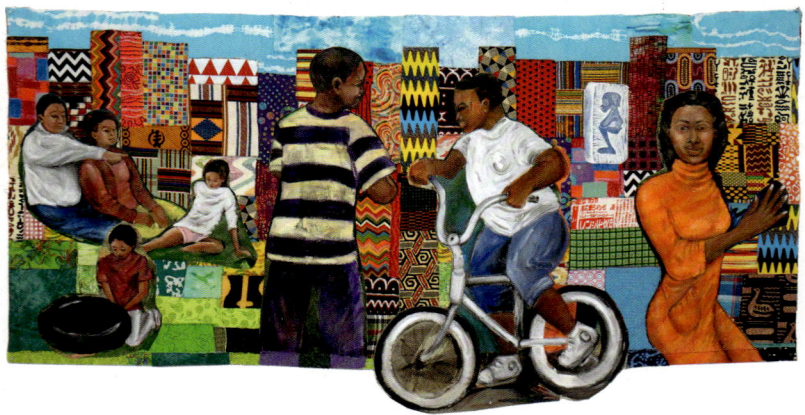

Fig. 107. Johnetta Tinker and Susan Thompson, *Deeply Rooted in the NeighborHOOD, Homage to Allan Rohan Crite,* 2021. Mixed-media quilt with applique, two panels of 104.1 × 226.1 cm each. Produced by Boston Public Art Triennial as part of Mentoring Murals

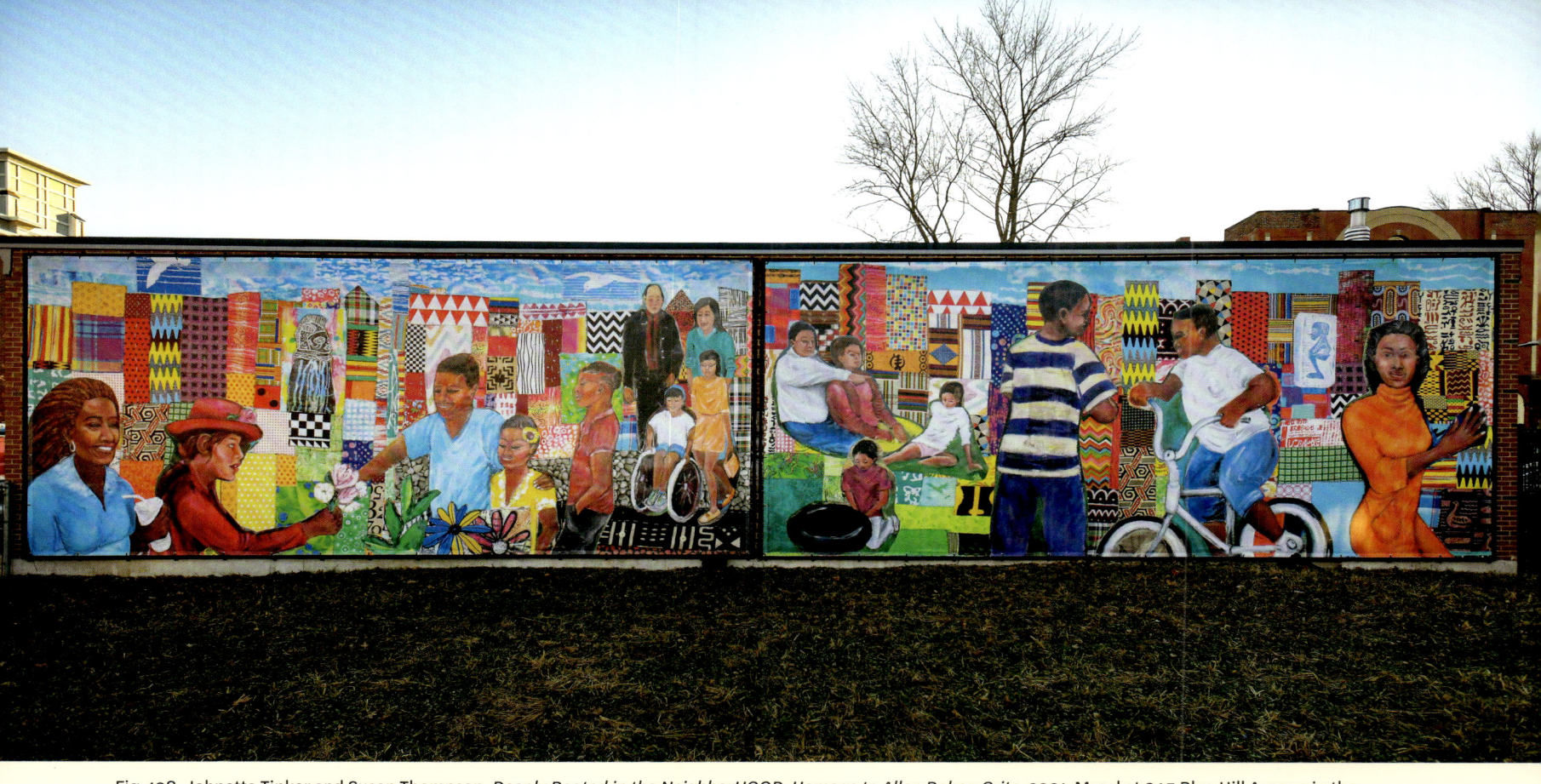

Fig. 108. Johnetta Tinker and Susan Thompson, *Deeply Rooted in the NeighborHOOD, Homage to Allan Rohan Crite,* 2021. Mural at 345 Blue Hill Avenue in the Grove Hall neighborhood, Dorchester, Massachusetts. Produced by Boston Public Art Triennial as part of Mentoring Murals

"[Artist and Boston Collective member Paul Goodnight] said that somebody called him and said there was a whole basket full of Allan's work at Goodwill. . . . By the time he got over there, somebody had taken most of it. . . . If we had known, the whole Boston Collective would have, you know, gone over there and gotten that work and, and saved it. . . . Amazing, huh? If people don't know the worth, they're gonna dump it somewhere. To think, the Smithsonian has his work and so does the Phillips Collection, and for it to be at Goodwill is just . . . you know."

Johnetta Tinker

"If there were one thing I'd want to underscore about Mr. Crite, it's that when we think of the art of African Americans in the twentieth century, we have to think of it as a living tradition. A living tradition isn't one generation of work. A living tradition is a stream of work that's being built upon and added to."

Barry Gaither

BIOGRAPHIES OF CONTRIBUTORS TO RECOLLECTIONS

Interviewer

Arielle Gray is a writer, reporter, and artist from and currently based in Boston. Her audio journalism and creative practice examine the spaces that thrive beneath the humus of Western hegemony—she believes this is where we find possibility and creation. She is the co-founder of Print Ain't Dead, a Black book space and text-based art collective in Boston.

Interviewees

Kathleen Bitetti is a practicing visual artist, curator, arts administrator, and public policy advocate based in Boston. She first met Crite when she mounted a show of his work at the art gallery at the University of Massachusetts, Boston, in the 1980s.

Aukram Burton is a photographer and the Executive Director of the Kentucky Center for African American Heritage. He and his wife, Nefertiti, are also the co-founders of the nonprofit organization Middle Passage Educational and Cultural Resources. A longtime friend of Crite's, he helped facilitate the artist's two trips to China in the 1980s.

Arthur Dion is Director Emeritus of Gallery NAGA, a fixture on Boston's Newbury Street since 1983. He first met Crite when he saw him speak at the Rhode Island Black Heritage Society.

Edmund Barry Gaither is the founding Director and Curator of the Museum of the National Center of Afro-American Artists (NCAAA). He is also a Special Consultant at the Museum of Fine Arts, Boston. He was friends with Crite for decades and mounted multiple exhibitions of his work at the NCAAA. He also oversaw the acquisition of dozens of Crite works for that institution's permanent collection.

Napoleon Jones-Henderson is a long-standing founding member of the influential artist collective African Commune of Bad Relevant Artists (AfriCOBRA). A multimedia artist and educator best known for his woven textiles, Jones-Henderson has been based in Boston since 1974 and was a member of the Boston Collective alongside Crite.

Ted Landsmark has been a civic planner, civil rights and equity advocate, higher education administrator, arts and culture researcher, and community-engaged social activist in Boston and nationally. He is currently Distinguished Professor of Public Policy and Urban Affairs at Northeastern University and the co-curator of the Isabella Stewart Gardner's Crite exhibition. He worked closely with Crite on the project of turning his home into a museum.

Denise Patmon is Professor of Education at the University of Massachusetts, Boston, where she has worked since 1995, serving in various leadership positions. She first met Crite when she was an undergraduate student new to Boston. Her mother put her in touch with the artist so he could keep an eye on her.

Hakim Raquib is a Boston-based photographer and is currently artist in residence at Northeastern University's African American Master Artists-in-Residence Program. He met Crite through the artist's wife, Jackie Cox-Crite.

Susan Thompson is a Boston-based textile artist who has exhibited widely and is a resident at Northeastern University's African American Master Artists-in-Residence Program. A member of the Boston Collective and one of Crite's mentees, she had studio space in his South End home for several years. She and Crite also collaborated on works of art.

Johnetta Tinker is an artist and educator who is a longtime Boston resident. Tinker's work has been shown in numerous art exhibits and traveling exhibitions throughout the United States and abroad. Tinker has created murals in Houston and Boston and designed interactive exhibits at multiple institutions. Crite became her mentor and friend when she returned to Boston after studying with the artist John Biggers at Texas Southern University.

BIBLIOGRAPHY

Abdul-Fattah 2020
Abdul-Fattah, Hakimah. "How Griots Tell Legendary Epics through Stories and Songs in West Africa." Metropolitan Museum of Art, April 20, 2020. https://www.metmuseum.org/perspectives/articles/2020/4/sahel-sunjata-stories-songs.

Adlow 1939
Adlow, Dorothy. "Allan Crite's Art Shown." *Christian Science Monitor,* December 15, 1939, 18.

Alexander 2020
Alexander, Elizabeth. "The Trayvon Generation." *New Yorker,* June 15, 2020. https://www.newyorker.com/magazine/2020/06/22/the-trayvon-generation.

American Negro Exposition 1940
American Negro Exposition. *Exhibition of the Art of the American Negro (1851 to 1940).* Exh. cat. Chicago, 1940. https://collections.library.yale.edu/catalog/16394250.

Angelou 2011
Angelou, Maya. "I Am a Human Being." Speech at the Organization of Women Writers of Africa, New York, October 14, 2011. Partial transcript at https://www.salon.com/2014/05/29/i_love_being_an_african_american_woman_the_maya_angelou_speech_that_changed_my_life/.

Athenaeum Items 1948
"Allan Rohan Crite Exhibition." *Athenaeum Items: A Library Letter from the Boston Athenaeum* 48 (1948): 2.

Baetens et al. 2018
Baetens, Jan, et al., eds. *The Cambridge History of the Graphic Novel.* Cambridge, 2018.

Bailey et al. 1993
Bailey, Ronald, et al. *Lower Roxbury: A Community of Treasures in the City of Boston.* Boston, 1993.

Ball 1986
Ball, Joanne. "A South End Tribute to an Artist." *Boston Globe,* August 29, 1986, 29.

Barlow 1986
Barlow, Ellen. "Boston Artists Show Their Work in China." *Boston Globe,* August 21, 1986.

Bassett 2016
Bassett, Mary T. "Beyond Berets: The Black Panthers as Health Activists." *American Journal of Public Health* 106 (2016): 1741–43.

Bay State Banner 1967
Bay State Banner. "List of Demands: MAW in U.S. Protest." June 10, 1967.

Benjamin 1994
Benjamin, Tritobia Hayes. *The Life and Art of Loïs Mailou Jones.* Rohnert Park, 1994.

Boone 2008
Boone, Emilie Chesnutt. "Envisioning the Crowd: The 1930s Neighborhood Series of Allan Rohan Crite." Master's thesis, Washington University in Saint Louis, 2008.

Boston Daily Globe 1922
Boston Daily Globe. "'Shuffle Along' Opens at Selwyn: Musical Comedy Produced Entirely by Negroes, Scenes Full of Laughter, Jazz and Excellent Singing; Cast Entirely Colored." July 30, 1922.

Boston Redevelopment Authority 1965
Boston Redevelopment Authority. "South End Urban Renewal Plan." 1965. https://ia600207.us.archive.org/33/items/southendurbanren01bost/southendurbanren01bost.pdf.

Boston Symphony Orchestra 2023
Boston Symphony Orchestra. "A Century of Song: Roland Hayes and the Boston Symphony Orchestra." October 26, 2023. https://www.bso.org/exhibits/a-century-of-song-roland-hayes-and-the-boston-symphony-orchestra.

Brooks-Key 2023
Brooks-Key, André E. "Holy Dashikis! Black Sartorial Nationalism and Black Israelite Religion." In *Religion, Attire, and Adornment in North America,* edited by Marie W. Dallam and Benjamin E. Zeller, 117–42. New York, 2023.

Carden 1989
Carden, Lance. *Witness: An Oral History of Black Politics in Boston, 1920–1960.* Eugene, 1989.

Caro 2008
Caro, Julie L. "Rooted in the Community: Black Middle-Class Identity Performance in the Early Works of Allan Rohan Crite, 1935–1948." PhD diss., University of Texas at Austin, 2008.

Caro 2017
Caro, Julie L. "Allan Rohan Crite's (Re)Visioning of the Spirituals." In *Beholding Christ and Christianity in African American Art,* edited by James Romaine and Phoebe Wolfskill, 101–12. University Park, PA, 2017.

Caro et al. 2001
Caro, Julie Levin, et al., eds. *Allan Rohan Crite: Artist-Reporter of the African American Community.* Exh. cat. Frye Art Museum, Seattle. Seattle, 2001.

Carvalho 2015
Carvalho, Joseph, III. "The Puerto Rican Community of Western Massachusetts, 1898–1960." *Historical Journal of Massachusetts* 43 (2015): 34–63. https://www.westfield.ma.edu/historical-journal/wp-content/uploads/2019/11/The-Puerto-Rican-Community-of-Western-Massachusetts-1898-1960-by-Joseph-Carvalho-III.pdf.

Chicago Defender 1922
Chicago Defender. "'Shuffle Along' Breezy Comedy." August 12, 1922.

Chicago Defender 1940
Chicago Defender. "Young Artist on Federal Project Wins Critics' Acclaim for Painting." February 17, 1940.

Clark 1979
Clark, Edward. "Annamae Palmer Crite and Allan Rohan Crite: Mother and Artist Son; An Interview." *MELUS* 6 (1979): 67–78.

Cochrane 1934
Cochrane, Albert. "An Improved Edition of the Society of Independent Artists' Joy Street Seventh Annual Is More Even in Its Performance." *Boston Evening Transcript,* February 10, 1934.

Coleman 1992
Coleman, Sandy. "Seeing the African-American: The Artists Speak for Themselves." *Boston Globe,* February 9, 1992, B33.

Crite 1927–68
Allan Rohan Crite Papers, 1927–1968. James Weldon Johnson Memorial Collection, Yale Collection of American Literature, Beinecke Rare Book and Manuscript Library, Yale University. https://hdl.handle.net/10079/bibid/15987439.

Crite 1930–79
Allan Rohan Crite Papers, 1930–1979. Archives of American Art, Smithsonian Institution, Washington, DC. Original copy at the African American Museum, Philadelphia.

Crite 1938
Crite, Allan Rohan. "Why I Illustrate the Spirituals." *World Horizons: A Magazine for Young People* 1 (1938): 44–55.

Crite 1944
Crite, Allan Rohan. *Were You There When They Crucified My Lord?* Cambridge, MA, 1944.

Crite 1947
Crite, Allan Rohan. *All Glory: Brush Drawing Meditations on the Prayer of Consecration.* Cambridge, MA, 1947.

Crite 1948
Crite, Allan Rohan. *Three Spirituals from Earth to Heaven.* Cambridge, MA, 1948.

Crite 1948–2002
Allan Rohan Crite Papers, 1948–2002, undated bulk 1955–1962. Boston Athenaeum. http://catalog .bostonathenaeum.org/vwebv /holdingsInfo?bibId=474192.

Crite 1949
Crite, Allan Rohan. "The Incarnation and the Arts." *Living Church,* December 25, 1949.

Crite 1954
Crite, Allan Rohan. "The Meaning of the Spirituals." *Catholic Art Quarterly* 17, no. 2 (1954): 69–70.

Crite 1958
Crite, Allan Rohan. "Talk It Over Session." Speech given at the Convention of Episcopal Young Churchmen, Oberlin College, 1958, included in the booklet *The Vocation of Christian Art,* n.d., Series III, Allan Rohan Crite Papers, 1948–2002, Boston Athenaeum, http://catalog .bostonathenaeum.org/vwebv /holdingsInfo?bibId=474192.

Crite 1959
Crite, Allan Rohan. "The Place of Religious Art." Lecture delivered at St. Anne's School for Girls, Arlington Heights, MA, May 29, 1959, included in the booklet *The Vocation of Christian Art,* n.d., Series III, Allan Rohan Crite Papers, 1948–2002, Boston Athenaeum, http://catalog .bostonathenaeum.org/vwebv /holdingsInfo?bibId=474192.

Crite 1977a
Crite, Allan Rohan. *An Artist's Sketchbook of the South End: A Walking Tour about Black People.* 1977. There are two complete copies of this work in the collection of the Boston Athenaeum, Prints and Photographs Department; see record 1977.1 (no. 1) and call number UT.9 U9 Cri.a. 1977. https://catalog .bostonathenaeum.org/vwebv /holdingsInfo?bibId=381089.

Crite 1977b
Crite, Allan Rohan. *An Autobiographical Sketch.* Self-published, 1977, copy in the Boston Public Library.

Crite 1978
Crite, Allan Rohan. *Combat Zone* (1977–1978). Boston Athenaeum, Prints and Photographs Department, UT.9 U9 Cri.a. 1978.c. (no. 2). https:// catalog.bostonathenaeum.org /vwebv/holdingsInfo?bibId=381211.

Crite 1979–80
Crite, Allan Rohan. Oral history interview for the Smithsonian Archives of American Art, January 16, 1979–October 22, 1980. Interview by Robert F. Brown with the participation of Susan Thompson. Transcript at https:// www.aaa.si.edu/collections /interviews/oral-history-interview -allan-rohan-crite-11458.

Crite 1985
Crite, Allan Rohan. *Reflections on the Afro-Asian-American Cultural Heritage of Peoples of Color.* Boston, 1985.

Crite 1990
Crite, Allan Rohan. *Men, Abortion, Sex, and Other Essays.* Self-published booklet. Boston, 1990. Collection of Johnetta Tinker, Boston.

Crite 2001
Crite, Allan Rohan. Interview by Julieanna L. Richardson for the HistoryMakers Digital Archive, February 12, 2001. https://www .thehistorymakers.org/sites /default/files/A2001_018_EAD.pdf.

Crite n.d. [after 1970]
Crite, Allan Rohan. *Autobiographical Sketch ('For Susan').* Self-published, n.d. [after 1970]. Collection of Susan Thompson.

Cromwell 1994
Cromwell, Adelaide. *The Other Brahmins: Boston's Black Upper Class, 1750–1950.* Fayetteville, AR, 1994.

Culver 1998
Culver, Michael, *Charles Woodbury and His Students.* Exh. cat. Ogunquit Museum of American Art, Ogunquit, ME. Ogunquit, 1998. https://www .tfaoi.org/newsmu/nmus104a.htm.

Daniels 1914
Daniels, John. *In Freedom's Birthplace: A Study of the Boston Negroes.* Boston, 1914.

Drake and Cayton 1962
Drake, St. Clair, and Horace R. Cayton. *Black Metropolis: A Study of Negro Life in a Northern City.* New York, 1945. Rev. and enl. ed., 2 vols. New York, 1962.

Du Bois 1969
Du Bois, W. E. B. "The Talented Tenth." In Booker T. Washington et al., *The Negro Problem: A Series of Articles by Representative Negroes of To-Day,* 31–76. New York, 1903. Reprint, New York, 1969.

Duran 1983
Duran, José. "Community Fellows 1983." *Department of Urban Studies and Planning News,* February 22, 1983. Massachusetts Institute of Technology, Department of Urban Studies and Planning Records, AC-0113. Massachusetts Institute of Technology Libraries, Department of Distinctive Collections, Community Fellows Program, 1971–97, box 35.

Equal Justice Initiative 2017
Equal Justice Initiative. *Lynching in America: Confronting the Legacy of Racial Terror.* 3rd ed. https:// lynchinginamerica.eji.org/report/.

Fairbrother 1986
Fairbrother, Trevor J. *The Bostonians: Painters of an Elegant Age.* Boston, 1986.

Farrington 2016
Farrington, Lisa. *African-American Art: A Visual and Cultural History.* New York, 2016.

Fischer 2022
Fischer, Anne Gray. *The Streets Belong to Us: Sex, Race, and Police Power from Segregation to Gentrification.* Chapel Hill, 2022.

Forsyth 2019
Forsyth, Ilene H. *Throne of Wisdom: Wood Sculptures of the Madonna in Romanesque France.* Princeton, 1972. Reprint, Princeton, 2019.

Fraden 1987
Fraden, Rena. "Feels Good, Can't Hurt: Black Representation on the FAP." *Journal of American Culture* 10 (1987): 21–29.

Francis 2000
Francis, Jacqueline. "Modern Art, 'Racial Art': The Work of Malvin Gray Johnson and the Challenges of Painting, 1928–1934." PhD diss., Emory University, 2000.

Francis 2003
Francis, Jacqueline. "Writing African American Art History." *American Art* 17 (2003): 2–10.

Frazier 1962
Frazier, E. Franklin. *Black Bourgeoisie: The Rise of a New Middle Class in the United States.* New York, 1957. Reprint, New York, 1962.

Fripp 1967
Fripp, William. "How Mothers' March Began." *Boston Globe,* June 3, 1967, 4.

Godfrey and Whitley 2017
Godfrey, Mark, and Zoé Whitley, eds. *Soul of a Nation: Art in the Age of Black Power.* Exh. cat. Tate Modern, London. London, 2017.

Gordon 2023
Gordon, Lisa. "Boston's Only Black Hospital Was Founded in 1908—in the South End Building Where I Lived." WBUR, February 9, 2023. https://www.wbur.org/cognoscenti /2023/02/09/historic-boston -plymouth-hospital-cornelius -garland-lisa-gordon.

Greenidge 2019
Greenidge, Kerri K. *Black Radical: The Life and Times of William Monroe Trotter.* New York, 2019.

Grimberg and Readdean 2023
Grimberg, Sharon, and Cyndee Readdean, dirs. *The Busing Battleground: The Decades-Long Road to School Desegregation.* PBS, aired September 11, 2023. https:// www.pbs.org/wgbh /americanexperience/films /busing-battleground/.

Gumprecht 2023
Gumprecht, Blake. *North to Boston: Life Histories from the Black Great Migration to New England.* New York, 2023.

Harris 1995
Harris, Jonathan. *Federal Art and National Culture: The Politics of Identity in New Deal America.* Cambridge, 1995.

Harvard Gazette 2007
Harvard Gazette. "Former Staff, Prestigious Artist Crite Dies at 97." September 20, 2007. https://news .harvard.edu/gazette/story/2007 /09/former-staff-prestigious -artist-crite-dies-at-97/.

Hayden 1991
Hayden, Robert C. *African Americans in Boston: More Than 350 Years.* Boston, 1991.

Haygood et al. 2018
Haygood, Will, et al. *I Too Sing America: The Harlem Renaissance at 100.* New York, 2018.

Heitner 2009
Heitner, Devorah. "Performing Black Power in the 'Cradle of Liberty': *Say Brother* Envisions New Principles of Blackness in Boston." *Television & New Media* 10 (2009): 392–415.

Hills 1983
Hills, Patricia. *Social Concern and Urban Realism: American Paintings of the 1930s.* Boston, 1983.

Holland et al. 1998
Holland, Juanita M., et al. *Narratives of African American Art and Identity: The David C. Driskell Collection.* College Park, MD, 1998.

Horton and Horton 1979
Horton, James Oliver, and Lois E. Horton. *Black Bostonians: Family Life and Community Struggle in the Antebellum North.* New York, 1979.

Hughes 1926
Hughes, Langston. "The Negro Artist and the Racial Mountain." *Nation* 122 (1926): 662–64. Reprinted in *The Portable Harlem Renaissance Reader,* edited by David Levering Lewis, 91–95. New York, 1994.

Jenkins 2021
Jenkins, Earnestine L. *Black Artists in America: From the Great Depression to Civil Rights.* New Haven, 2021.

King-Hammond et al. 1993
King-Hammond, Leslie, et al. *Alone in a Crowd: Prints of the 1930s–40s by African-American Artists from the Collection of Reba and Dave Williams.* Exh. cat. Newark Museum of Art, Newark, and the Equitable Gallery, New York. New York, 1993.

Levey 1965a
Levey, Robert L. "Dr. King's March Draws Support as School Meeting Sags." *Boston Globe,* April 20, 1965, 5. https://www.newspapers.com /article/the-boston-globe-dr -martin-luther-king-w/139731198/.

Levey 1965b
Levey, Robert L. "A Mile of Marchers." *Boston Globe,* April 24, 1965, 1. https://www.newspapers .com/article/the-boston-globe-king -boston-march-bo/36165877/.

Levine 2021
Levine, Jeremy R. *Constructing Community: Urban Governance, Development, and Inequality in Boston.* Princeton, 2021.

Locke 1925
Locke, Alain. "The Legacy of the Ancestral Arts." In *The New Negro: An Interpretation,* 254–67. New York, 1925. Reprint, New York, 1992.

Locke 2012
Locke, Alain. *The Works of Alain Locke.* Edited by Charles Molesworth. Oxford, 2012.

Locke 2020
Locke, Alain. *Negro Art: Past and Present.* Washington, DC, 1936. Reprint, Eastford, CT, 2020.

MAAH and NCAAA 1974
Museum of Afro-American History and Museum of the National Center of Afro-American Artists. *Roxbury: Yesteryears.* Exh. cat. Museum of Afro-American History and Museum of the National Center of Afro-American Artists, Boston. Boston, 1974.

Matney 1978
Matney, William C., ed. *Who's Who Among Black Americans: 1977–1978.* 2nd ed., vol. 1. Northbrook, IL, 1978.

MBTA 1981
Massachusetts Bay Transportation Authority. *A Chronicle of the Boston Transit System.* Boston, 1981.

McLaughlin 1981
McLaughlin, Jeff. "A Griot with Graphic Stories to Tell: Lives in the Arts." *Boston Globe,* June 24, 1981, 38.

Medvedow 1994
Medvedow, Jill, ed. *The Eye of the Beholder.* Boston, 1994.

Meeks and Murphy 2016
Meeks, Stephen, and Kevin Murphy. *The Past and Future City: How Historic Preservation Is Reviving America's Communities.* Washington DC, 2016.

Mellin 1997–98
Mellin, Barbara Rizza. *Arts Around Boston* (1997–98): 28–29, 49.

MIT Colab 2022
MIT Colab. "The Mel King Community Fellows." 2022. https://www.colab.mit.edu/mkcf.

MoMA 1936
Museum of Modern Art. *New Horizons in American Art.* Exh. cat. New York, 1936. https://www.moma .org/calendar/exhibitions/2942.

Murrell 2024
Murrell, Denise. *The Harlem Renaissance and Transatlantic Modernism.* Exh. cat. Metropolitan Museum of Art, New York. New York, 2024.

Nally 2022
Nally, Megan. "The (Unrealized) Metropolitan Master Highway Plan of 1948." Norman B. Leventhal Map & Education Center at the Boston Public Library, September 19, 2022. https://www.leventhalmap.org /articles/visualizing-change-in -boston-activism-over-time/.

National Park Service 2024
National Park Service. "Allan Rohan Crite: The Artist in the Shipyard." Boston National Historical Park. https://www.nps.gov/articles/000 /cny-allan-crite.htm.

New York Times 1961
New York Times. "Religious Art Show Planned in Trieste." April 23, 1961. https://timesmachine.nytimes.com /timesmachine/1961/04/23 /109563545.html?pageNumber=32.

O'Connor 2023
O'Connor, Brian Wright. "The Union United Methodist Church: A South End Survivor." *Bay State Banner,* December 6, 2023. https:// baystatebanner.com/2023/12/06 /the-union-united-methodist -church-a-south-end-survivor/.

O'Connor 1993
O'Connor, Thomas H. *Building a New Boston: Politics and Urban Renewal, 1950–1970.* Boston, 1993.

Park and Markowitz 1977
Park, Marlene, and Gerald E. Markowitz. *The New Deal for Art.* New York, 1977.

Passantino and Scott 1999
Passantino, Erika D., and David W. Scott, eds. *The Eye of Duncan Phillips: A Collection in the Making.* New Haven, 1999.

Patton 1998
Patton, Sharon F. *African-American Art.* New York, 1998.

Perry 1992
Perry, Regina. *Free within Ourselves: African-American Artists in the Collection of the National Museum of American Art.* Washington, DC, 1992.

Pinder 1999
Pinder, Kymberly N. "Black Representation and Western Survey Textbooks." *Art Bulletin* 81 (1999): 533–38.

Porter 1992
Porter, James A. *Modern Negro Art.* Washington, DC, 1943. Reprint, Washington, DC, 1992.

Powell 1999
Powell, Richard J. *Black Art: A Cultural History.* London, 1999. 3rd ed., London, 2021.

Queen 1998
Queen, Christopher. "Allan Crite at Home: A Tour of His House Museum in Boston's South End." *Harvard University Alumni Bulletin* 32 (1998): 10–13.

Recken 1993
Recken, Stephen L. "Fitting-In: The Redefinition of Success in the 1930s." *Journal of Popular Culture* 27 (1993): 205–22.

Reddy 2019
Reddy, Karina. "1940–1949." Fashion History Timeline. Fashion Institute of Technology, State University of New York, May 8, 2019. https://fashionhistory.fitnyc.edu /1940-1949/.

Reynolds and Wright 1989
Reynolds, Gary A., and Beryl J. Wright. *Against the Odds: African-American Artists and the Harmon Foundation.* Exh. cat. Newark Museum of Art, Newark. Newark, 1989.

Roses 2017
Roses, Lorraine Elena. "Gender and Culture: Black Women as Arts Organizers, 1917–1930." In *Black Bostonians and the Politics of Culture, 1920–1940,* 51–71. Amherst, MA, 2017.

Rubenfeld 1999
Rubenfeld, Richard L. "Allan Rohan Crite, *Parade on Hammond Street*." In *The Eye of Duncan Phillips: A Collection in the Making,* edited by Erika D. Passantino and David W. Scott, 496–97. New Haven, 1999.

Schacht et al. 2023
Schacht, Kayley R., et al. *A History and Analysis of the WPA Exhibit of Black Art at the Fort Huachuca Mountain View Officers' Club, 1943–1946.* US Army Corps of Engineers, Engineer Research and Development Center, June 2023. https://apps.dtic.mil/sti/trecms /pdf/AD1203977.pdf.

Schickler 2016
Schickler, Eric. *Racial Realignment: The Transformation of American Liberalism, 1932–1965.* Princeton, 2016.

Schorow 2017
Schorow, Stephanie. *Inside the Combat Zone: The Stripped Down History of Boston's Most Notorious Neighborhood.* Boston, 2017.

Segal 2016
Segal, Corinne. "This Flag Once Protested Lynching; Now It's an Artist's Response to Police Violence." PBS News, July 10, 2016. https://www.pbs.org/newshour /arts/this-flag-once-protested -lynching-now-its-an-artists -response-to-police-violence.

Smalls 1994
Smalls, James. "A Ghost of a Chance: Invisibility and Elision in African American Art Historical Practice." *Art Documentation* 13 (1994): 3–8.

Smith 1942
Smith, Henry Ladd. *Airways: The History of Commercial Aviation in the United States.* New York, 1942.

Stapen 1992
Stapen, Nancy. "Allan Crite's Erotic Pleasures." *Boston Globe,* December 22, 1992, 55.

Sullivan 2016
Sullivan, John Jeremiah. "'Shuffle Along' and the Lost History of Black Performance in America." *New York Times,* March 24, 2016.

Nelson and Copeland 2023
Nelson, Steven, and Huey Copeland, eds. *Black Modernisms in the Transatlantic World.* New Haven, 2023.

Tanga 2024a
Tanga, Martina. "The Boston Collective: Assembled at the Right Time and Place." *Boston Art Review* 12 (2024): 26–31.

Tanga 2024b
Tanga, Martina. "From Local to Global: The Boston Collective." Lecture, April 4, 2024, posted by Museum of Fine Arts, Boston. https://youtu.be/CB0wwfWda0U.

Thernstrom 1973
Thernstrom, Stephan. *The Other Bostonians: Poverty and Progress in the American Metropolis, 1880– 1970.* Cambridge, MA, 1973.

Tonelli 1990
Tonelli, Edith A. "The Avant-Garde in Boston: The Experiment of the WPA Federal Art Project." *Archives of American Art Journal* 30 (1990): 41–47.

Truettner and Stein 1999
Truettner, William H., and Roger B. Stein, eds. *Picturing Old New England: Image and Memory.* Exh. cat. National Museum of American Art, Washington, DC. Washington, DC, 1999.

Walshin 1997
Walshin, Lydia. "Walking Tour." *Glue* magazine, September 1997, 17–20.

Wardlaw 1989
Wardlaw, Alvia. *Black Art Ancestral Legacy: The African Impulse in African American Art.* Exh. cat. Dallas Museum of Art. Dallas, 1989.

West 1982
West, Dorothy. *The Living Is Easy.* New York, 1948. Reprint, New York, 1982.

West End Museum 2017
West End Museum. "The New York Streets: Boston's First Urban Renewal Project." January 31, 2017. https://thewestendmuseum.org /exhibits/the-new-york-streets -bostons-first-urban-renewal -project/.

WGBH 1977
"Affirmative Action or Discrimination [Part 2 of 2]." *Say Brother,* episode 805, WGBH Boston, October 14, 1977. http:// americanarchive.org/catalog /cpb-aacip-15-9j38kh4t.

Wolfskill 2017
Wolfskill, Phoebe. *Archibald Motley, Jr. and Racial Reinvention: The Old Negro in New Negro Art.* Champaign, 2017.

Woodbury and Perkins 1925
Woodbury, Charles H., and Elizabeth Ward Perkins. *The Art of Seeing: Mental Training through Drawing.* New York, 1925.

INDEX

CRITE'S IMPORTANCE AS AN ARTIST

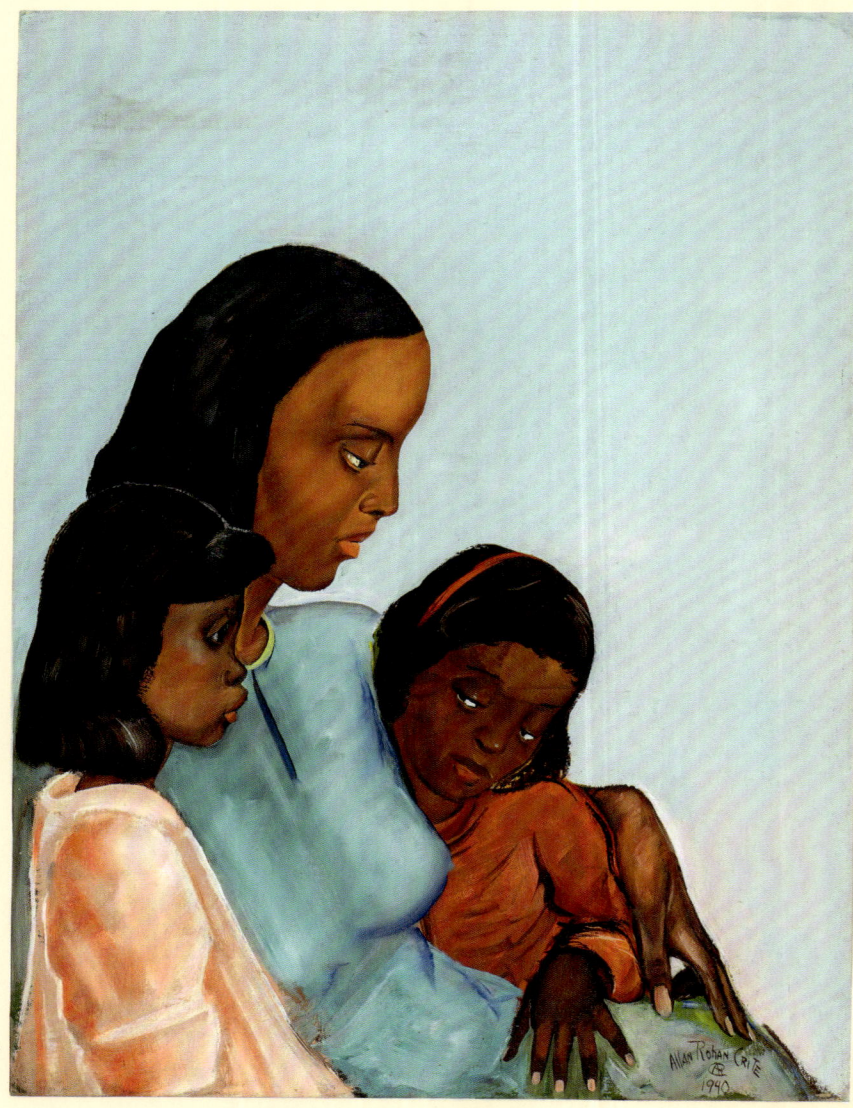

Fig. 1. Allan Rohan Crite, *Untitled (Mother and Children),* 1940. Oil on canvas board, 61 × 45.7 cm. Courtesy of Museum of African American History Boston | Nantucket

"Allan was really a griot, a storyteller."
Ted Landsmark

"He was comfortable later on being referred to as a griot. I think he embraced that. People saw him that way. He was sort of a historian of the Black experience."
Arthur Dion

"It was the practice of the [Clark] Atlanta University Annual to purchase the prize-winners from every year, and those became the works which were in the collection of the university, and they were the works that were in those various reading rooms and offices across the campus. So [from my time as a student there] I knew this

little group of Boston artists, including Mr. Crite, by their work out in the world before I met any of them directly and personally. One of the striking things about [Crite's] work was his interest in Black figuration.

The most important movement in the visual arts in the first half of the twentieth century for African American artists is establishing Black portraiture and figures. That mattered because much of the imagery that was built around Black physical presence was so distorted, with so many caricatures. Much of it was the Aunt Jemima kind of image, the southern bumpkin, and that was a wide representation. Mr. Crite was . . . always making a different argument for the figure. And that different argument becomes increasingly important over the century, because those distorted images, which came from the movies and from advertising, had so sullied the representation of Black figures that even some Blacks themselves had begun to use them. It was like an antidote to come up with a representation that went in a different direction. (Fig. 1)

The argument that Mr. Crite's work made was that the majesty of Black people resided in their simple humanity, and that they were people first. You were not there for someone else's entertainment. You were not the exotic jazz character. You were not necessarily the rural bumpkin. And when any of those had to be represented, the strategy had to be different. So when the rural image appears in Mr. Crite's work, it's the plowman standing in dignity in their field, like the shepherds in the New Testament, standing in the fields and watching. So he brought the representation of fundamental dignity, and steered very clear of the work of the several artists who were working in the same time period but with a more stereotypical treatment of Black subjects." (Fig. 2)

Barry Gaither

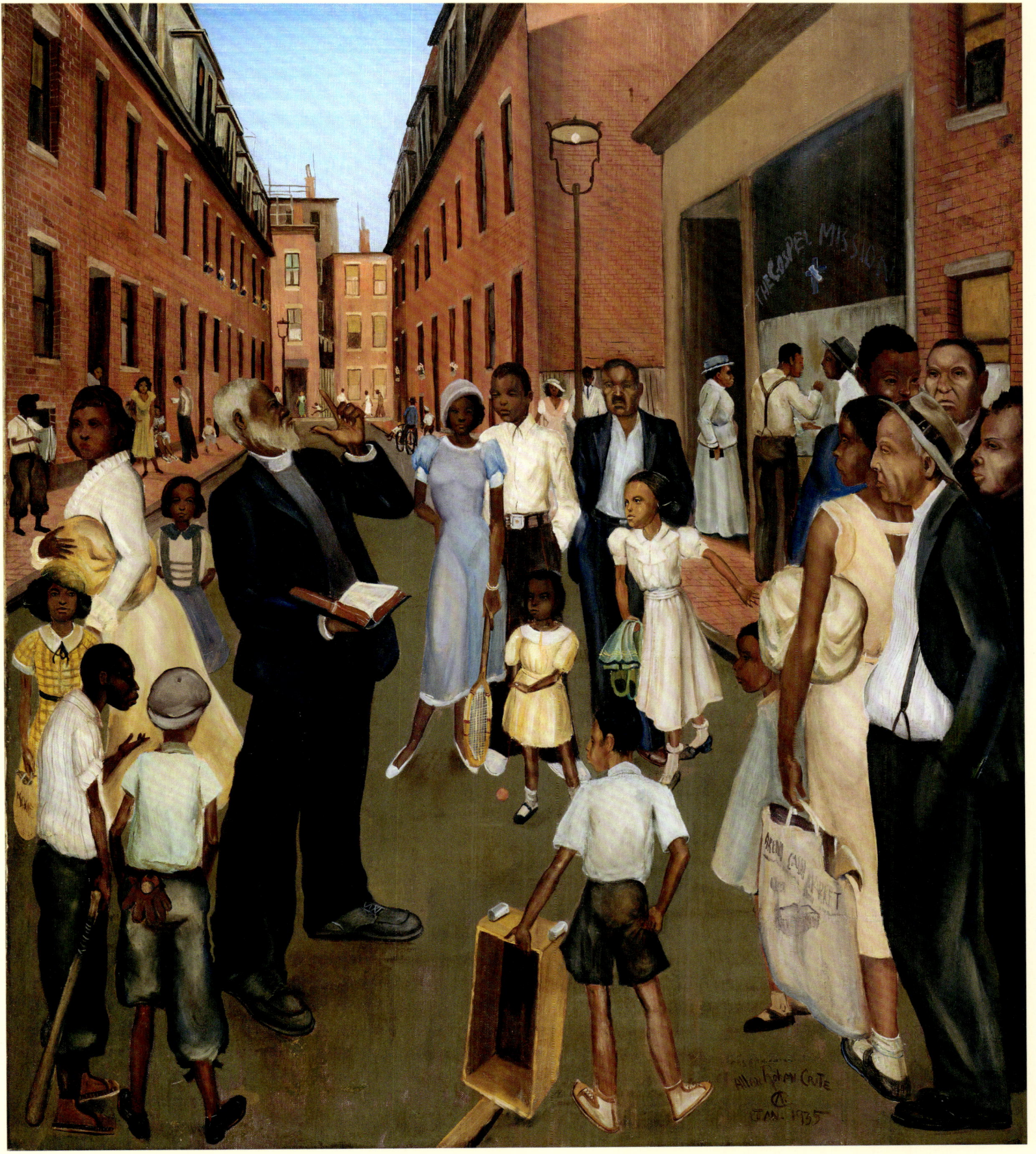

Fig. 2. Allan Rohan Crite, *Thus Saith the Lord,* January 1935. Oil on canvas, 104.1 × 89.9 cm. Courtesy of Museum of African American History Boston | Nantucket

"People see themselves in Allan's work because they are in Allan's work . . . and could feel as though he was not only empathetic to their lives but willing to tell their stories through visual representation." (Fig. 3)

Ted Landsmark

"Mr. Crite's work has always been relevant, and I'm speaking about his astute intellectual exercises that were translated and interpreted and put forward to the larger community in his artwork. [In the 1970s,] he did begin to do works that combine traditional African formats with contemporary formats he saw here in the community." (Fig. 4)

Napoleon Jones-Henderson

"The beauty and how he portrays Black people as royal. It's never demeaning . . . it's always this royal kind of thing."

Susan Thompson

"I learned that . . . everybody was regal because he painted everybody. A couple, lots of kids on the street, school's out, you know, just everybody. And so here was always a place and a space for you as an individual to identify with someone in a piece of art and not something that was highlighting only the aristocrats of the Black community or, you know, a certain type."

Denise Patmon

"In terms of the arc of his career, the capper was in the '60s. He comes out of the church, and he's an experienced senior recognized figure who is now down with Black Is Beautiful and becomes as relevant to the moment as anyone of any age. He was hip to what was happening in Black consciousness. Consciousness included not just the relationship between Blackness in America and Blackness in Africa but a kind of simultaneity of the two. And he returned to depicting the community around him as he had at the beginning of his career, only now he saw it in kind of combined American and African terms."

Arthur Dion

"He had a style. I mean, that's the greatest accomplishment any artist can have. It's to have a style that's unique. It's a distinctive [style], like Picasso."

Hakim Raquib

"He's our [the Black community's] John Singer Sargent, you know . . . he's it."

Denise Patmon

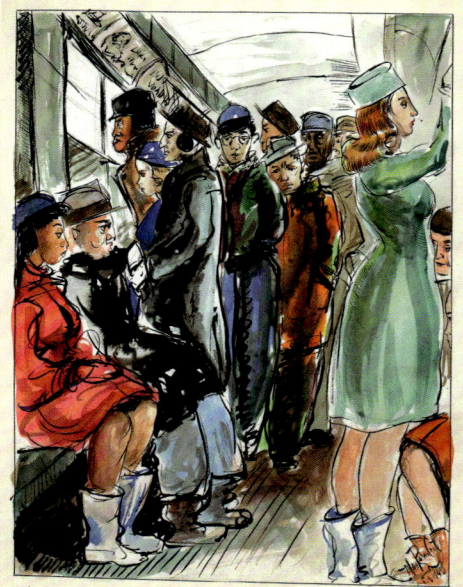

Fig. 3. Allan Rohan Crite, *7:45 a.m.,* February 1945. Watercolor and black ink over graphite, 37.1 × 29.2 cm. Boston Athenaeum

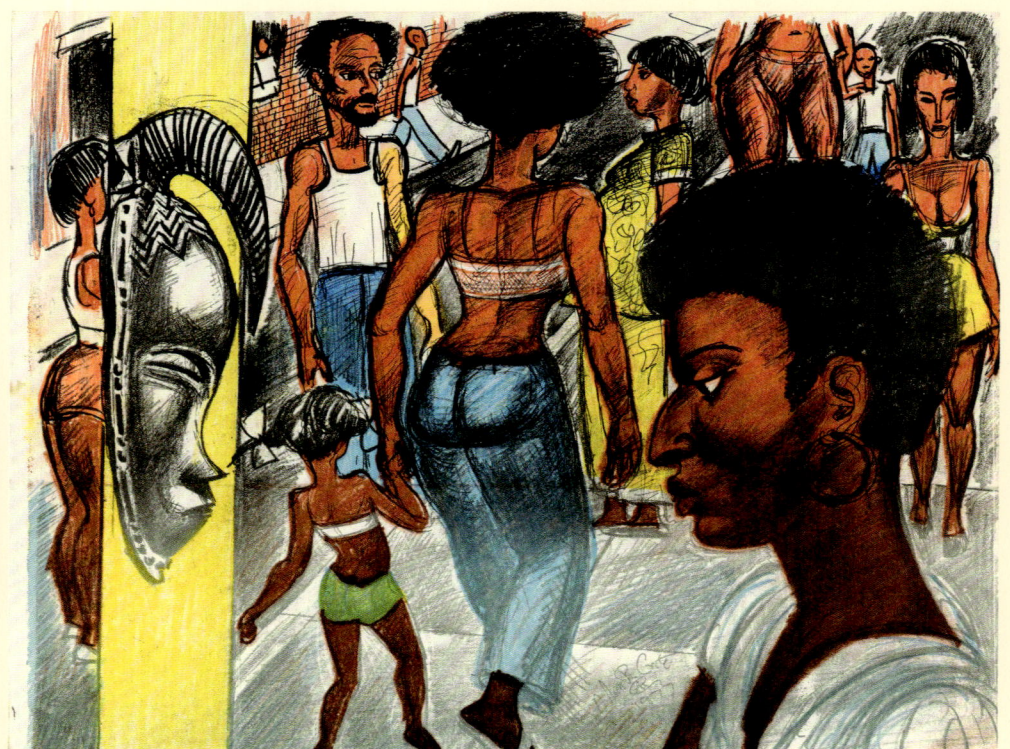

Fig. 4. Allan Rohan Crite, *Untitled (Mask and Woman in Profile),* 1977. Colored Multilith print, 21.6 × 27.9 cm. Collection of Susan Thompson

CRITE'S INTELLECTUAL CURIOSITY

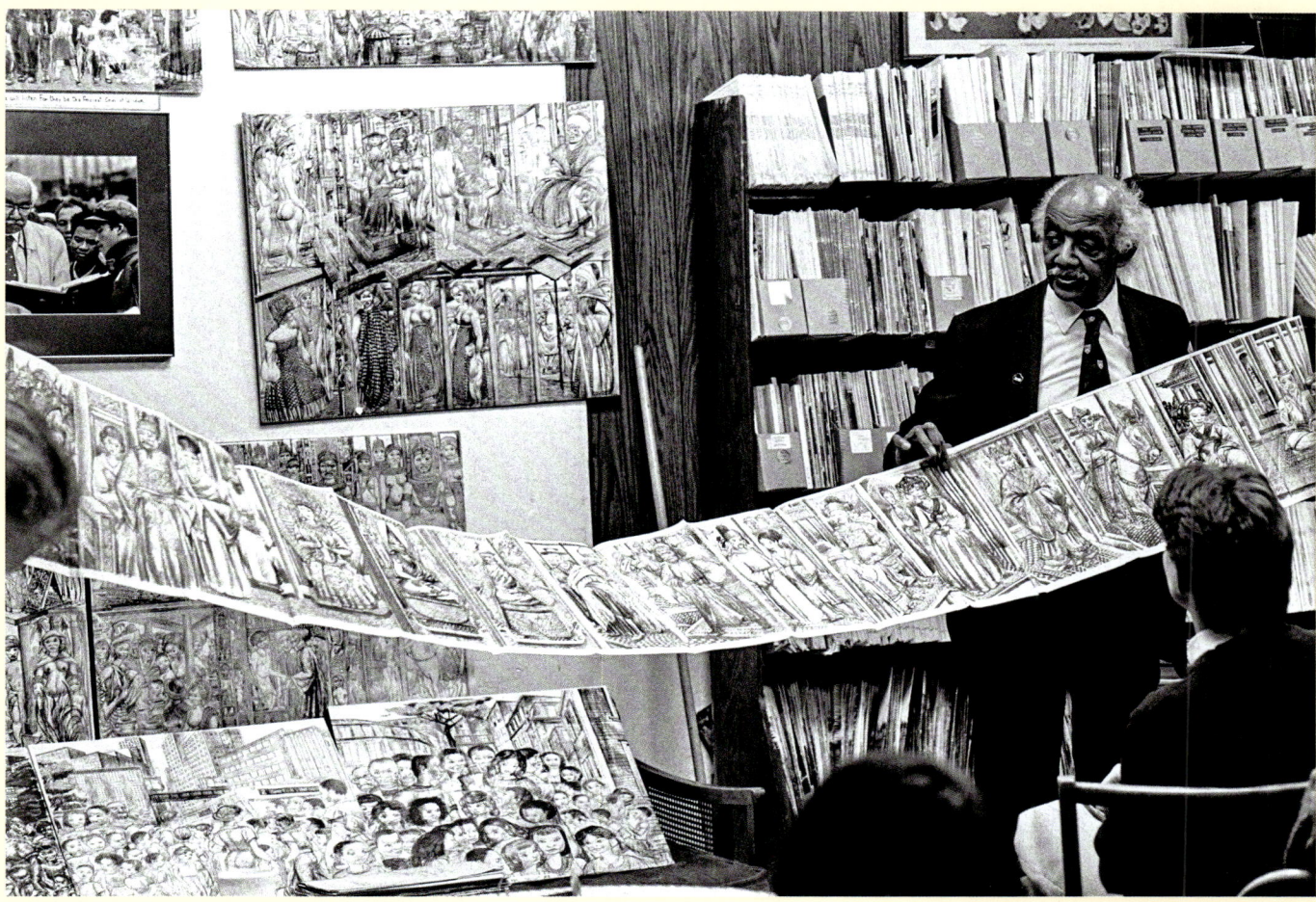

Fig. 5. Allan Crite presents one of his pictorial series of Multilith prints in his studio at 410 Columbus Avenue. Photograph by Reginald L. Jackson, PhD

"I would say that his intellectual curiosity is the bedrock of all of his image-making output. So, for me, that would be the most important of Allan's attributes that I hold in high esteem. . . . You gotta stay curious."

Napoleon Jones-Henderson

"Another thing that . . . [is] distinctive in his work was his great interest in history as a subject, especially the Nile Valley and the ancient worlds of Asia and of the Indigenous Americas. And these he translated into very large scroll-like works . . . accordion books. And if you look at those . . . like his *Reflections on the [Afro-Asian-American Cultural Heritage of] Peoples of Color,* it starts in the South End with his

house and with him. . . . [The] f rst cluster of figures you see there are all known figures. Byron Rushing is in there. Paul Goodnight is in there. I'm in there with Harriet Kennedy, who was assistant director of the National Center of Afro-American Artists at the time. Starting from this core of people, it multiplies almost endlessly until it reaches Japan in one direction and South America in the other direction. . . . That is a manifest love of humanity." (Fig. 5)

Barry Gaither

"We always talked about history. His mind was—he was a genius, that's all I can say. He knew everything about history. And I

said, 'I wish I had you as a history teacher. Because you gave me the details of what was going on and the parallels of what's going on today.' We would look at Channel 2 together via telephone. He would be at home, and I would be at home, and if something came on Channel 2 that was interesting, I would call him, and I would say, 'Mr. Crite, you know, they're doing the Civil War on Channel 2.' He'd turn it on, and we would look at episodes together on the phone, and he would be explaining to me the other side of the story, the one that you don't hear in the news, and the background of everything."

Johnetta Tinker

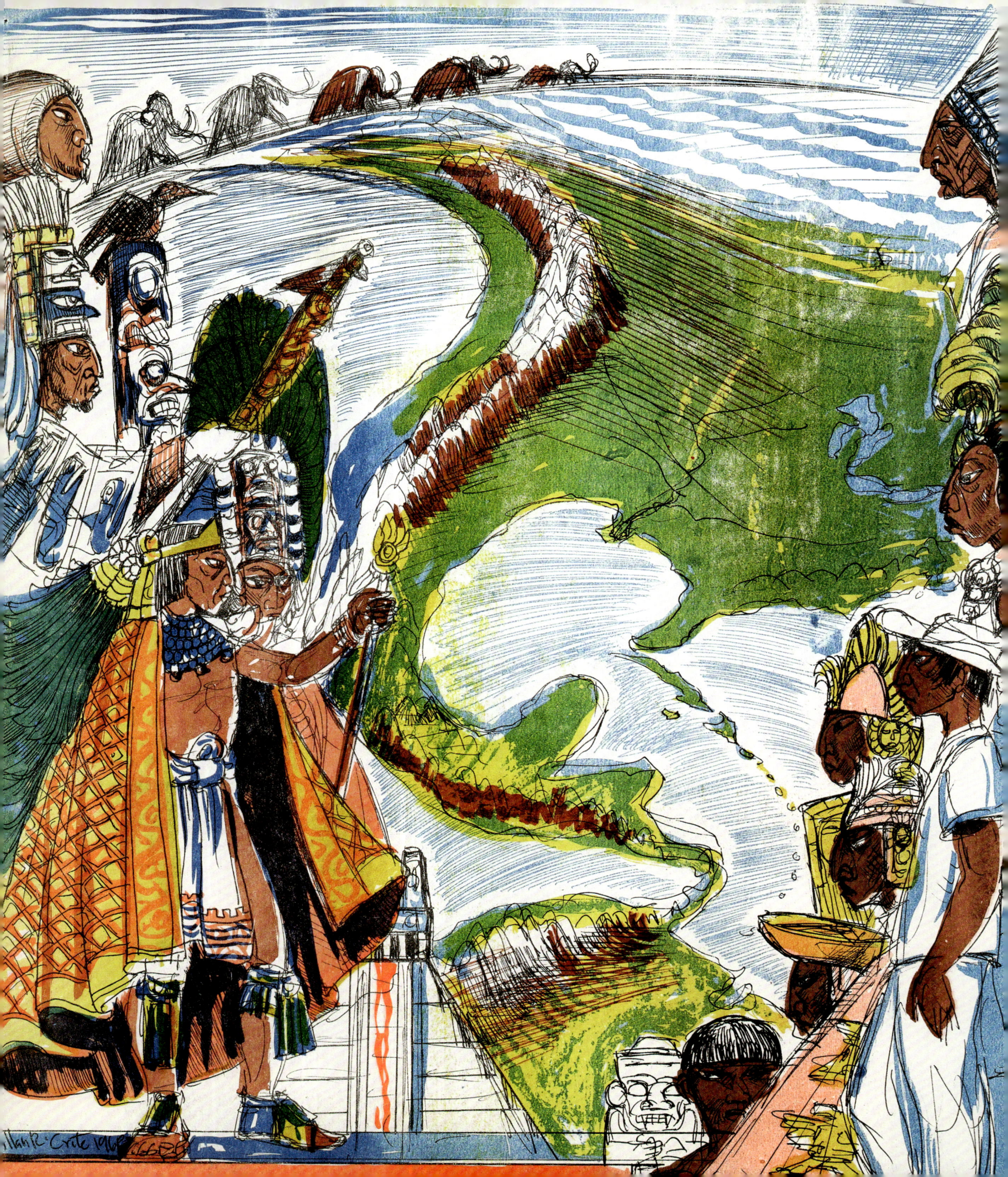

CRITE, CITIZEN OF BOSTON, CITIZEN OF THE WORLD

"I think that it's really important for us to locate him, not just, you know, as a Bostonian, which he was very proud to be, not just as an artist . . . and not [just] as a person who spent most of his life in Massachusetts, but truly as a citizen of the world. . . . I didn't love Boston automatically, but I learned to love Boston through him." (Fig. 6)

Denise Patmon

"When he was growing up, the South End was a pretty diverse place, with folks from all backgrounds, immigrants . . . a community that was Black and brown. A significant Chinese community, a Lebanese community, a community that was welcoming to Boston's gay population, and people got along very well with each other."

Ted Landsmark

"So my whole crew and I, we went over there, and his home was an amazing living museum. And my staff [at the Harbor Art Gallery at UMass Boston] at the time, we're punk rockers with mohawks and piercings and black leather. So we just show up to his house and he doesn't blink an eye and invites us in; he was a quiet radical."

Kathleen Bitetti

"His doors were open to everybody. He had no judgment, couldn't care [less]. People gay, straight, whatever, didn't care."

Kathleen Bitetti

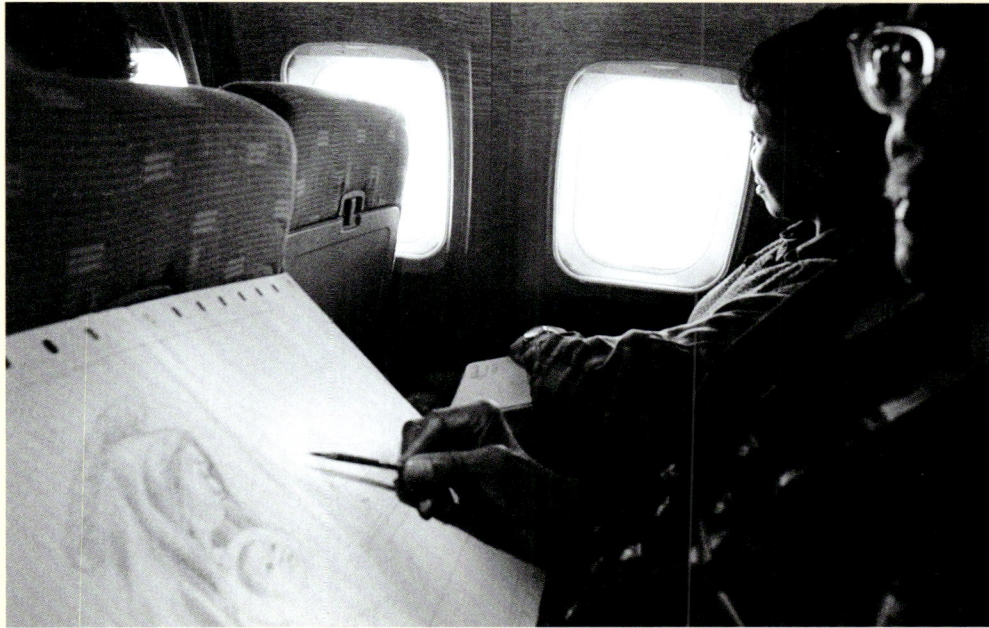

Opposite: Detail of *The Cultural Foundations of America: The Indian*, plate 32

Fig. 6. Allan Rohan Crite drawing in flight with Susan Thompson en route to Haiti, 1986. Photograph by Reginald L. Jackson, PhD

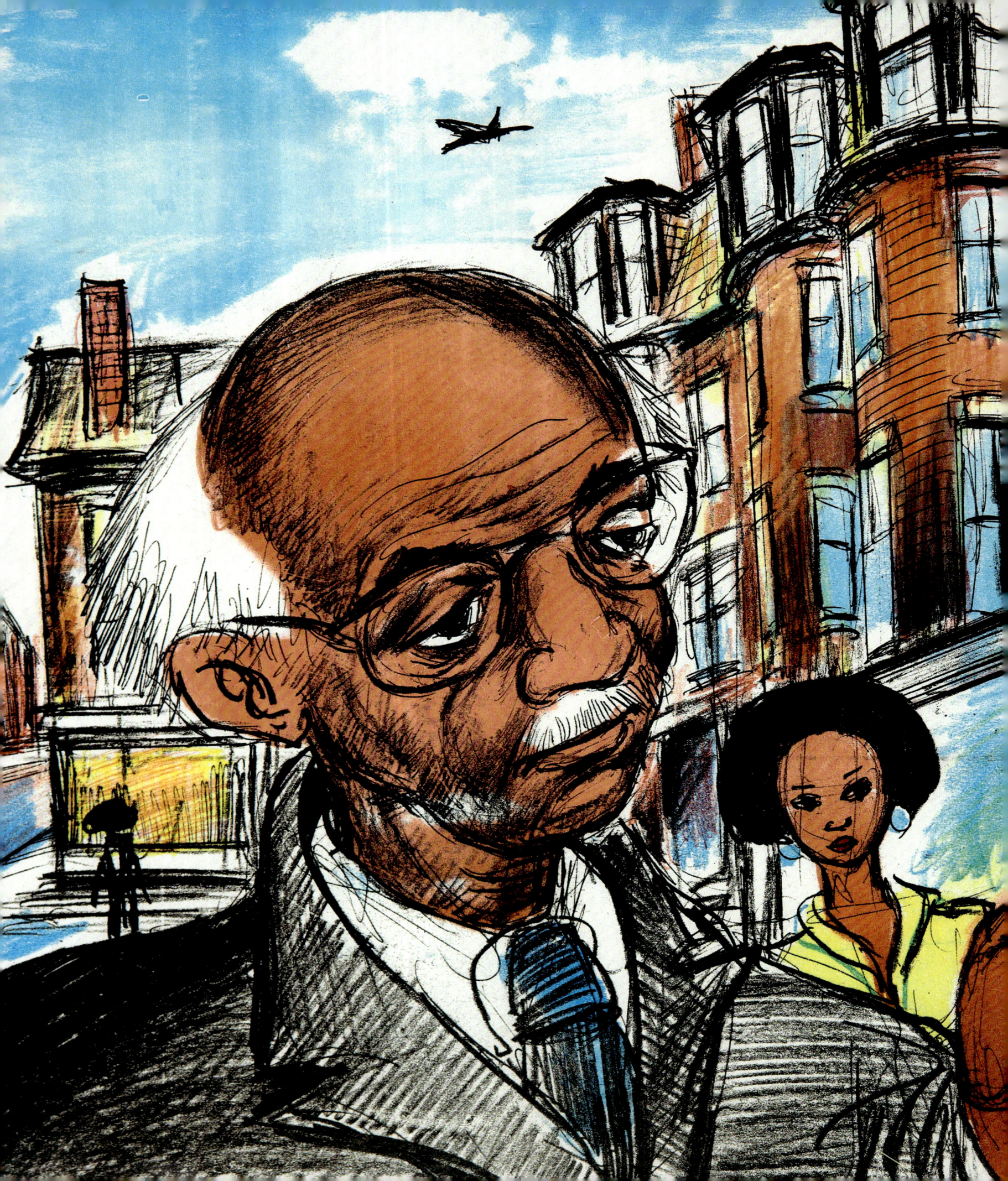

ALLAN ROHAN CRITE

THE OMNIPRESENT ARTIST

Diana Seave Greenwald and Christina Michelon

INTRODUCTION

Allan Rohan Crite (1910–2007) is everywhere. The traces of his art and generosity pervade Boston, his home for almost a century. Over a lifetime that spanned incredible social and economic change—he lived through both world wars, the Depression, the Civil Rights Movement, the Women's Rights Movement, and the advent of the personal computer—he produced thousands of works spanning a range of media. They include oil paintings, watercolors, and wooden icons made for churches, as well as prints produced with innovative technologies like linoleum cuts, lithography, and even Xerox photocopies. This diversity of media is echoed in the diversity of subject matter that Crite tackled: from his best-known depictions of the Boston neighborhoods of Lower Roxbury and the South End to liturgical images produced for Episcopal worship, to visual travelogues of a voyage to southern China, to erotic studies of human sexuality.

The limited scholarship about Crite has focused almost exclusively on oil paintings showing life in Boston—mostly but not exclusively the lives of Black people—from the 1930s and '40s.[1] These works are compelling artistic contributions; they feature prominently in these exhibitions and this volume. However, they are only an early stage of what became a rich decades-long artistic career. To focus on these paintings alone neglects Crite's prescient artistic and intellectual responsiveness to the dizzying social change that occurred around him—social change that had a particular impact on him as a Black man living in a northern American city known for its struggles with racial integration in the late twentieth century. This catalogue represents a first effort to grapple with a broader span of the artist's works: from drawings made as a teenager in the 1920s to projects dating to the 1990s, when he was an octogenarian. Zooming out to this broader career-spanning view makes clear that Crite, whose current artistic reputation in the broader art historical literature is one of academic Bostonian conservatism, was something of a radical. The artist—who often wore a suit and tie and was dedicated to the buttoned-up world of Episcopal worship—can hardly be characterized as conservative (fig. 7). Both his extensive writings and his artworks reveal not only progressive political views but wide-ranging artistic experimentation with different subject matter and media.

Opposite: Detail of 410 Columbus Avenue, from An Artist's Sketchbook of the South End: A Walking Tour about Black People, plate 38

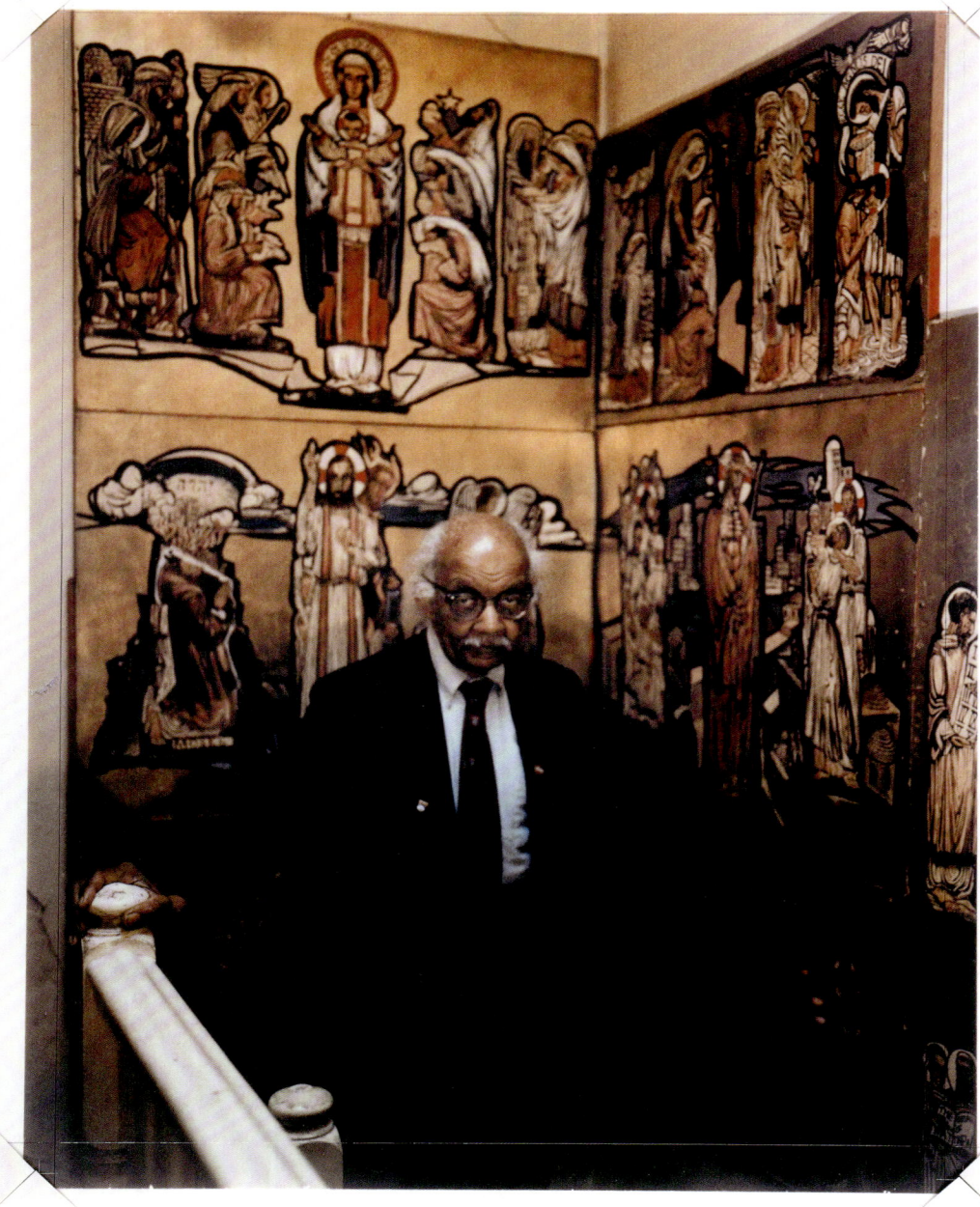

From creating liturgical images that explicitly rendered holy figures as Black, to a "walking tour" of Boston's South End that confronted the destructive realities of urban renewal and gentrification, to graphic-novel-like publications, Crite was constantly innovating. Perhaps his most compelling innovation was that after the 1940s he eschewed singular original oil paintings; he stopped making pure watercolors in the '50s. Instead, he embraced the printed multiple. This contributed to the marginalization of his work in the history of art. Producing multiples made his work less "valuable" in art historical and economic estimations that privilege the original. However, this choice made his work far more accessible to his community.

Community was at the center of Crite's life and practice. His art was often grounded in his immediate surroundings—in the places and people he enjoyed seeing daily. As a result, he was a key player in the preservation of community memory. In an oral history from the 1970s, he described himself as "something like what they call the *griot,* so far as the African tradition is concerned."[2] A griot is a West African holder of oral traditions and history. Both a storyteller and a sage advisor and mediator, the griot was a pillar of a range of West African communities.[3] Crite's choice of this term is telling. He was both an artistic repository of community memory *and* a pillar of the community. Unsurprisingly, perhaps the most poignant traces of his impact are in the memories of those who knew him and were mentored by him—memories that are extensively recorded in this book. Called the Dean of the African American arts community, these recollections make clear that his influence is still alive and well.

This one book and two concurrent exhibitions are not enough to comprehensively cover the life and work of Allan Rohan Crite. However, our goal is to direct attention toward an artist who, at least in the scholarly literature, has been largely overlooked. This essay provides a brief introduction to Crite and his vast oeuvre. It focuses particularly on his connections to the exhibitions' two host institutions: the Boston Athenaeum and the Isabella Stewart Gardner Museum. The first is one of the most important repositories of Crite's work and a longtime intellectual home for the artist; the latter was a lifelong source of inspiration. From Boston's most rarefied institutions to the sidewalks of its many neighborhoods, Crite was omnipresent and influential. Using new primary source material and select case studies presented chronologically, we aim to describe and document just a portion of that presence and influence.

ORIGINS AND EARLY CAREER: 1910–1939

Allan Rohan Crite was born in 1910 in North Plainfield, New Jersey. His father, Oscar William Crite (1875–1937), was a stationary engineer, and his mother, Annamae Palmer Crite (1891–1977), was a poet, lifelong learner, and homemaker.[4] The family moved to Boston when Crite was an infant, first settling on Shawmut Avenue in the South End. Annamae had a strong influence on Crite's academic and spiritual life from an early age. Mother and son became parishioners at St. Bartholomew's Episcopal Church in Cambridge and would both become pillars of Boston's Episcopal community. Annamae made sure to supplement her son's Boston public school education with visits to historical sites around the city, Bible study, and—critically—enrollment in classes at the South End's Children's Art Centre (fig. 8). During his studies at the Children's Art Centre, he took a range of field trips to local museums, including the Museum of Fine Arts and often the Gardner. The trips to the Gardner were organized by Charles Woodbury and Elizabeth Perkins.[5] In an oral history from 1979, Crite recalled:

> We used to make trips up to the Isabel Stewart/Jack Gardner palace. I remember going there. Of course, the collection they have there is just a blaze of color, the courtyard. I made several drawings. One of them was sent to Mrs. Gardner and she was rather pleased—she was still alive at the time. . . . My mother tells me—she came out with a group of children from the Art Centre, and Mrs. Gardner saw her and asked her to come in and sit down and have a cup of tea with her, so she did. That's one of those little pleasant incidents—sitting and having tea with this rather fabulous woman. . . . I just remember this blaze of glory, of color, of flowers . . . streaming down in the courtyard; and then of course the mysterious nooks and corners, with bits of Italian paintings and carvings.[6]

It is clear that Crite was an avid museumgoer from a young age, copying from and being inspired by the rich collections conserved around the city. Many of Crite's exceptional childhood drawings survive; they feature animated stick figures, fantastical creatures, and scenes of adventure (fig. 9). "One of the features of drawing classes at the Art Centre," he recalled, "was 'stickman' figure drawing, action figures stressing movement and action. I remember one occasion . . . when a few of us selected children made drawings, action drawings from movies. We were impressed with the idea of seeing, understanding movement and translating that movement on to our drawings. I suppose in a way

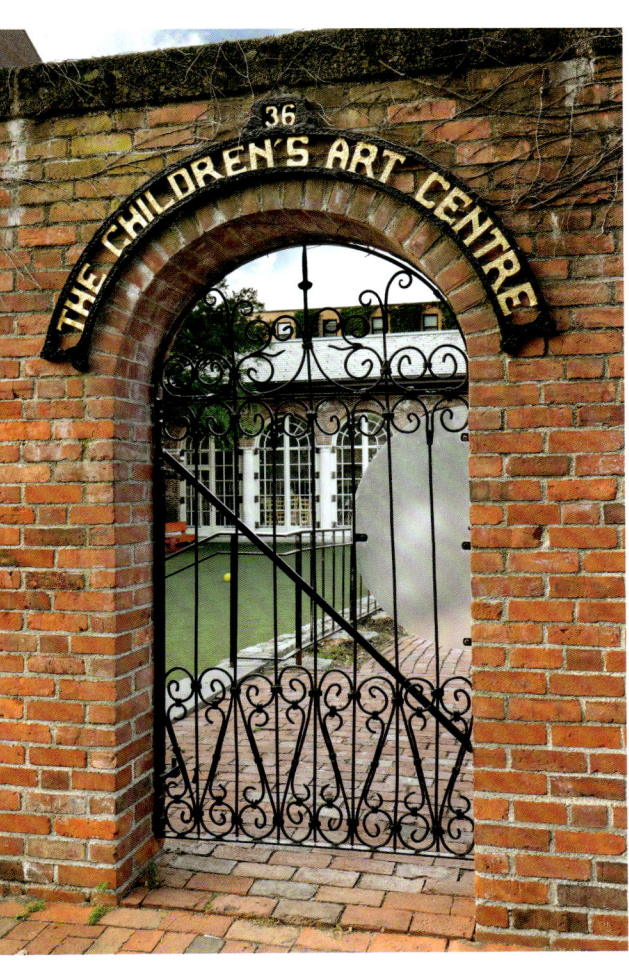

Fig. 8. The gate for the Children's Art Centre in Boston's South End neighborhood, 2024

Mr. Woodbury was translating to us children that sense of movement in nature which he, as a famous marine painter, felt in the movement of the waves of the sea."[7] Some of Crite's early drawings depict biblical scenes, anticipating the importance of spirituality in his later work.[8] Woodbury and Perkins surely recognized Crite's talent from an early age, and they included his drawings in their book *The Art of Seeing: Mental Training through Drawing* (1925).[9] In a sense, at just fifteen years old, Crite was already a published illustrator.

Crite attended English High School, one of the oldest and best public schools in Boston. After graduating in 1929, he enrolled at the School of the Museum of Fine Arts (SMFA) to study industrial design but also to receive an academic art education.[10] A sketchbook from 1932 encapsulates Crite's range of interests and talents even at this early point in his career. Its pages are full of portraits (fig. 10), stained-glass windows, notes on famous artists, figure studies, caricatures, and Shakespearean costume designs, along with a handwritten report on human rights in Russia, a sociological interest foreshadowing his deeper dive into world cultures later in his career.

Just as Crite started at the SMFA, tragedy struck his family. His father, Oscar, had an accident at work and consequently suffered a stroke. He was incapacitated, and the family's financial situation became tenuous—just on the eve of the Great Depression. Annamae went to work cleaning office buildings and homes to continue to support her son's education.[11] If mother and son were already close, this sacrifice seems to have cemented a lifelong bond between them. They shared caregiving responsibilities for Oscar until he died in 1937, and lived together for the next four decades, until Annamae's death, first at 2 Dilworth Street in Lower Roxbury and later at 410 Columbus Avenue in the South End. Annamae had an enormous influence—particularly on Crite's dedication to the Episcopal Church and his later-in-life decision to earn a bachelor's degree from the Harvard Extension School. As she said in an oral history in 1976, "Harvard University and the Episcopal Church have been my two loves. I went to church, that was on a Sunday, and the next day went to Harvard. . . . I love Harvard. . . . My son has inherited the same affection for Harvard."[12]

In the wake of Oscar's illness, Crite received several early breaks in his career. He had illustrations published in national magazines, was added to a roster of artists represented by a gallery on Boston's Newbury Street, and earned a prestigious prize in painting from the SMFA. During the Great Depression, he joined two government programs designed to support artists: first, the short-lived Public Works of Art Project in 1934 and later the Federal Art Project, although he resigned several months later, when the government required that he file as someone in need of financial assistance in order to continue to participate in the project.[13]

While working for the Federal Art Project, Crite completed a masterpiece that exemplifies his best-known images of the Black neighborhoods of Boston at midcentury and attests to his self-described role as an "artist-reporter." In *School's Out* (1936) (see fig. 48), the sidewalks are full of people.[14] Girls and women—presumably mothers and daughters, sisters and aunts—wear brightly colored dresses. With lightweight flowing material and relatively short skirts, this is probably a spring or even a summer day. The title of the painting could refer to a daily dismissal time, although the summery garments may suggest a more definitive "out"—that sweet last day of school when kids are free to roam for the next few months. The brick buildings and mostly Black population situate this abundant, figure-filled canvas in the neighborhood of Lower Roxbury or the South End. Scenes like this one testify to Crite's documentation of Black life in Boston during the twentieth century. But it would be a mistake to overemphasize the second of Crite's roles—that of reporter—to the detriment of his artistry.

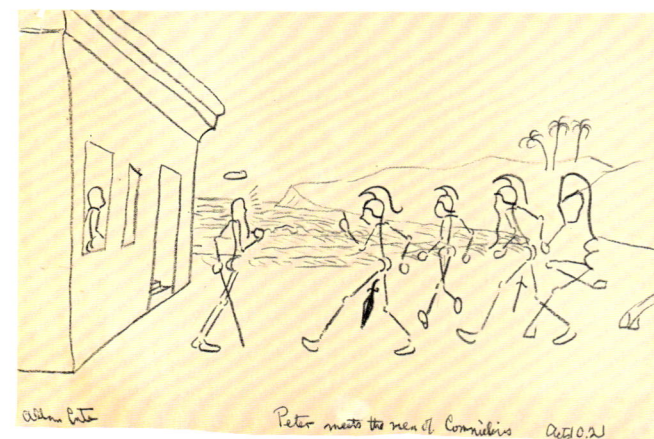

Fig. 9. Allan Rohan Crite, *Peter Meets the Men of Cornelius (Acts 10.21),* 1920–27. Crayon on paper, 30.4 × 45.5 cm. Boston Athenaeum